NEWS TIMES
Tsugumi Ohba has an illegitimate child?!

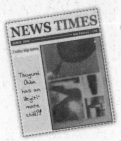

There was a time when I, too, wanted to illustrate my own long-running series. It's true. You have to believe me!

—Tsugumi Ohba

I was in middle school when I started drawing longer manga in my notebook. I stopped showing them to other people, though.

—Takeshi Obata

NO PEEKING!

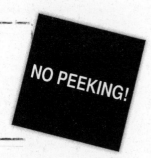

Tsugumi Ohba

Born in Tokyo, Tsugumi Ohba is the author of the hit series *Death Note*. His current series *Bakuman。* is serialized in *Weekly Shonen Jump*.

Takeshi Obata

Takeshi Obata was born in 1969 in Niigata, Japan, and is the artist of the wildly popular SHONEN JUMP title *Hikaru no Go*, which won the 2003 Tezuka Osamu Cultural Prize: Shinsei "New Hope" award and the 2000 Shogakukan Manga award. Obata is also the artist of *Arabian Majin Bokentan Lamp Lamp*, *Ayatsuri Sakon*, *Cyborg Jichan G.*, and the smash hit manga *Death Note*. His current series *Bakuman。* is serialized in *Weekly Shonen Jump*.

BAKUMAN。

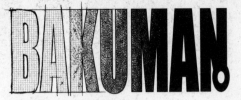

Volume 7

SHONEN JUMP Manga Edition

Story by **TSUGUMI OHBA**
Art by **TAKESHI OBATA**

Translation | **Tetsuichiro Miyaki**
English Adaptation | **Hope Donovan**
Touch-up Art & Lettering | **James Gaubatz**
Design | **Fawn Lau**
Editor | **Alexis Kirsch**

Printed in the U.S.A.

Published by VIZ Media, LLC
P.O. Box 77010
San Francisco, CA 94107

10 9 8 7 6 5 4 3 2 1
First printing, October 2011

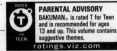

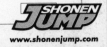

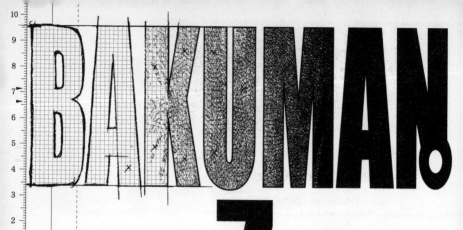

BAKUMAN。

7

GAG
and
SERIOUS

STORY BY

ART BY

TSUGUMI OHBA

TAKESHI OBATA

MAN。
バクマン。
vol. 7
J
F
G
H
K
L
LOVE

*These ages are from December 2011.

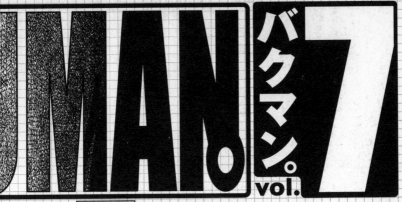

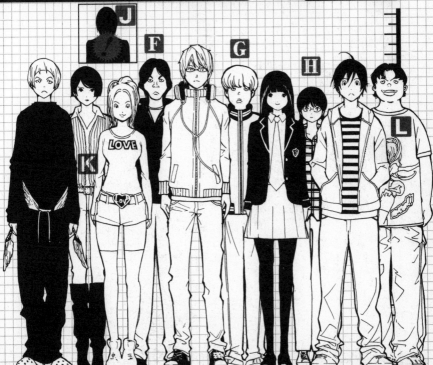

EIJI
Nizuma

A manga prodigy and Tezuka Award winner at the age of 15. One of the most popular creators in *Jump*.

Age: 19

KAYA
Miyoshi

Miho's friend and Akito's girlfriend. A nice girl who actively works as the interceder between Moritaka and Azuki.

Age: 18

AKITO
Takagi

Manga writer. An extremely smart guy who gets the best grades in his class. A cool guy who becomes very passionate when it comes to manga.

Age: 17

MIHO
Azuki

A girl who dreams of becoming a voice actress. She promised to marry Moritaka under the condition that they not see each other until their dreams come true.

Age: 18

MORITAKA
Mashiro

Manga artist. An extreme romantic who believes that he will marry Miho Azuki once their dreams come true.

Age: 17

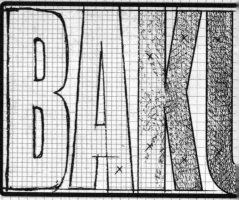

STORY In order to attain the glory that only a handful of people can, two young men decide to walk the rough "path of manga" and become professional manga creators. This is the story of a great artist, Moritaka Mashiro, a talented writer, Akito Takagi, and their quest to become manga legends!

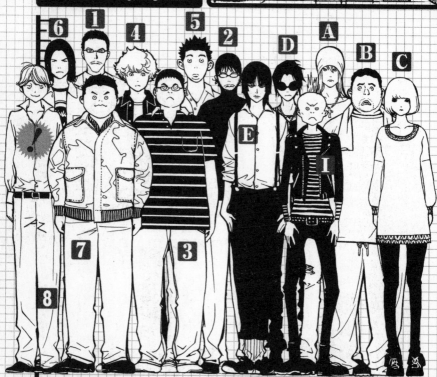

The characters with this mark appear for the first time in volume 7.

WEEKLY SHONEN JUMP
Editorial Office

1 Editor in Chief Sasaki		Age: 48
2 Deputy Editor in Chief Heishi		Age: 43
3 Soichi Aida		Age: 36
4 Yujiro Hattori		Age: 29
5 Akira Hattori		Age: 31
6 Koji Yoshida		Age: 33
7 Goro Miura		Age: 24
8 Masakazu Yamahisa		Age: 24

THE MANGA ARTISTS

A SHINTA FUKUDA		Age: 21
B TAKURO NAKAI		Age: 34
C KO AOKI		Age: 21
D KOJI MAKAINO		Age: 31
E KAZUYA HIRAMARU		Age: 27
J RYU SHIZUKA		Age: 18
K AIKO IWASE		Age: 18
L ISHIZAWA		Age: 18
F Ogawa **G** Takahama **N** Kato **I** Yasuoka		

The Assistants

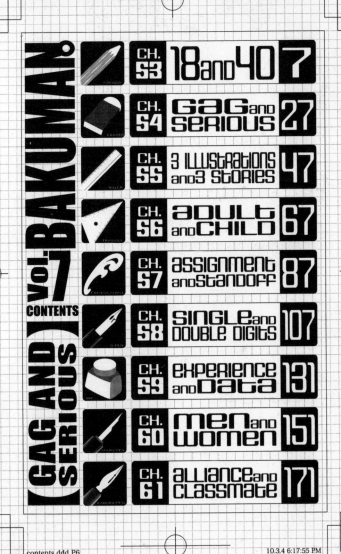

BAKUMAN.

VOL. 7 — GAG AND SERIOUS

CONTENTS

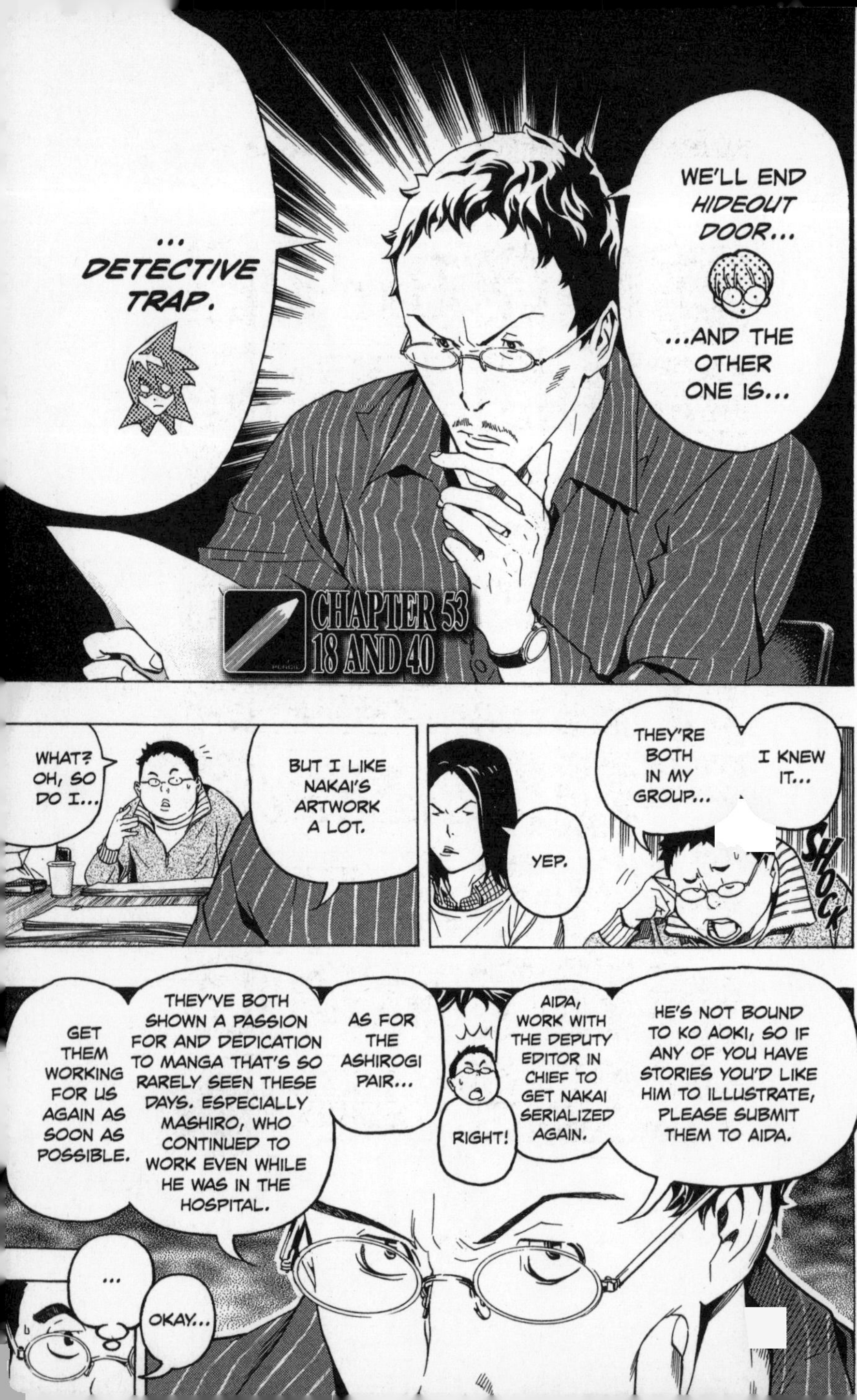
WE'LL END HIDEOUT DOOR...
...AND THE OTHER ONE IS...
...DETECTIVE TRAP.
CHAPTER 53
18 AND 40
I KNEW IT...
THEY'RE BOTH IN MY GROUP...
YEP.
SHOCK
BUT I LIKE NAKAI'S ARTWORK A LOT.
WHAT? OH, SO DO I...
HE'S NOT BOUND TO KO AOKI, SO IF ANY OF YOU HAVE STORIES YOU'D LIKE HIM TO ILLUSTRATE, PLEASE SUBMIT THEM TO AIDA.
AIDA, WORK WITH THE DEPUTY EDITOR IN CHIEF TO GET NAKAI SERIALIZED AGAIN.
RIGHT!
AS FOR THE ASHIROGI PAIR...
THEY'VE BOTH SHOWN A PASSION FOR AND DEDICATION TO MANGA THAT'S SO RARELY SEEN THESE DAYS. ESPECIALLY MASHIRO, WHO CONTINUED TO WORK EVEN WHILE HE WAS IN THE HOSPITAL.
GET THEM WORKING FOR US AGAIN AS SOON AS POSSIBLE.
...
OKAY...

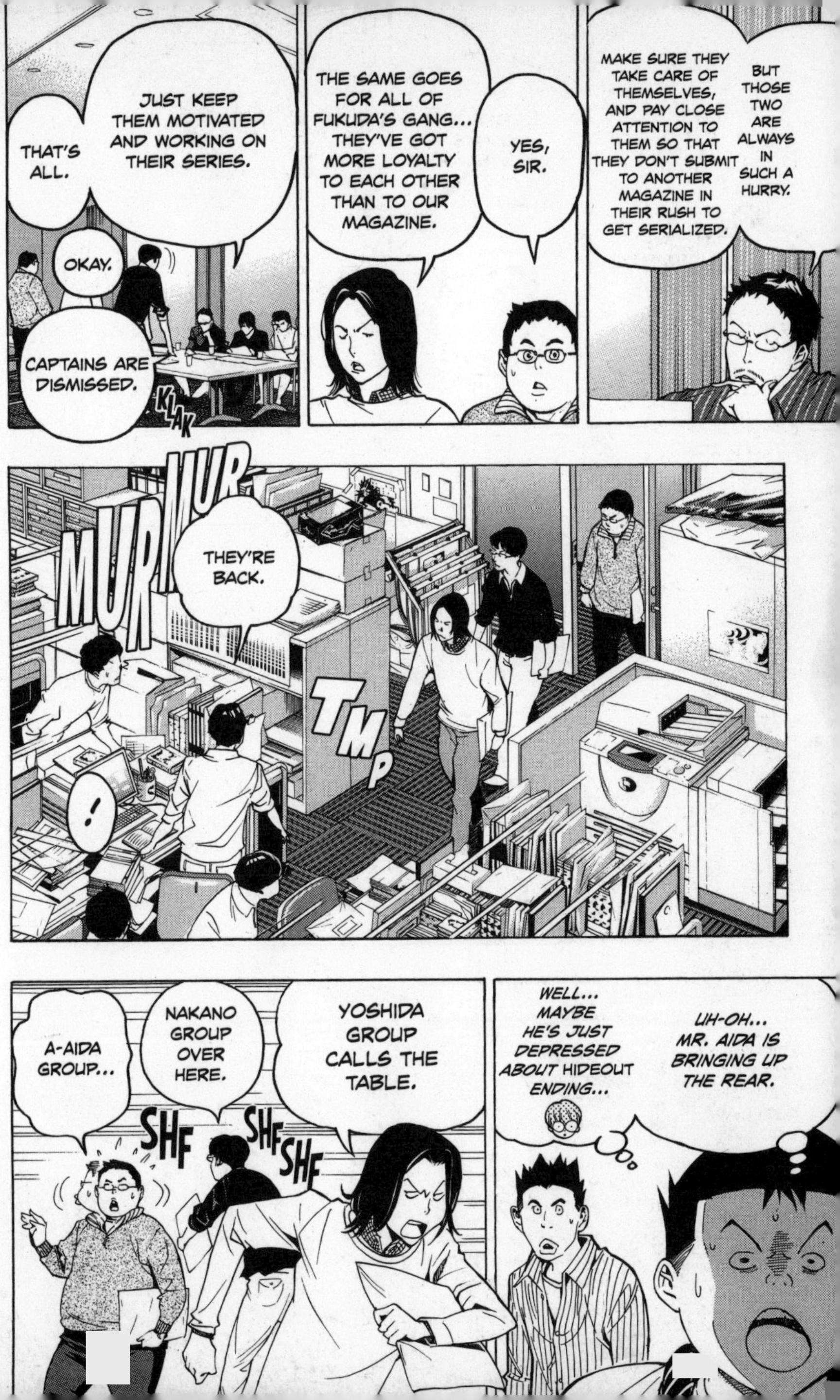
BUT THOSE TWO ARE ALWAYS IN SUCH A HURRY.
MAKE SURE THEY TAKE CARE OF THEMSELVES, AND PAY CLOSE ATTENTION TO THEM SO THAT THEY DON'T SUBMIT TO ANOTHER MAGAZINE IN THEIR RUSH TO GET SERIALIZED.
THE SAME GOES FOR ALL OF FUKUDA'S GANG... THEY'VE GOT MORE LOYALTY TO EACH OTHER THAN TO OUR MAGAZINE.
YES, SIR.
JUST KEEP THEM MOTIVATED AND WORKING ON THEIR SERIES.
THAT'S ALL.
OKAY.
CAPTAINS ARE DISMISSED.
KLAK
MUR MUR
THEY'RE BACK.
TMP
!
UH-OH... MR. AIDA IS BRINGING UP THE REAR.
WELL... MAYBE HE'S JUST DEPRESSED ABOUT HIDEOUT ENDING...
YOSHIDA GROUP CALLS THE TABLE.
NAKANO GROUP OVER HERE.
A-AIDA GROUP...
SHF SHF SHF

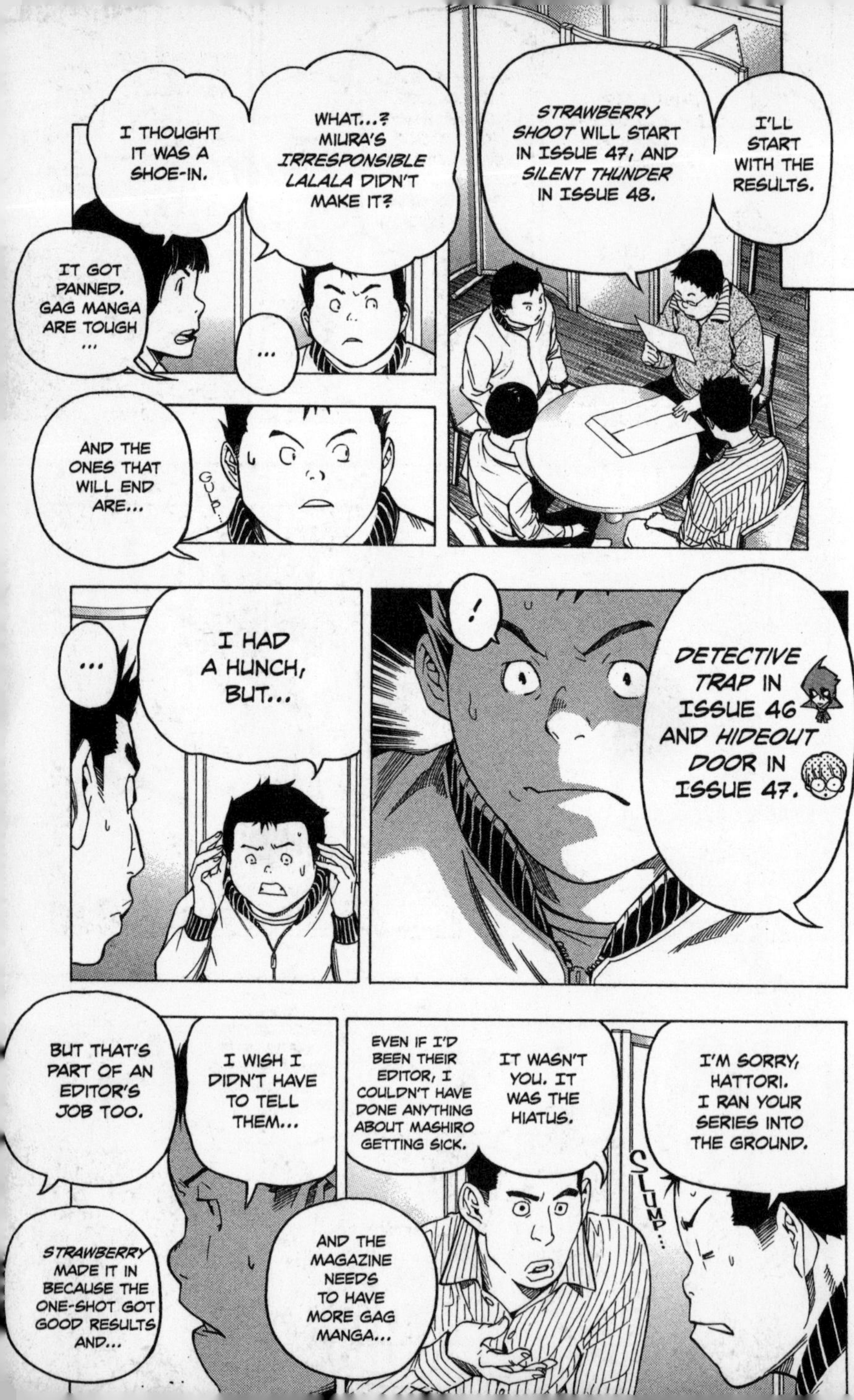
I'LL START WITH THE RESULTS.
STRAWBERRY SHOOT WILL START IN ISSUE 47, AND *SILENT THUNDER* IN ISSUE 48.
WHAT...? MIURA'S *IRRESPONSIBLE LALALA* DIDN'T MAKE IT?
I THOUGHT IT WAS A SHOE-IN.
...
IT GOT PANNED. GAG MANGA ARE TOUGH ...
AND THE ONES THAT WILL END ARE...
GULP...
DETECTIVE TRAP IN ISSUE 46 AND *HIDEOUT DOOR* IN ISSUE 47.
!
I HAD A HUNCH, BUT...
...
I'M SORRY, HATTORI. I RAN YOUR SERIES INTO THE GROUND.
SLUMP...
IT WASN'T YOU. IT WAS THE HIATUS.
EVEN IF I'D BEEN THEIR EDITOR, I COULDN'T HAVE DONE ANYTHING ABOUT MASHIRO GETTING SICK.
AND THE MAGAZINE NEEDS TO HAVE MORE GAG MANGA...
I WISH I DIDN'T HAVE TO TELL THEM...
BUT THAT'S PART OF AN EDITOR'S JOB TOO.
STRAWBERRY MADE IT IN BECAUSE THE ONE-SHOT GOT GOOD RESULTS AND...

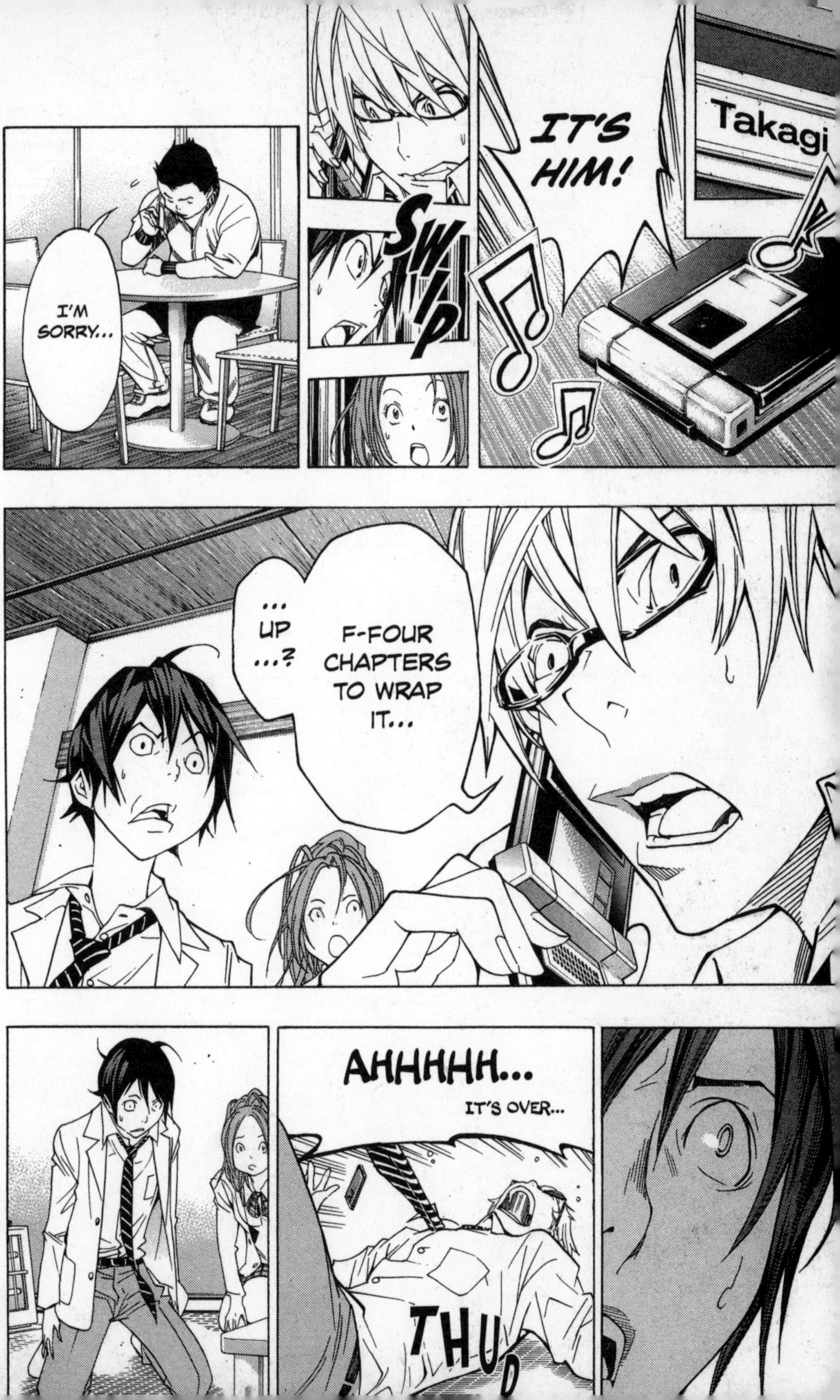
Takagi
IT'S HIM!
SWIP
I'M SORRY...
F-FOUR CHAPTERS TO WRAP IT...
... UP ...?
AHHHHH...
IT'S OVER...
THUD

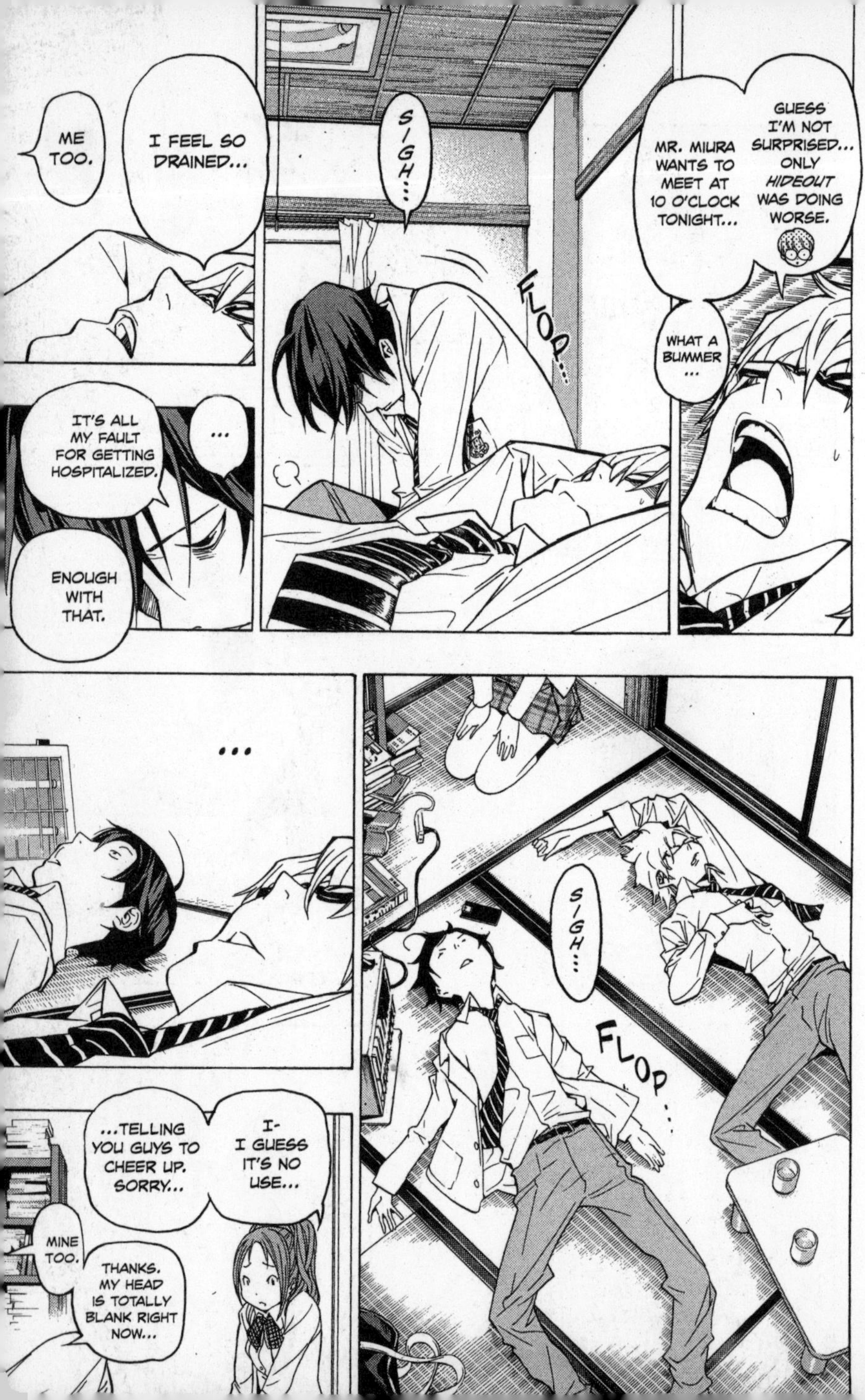
GUESS I'M NOT SURPRISED... ONLY *HIDEOUT* WAS DOING WORSE.
MR. MIURA WANTS TO MEET AT 10 O'CLOCK TONIGHT...
WHAT A BUMMER...
SIGH...
FLOP...
I FEEL SO DRAINED...
ME TOO.
...
IT'S ALL MY FAULT FOR GETTING HOSPITALIZED.
ENOUGH WITH THAT.
SIGH...
FLOP...
...
I- I GUESS IT'S NO USE...
...TELLING YOU GUYS TO CHEER UP. SORRY...
THANKS. MY HEAD IS TOTALLY BLANK RIGHT NOW...
MINE TOO.

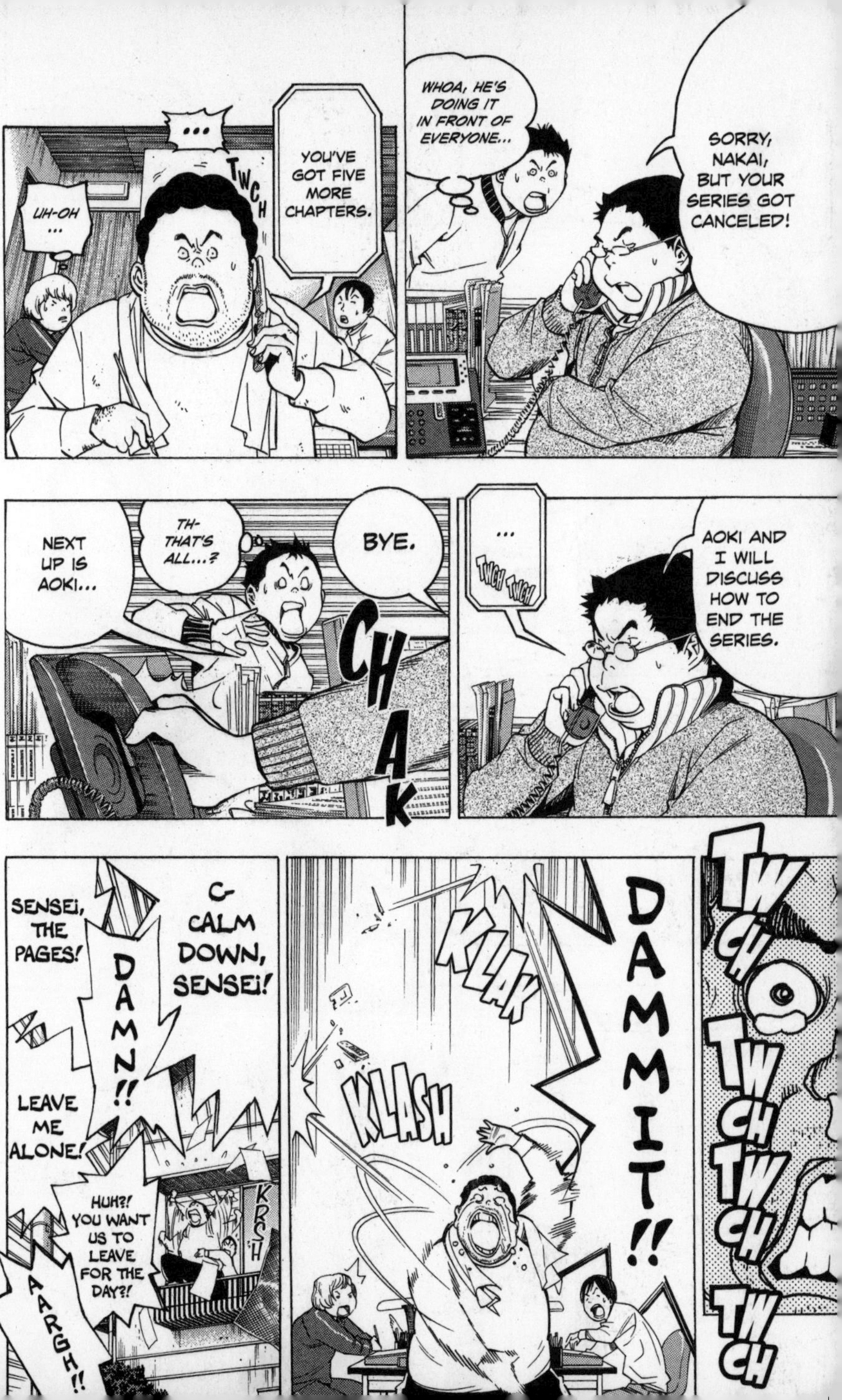
SORRY, NAKAI, BUT YOUR SERIES GOT CANCELED!
WHOA, HE'S DOING IT IN FRONT OF EVERYONE...
YOU'VE GOT FIVE MORE CHAPTERS.
TWCH
...
UH-OH...
AOKI AND I WILL DISCUSS HOW TO END THE SERIES.
...
TWCH TWCH
BYE.
TH-THAT'S ALL...?
NEXT UP IS AOKI...
CHAK
TWCH TWCH TWCH TWCH
DAMMIT!!
KLAK
KLASH
C-CALM DOWN, SENSEI!
SENSEI, THE PAGES!
DAMN!!
LEAVE ME ALONE!
KRCH
HUH?! YOU WANT US TO LEAVE FOR THE DAY?!
AARGH!!

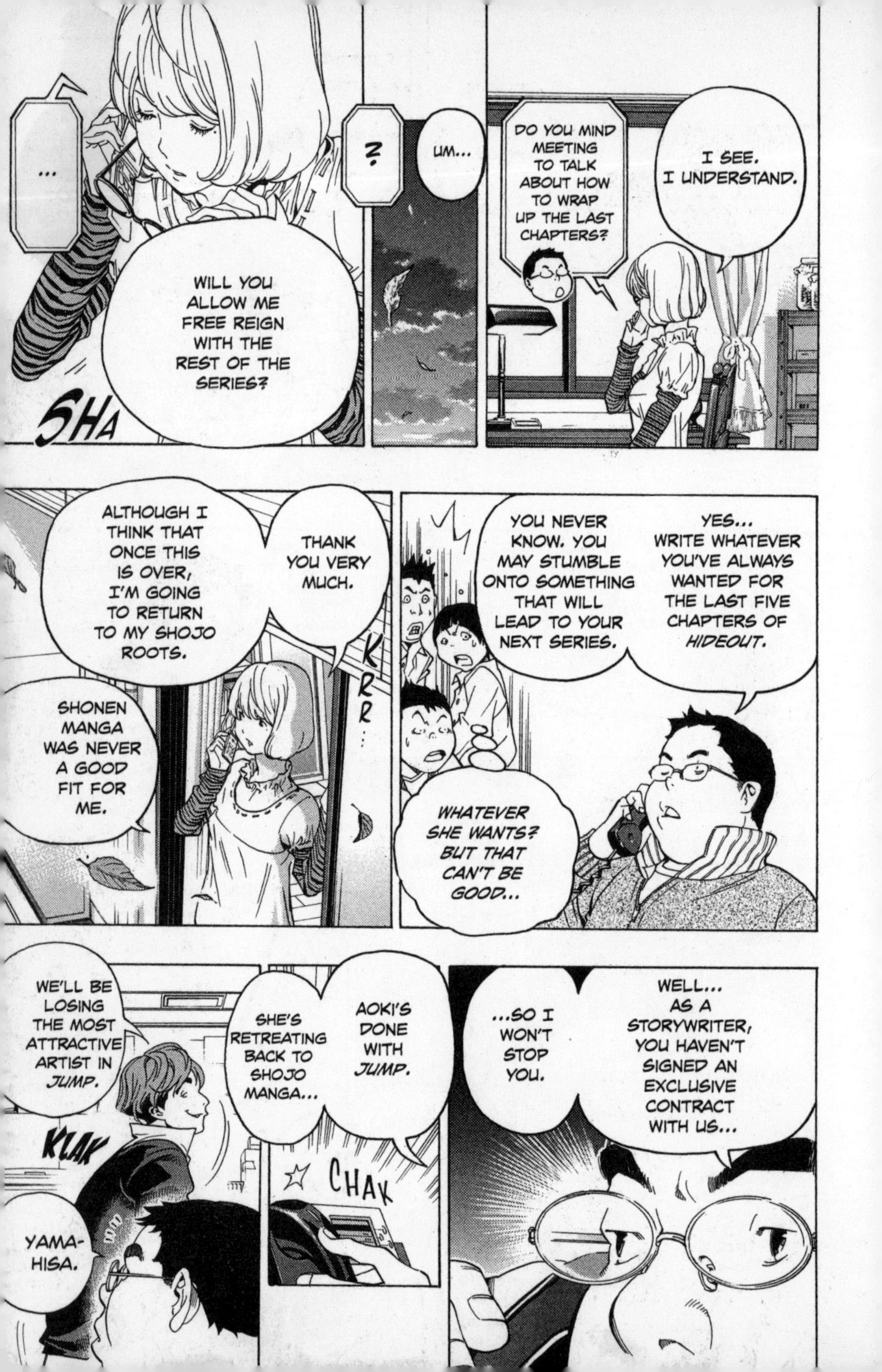
I SEE. I UNDERSTAND.
DO YOU MIND MEETING TO TALK ABOUT HOW TO WRAP UP THE LAST CHAPTERS?
UM...
?
WILL YOU ALLOW ME FREE REIGN WITH THE REST OF THE SERIES?
...
SHA
YES... WRITE WHATEVER YOU'VE ALWAYS WANTED FOR THE LAST FIVE CHAPTERS OF *HIDEOUT*.
YOU NEVER KNOW. YOU MAY STUMBLE ONTO SOMETHING THAT WILL LEAD TO YOUR NEXT SERIES.
WHATEVER SHE WANTS? BUT THAT CAN'T BE GOOD...
THANK YOU VERY MUCH.
KRRR...
ALTHOUGH I THINK THAT ONCE THIS IS OVER, I'M GOING TO RETURN TO MY SHOJO ROOTS.
SHONEN MANGA WAS NEVER A GOOD FIT FOR ME.
WELL... AS A STORYWRITER, YOU HAVEN'T SIGNED AN EXCLUSIVE CONTRACT WITH US...
...SO I WON'T STOP YOU.
AOKI'S DONE WITH *JUMP*.
SHE'S RETREATING BACK TO SHOJO MANGA...
CHAK
WE'LL BE LOSING THE MOST ATTRACTIVE ARTIST IN *JUMP*.
KLAK
YAMA-HISA.

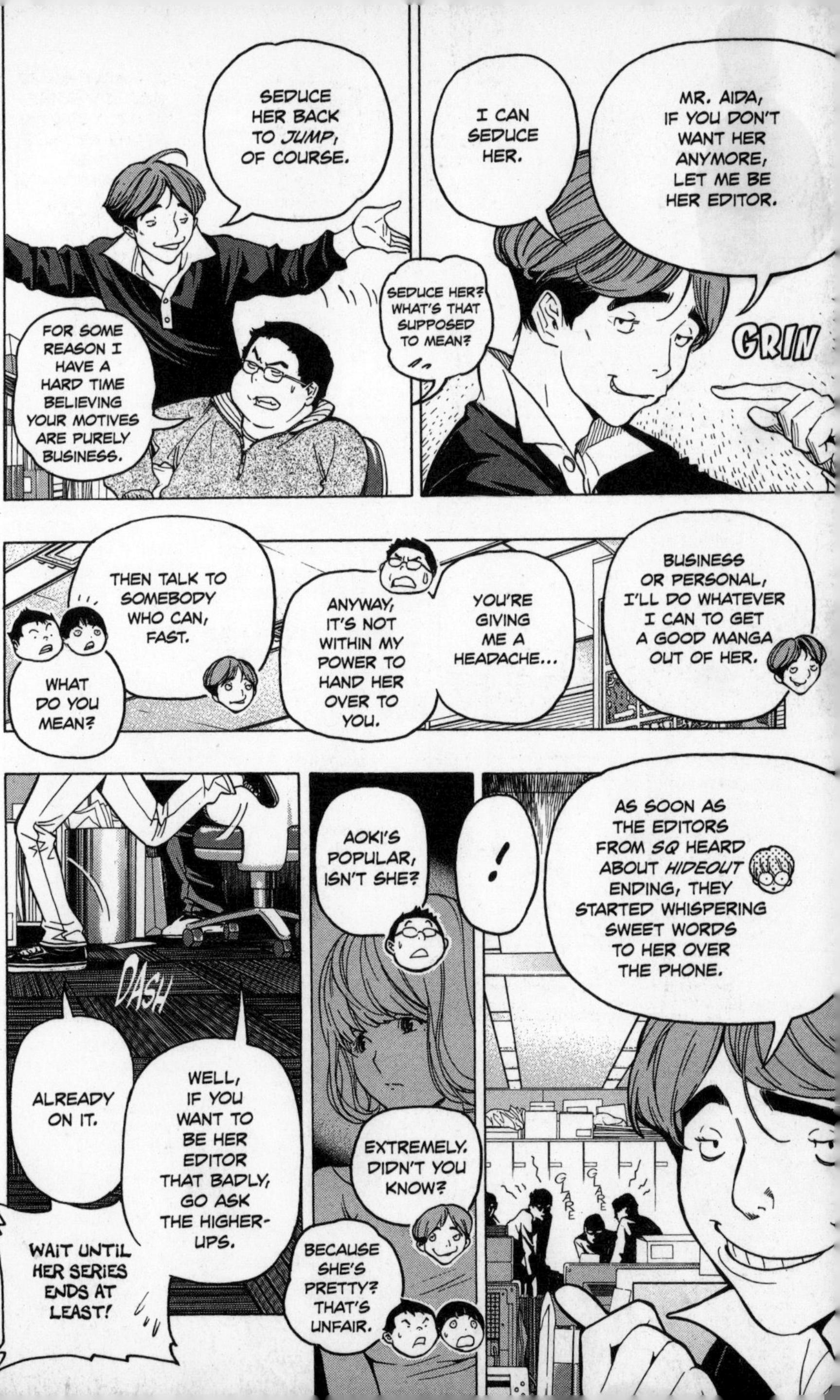
MR. AIDA, IF YOU DON'T WANT HER ANYMORE, LET ME BE HER EDITOR.
GRIN
I CAN SEDUCE HER.
SEDUCE HER? WHAT'S THAT SUPPOSED TO MEAN?
SEDUCE HER BACK TO *JUMP*, OF COURSE.
FOR SOME REASON I HAVE A HARD TIME BELIEVING YOUR MOTIVES ARE PURELY BUSINESS.
BUSINESS OR PERSONAL, I'LL DO WHATEVER I CAN TO GET A GOOD MANGA OUT OF HER.
YOU'RE GIVING ME A HEADACHE...
ANYWAY, IT'S NOT WITHIN MY POWER TO HAND HER OVER TO YOU.
THEN TALK TO SOMEBODY WHO CAN, FAST.
WHAT DO YOU MEAN?
AS SOON AS THE EDITORS FROM *SQ* HEARD ABOUT *HIDEOUT* ENDING, THEY STARTED WHISPERING SWEET WORDS TO HER OVER THE PHONE.
!
GLARE
GLARE
AOKI'S POPULAR, ISN'T SHE?
EXTREMELY. DIDN'T YOU KNOW?
BECAUSE SHE'S PRETTY? THAT'S UNFAIR.
DASH
WELL, IF YOU WANT TO BE HER EDITOR THAT BADLY, GO ASK THE HIGHER-UPS.
ALREADY ON IT.
WAIT UNTIL HER SERIES ENDS AT LEAST!

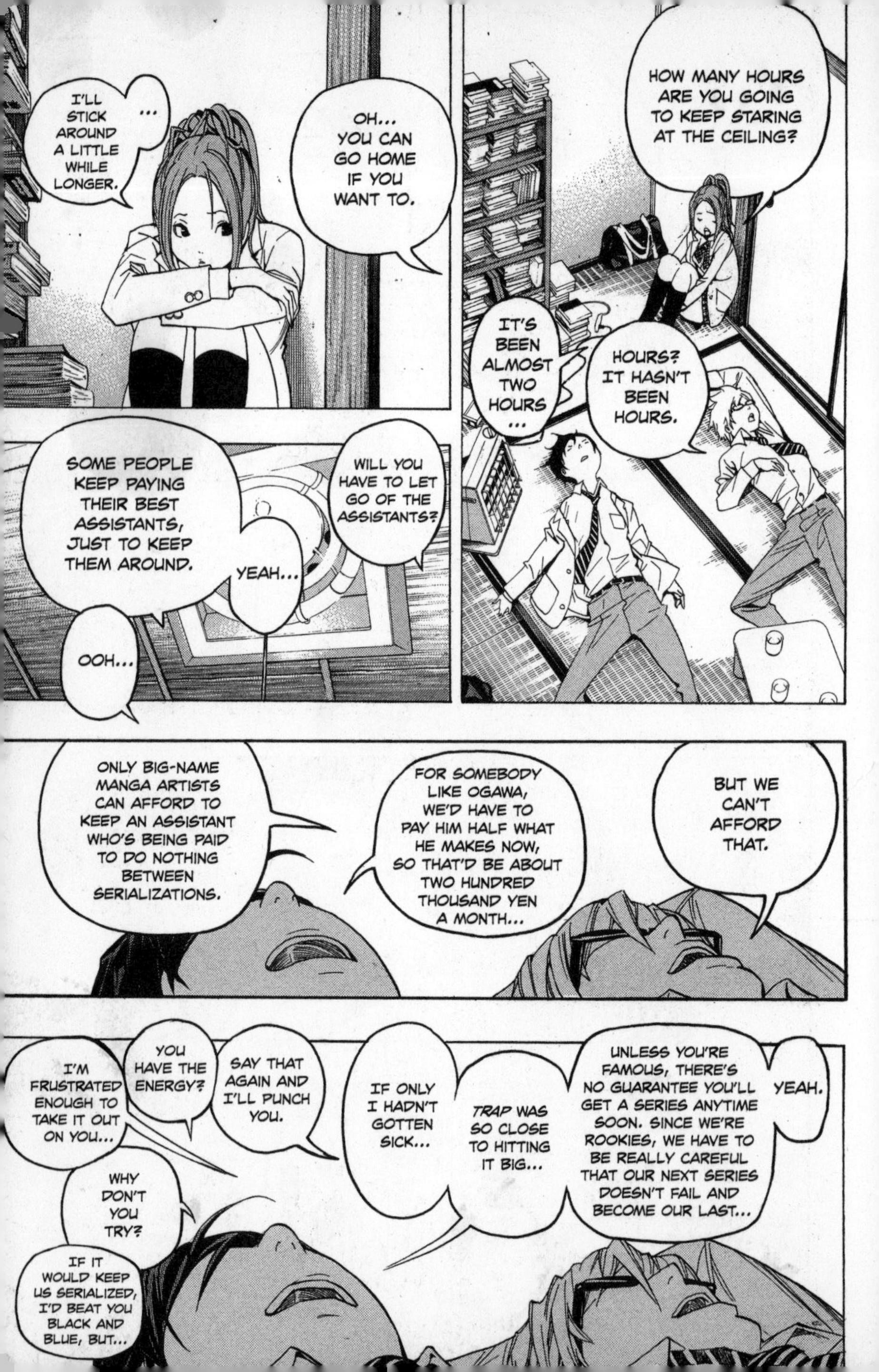
HOW MANY HOURS ARE YOU GOING TO KEEP STARING AT THE CEILING?
HOURS? IT HASN'T BEEN HOURS.
IT'S BEEN ALMOST TWO HOURS...
OH... YOU CAN GO HOME IF YOU WANT TO.
...
I'LL STICK AROUND A LITTLE WHILE LONGER.
WILL YOU HAVE TO LET GO OF THE ASSISTANTS?
YEAH...
SOME PEOPLE KEEP PAYING THEIR BEST ASSISTANTS, JUST TO KEEP THEM AROUND.
OOH...
BUT WE CAN'T AFFORD THAT.
FOR SOMEBODY LIKE OGAWA, WE'D HAVE TO PAY HIM HALF WHAT HE MAKES NOW, SO THAT'D BE ABOUT TWO HUNDRED THOUSAND YEN A MONTH...
ONLY BIG-NAME MANGA ARTISTS CAN AFFORD TO KEEP AN ASSISTANT WHO'S BEING PAID TO DO NOTHING BETWEEN SERIALIZATIONS.
YEAH.
UNLESS YOU'RE FAMOUS, THERE'S NO GUARANTEE YOU'LL GET A SERIES ANYTIME SOON. SINCE WE'RE ROOKIES, WE HAVE TO BE REALLY CAREFUL THAT OUR NEXT SERIES DOESN'T FAIL AND BECOME OUR LAST...
TRAP WAS SO CLOSE TO HITTING IT BIG...
IF ONLY I HADN'T GOTTEN SICK...
SAY THAT AGAIN AND I'LL PUNCH YOU.
YOU HAVE THE ENERGY?
I'M FRUSTRATED ENOUGH TO TAKE IT OUT ON YOU...
WHY DON'T YOU TRY?
IF IT WOULD KEEP US SERIALIZED, I'D BEAT YOU BLACK AND BLUE, BUT...

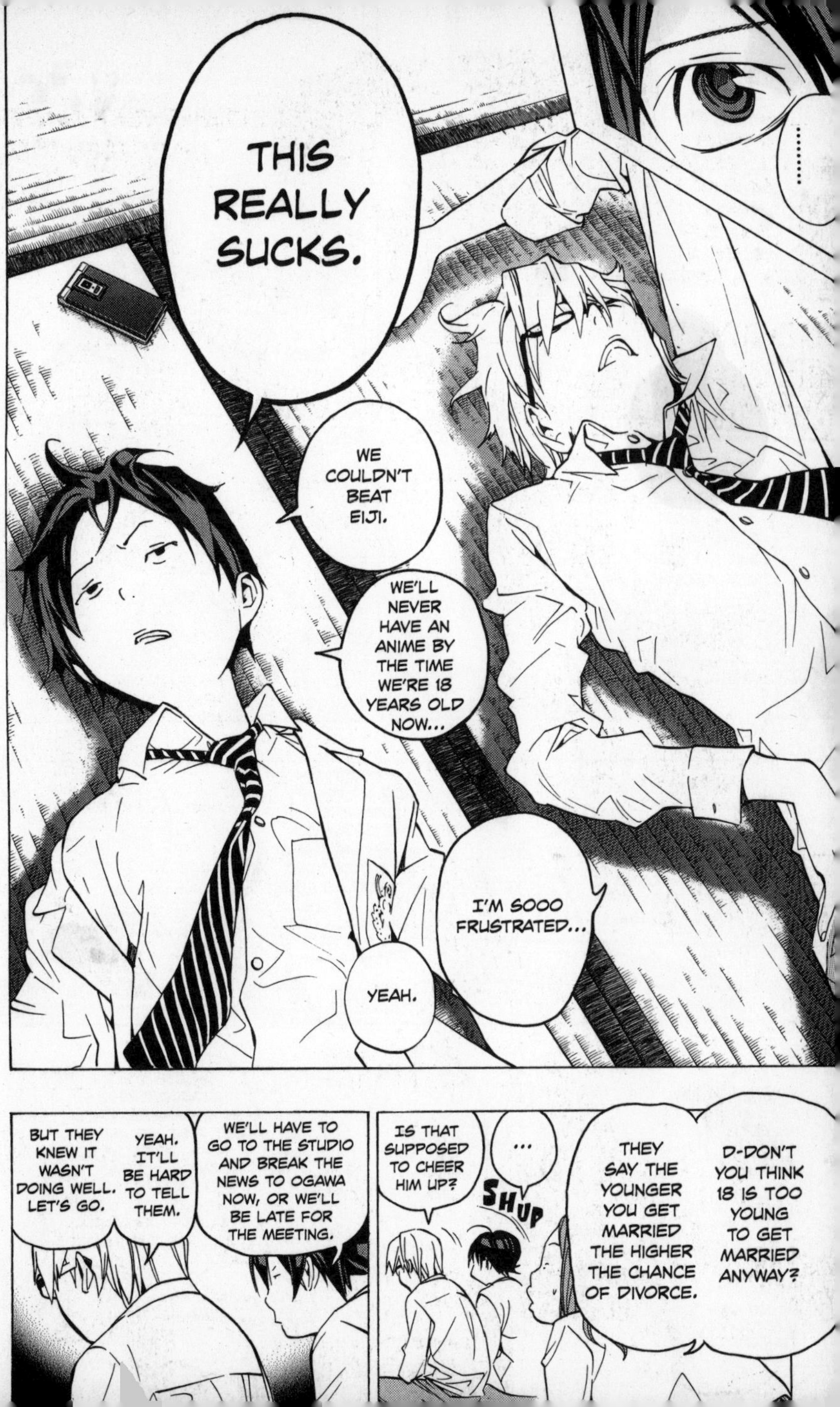
......
THIS REALLY SUCKS.
WE COULDN'T BEAT EIJI.
WE'LL NEVER HAVE AN ANIME BY THE TIME WE'RE 18 YEARS OLD NOW...
I'M SOOO FRUSTRATED...
YEAH.
D-DON'T YOU THINK 18 IS TOO YOUNG TO GET MARRIED ANYWAY?
THEY SAY THE YOUNGER YOU GET MARRIED THE HIGHER THE CHANCE OF DIVORCE.
...
IS THAT SUPPOSED TO CHEER HIM UP?
SHUP
WE'LL HAVE TO GO TO THE STUDIO AND BREAK THE NEWS TO OGAWA NOW, OR WE'LL BE LATE FOR THE MEETING.
YEAH. IT'LL BE HARD TO TELL THEM.
BUT THEY KNEW IT WASN'T DOING WELL. LET'S GO.

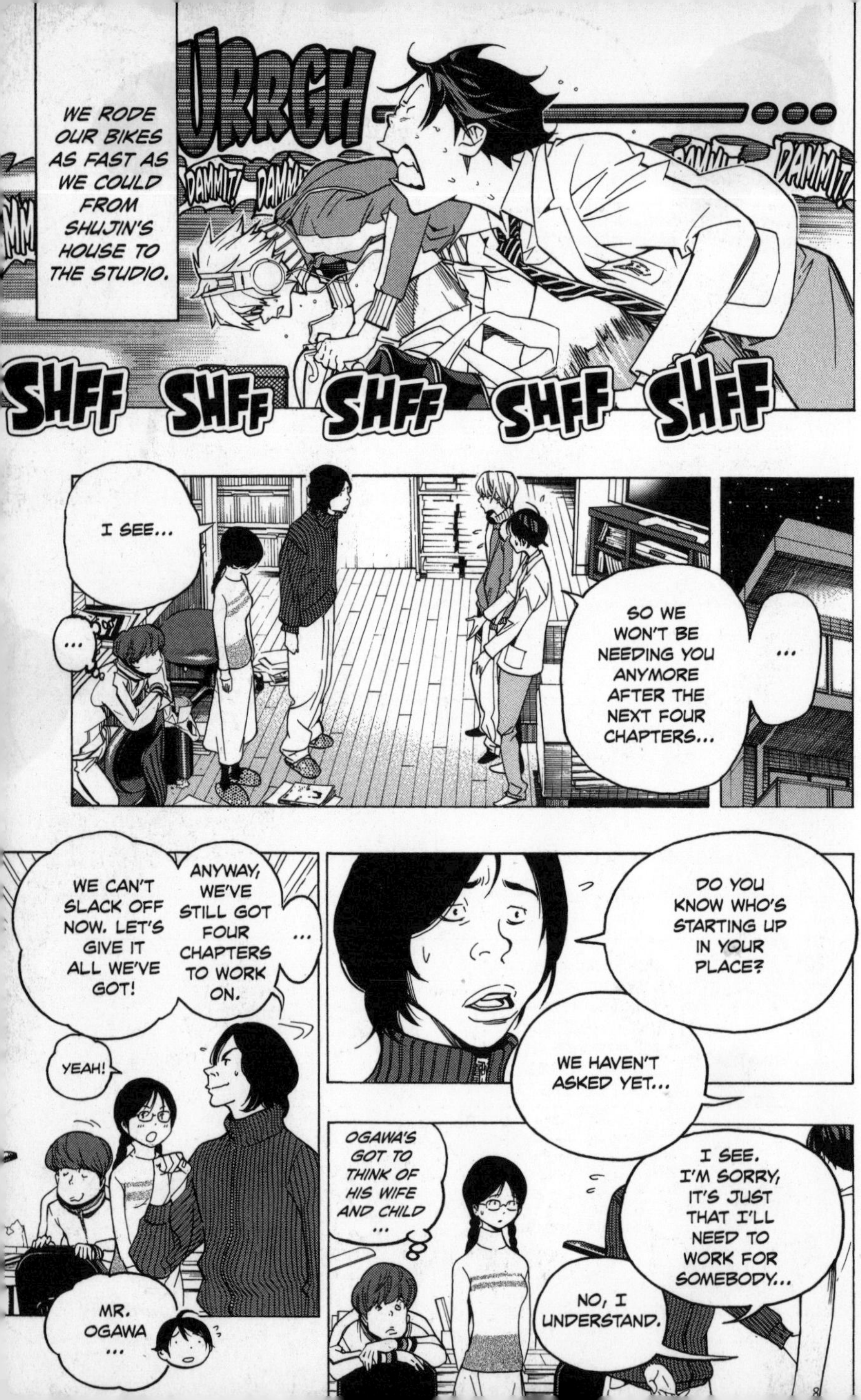
DAMMIT!
DAMMIT!
URRGH———...
DAMMIT!
DAMMIT!
WE RODE OUR BIKES AS FAST AS WE COULD FROM SHUJIN'S HOUSE TO THE STUDIO.
SHFF
SHFF
SHFF
SHFF
SHFF
...
SO WE WON'T BE NEEDING YOU ANYMORE AFTER THE NEXT FOUR CHAPTERS...
I SEE...
...
DO YOU KNOW WHO'S STARTING UP IN YOUR PLACE?
WE HAVEN'T ASKED YET...
I SEE. I'M SORRY, IT'S JUST THAT I'LL NEED TO WORK FOR SOMEBODY...
OGAWA'S GOT TO THINK OF HIS WIFE AND CHILD ...
NO, I UNDERSTAND.
...
ANYWAY, WE'VE STILL GOT FOUR CHAPTERS TO WORK ON.
WE CAN'T SLACK OFF NOW. LET'S GIVE IT ALL WE'VE GOT!
YEAH!
MR. OGAWA ...

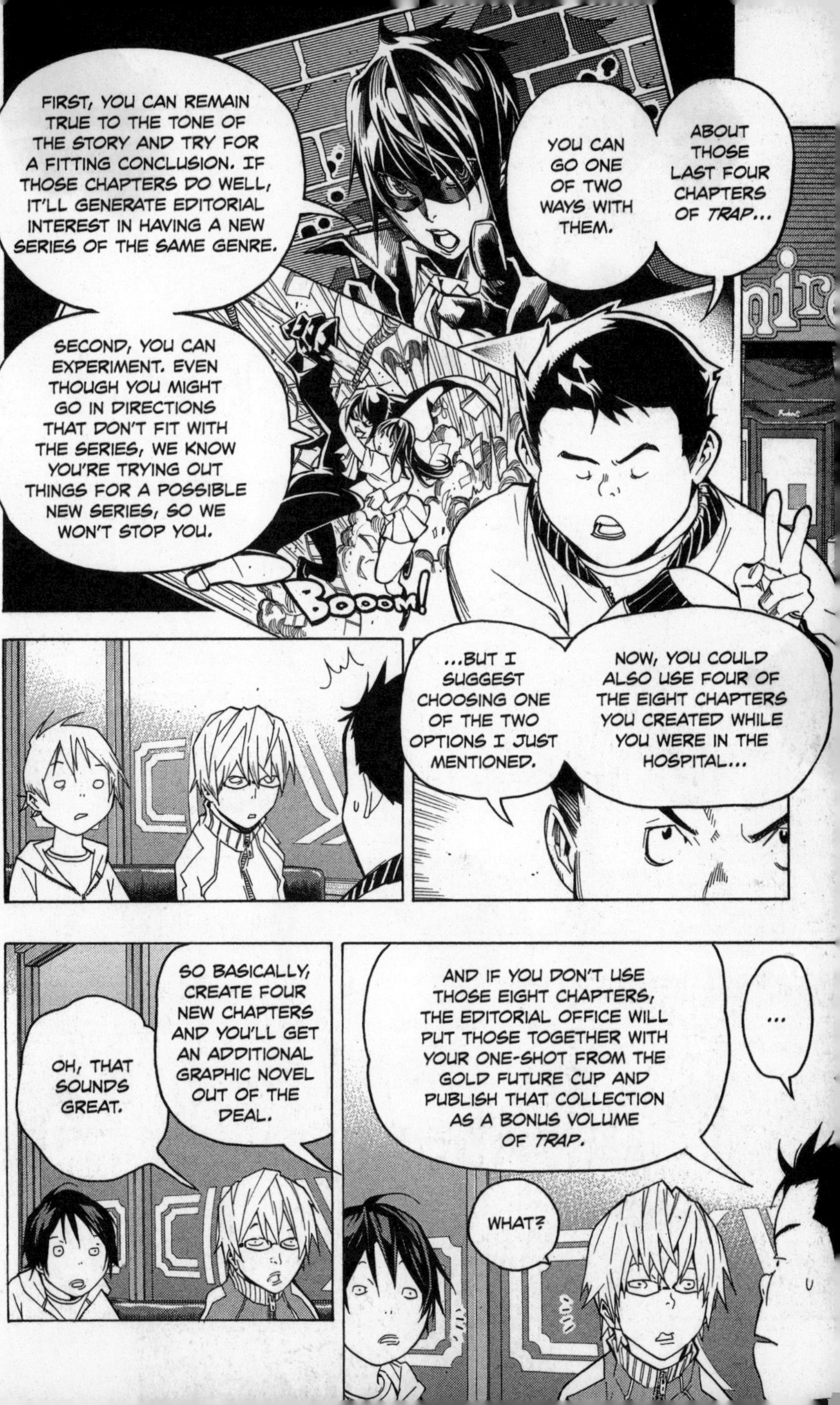
ABOUT THOSE LAST FOUR CHAPTERS OF *TRAP*...
YOU CAN GO ONE OF TWO WAYS WITH THEM.
FIRST, YOU CAN REMAIN TRUE TO THE TONE OF THE STORY AND TRY FOR A FITTING CONCLUSION. IF THOSE CHAPTERS DO WELL, IT'LL GENERATE EDITORIAL INTEREST IN HAVING A NEW SERIES OF THE SAME GENRE.
SECOND, YOU CAN EXPERIMENT. EVEN THOUGH YOU MIGHT GO IN DIRECTIONS THAT DON'T FIT WITH THE SERIES, WE KNOW YOU'RE TRYING OUT THINGS FOR A POSSIBLE NEW SERIES, SO WE WON'T STOP YOU.
BOOOM!
NOW, YOU COULD ALSO USE FOUR OF THE EIGHT CHAPTERS YOU CREATED WHILE YOU WERE IN THE HOSPITAL...
...BUT I SUGGEST CHOOSING ONE OF THE TWO OPTIONS I JUST MENTIONED.
...
AND IF YOU DON'T USE THOSE EIGHT CHAPTERS, THE EDITORIAL OFFICE WILL PUT THOSE TOGETHER WITH YOUR ONE-SHOT FROM THE GOLD FUTURE CUP AND PUBLISH THAT COLLECTION AS A BONUS VOLUME OF *TRAP*.
WHAT?
SO BASICALLY, CREATE FOUR NEW CHAPTERS AND YOU'LL GET AN ADDITIONAL GRAPHIC NOVEL OUT OF THE DEAL.
OH, THAT SOUNDS GREAT.

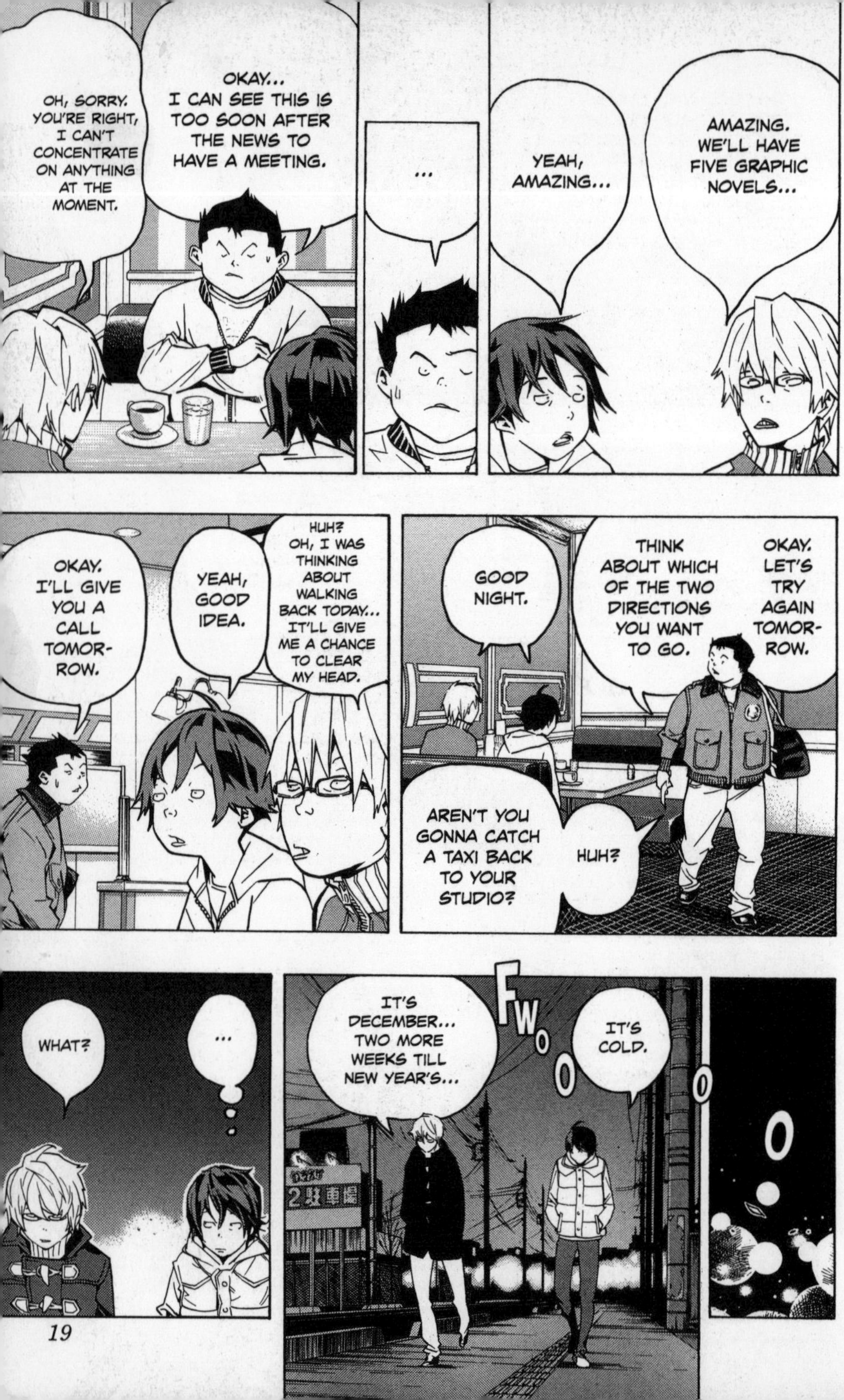
AMAZING. WE'LL HAVE FIVE GRAPHIC NOVELS...
YEAH, AMAZING...
...
OKAY... I CAN SEE THIS IS TOO SOON AFTER THE NEWS TO HAVE A MEETING.
OH, SORRY. YOU'RE RIGHT, I CAN'T CONCENTRATE ON ANYTHING AT THE MOMENT.
OKAY. LET'S TRY AGAIN TOMOR-ROW.
THINK ABOUT WHICH OF THE TWO DIRECTIONS YOU WANT TO GO.
GOOD NIGHT.
HUH?
AREN'T YOU GONNA CATCH A TAXI BACK TO YOUR STUDIO?
HUH? OH, I WAS THINKING ABOUT WALKING BACK TODAY... IT'LL GIVE ME A CHANCE TO CLEAR MY HEAD.
YEAH, GOOD IDEA.
OKAY. I'LL GIVE YOU A CALL TOMOR-ROW.
IT'S COLD.
FWOOOO
IT'S DECEMBER... TWO MORE WEEKS TILL NEW YEAR'S...
...
WHAT?

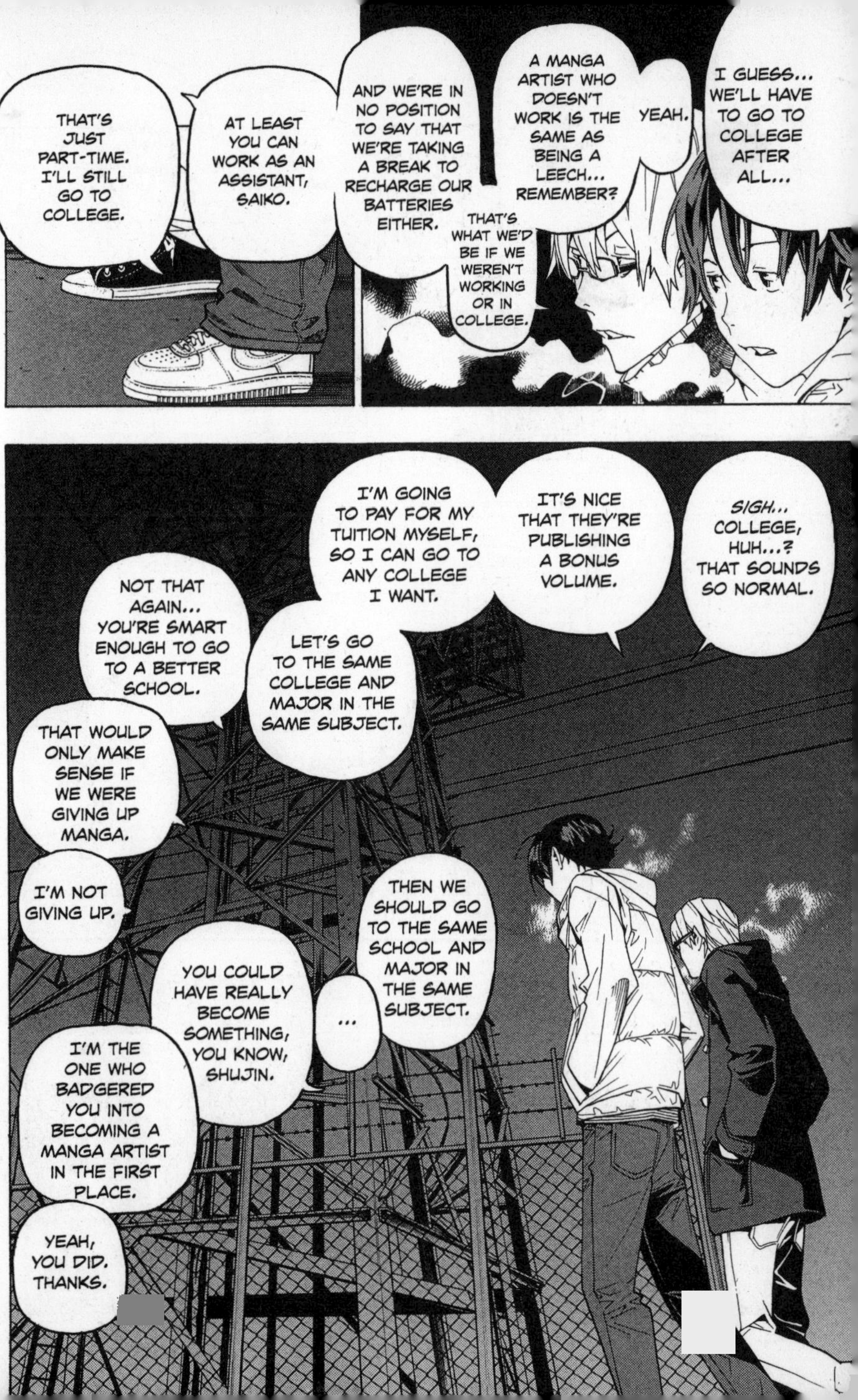
I GUESS... WE'LL HAVE TO GO TO COLLEGE AFTER ALL...
YEAH.
A MANGA ARTIST WHO DOESN'T WORK IS THE SAME AS BEING A LEECH... REMEMBER?
THAT'S WHAT WE'D BE IF WE WEREN'T WORKING OR IN COLLEGE.
AND WE'RE IN NO POSITION TO SAY THAT WE'RE TAKING A BREAK TO RECHARGE OUR BATTERIES EITHER.
AT LEAST YOU CAN WORK AS AN ASSISTANT, SAIKO.
THAT'S JUST PART-TIME. I'LL STILL GO TO COLLEGE.
SIGH... COLLEGE, HUH...? THAT SOUNDS SO NORMAL.
IT'S NICE THAT THEY'RE PUBLISHING A BONUS VOLUME.
I'M GOING TO PAY FOR MY TUITION MYSELF, SO I CAN GO TO ANY COLLEGE I WANT.
NOT THAT AGAIN... YOU'RE SMART ENOUGH TO GO TO A BETTER SCHOOL.
LET'S GO TO THE SAME COLLEGE AND MAJOR IN THE SAME SUBJECT.
THAT WOULD ONLY MAKE SENSE IF WE WERE GIVING UP MANGA.
I'M NOT GIVING UP.
THEN WE SHOULD GO TO THE SAME SCHOOL AND MAJOR IN THE SAME SUBJECT.
...
YOU COULD HAVE REALLY BECOME SOMETHING, YOU KNOW, SHUJIN.
I'M THE ONE WHO BADGERED YOU INTO BECOMING A MANGA ARTIST IN THE FIRST PLACE.
YEAH, YOU DID. THANKS.

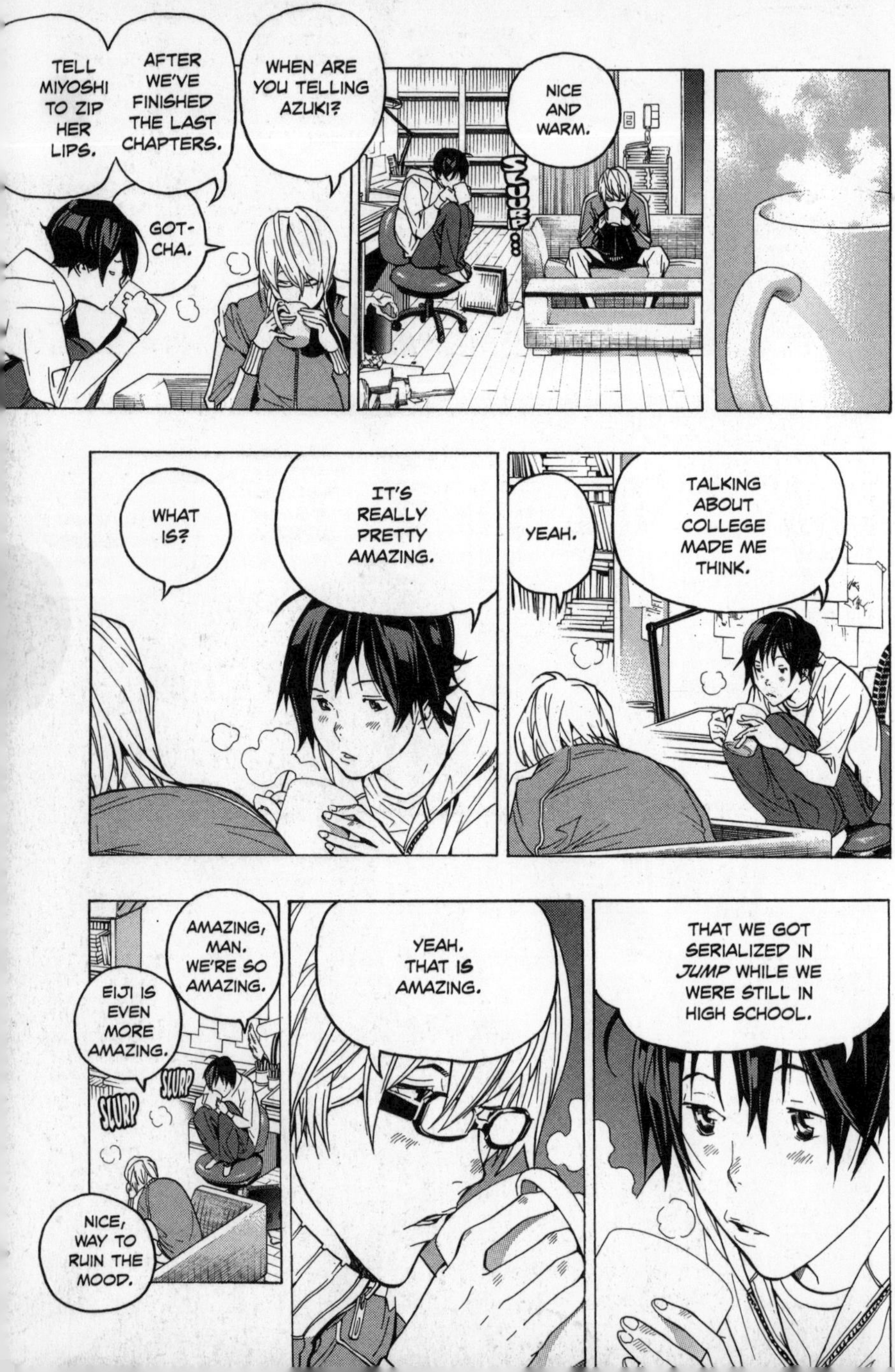
NICE AND WARM.
SLUURP...
WHEN ARE YOU TELLING AZUKI?
AFTER WE'VE FINISHED THE LAST CHAPTERS.
TELL MIYOSHI TO ZIP HER LIPS.
GOT-CHA.
TALKING ABOUT COLLEGE MADE ME THINK.
YEAH.
IT'S REALLY PRETTY AMAZING.
WHAT IS?
THAT WE GOT SERIALIZED IN *JUMP* WHILE WE WERE STILL IN HIGH SCHOOL.
YEAH. THAT IS AMAZING.
AMAZING, MAN. WE'RE SO AMAZING.
EIJI IS EVEN MORE AMAZING.
SLURP
SLURP
NICE, WAY TO RUIN THE MOOD.

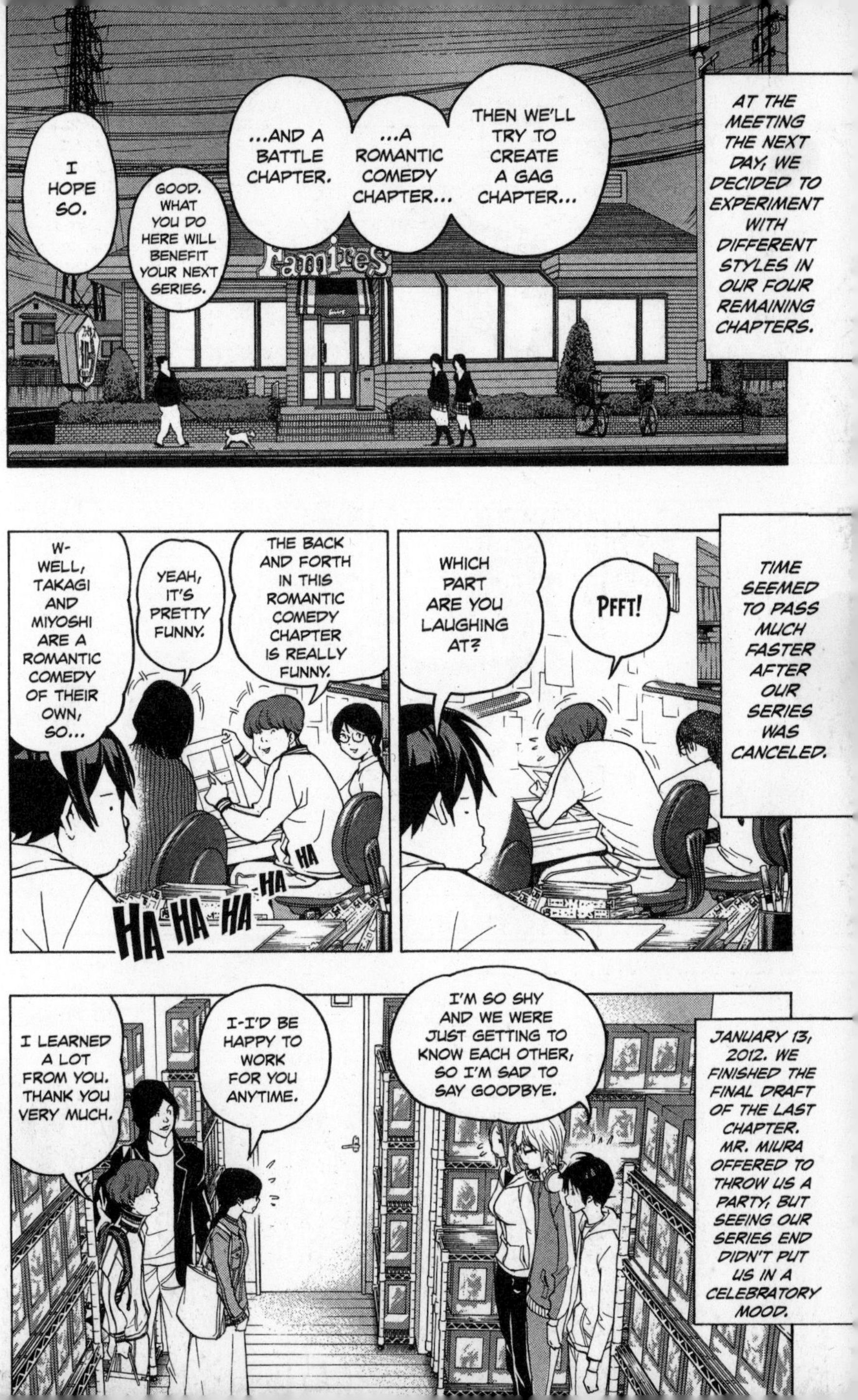
AT THE MEETING THE NEXT DAY, WE DECIDED TO EXPERIMENT WITH DIFFERENT STYLES IN OUR FOUR REMAINING CHAPTERS.
THEN WE'LL TRY TO CREATE A GAG CHAPTER...
...A ROMANTIC COMEDY CHAPTER...
...AND A BATTLE CHAPTER.
GOOD. WHAT YOU DO HERE WILL BENEFIT YOUR NEXT SERIES.
I HOPE SO.
Famires
TIME SEEMED TO PASS MUCH FASTER AFTER OUR SERIES WAS CANCELED.
PFFT!
WHICH PART ARE YOU LAUGHING AT?
THE BACK AND FORTH IN THIS ROMANTIC COMEDY CHAPTER IS REALLY FUNNY.
YEAH, IT'S PRETTY FUNNY.
W-WELL, TAKAGI AND MIYOSHI ARE A ROMANTIC COMEDY OF THEIR OWN, SO...
HA HA HA HA HA HA
JANUARY 13, 2012. WE FINISHED THE FINAL DRAFT OF THE LAST CHAPTER. MR. MIURA OFFERED TO THROW US A PARTY, BUT SEEING OUR SERIES END DIDN'T PUT US IN A CELEBRATORY MOOD.
I'M SO SHY AND WE WERE JUST GETTING TO KNOW EACH OTHER, SO I'M SAD TO SAY GOODBYE.
I-I'D BE HAPPY TO WORK FOR YOU ANYTIME.
I LEARNED A LOT FROM YOU. THANK YOU VERY MUCH.

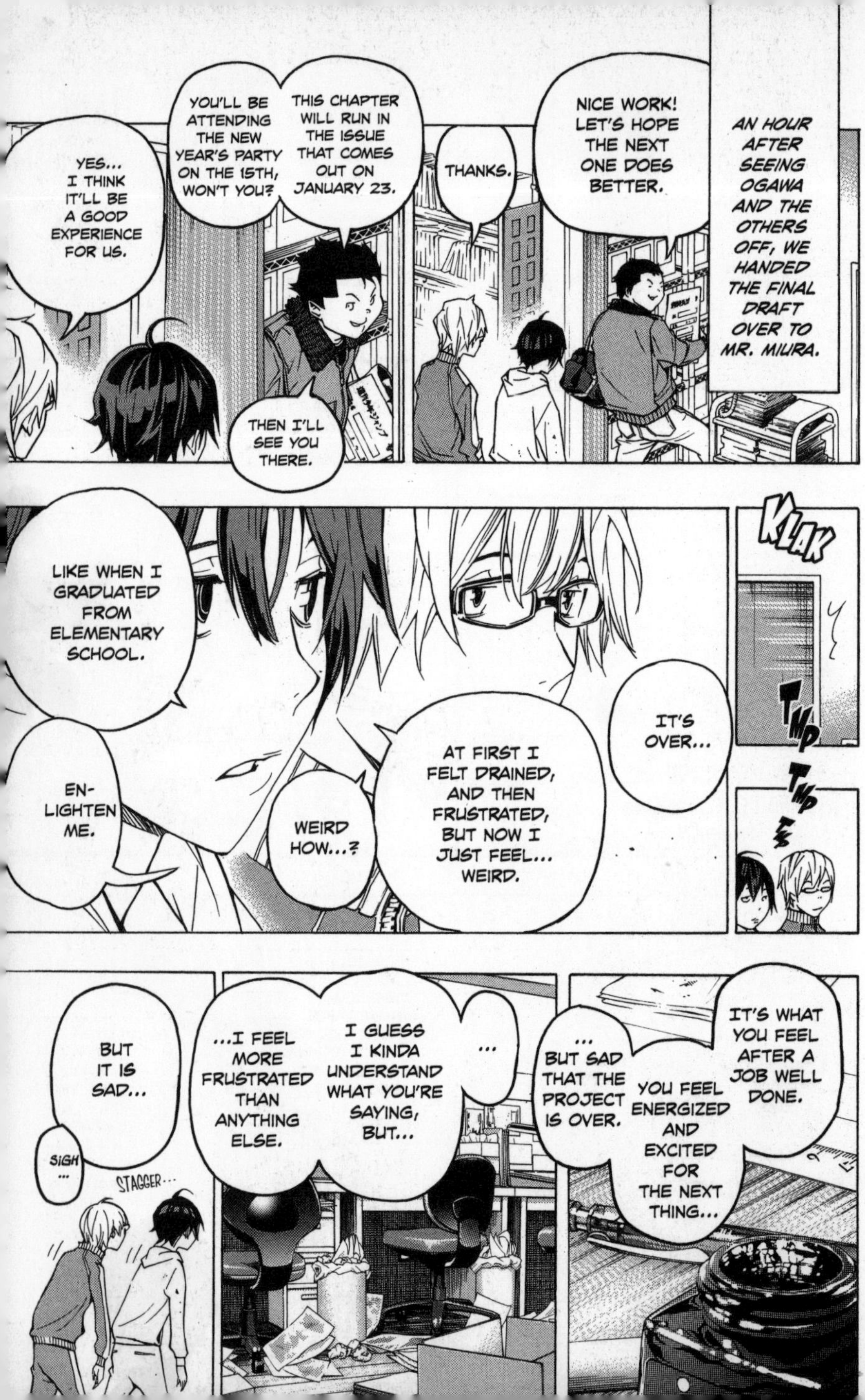
AN HOUR AFTER SEEING OGAWA AND THE OTHERS OFF, WE HANDED THE FINAL DRAFT OVER TO MR. MIURA.
NICE WORK! LET'S HOPE THE NEXT ONE DOES BETTER.
THANKS.
THIS CHAPTER WILL RUN IN THE ISSUE THAT COMES OUT ON JANUARY 23.
YOU'LL BE ATTENDING THE NEW YEAR'S PARTY ON THE 15TH, WON'T YOU?
YES... I THINK IT'LL BE A GOOD EXPERIENCE FOR US.
THEN I'LL SEE YOU THERE.
KLAK
TMP
TMP
TMP
IT'S OVER...
AT FIRST I FELT DRAINED, AND THEN FRUSTRATED, BUT NOW I JUST FEEL... WEIRD.
WEIRD HOW...?
LIKE WHEN I GRADUATED FROM ELEMENTARY SCHOOL.
EN-LIGHTEN ME.
IT'S WHAT YOU FEEL AFTER A JOB WELL DONE.
YOU FEEL ENERGIZED AND EXCITED FOR THE NEXT THING...
...BUT SAD THAT THE PROJECT IS OVER.
...
I GUESS I KINDA UNDERSTAND WHAT YOU'RE SAYING, BUT...
...I FEEL MORE FRUSTRATED THAN ANYTHING ELSE.
BUT IT IS SAD...
SIGH...
STAGGER...

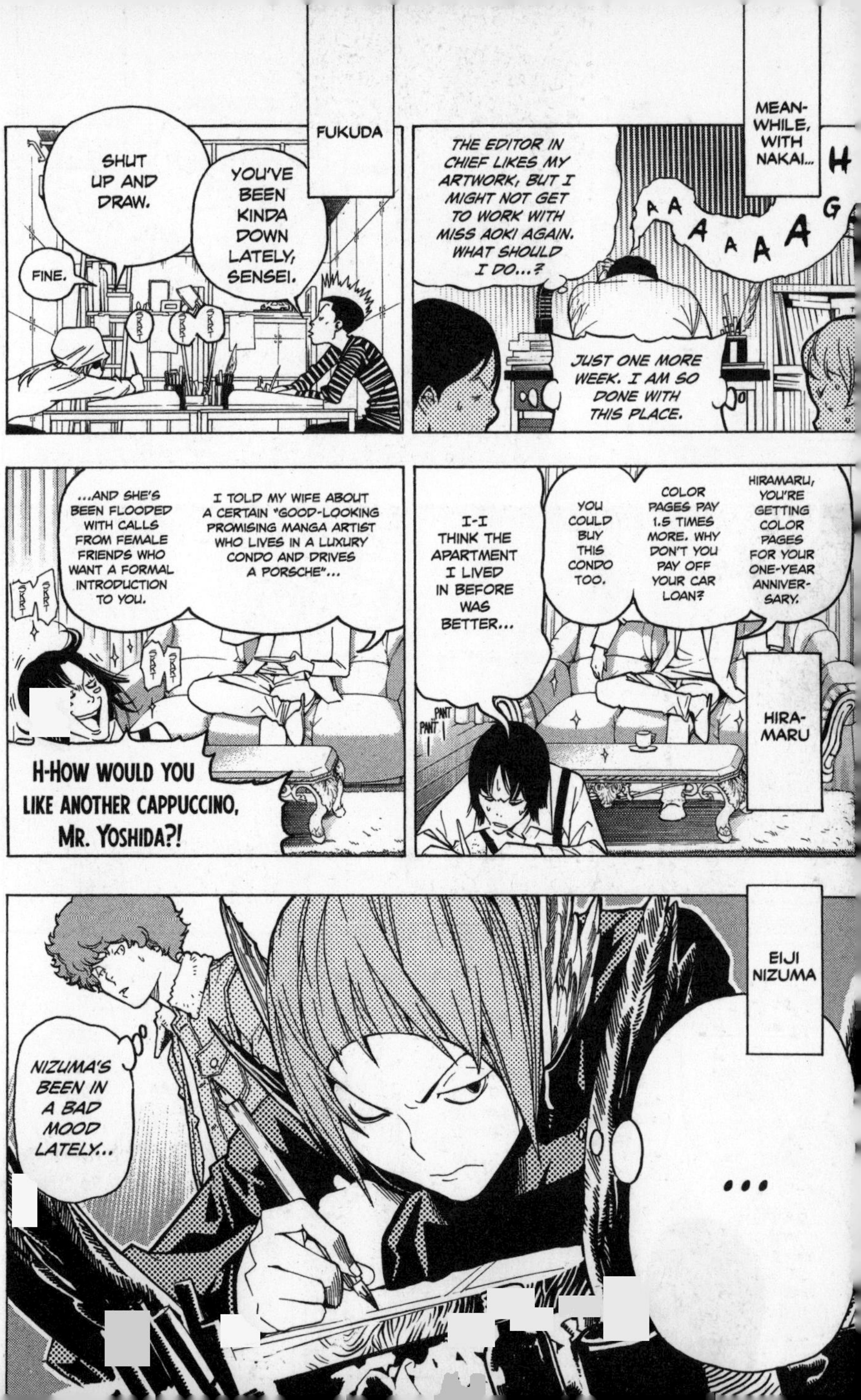
MEAN-WHILE, WITH NAKAI...
HAAAAAAG
THE EDITOR IN CHIEF LIKES MY ARTWORK, BUT I MIGHT NOT GET TO WORK WITH MISS AOKI AGAIN. WHAT SHOULD I DO...?
JUST ONE MORE WEEK. I AM SO DONE WITH THIS PLACE.
FUKUDA
YOU'VE BEEN KINDA DOWN LATELY, SENSEI.
SHUT UP AND DRAW.
FINE.
SKRT
SKRT
SKRT
HIRAMARU
HIRAMARU, YOU'RE GETTING COLOR PAGES FOR YOUR ONE-YEAR ANNIVERSARY.
COLOR PAGES PAY 1.5 TIMES MORE. WHY DON'T YOU PAY OFF YOUR CAR LOAN?
YOU COULD BUY THIS CONDO TOO.
I-I THINK THE APARTMENT I LIVED IN BEFORE WAS BETTER...
PANT PANT
I TOLD MY WIFE ABOUT A CERTAIN "GOOD-LOOKING PROMISING MANGA ARTIST WHO LIVES IN A LUXURY CONDO AND DRIVES A PORSCHE"...
...AND SHE'S BEEN FLOODED WITH CALLS FROM FEMALE FRIENDS WHO WANT A FORMAL INTRODUCTION TO YOU.
SKRT SKRT
SKRT SKRT
H-HOW WOULD YOU LIKE ANOTHER CAPPUCCINO, MR. YOSHIDA?!
EIJI NIZUMA
...
NIZUMA'S BEEN IN A BAD MOOD LATELY...

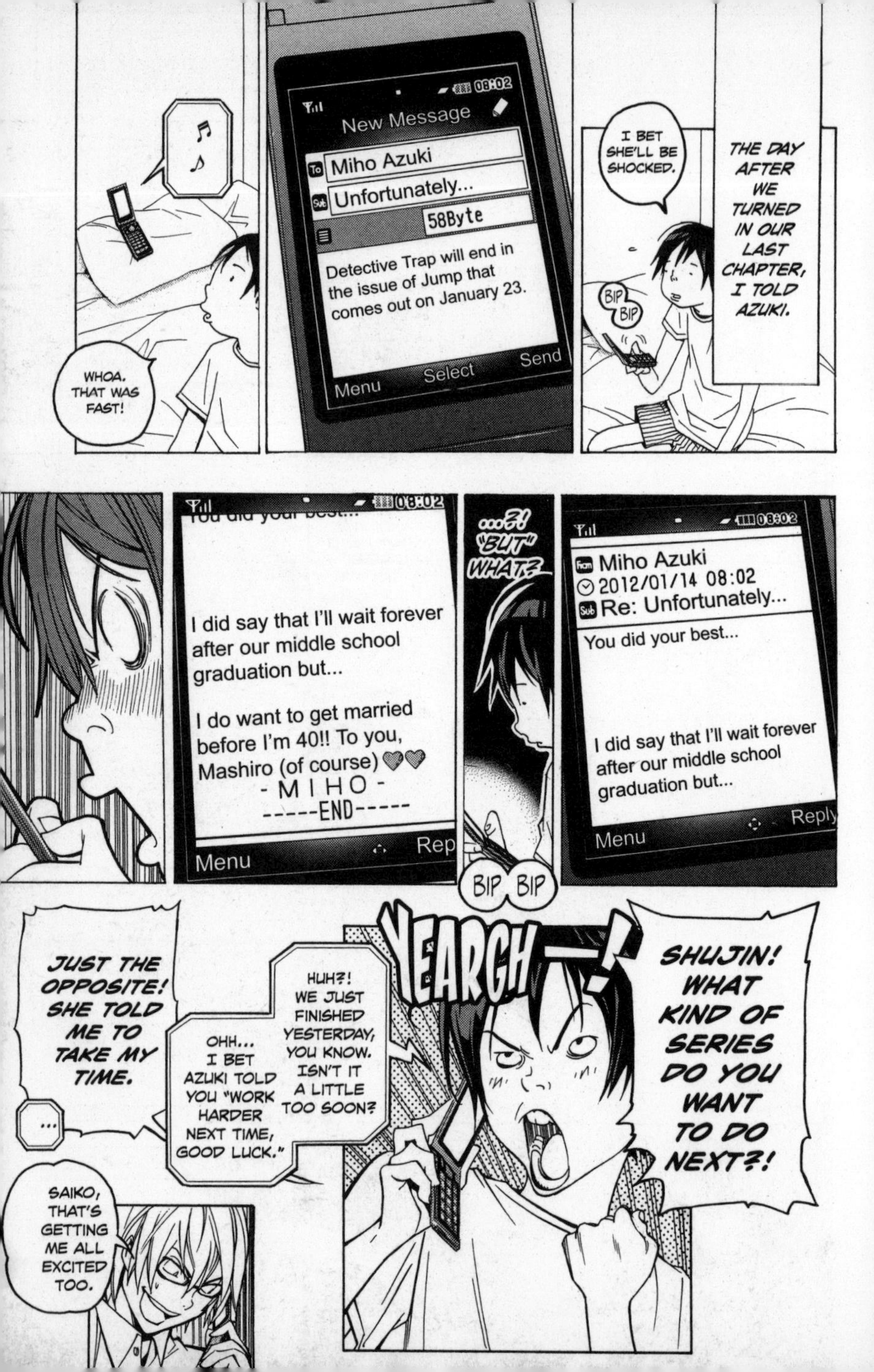
THE DAY AFTER WE TURNED IN OUR LAST CHAPTER, I TOLD AZUKI.
I BET SHE'LL BE SHOCKED.
BIP BIP
08:02
New Message
To Miho Azuki
Sub Unfortunately...
58Byte
Detective Trap will end in the issue of Jump that comes out on January 23.
Menu
Select
Send
♪ ♪
WHOA. THAT WAS FAST!
08:02
From Miho Azuki
2012/01/14 08:02
Sub Re: Unfortunately...
You did your best...
I did say that I'll wait forever after our middle school graduation but...
Menu
Reply
...?! "BUT" WHAT?
BIP BIP
08:02
I did say that I'll wait forever after our middle school graduation but...
I do want to get married before I'm 40!! To you, Mashiro (of course) ♥♥
-MIHO-
-----END-----
Menu
Rep
YEARGH—!
SHUJIN! WHAT KIND OF SERIES DO YOU WANT TO DO NEXT?!
HUH?! WE JUST FINISHED YESTERDAY, YOU KNOW. ISN'T IT A LITTLE TOO SOON?
OHH... I BET AZUKI TOLD YOU "WORK HARDER NEXT TIME, GOOD LUCK."
JUST THE OPPOSITE! SHE TOLD ME TO TAKE MY TIME.
...
SAIKO, THAT'S GETTING ME ALL EXCITED TOO.

OHBA'S STORYBOARD

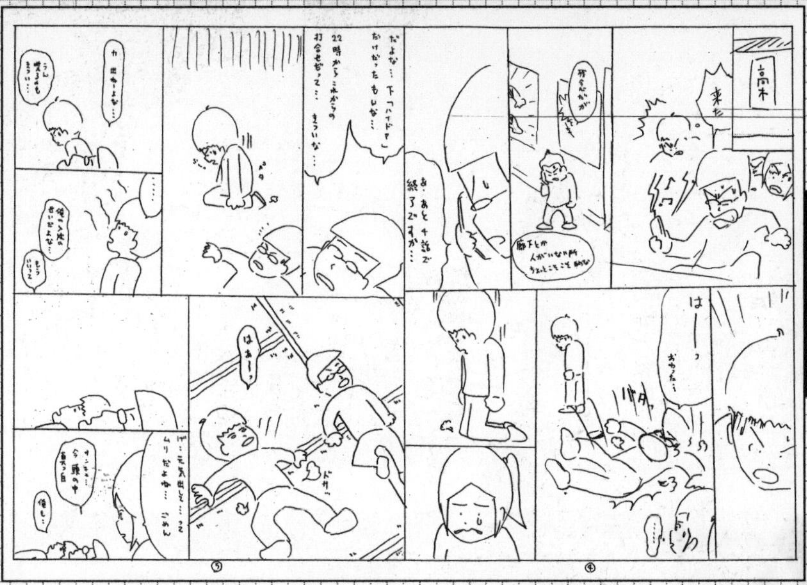

OBATA'S STORYBOARD

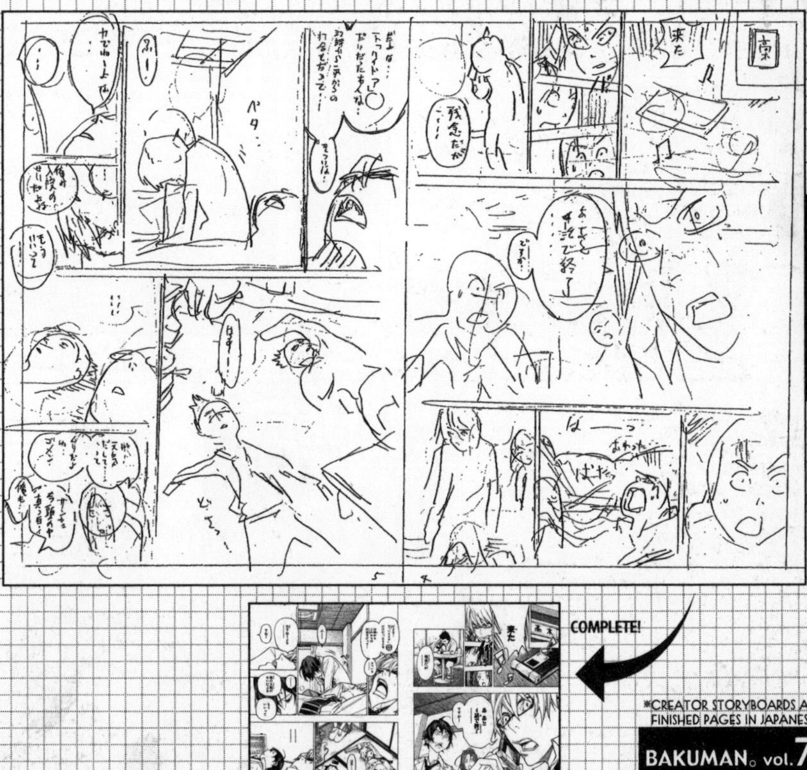

COMPLETE!

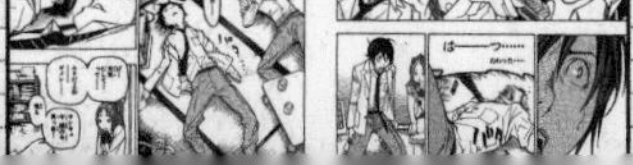

*CREATOR STORYBOARDS AND FINISHED PAGES IN JAPANESE

BAKUMAN。vol.7
"Until the Final Draft Is Complete"
Chapter 53, pp. 10-11

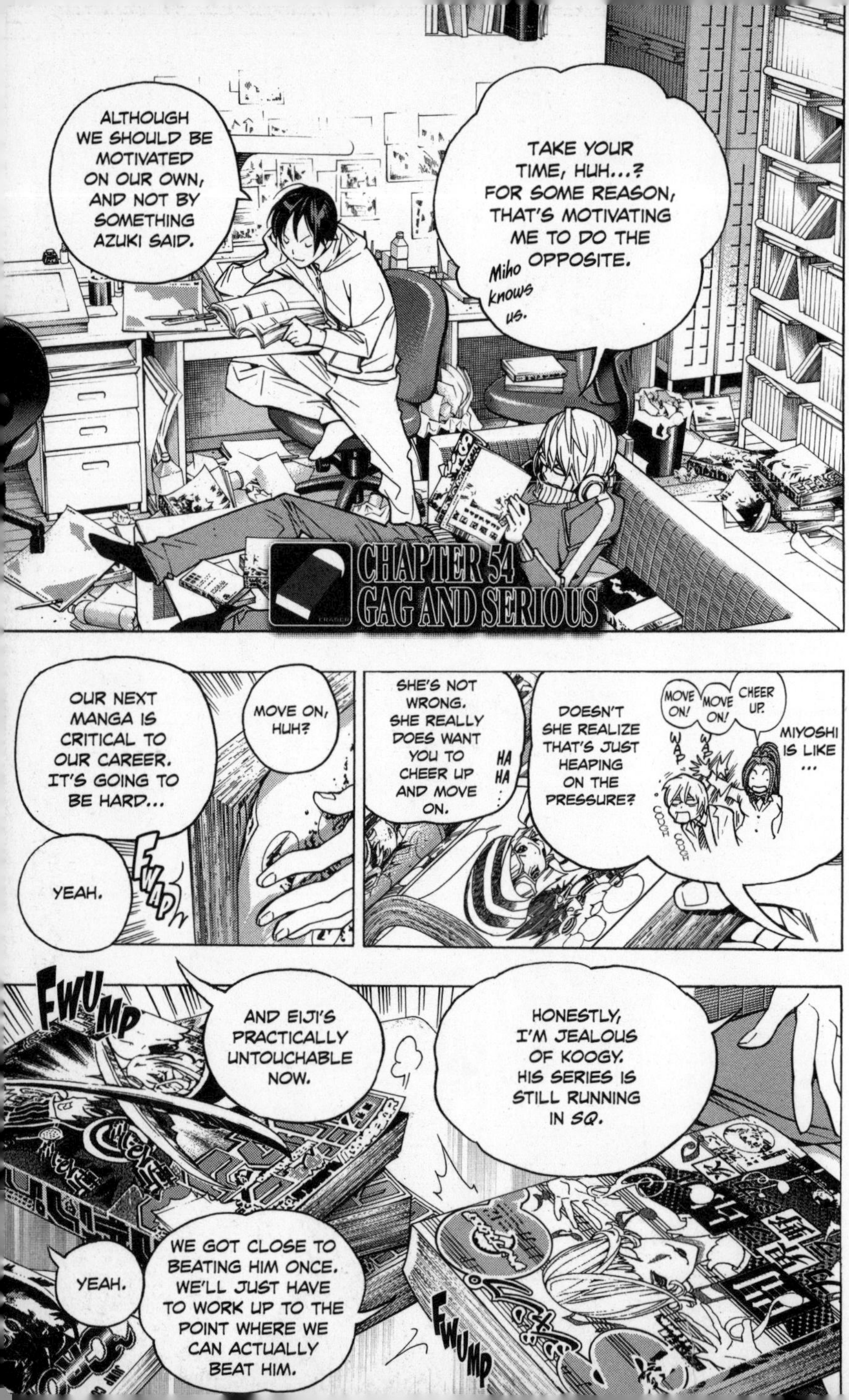
TAKE YOUR TIME, HUH...? FOR SOME REASON, THAT'S MOTIVATING ME TO DO THE OPPOSITE.
Miho knows us.
ALTHOUGH WE SHOULD BE MOTIVATED ON OUR OWN, AND NOT BY SOMETHING AZUKI SAID.
CHAPTER 54 GAG AND SERIOUS
ERASER
CHEER UP.
MOVE ON!
MOVE ON!
WAP
WAP
MIYOSHI IS LIKE ...
DOESN'T SHE REALIZE THAT'S JUST HEAPING ON THE PRESSURE?
HA HA
SHE'S NOT WRONG. SHE REALLY DOES WANT YOU TO CHEER UP AND MOVE ON.
MOVE ON, HUH?
OUR NEXT MANGA IS CRITICAL TO OUR CAREER. IT'S GOING TO BE HARD...
FWAP
YEAH.
HONESTLY, I'M JEALOUS OF KOOGY. HIS SERIES IS STILL RUNNING IN SQ.
AND EIJI'S PRACTICALLY UNTOUCHABLE NOW.
FWUMP
FWUMP
WE GOT CLOSE TO BEATING HIM ONCE. WE'LL JUST HAVE TO WORK UP TO THE POINT WHERE WE CAN ACTUALLY BEAT HIM.
YEAH.

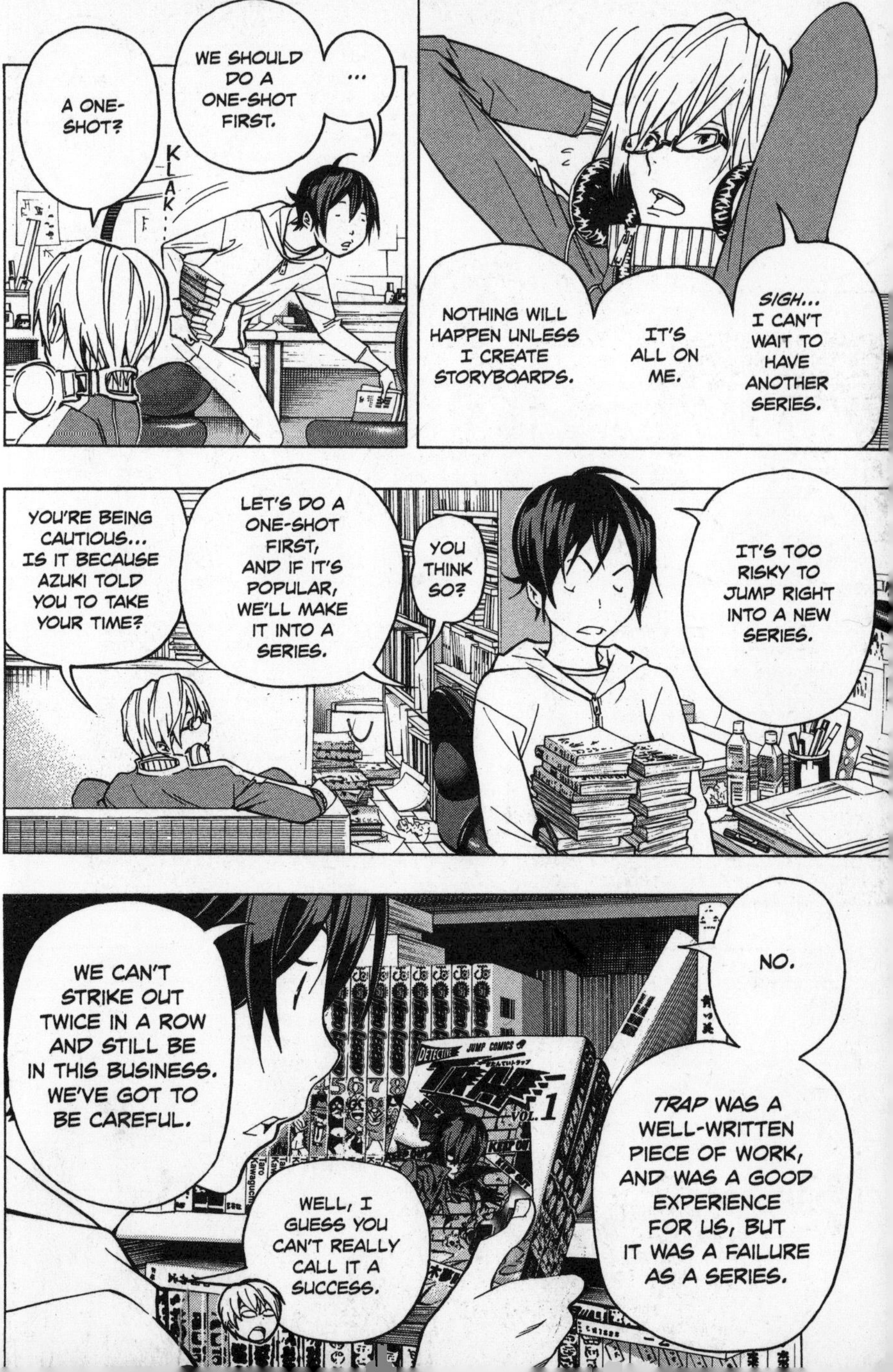
SIGH... I CAN'T WAIT TO HAVE ANOTHER SERIES.
IT'S ALL ON ME.
NOTHING WILL HAPPEN UNLESS I CREATE STORYBOARDS.
...
WE SHOULD DO A ONE-SHOT FIRST.
KLAK...
A ONE-SHOT?
IT'S TOO RISKY TO JUMP RIGHT INTO A NEW SERIES.
YOU THINK SO?
LET'S DO A ONE-SHOT FIRST, AND IF IT'S POPULAR, WE'LL MAKE IT INTO A SERIES.
YOU'RE BEING CAUTIOUS... IS IT BECAUSE AZUKI TOLD YOU TO TAKE YOUR TIME?
NO.
TRAP WAS A WELL-WRITTEN PIECE OF WORK, AND WAS A GOOD EXPERIENCE FOR US, BUT IT WAS A FAILURE AS A SERIES.
WELL, I GUESS YOU CAN'T REALLY CALL IT A SUCCESS.
WE CAN'T STRIKE OUT TWICE IN A ROW AND STILL BE IN THIS BUSINESS. WE'VE GOT TO BE CAREFUL.

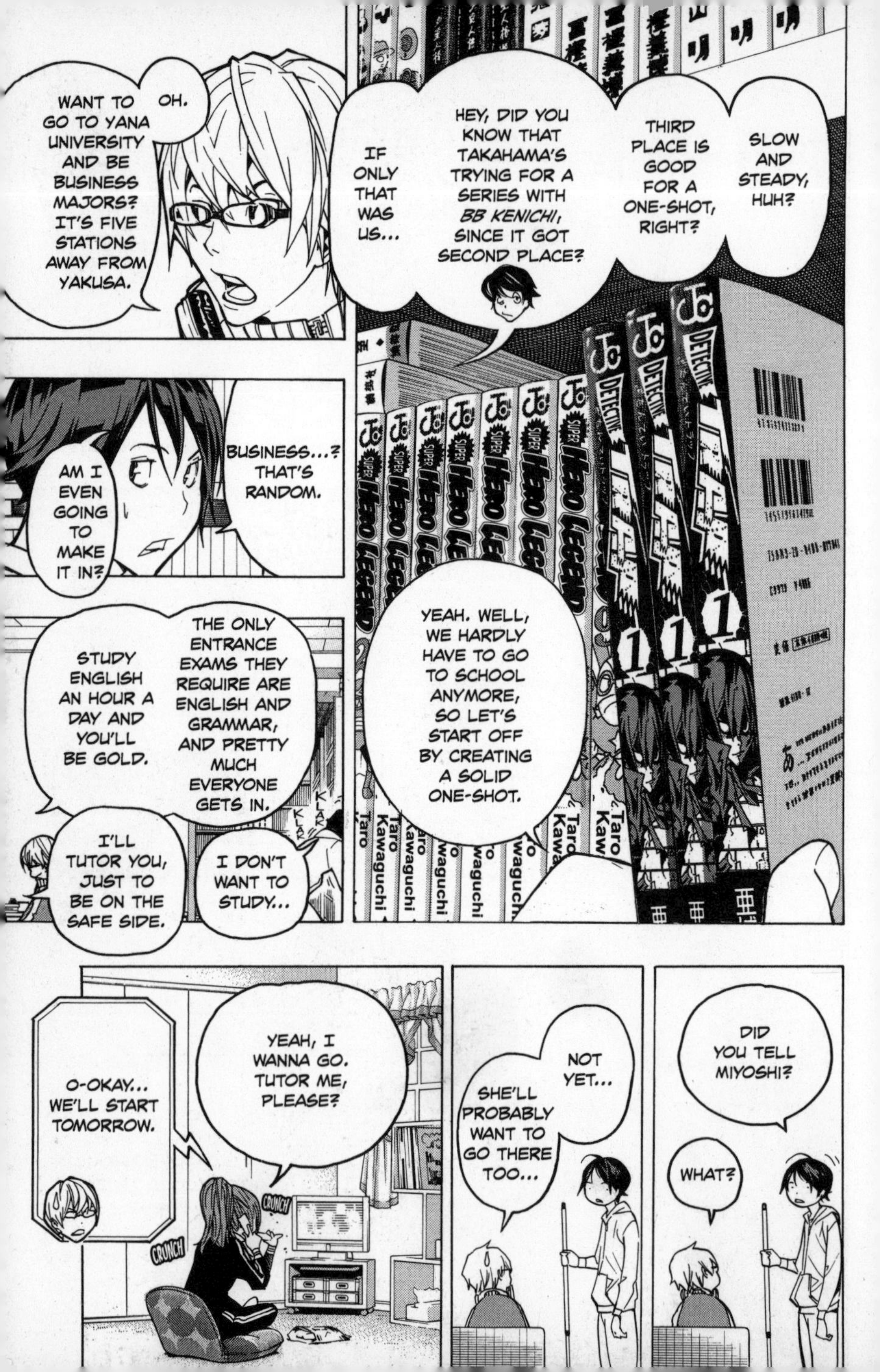
SLOW AND STEADY, HUH?
THIRD PLACE IS GOOD FOR A ONE-SHOT, RIGHT?
HEY, DID YOU KNOW THAT TAKAHAMA'S TRYING FOR A SERIES WITH *BB KENICHI*, SINCE IT GOT SECOND PLACE?
IF ONLY THAT WAS US...
DETECTIVE
SUPER HERO LEGEND
Taro Kawaguchi
YEAH. WELL, WE HARDLY HAVE TO GO TO SCHOOL ANYMORE, SO LET'S START OFF BY CREATING A SOLID ONE-SHOT.
OH.
WANT TO GO TO YANA UNIVERSITY AND BE BUSINESS MAJORS? IT'S FIVE STATIONS AWAY FROM YAKUSA.
BUSINESS...? THAT'S RANDOM.
AM I EVEN GOING TO MAKE IT IN?
THE ONLY ENTRANCE EXAMS THEY REQUIRE ARE ENGLISH AND GRAMMAR, AND PRETTY MUCH EVERYONE GETS IN.
STUDY ENGLISH AN HOUR A DAY AND YOU'LL BE GOLD.
KLAK KLAK
I DON'T WANT TO STUDY...
I'LL TUTOR YOU, JUST TO BE ON THE SAFE SIDE.
DID YOU TELL MIYOSHI?
WHAT?
NOT YET...
SHE'LL PROBABLY WANT TO GO THERE TOO...
YEAH, I WANNA GO. TUTOR ME, PLEASE?
CRUNCH
CRUNCH
O-OKAY... WE'LL START TOMORROW.

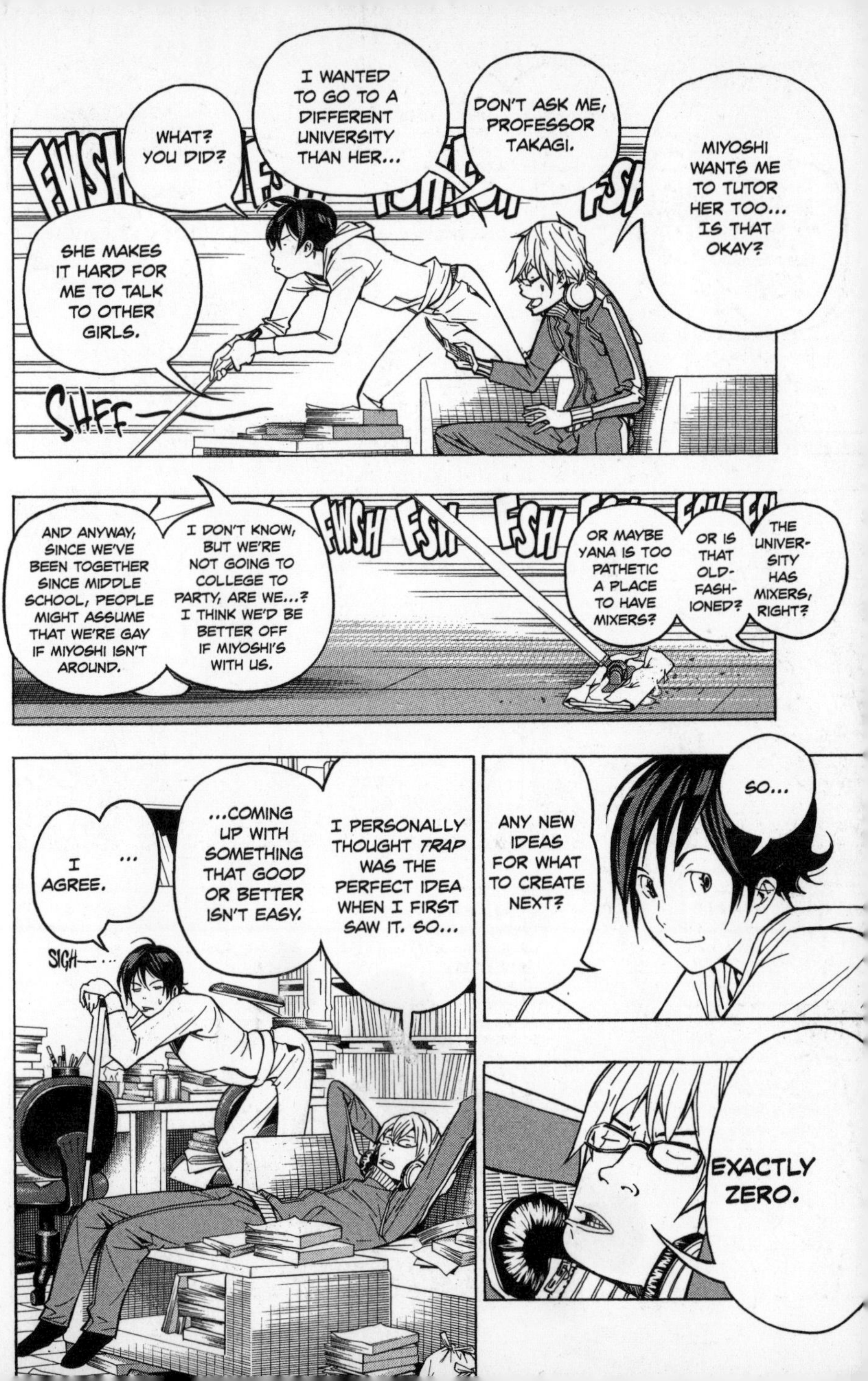
MIYOSHI WANTS ME TO TUTOR HER TOO... IS THAT OKAY?
FSH
DON'T ASK ME, PROFESSOR TAKAGI.
I WANTED TO GO TO A DIFFERENT UNIVERSITY THAN HER...
WHAT? YOU DID?
FWSH
SHE MAKES IT HARD FOR ME TO TALK TO OTHER GIRLS.
SHFF—
THE UNIVER-SITY HAS MIXERS, RIGHT?
OR IS THAT OLD-FASHIONED?
OR MAYBE YANA IS TOO PATHETIC A PLACE TO HAVE MIXERS?
FSH
FSH
FWSH
I DON'T KNOW, BUT WE'RE NOT GOING TO COLLEGE TO PARTY, ARE WE...? I THINK WE'D BE BETTER OFF IF MIYOSHI'S WITH US.
AND ANYWAY, SINCE WE'VE BEEN TOGETHER SINCE MIDDLE SCHOOL, PEOPLE MIGHT ASSUME THAT WE'RE GAY IF MIYOSHI ISN'T AROUND.
SO...
ANY NEW IDEAS FOR WHAT TO CREATE NEXT?
EXACTLY ZERO.
I PERSONALLY THOUGHT *TRAP* WAS THE PERFECT IDEA WHEN I FIRST SAW IT. SO...
...COMING UP WITH SOMETHING THAT GOOD OR BETTER ISN'T EASY.
...
I AGREE.
SIGH—...

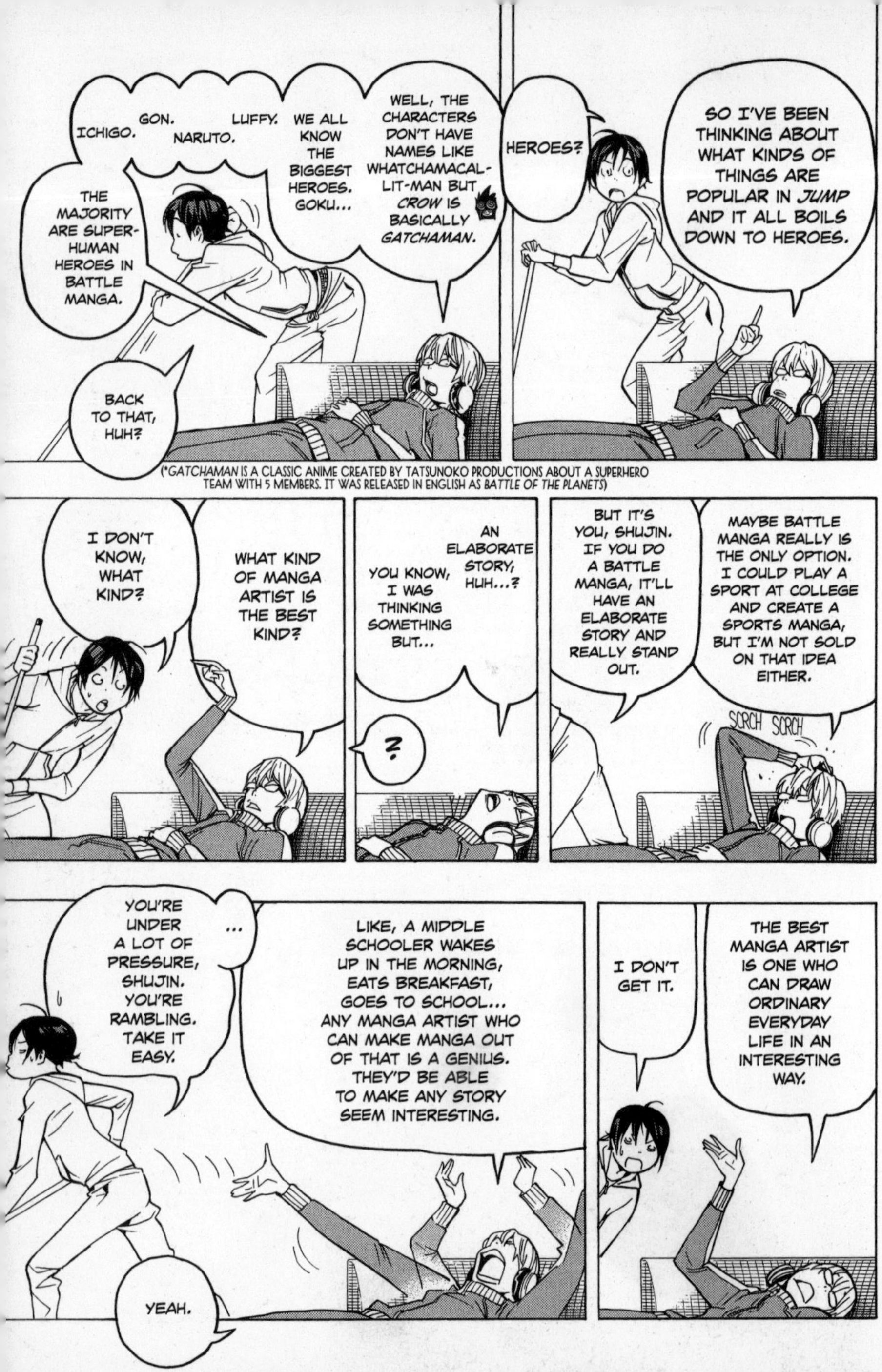
SO I'VE BEEN THINKING ABOUT WHAT KINDS OF THINGS ARE POPULAR IN *JUMP* AND IT ALL BOILS DOWN TO HEROES.
HEROES?
WELL, THE CHARACTERS DON'T HAVE NAMES LIKE WHATCHAMACAL-LIT-MAN BUT *CROW* IS BASICALLY *GATCHAMAN*.
WE ALL KNOW THE BIGGEST HEROES. GOKU...
LUFFY.
NARUTO.
GON.
ICHIGO.
THE MAJORITY ARE SUPER-HUMAN HEROES IN BATTLE MANGA.
BACK TO THAT, HUH?
MAYBE BATTLE MANGA REALLY IS THE ONLY OPTION. I COULD PLAY A SPORT AT COLLEGE AND CREATE A SPORTS MANGA, BUT I'M NOT SOLD ON THAT IDEA EITHER.
BUT IT'S YOU, SHUJIN. IF YOU DO A BATTLE MANGA, IT'LL HAVE AN ELABORATE STORY AND REALLY STAND OUT.
SCRCH SCRCH
AN ELABORATE STORY, HUH...?
YOU KNOW, I WAS THINKING SOMETHING BUT...
?
WHAT KIND OF MANGA ARTIST IS THE BEST KIND?
I DON'T KNOW, WHAT KIND?
THE BEST MANGA ARTIST IS ONE WHO CAN DRAW ORDINARY EVERYDAY LIFE IN AN INTERESTING WAY.
I DON'T GET IT.
LIKE, A MIDDLE SCHOOLER WAKES UP IN THE MORNING, EATS BREAKFAST, GOES TO SCHOOL... ANY MANGA ARTIST WHO CAN MAKE MANGA OUT OF THAT IS A GENIUS. THEY'D BE ABLE TO MAKE ANY STORY SEEM INTERESTING.
...
YOU'RE UNDER A LOT OF PRESSURE, SHUJIN. YOU'RE RAMBLING. TAKE IT EASY.
YEAH.

(**GATCHAMAN* IS A CLASSIC ANIME CREATED BY TATSUNOKO PRODUCTIONS ABOUT A SUPERHERO TEAM WITH 5 MEMBERS. IT WAS RELEASED IN ENGLISH AS *BATTLE OF THE PLANETS*)

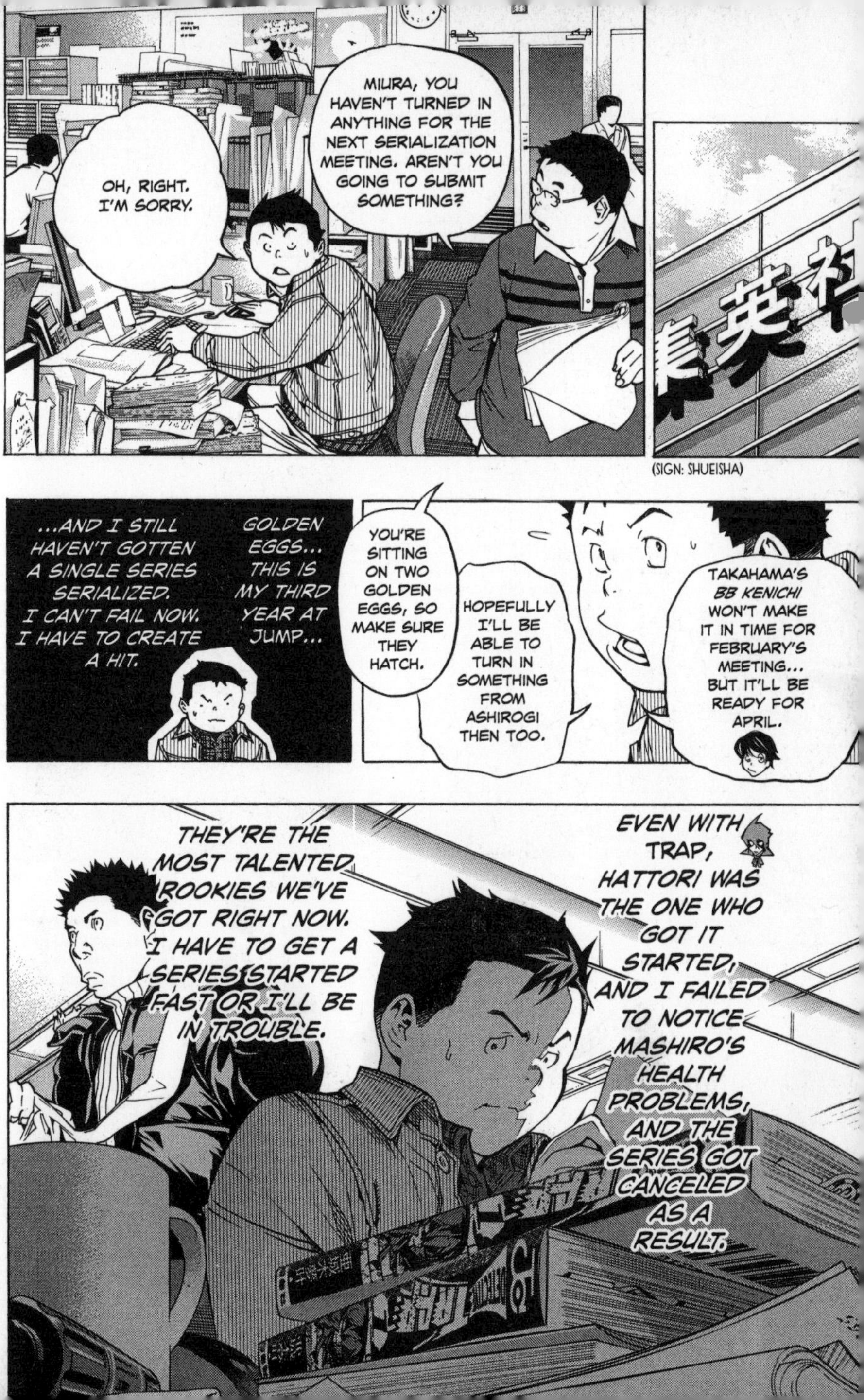
(SIGN: SHUEISHA)
MIURA, YOU HAVEN'T TURNED IN ANYTHING FOR THE NEXT SERIALIZATION MEETING. AREN'T YOU GOING TO SUBMIT SOMETHING?
OH, RIGHT. I'M SORRY.
TAKAHAMA'S BB KENICHI WON'T MAKE IT IN TIME FOR FEBRUARY'S MEETING... BUT IT'LL BE READY FOR APRIL.
HOPEFULLY I'LL BE ABLE TO TURN IN SOMETHING FROM ASHIROGI THEN TOO.
YOU'RE SITTING ON TWO GOLDEN EGGS, SO MAKE SURE THEY HATCH.
GOLDEN EGGS... THIS IS MY THIRD YEAR AT JUMP...
...AND I STILL HAVEN'T GOTTEN A SINGLE SERIES SERIALIZED. I CAN'T FAIL NOW. I HAVE TO CREATE A HIT.
EVEN WITH TRAP, HATTORI WAS THE ONE WHO GOT IT STARTED, AND I FAILED TO NOTICE MASHIRO'S HEALTH PROBLEMS, AND THE SERIES GOT CANCELED AS A RESULT.
THEY'RE THE MOST TALENTED ROOKIES WE'VE GOT RIGHT NOW. I HAVE TO GET A SERIES STARTED FAST OR I'LL BE IN TROUBLE.

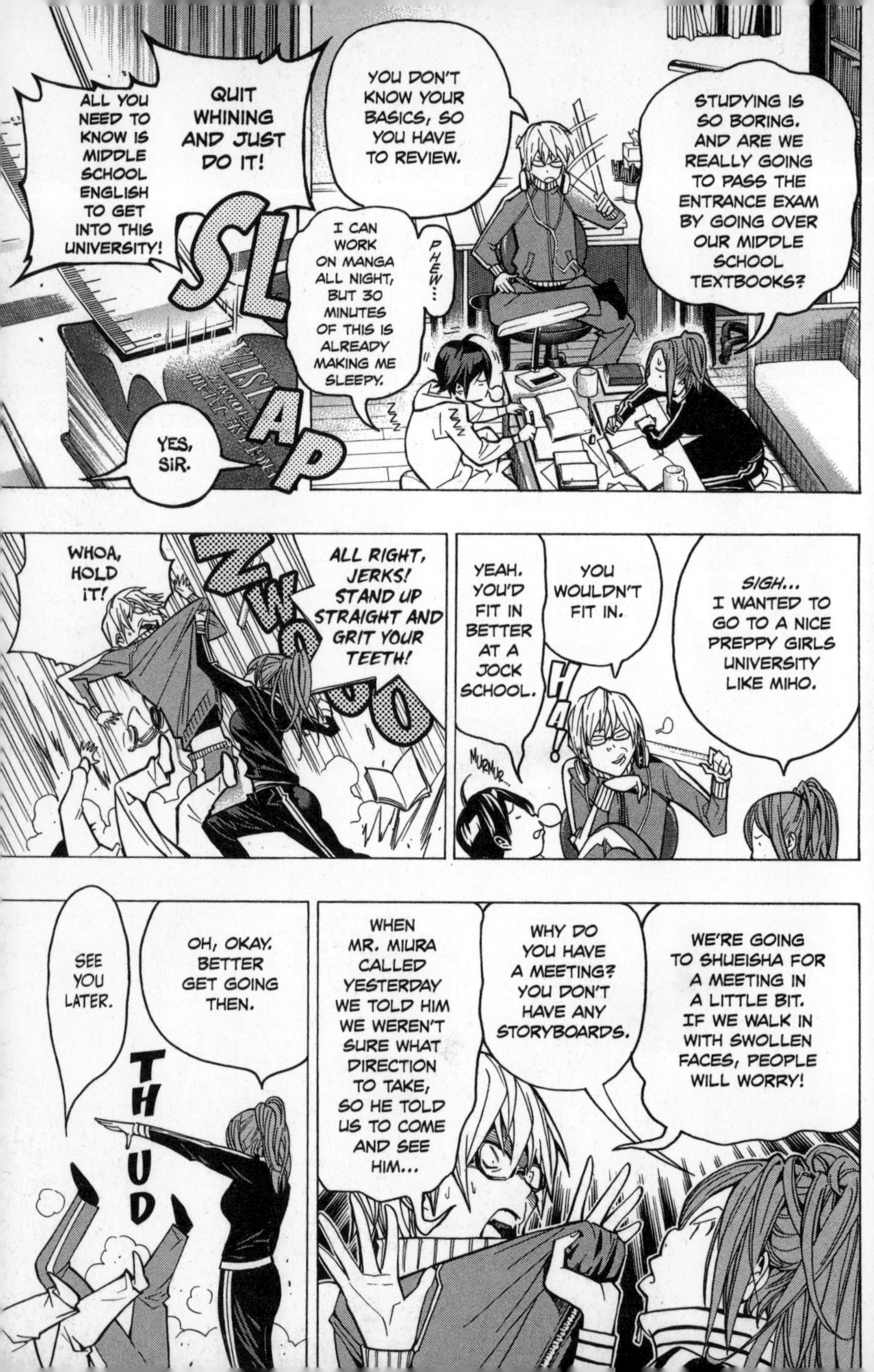
STUDYING IS SO BORING. AND ARE WE REALLY GOING TO PASS THE ENTRANCE EXAM BY GOING OVER OUR MIDDLE SCHOOL TEXTBOOKS?
YOU DON'T KNOW YOUR BASICS, SO YOU HAVE TO REVIEW.
PHEW...
I CAN WORK ON MANGA ALL NIGHT, BUT 30 MINUTES OF THIS IS ALREADY MAKING ME SLEEPY.
QUIT WHINING AND JUST DO IT!
ALL YOU NEED TO KNOW IS MIDDLE SCHOOL ENGLISH TO GET INTO THIS UNIVERSITY!
SLAP
YES, SIR.
SIGH... I WANTED TO GO TO A NICE PREPPY GIRLS UNIVERSITY LIKE MIHO.
YOU WOULDN'T FIT IN.
YEAH. YOU'D FIT IN BETTER AT A JOCK SCHOOL.
HA!
MURMUR...
ALL RIGHT, JERKS! STAND UP STRAIGHT AND GRIT YOUR TEETH!
WHOA, HOLD IT!
WE'RE GOING TO SHUEISHA FOR A MEETING IN A LITTLE BIT. IF WE WALK IN WITH SWOLLEN FACES, PEOPLE WILL WORRY!
WHY DO YOU HAVE A MEETING? YOU DON'T HAVE ANY STORYBOARDS.
WHEN MR. MIURA CALLED YESTERDAY WE TOLD HIM WE WEREN'T SURE WHAT DIRECTION TO TAKE, SO HE TOLD US TO COME AND SEE HIM...
OH, OKAY. BETTER GET GOING THEN.
SEE YOU LATER.
THUD

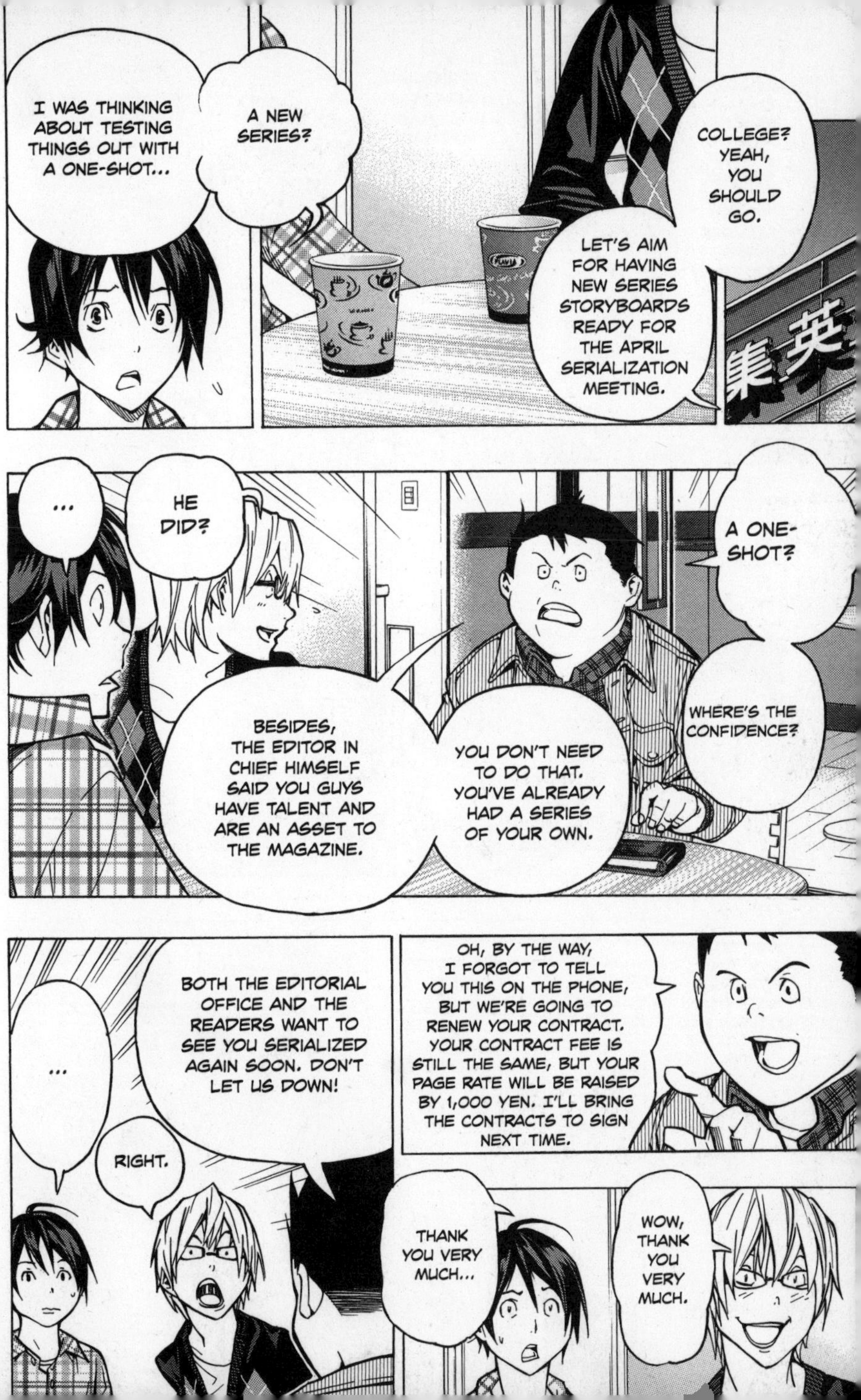
COLLEGE? YEAH, YOU SHOULD GO.
LET'S AIM FOR HAVING NEW SERIES STORYBOARDS READY FOR THE APRIL SERIALIZATION MEETING.
集英
A NEW SERIES?
I WAS THINKING ABOUT TESTING THINGS OUT WITH A ONE-SHOT...
A ONE-SHOT?
WHERE'S THE CONFIDENCE?
YOU DON'T NEED TO DO THAT. YOU'VE ALREADY HAD A SERIES OF YOUR OWN.
BESIDES, THE EDITOR IN CHIEF HIMSELF SAID YOU GUYS HAVE TALENT AND ARE AN ASSET TO THE MAGAZINE.
HE DID?
...
OH, BY THE WAY, I FORGOT TO TELL YOU THIS ON THE PHONE, BUT WE'RE GOING TO RENEW YOUR CONTRACT. YOUR CONTRACT FEE IS STILL THE SAME, BUT YOUR PAGE RATE WILL BE RAISED BY 1,000 YEN. I'LL BRING THE CONTRACTS TO SIGN NEXT TIME.
WOW, THANK YOU VERY MUCH.
THANK YOU VERY MUCH...
BOTH THE EDITORIAL OFFICE AND THE READERS WANT TO SEE YOU SERIALIZED AGAIN SOON. DON'T LET US DOWN!
...
RIGHT.

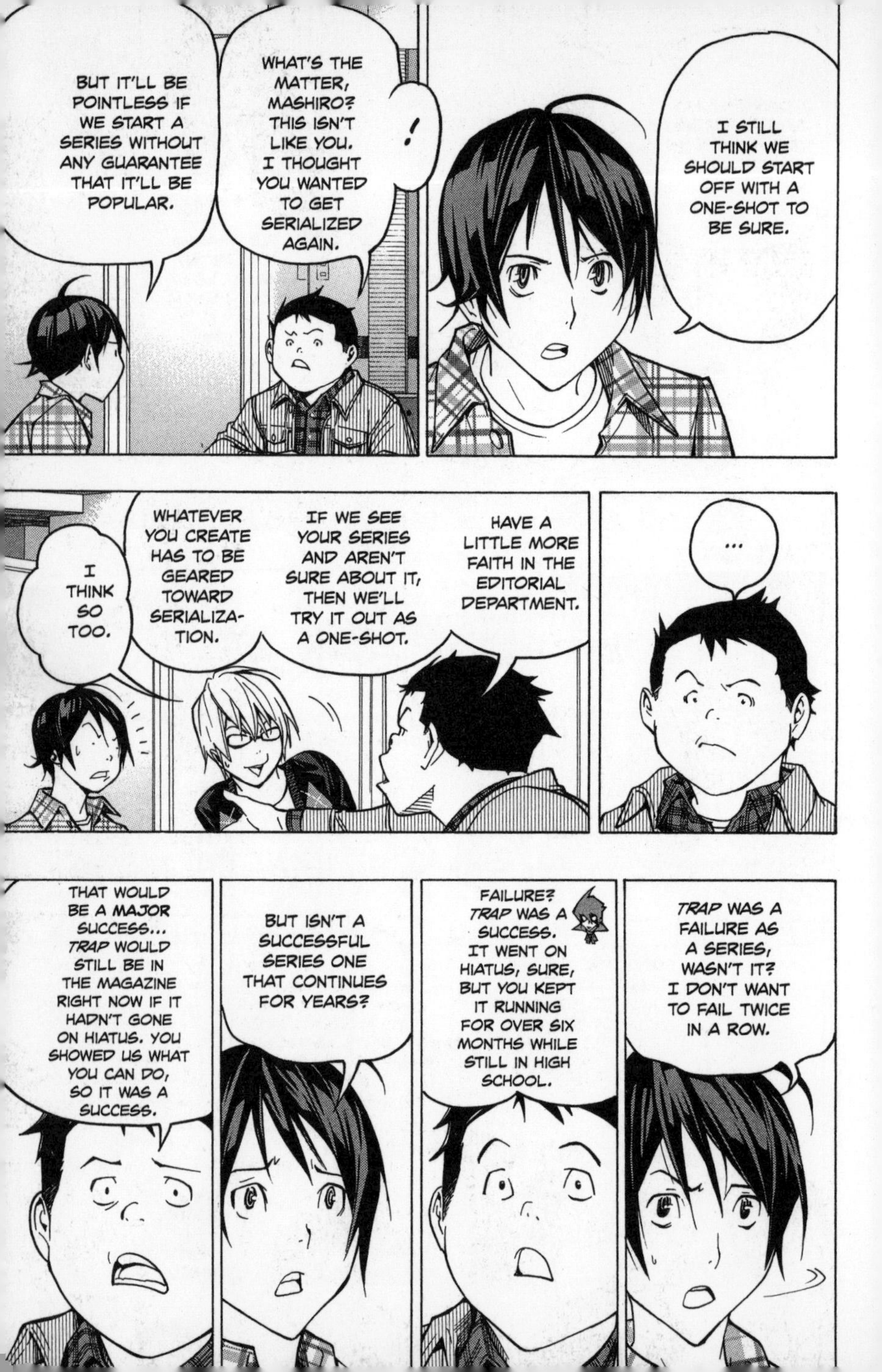
I STILL THINK WE SHOULD START OFF WITH A ONE-SHOT TO BE SURE.
WHAT'S THE MATTER, MASHIRO? THIS ISN'T LIKE YOU. I THOUGHT YOU WANTED TO GET SERIALIZED AGAIN.
!
BUT IT'LL BE POINTLESS IF WE START A SERIES WITHOUT ANY GUARANTEE THAT IT'LL BE POPULAR.
...
HAVE A LITTLE MORE FAITH IN THE EDITORIAL DEPARTMENT.
IF WE SEE YOUR SERIES AND AREN'T SURE ABOUT IT, THEN WE'LL TRY IT OUT AS A ONE-SHOT.
WHATEVER YOU CREATE HAS TO BE GEARED TOWARD SERIALIZA-TION.
I THINK SO TOO.
TRAP WAS A FAILURE AS A SERIES, WASN'T IT? I DON'T WANT TO FAIL TWICE IN A ROW.
FAILURE? TRAP WAS A SUCCESS. IT WENT ON HIATUS, SURE, BUT YOU KEPT IT RUNNING FOR OVER SIX MONTHS WHILE STILL IN HIGH SCHOOL.
BUT ISN'T A SUCCESSFUL SERIES ONE THAT CONTINUES FOR YEARS?
THAT WOULD BE A MAJOR SUCCESS... TRAP WOULD STILL BE IN THE MAGAZINE RIGHT NOW IF IT HADN'T GONE ON HIATUS. YOU SHOWED US WHAT YOU CAN DO, SO IT WAS A SUCCESS.

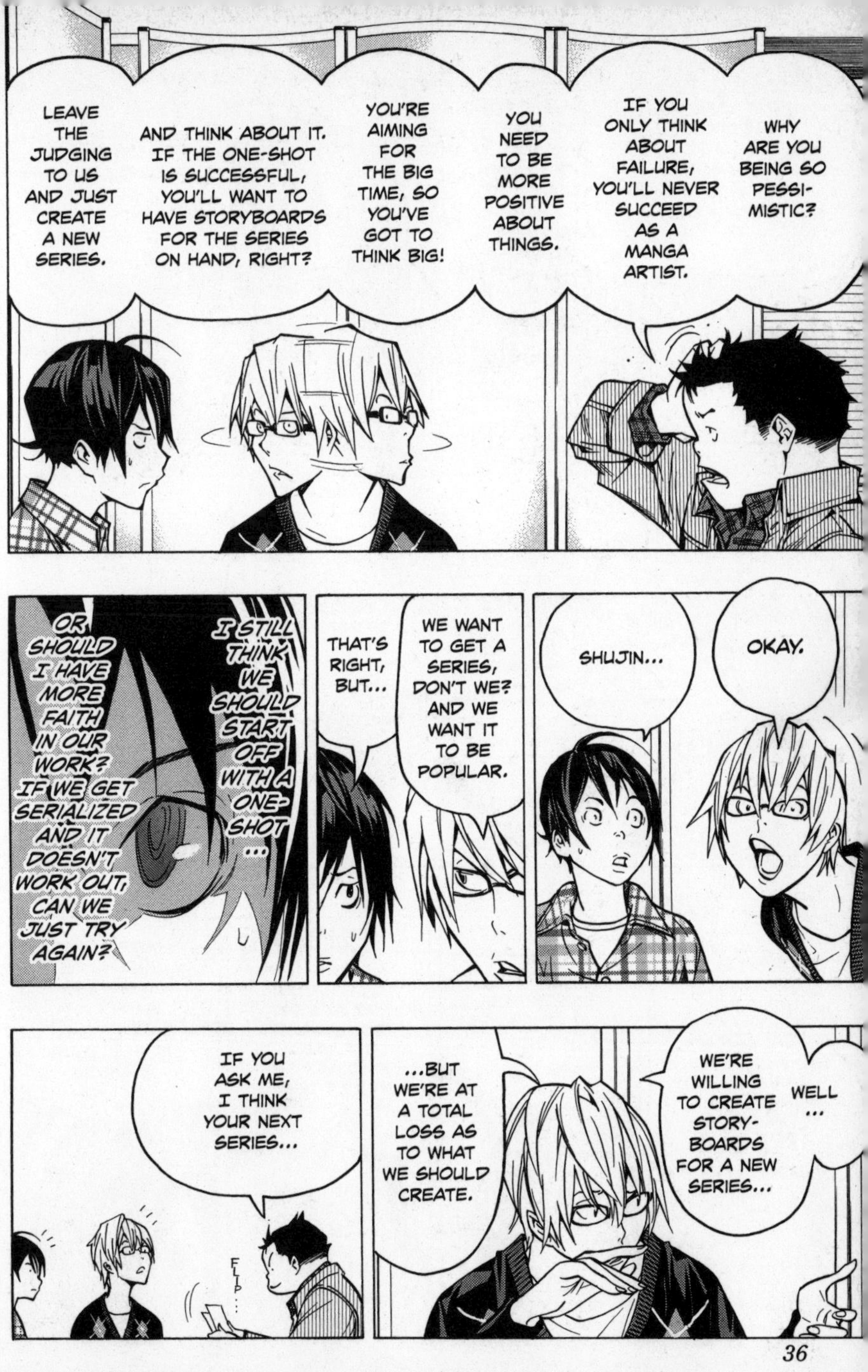
WHY ARE YOU BEING SO PESSIMISTIC?
IF YOU ONLY THINK ABOUT FAILURE, YOU'LL NEVER SUCCEED AS A MANGA ARTIST.
YOU NEED TO BE MORE POSITIVE ABOUT THINGS.
YOU'RE AIMING FOR THE BIG TIME, SO YOU'VE GOT TO THINK BIG!
AND THINK ABOUT IT. IF THE ONE-SHOT IS SUCCESSFUL, YOU'LL WANT TO HAVE STORYBOARDS FOR THE SERIES ON HAND, RIGHT?
LEAVE THE JUDGING TO US AND JUST CREATE A NEW SERIES.
OKAY.
SHUJIN...
WE WANT TO GET A SERIES, DON'T WE? AND WE WANT IT TO BE POPULAR.
THAT'S RIGHT, BUT...
I STILL THINK WE SHOULD START OFF WITH A ONE-SHOT...
OR SHOULD I HAVE MORE FAITH IN OUR WORK? IF WE GET SERIALIZED AND IT DOESN'T WORK OUT, CAN WE JUST TRY AGAIN?
WELL...
WE'RE WILLING TO CREATE STORY-BOARDS FOR A NEW SERIES...
...BUT WE'RE AT A TOTAL LOSS AS TO WHAT WE SHOULD CREATE.
IF YOU ASK ME, I THINK YOUR NEXT SERIES...
FLIP...

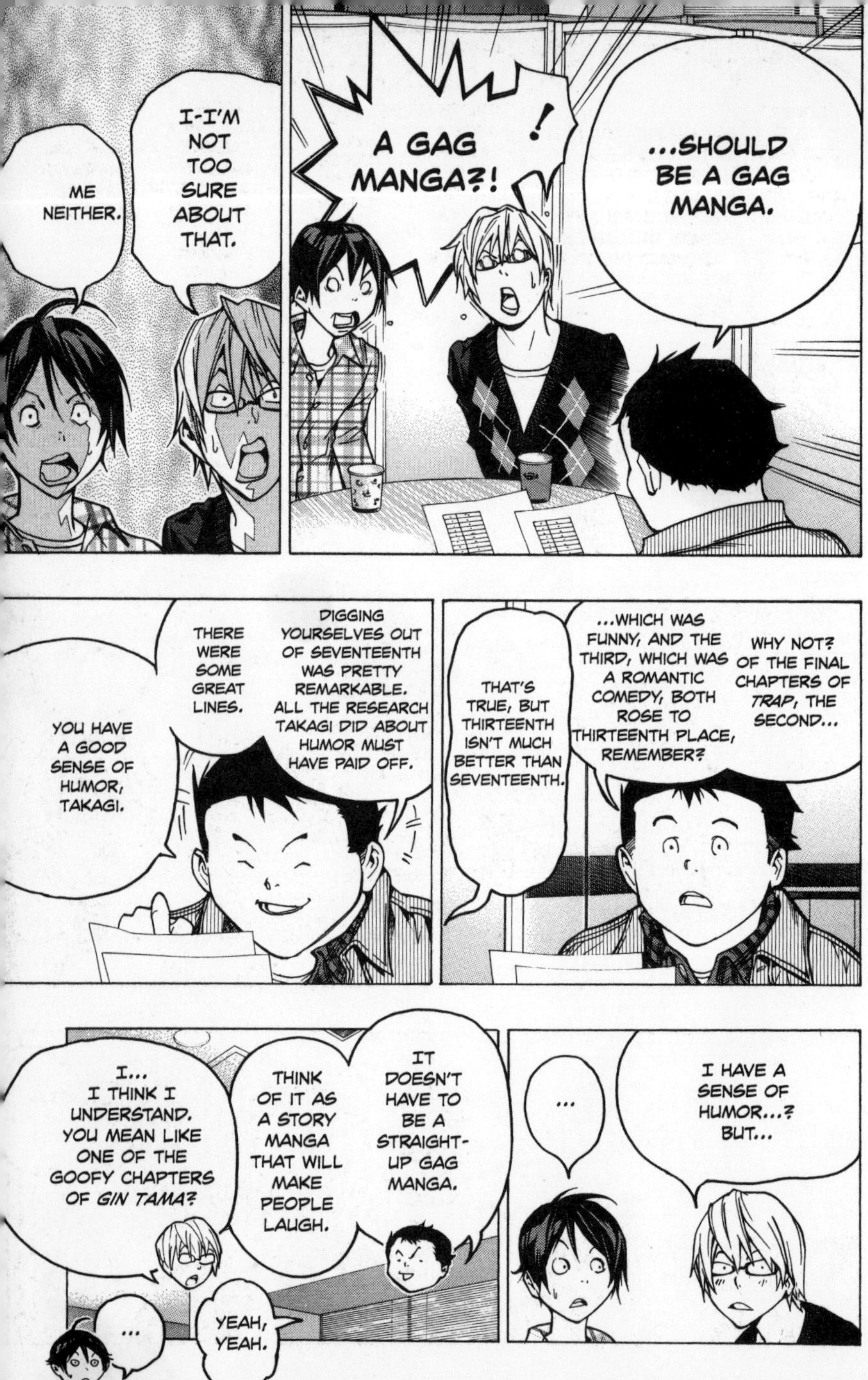
...SHOULD BE A GAG MANGA.
A GAG MANGA?!
!
I-I'M NOT TOO SURE ABOUT THAT.
ME NEITHER.
WHY NOT? OF THE FINAL CHAPTERS OF *TRAP*, THE SECOND...
...WHICH WAS FUNNY, AND THE THIRD, WHICH WAS A ROMANTIC COMEDY, BOTH ROSE TO THIRTEENTH PLACE, REMEMBER?
THAT'S TRUE, BUT THIRTEENTH ISN'T MUCH BETTER THAN SEVENTEENTH.
DIGGING YOURSELVES OUT OF SEVENTEENTH WAS PRETTY REMARKABLE. ALL THE RESEARCH TAKAGI DID ABOUT HUMOR MUST HAVE PAID OFF.
THERE WERE SOME GREAT LINES.
YOU HAVE A GOOD SENSE OF HUMOR, TAKAGI.
I HAVE A SENSE OF HUMOR...? BUT...
...
IT DOESN'T HAVE TO BE A STRAIGHT-UP GAG MANGA.
THINK OF IT AS A STORY MANGA THAT WILL MAKE PEOPLE LAUGH.
I... I THINK I UNDERSTAND. YOU MEAN LIKE ONE OF THE GOOFY CHAPTERS OF *GIN TAMA*?
YEAH, YEAH.
...

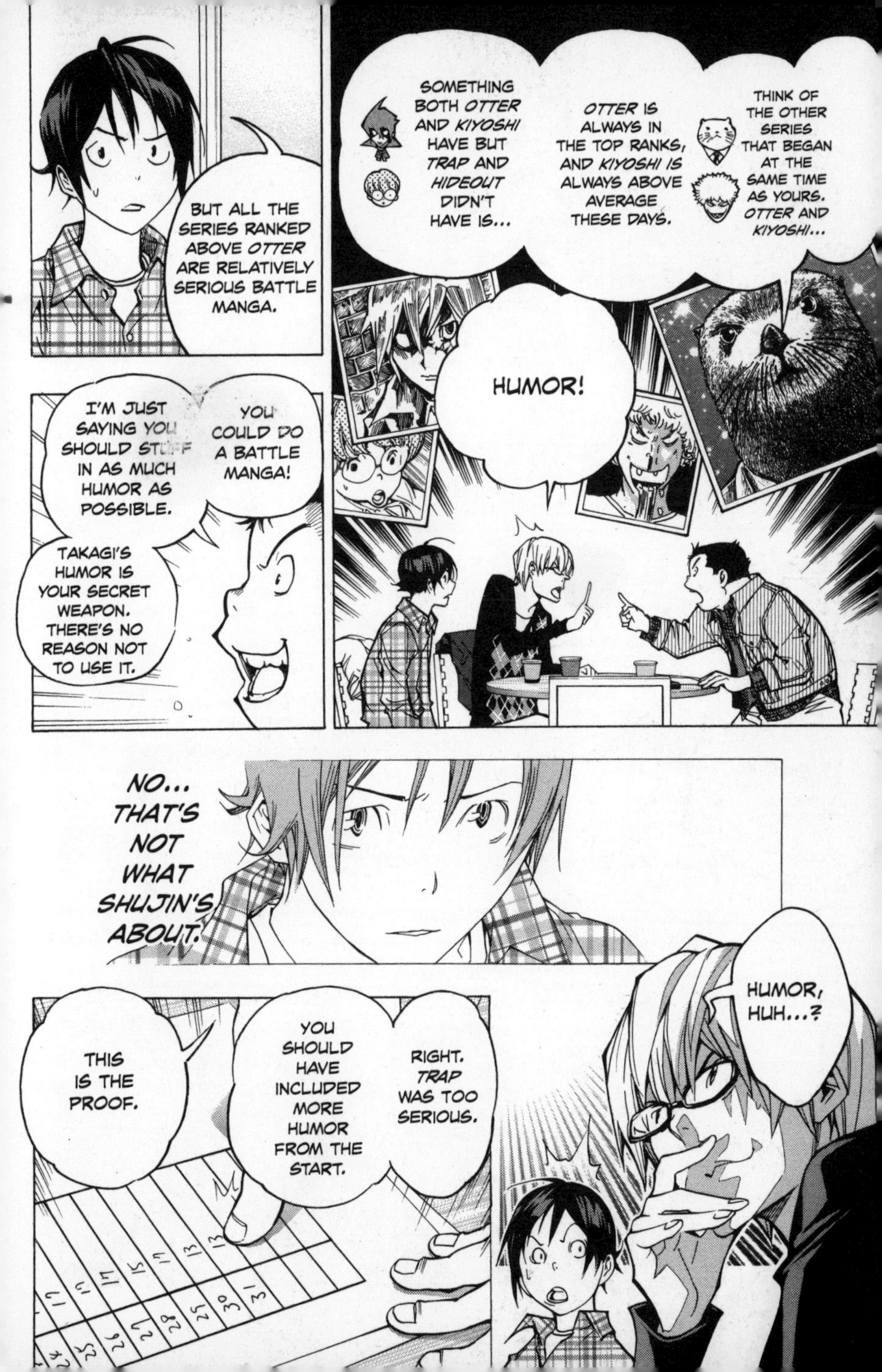
THINK OF THE OTHER SERIES THAT BEGAN AT THE SAME TIME AS YOURS. *OTTER* AND *KIYOSHI*...
OTTER IS ALWAYS IN THE TOP RANKS, AND *KIYOSHI* IS ALWAYS ABOVE AVERAGE THESE DAYS.
SOMETHING BOTH *OTTER* AND *KIYOSHI* HAVE BUT *TRAP* AND *HIDEOUT* DIDN'T HAVE IS...
HUMOR!
BUT ALL THE SERIES RANKED ABOVE *OTTER* ARE RELATIVELY SERIOUS BATTLE MANGA.
YOU COULD DO A BATTLE MANGA!
I'M JUST SAYING YOU SHOULD STUFF IN AS MUCH HUMOR AS POSSIBLE.
TAKAGI'S HUMOR IS YOUR SECRET WEAPON. THERE'S NO REASON NOT TO USE IT.
NO... THAT'S NOT WHAT SHUJIN'S ABOUT.
HUMOR, HUH...?
RIGHT. *TRAP* WAS TOO SERIOUS.
YOU SHOULD HAVE INCLUDED MORE HUMOR FROM THE START.
THIS IS THE PROOF.

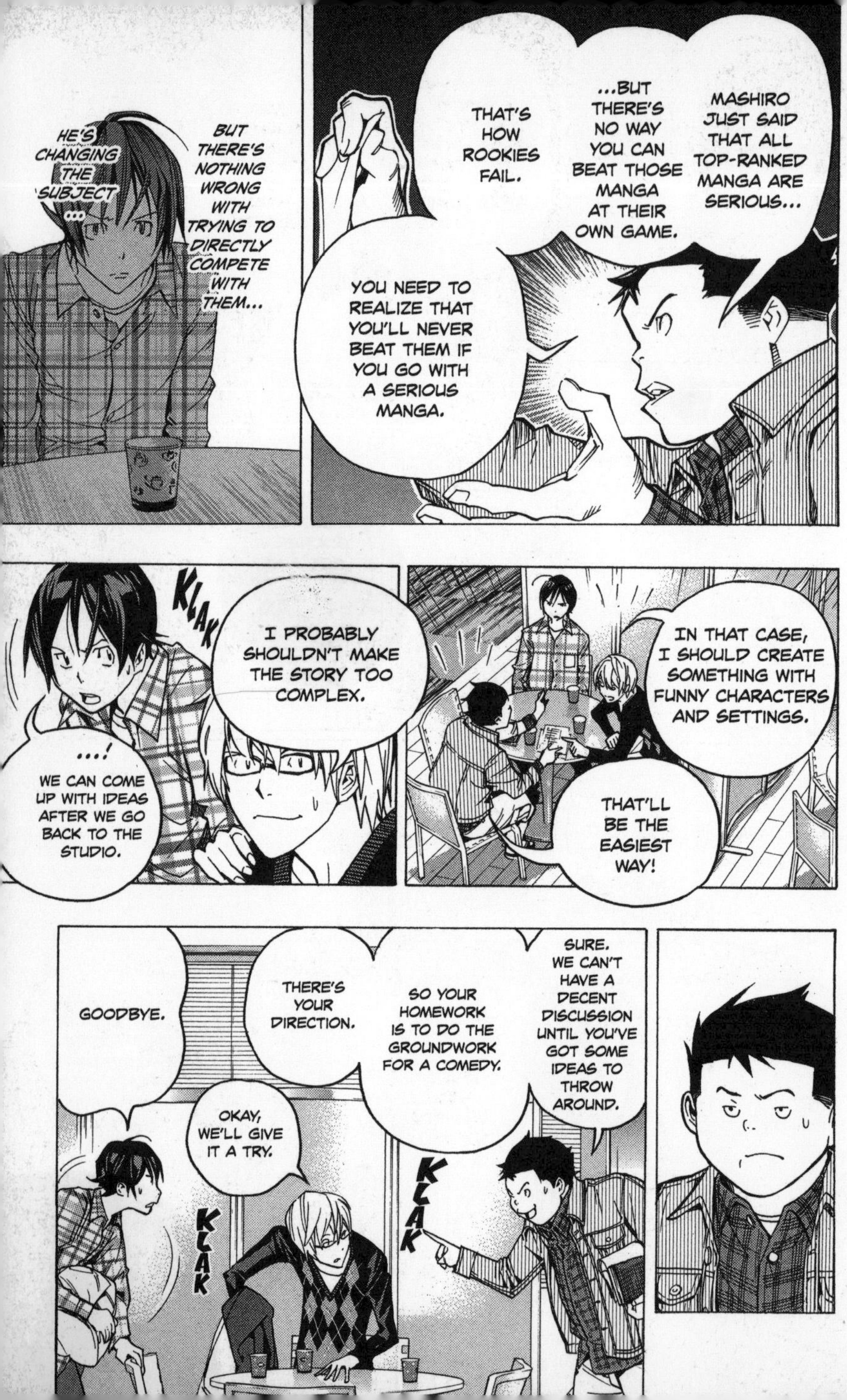
MASHIRO JUST SAID THAT ALL TOP-RANKED MANGA ARE SERIOUS...
...BUT THERE'S NO WAY YOU CAN BEAT THOSE MANGA AT THEIR OWN GAME.
THAT'S HOW ROOKIES FAIL.
YOU NEED TO REALIZE THAT YOU'LL NEVER BEAT THEM IF YOU GO WITH A SERIOUS MANGA.
BUT THERE'S NOTHING WRONG WITH TRYING TO DIRECTLY COMPETE WITH THEM...
HE'S CHANGING THE SUBJECT...
IN THAT CASE, I SHOULD CREATE SOMETHING WITH FUNNY CHARACTERS AND SETTINGS.
THAT'LL BE THE EASIEST WAY!
KLAK
I PROBABLY SHOULDN'T MAKE THE STORY TOO COMPLEX.
...!
WE CAN COME UP WITH IDEAS AFTER WE GO BACK TO THE STUDIO.
SURE. WE CAN'T HAVE A DECENT DISCUSSION UNTIL YOU'VE GOT SOME IDEAS TO THROW AROUND.
SO YOUR HOMEWORK IS TO DO THE GROUNDWORK FOR A COMEDY.
THERE'S YOUR DIRECTION.
KLAK
OKAY, WE'LL GIVE IT A TRY.
KLAK
GOODBYE.

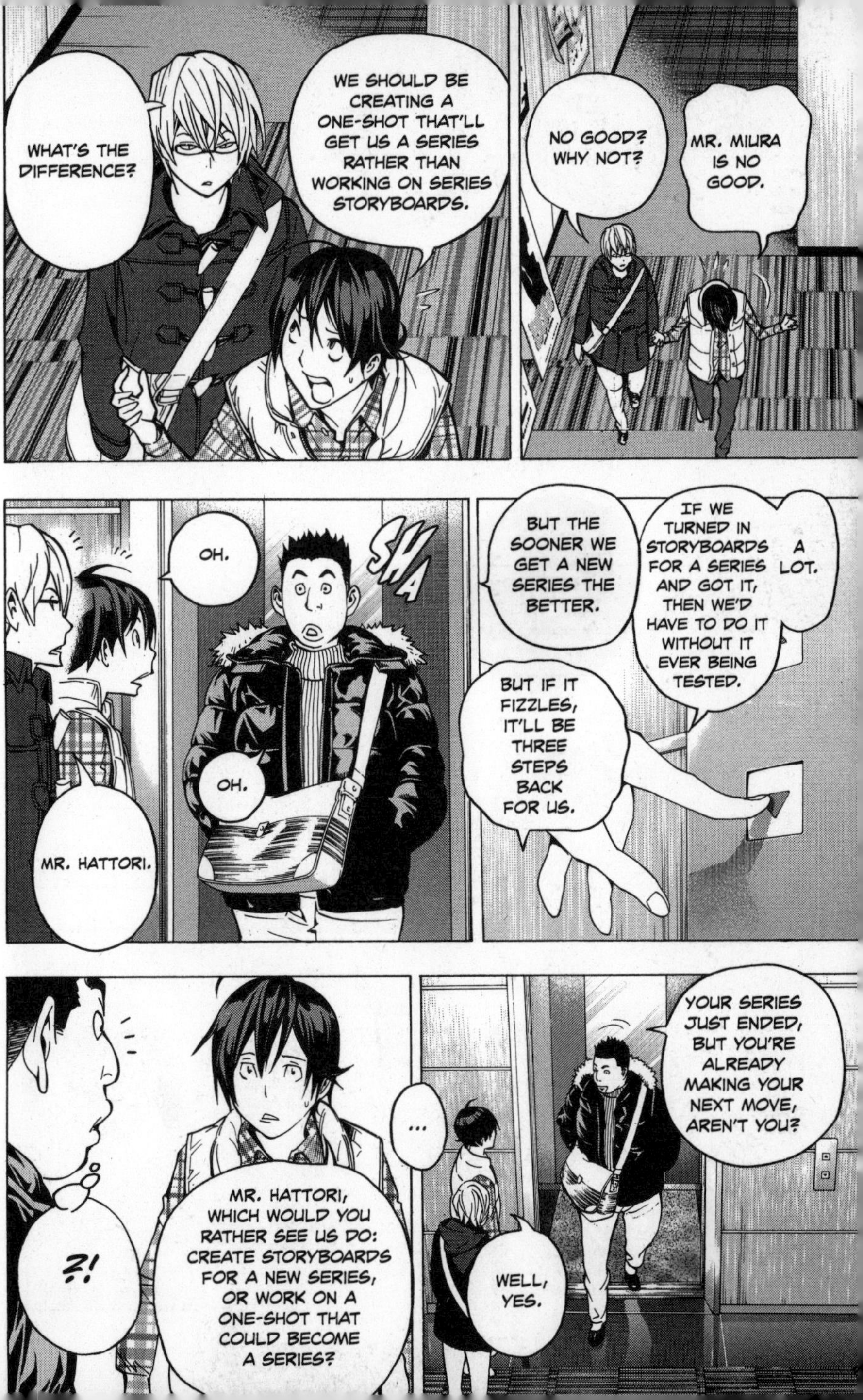
MR. MIURA IS NO GOOD.
NO GOOD? WHY NOT?
WE SHOULD BE CREATING A ONE-SHOT THAT'LL GET US A SERIES RATHER THAN WORKING ON SERIES STORYBOARDS.
WHAT'S THE DIFFERENCE?
A LOT.
IF WE TURNED IN STORYBOARDS FOR A SERIES AND GOT IT, THEN WE'D HAVE TO DO IT WITHOUT IT EVER BEING TESTED.
BUT THE SOONER WE GET A NEW SERIES THE BETTER.
BUT IF IT FIZZLES, IT'LL BE THREE STEPS BACK FOR US.
SHA
OH.
OH.
MR. HATTORI.
YOUR SERIES JUST ENDED, BUT YOU'RE ALREADY MAKING YOUR NEXT MOVE, AREN'T YOU?
WELL, YES.
...
MR. HATTORI, WHICH WOULD YOU RATHER SEE US DO: CREATE STORYBOARDS FOR A NEW SERIES, OR WORK ON A ONE-SHOT THAT COULD BECOME A SERIES?
?!

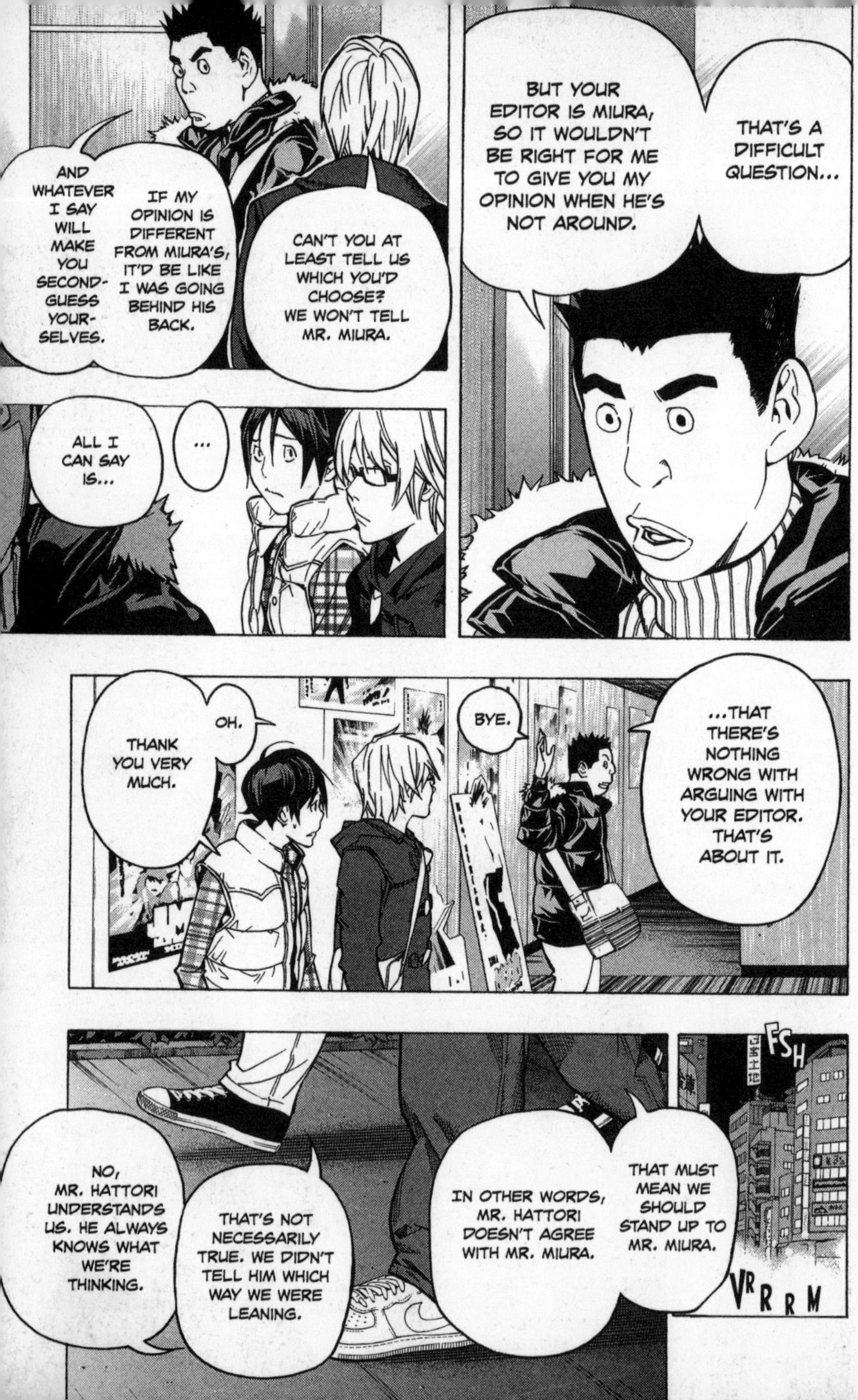
THAT'S A DIFFICULT QUESTION...
BUT YOUR EDITOR IS MIURA, SO IT WOULDN'T BE RIGHT FOR ME TO GIVE YOU MY OPINION WHEN HE'S NOT AROUND.
CAN'T YOU AT LEAST TELL US WHICH YOU'D CHOOSE? WE WON'T TELL MR. MIURA.
IF MY OPINION IS DIFFERENT FROM MIURA'S, IT'D BE LIKE I WAS GOING BEHIND HIS BACK.
AND WHATEVER I SAY WILL MAKE YOU SECOND-GUESS YOURSELVES.
...
ALL I CAN SAY IS...
...THAT THERE'S NOTHING WRONG WITH ARGUING WITH YOUR EDITOR. THAT'S ABOUT IT.
BYE.
OH.
THANK YOU VERY MUCH.
FSH
VRRRM
THAT MUST MEAN WE SHOULD STAND UP TO MR. MIURA.
IN OTHER WORDS, MR. HATTORI DOESN'T AGREE WITH MR. MIURA.
THAT'S NOT NECESSARILY TRUE. WE DIDN'T TELL HIM WHICH WAY WE WERE LEANING.
NO, MR. HATTORI UNDERSTANDS US. HE ALWAYS KNOWS WHAT WE'RE THINKING.

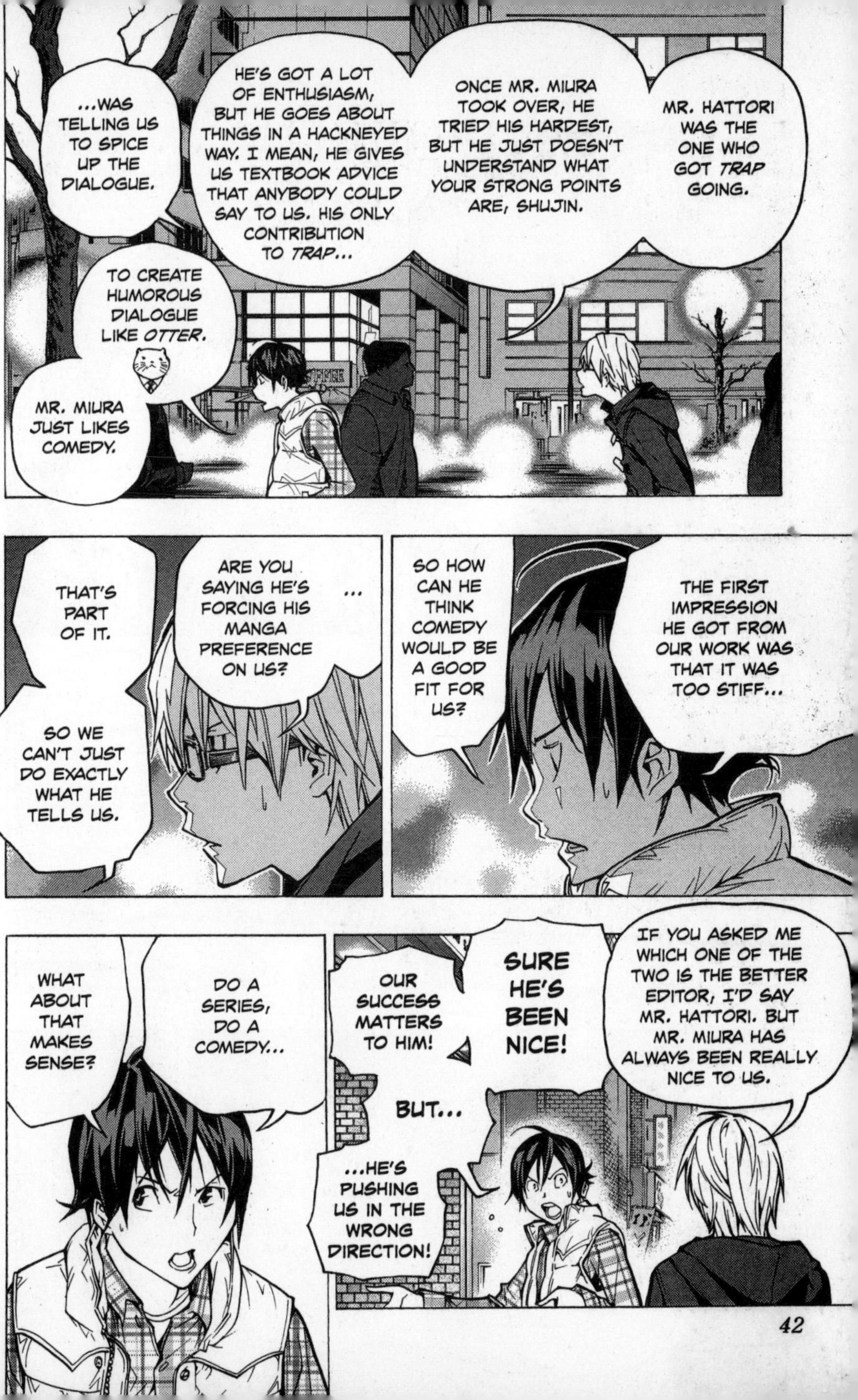
MR. HATTORI WAS THE ONE WHO GOT *TRAP* GOING.
ONCE MR. MIURA TOOK OVER, HE TRIED HIS HARDEST, BUT HE JUST DOESN'T UNDERSTAND WHAT YOUR STRONG POINTS ARE, SHUJIN.
HE'S GOT A LOT OF ENTHUSIASM, BUT HE GOES ABOUT THINGS IN A HACKNEYED WAY. I MEAN, HE GIVES US TEXTBOOK ADVICE THAT ANYBODY COULD SAY TO US. HIS ONLY CONTRIBUTION TO *TRAP*...
...WAS TELLING US TO SPICE UP THE DIALOGUE.
TO CREATE HUMOROUS DIALOGUE LIKE *OTTER*.
MR. MIURA JUST LIKES COMEDY.
THE FIRST IMPRESSION HE GOT FROM OUR WORK WAS THAT IT WAS TOO STIFF...
SO HOW CAN HE THINK COMEDY WOULD BE A GOOD FIT FOR US?
...
ARE YOU SAYING HE'S FORCING HIS MANGA PREFERENCE ON US?
THAT'S PART OF IT.
SO WE CAN'T JUST DO EXACTLY WHAT HE TELLS US.
IF YOU ASKED ME WHICH ONE OF THE TWO IS THE BETTER EDITOR, I'D SAY MR. HATTORI. BUT MR. MIURA HAS ALWAYS BEEN REALLY NICE TO US.
SURE HE'S BEEN NICE!
OUR SUCCESS MATTERS TO HIM!
BUT...
...HE'S PUSHING US IN THE WRONG DIRECTION!
DO A SERIES, DO A COMEDY...
WHAT ABOUT THAT MAKES SENSE?

READ THIS WAY

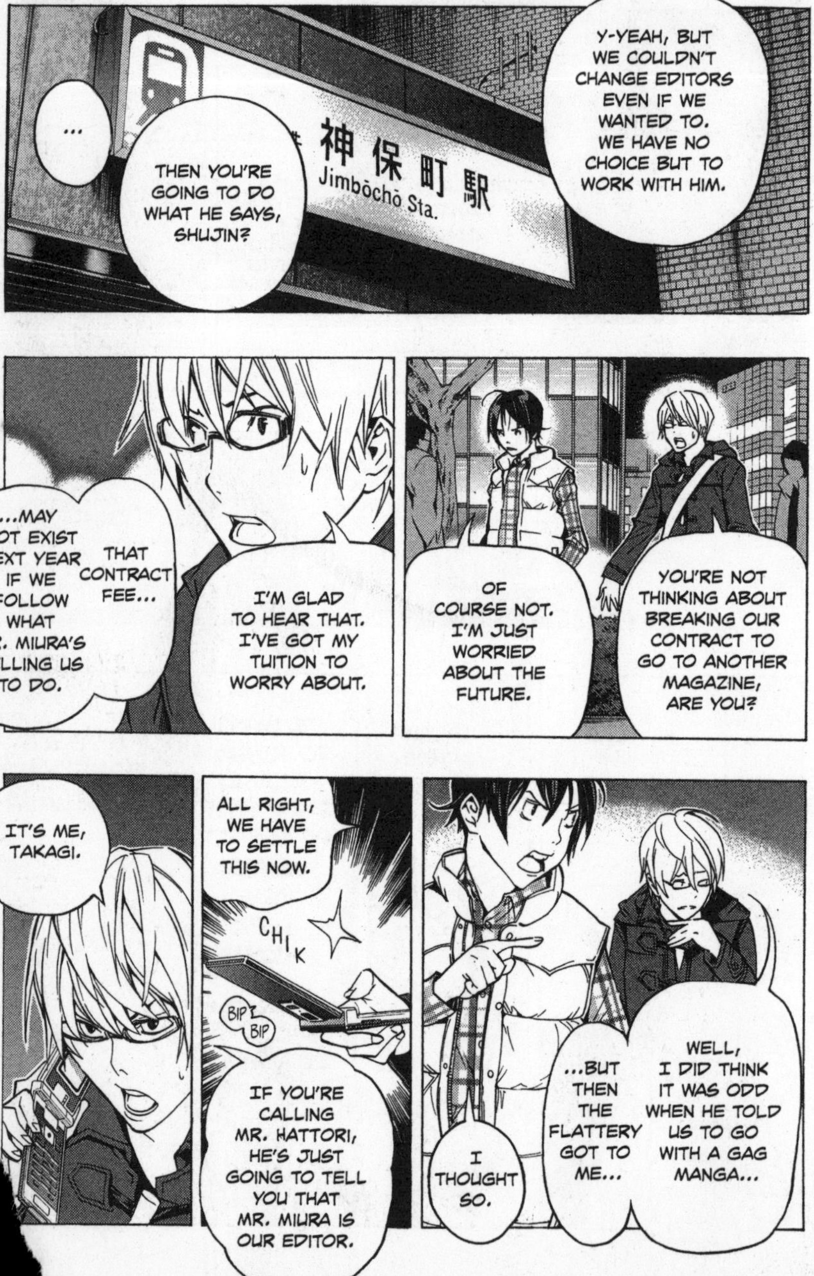
Y-YEAH, BUT WE COULDN'T CHANGE EDITORS EVEN IF WE WANTED TO. WE HAVE NO CHOICE BUT TO WORK WITH HIM.
THEN YOU'RE GOING TO DO WHAT HE SAYS, SHUJIN?
...
神保町駅
Jimbōchō Sta.
YOU'RE NOT THINKING ABOUT BREAKING OUR CONTRACT TO GO TO ANOTHER MAGAZINE, ARE YOU?
OF COURSE NOT. I'M JUST WORRIED ABOUT THE FUTURE.
I'M GLAD TO HEAR THAT. I'VE GOT MY TUITION TO WORRY ABOUT.
THAT CONTRACT FEE...
...MAY NOT EXIST NEXT YEAR IF WE FOLLOW WHAT MR. MIURA'S TELLING US TO DO.
WELL, I DID THINK IT WAS ODD WHEN HE TOLD US TO GO WITH A GAG MANGA...
...BUT THEN THE FLATTERY GOT TO ME...
I THOUGHT SO.
ALL RIGHT, WE HAVE TO SETTLE THIS NOW.
CHIK
BIP BIP
IF YOU'RE CALLING MR. HATTORI, HE'S JUST GOING TO TELL YOU THAT MR. MIURA IS OUR EDITOR.
IT'S ME, TAKAGI.

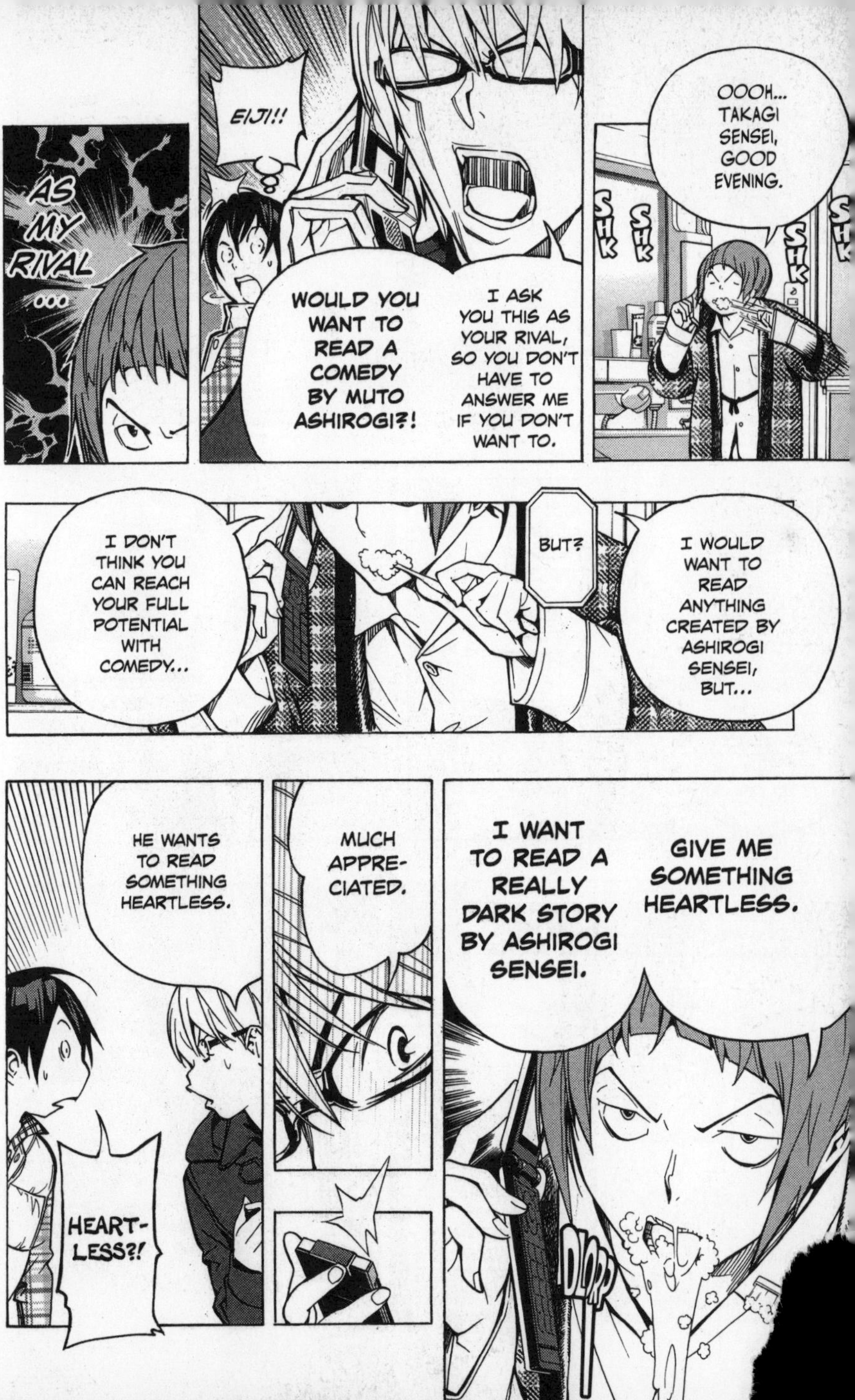
OOOH... TAKAGI SENSEI, GOOD EVENING.
SHK
SHK
SHK
EIJI!!
I ASK YOU THIS AS YOUR RIVAL, SO YOU DON'T HAVE TO ANSWER ME IF YOU DON'T WANT TO.
WOULD YOU WANT TO READ A COMEDY BY MUTO ASHIROGI?!
AS MY RIVAL...
I WOULD WANT TO READ ANYTHING CREATED BY ASHIROGI SENSEI, BUT...
BUT?
I DON'T THINK YOU CAN REACH YOUR FULL POTENTIAL WITH COMEDY...
GIVE ME SOMETHING HEARTLESS.
I WANT TO READ A REALLY DARK STORY BY ASHIROGI SENSEI.
MUCH APPRECIATED.
HE WANTS TO READ SOMETHING HEARTLESS.
HEART-LESS?!

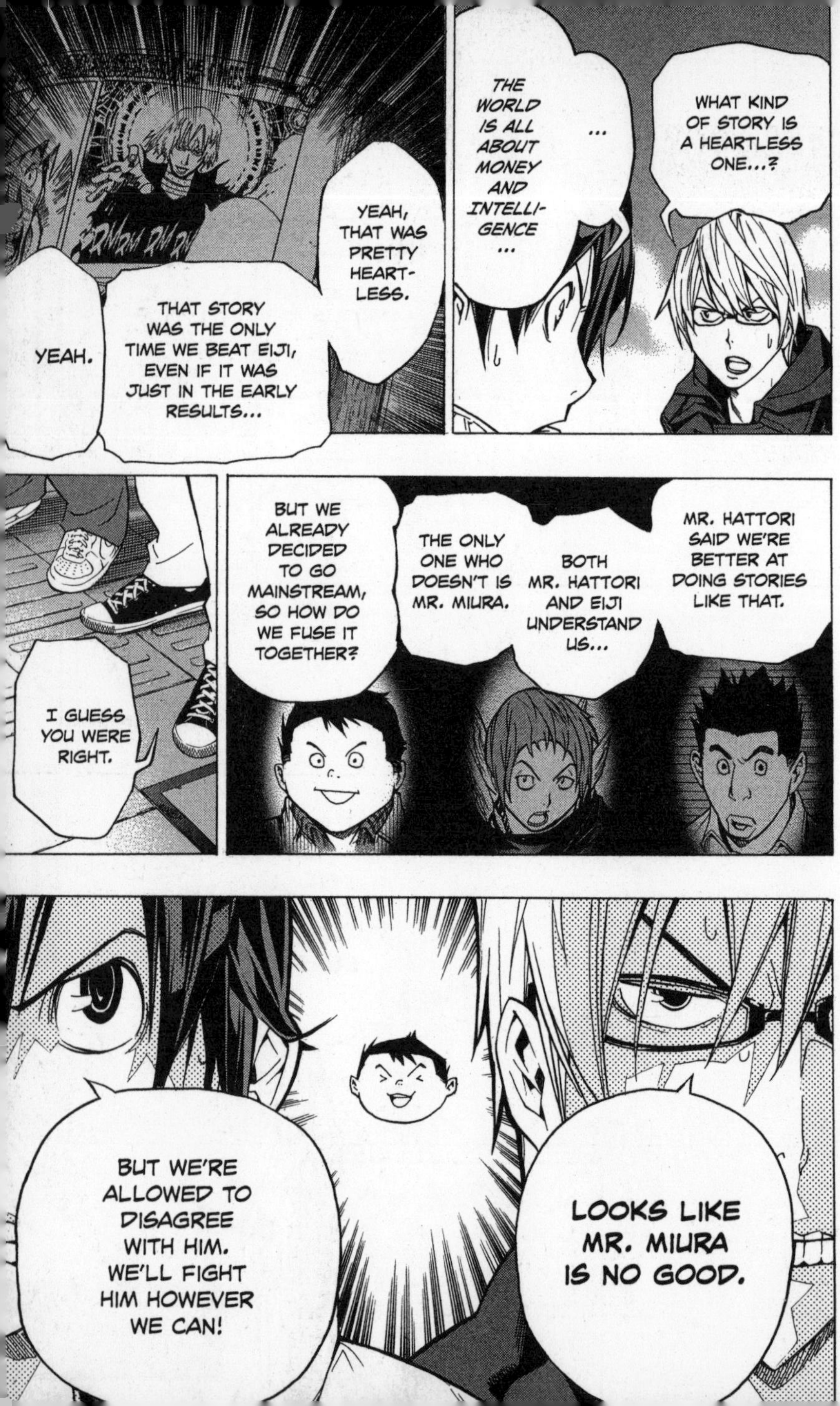
WHAT KIND OF STORY IS A HEARTLESS ONE...?
...
THE WORLD IS ALL ABOUT MONEY AND INTELLIGENCE ...
YEAH, THAT WAS PRETTY HEARTLESS.
THAT STORY WAS THE ONLY TIME WE BEAT EIJI, EVEN IF IT WAS JUST IN THE EARLY RESULTS...
YEAH.
MR. HATTORI SAID WE'RE BETTER AT DOING STORIES LIKE THAT.
BOTH MR. HATTORI AND EIJI UNDERSTAND US...
THE ONLY ONE WHO DOESN'T IS MR. MIURA.
BUT WE ALREADY DECIDED TO GO MAINSTREAM, SO HOW DO WE FUSE IT TOGETHER?
I GUESS YOU WERE RIGHT.
LOOKS LIKE MR. MIURA IS NO GOOD.
BUT WE'RE ALLOWED TO DISAGREE WITH HIM. WE'LL FIGHT HIM HOWEVER WE CAN!

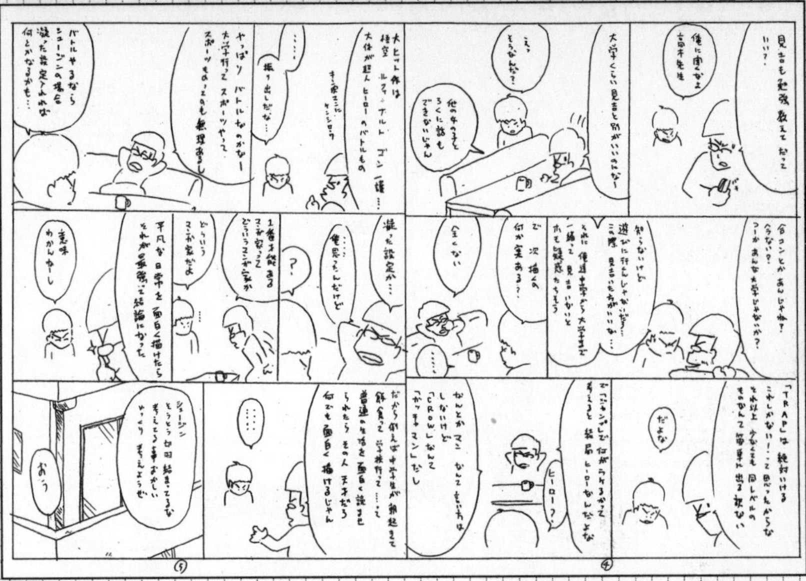
見吉も勉強教えてなって いい?
俺に聞くなよ 高木先生
大学くらい見吉と別がいいのになー
え? そうなんだ?
他の女の子とろくに話もできないじゃん
合コンとかあんじゃねぇ? ぺうない? つーかあんな大学じゃないか?
知らないけど 遊びに行くんじゃないだろ… この際 見吉いたちがいいな…
それに俺達中学から大学まで一緒って見吉いないとホモ疑惑たちそう
で 次描くの何か案ある?
全くない
……
「TRAP」は絶対いける これしかない!って思ったからな それ以上 少なくても同レベルのものなんて簡単に出る訳ない
だよな
で「ジャンプ」で何がうけるかって考えると結局ヒーローなんだよな
ヒーロー?
なんとかマン なんて言い方はしないけど「CROW」なんて「カッチマン」だし
④
大ヒット作は 悟空 ルフィ ナルト ゴン 一護… 大体が超人ヒーローのバトルもの
キン肉マンにケンシロウ
……
振り出しだな…
やっぱりバトルなのかなー 大学行ってスポーツやってスポーツものってのも無理あるし
バトルやるならシュージンの場合凝った設定入れれば何とかなるかも…
凝った設定か…
……俺思ったんだけど
?
1番才能あるマンガ家ってどういうマンガ家か
どういうマンガ家だよ
……
平凡な日常を面白く描けたらそれが最強って結論になった
意味わかんねーし
だから例えば中学生が朝起きて飯食って学校行って……って普通の生活を面白く読ませられたらその人天才だろ 何でも面白く描けるじゃん
……
シュージン とうとう切羽詰まってるな 考えてる事おかしい ゆっくり考えようぜ
おう
⑤

OHBA'S STORYBOARD

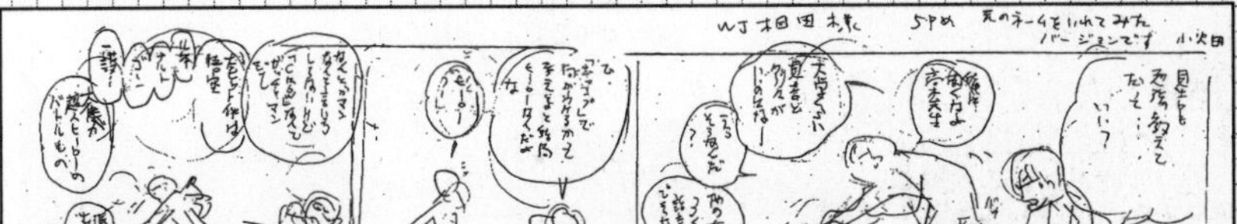
WJ相田様 5Pめ 元のネームを入れてみたバージョンです 小畑

OBATA'S STORYBOARD

COMPLETE!

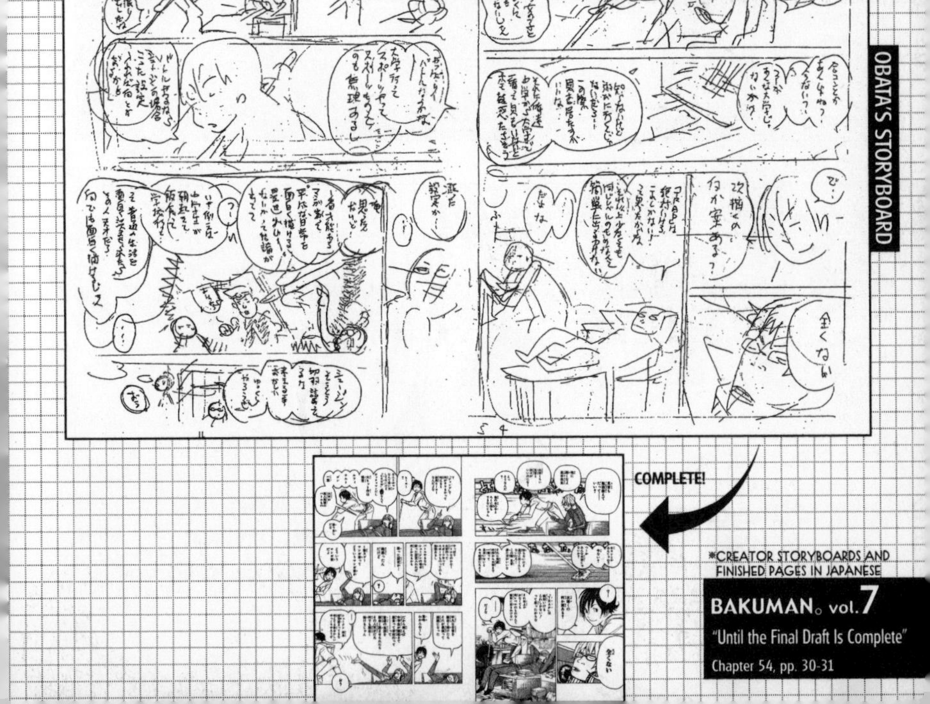

*CREATOR STORYBOARDS AND FINISHED PAGES IN JAPANESE

BAKUMAN。 vol. 7

"Until the Final Draft Is Complete"

Chapter 54, pp. 30-31

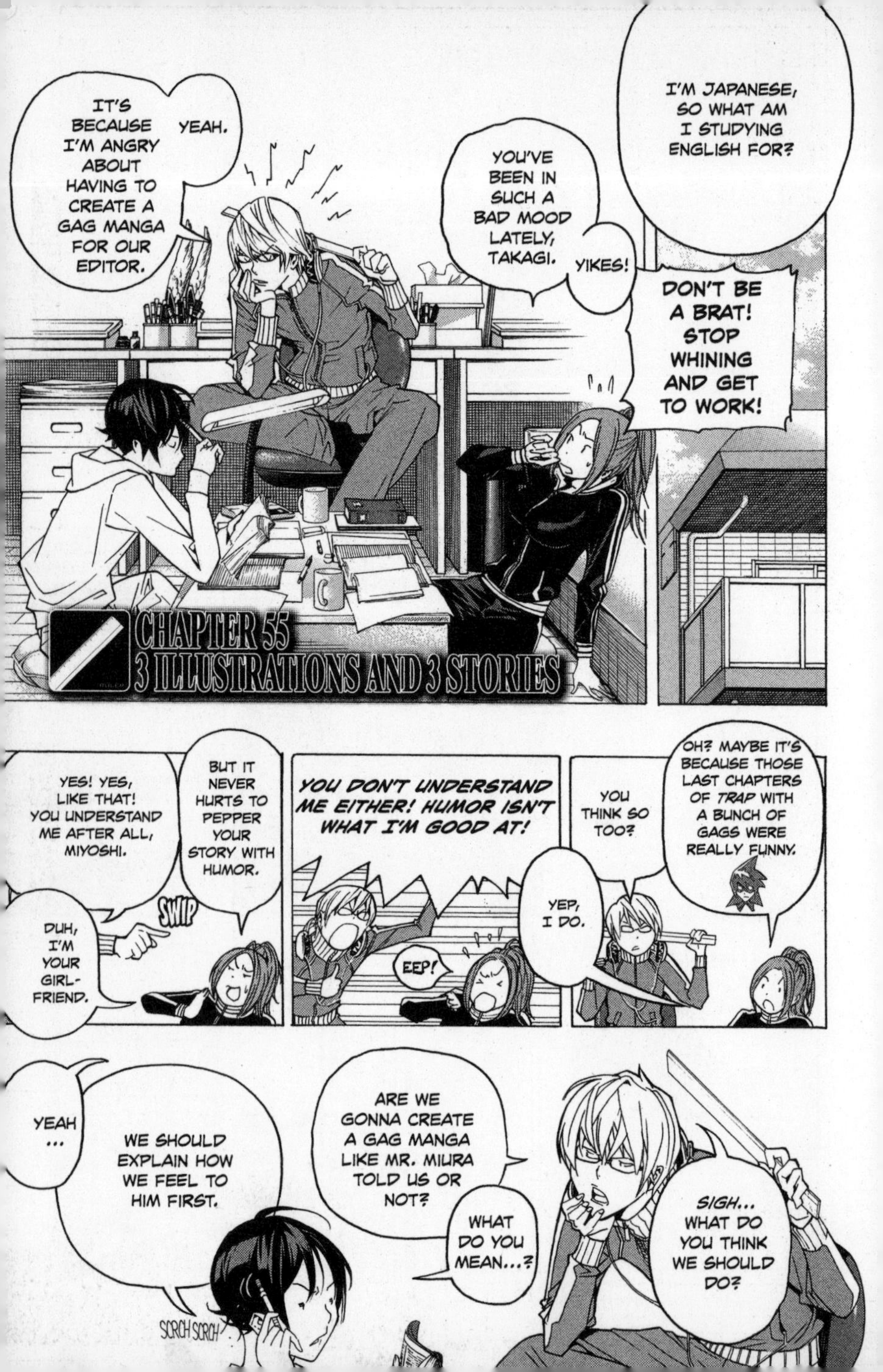
I'M JAPANESE, SO WHAT AM I STUDYING ENGLISH FOR?
DON'T BE A BRAT! STOP WHINING AND GET TO WORK!
YIKES!
YOU'VE BEEN IN SUCH A BAD MOOD LATELY, TAKAGI.
YEAH.
IT'S BECAUSE I'M ANGRY ABOUT HAVING TO CREATE A GAG MANGA FOR OUR EDITOR.
CHAPTER 55
3 ILLUSTRATIONS AND 3 STORIES
OH? MAYBE IT'S BECAUSE THOSE LAST CHAPTERS OF *TRAP* WITH A BUNCH OF GAGS WERE REALLY FUNNY.
YOU THINK SO TOO?
YEP, I DO.
YOU DON'T UNDERSTAND ME EITHER! HUMOR ISN'T WHAT I'M GOOD AT!
EEP!
BUT IT NEVER HURTS TO PEPPER YOUR STORY WITH HUMOR.
YES! YES, LIKE THAT! YOU UNDERSTAND ME AFTER ALL, MIYOSHI.
SWIP
DUH, I'M YOUR GIRL-FRIEND.
SIGH... WHAT DO YOU THINK WE SHOULD DO?
ARE WE GONNA CREATE A GAG MANGA LIKE MR. MIURA TOLD US OR NOT?
WHAT DO YOU MEAN...?
WE SHOULD EXPLAIN HOW WE FEEL TO HIM FIRST.
YEAH...
SCRCH SCRCH

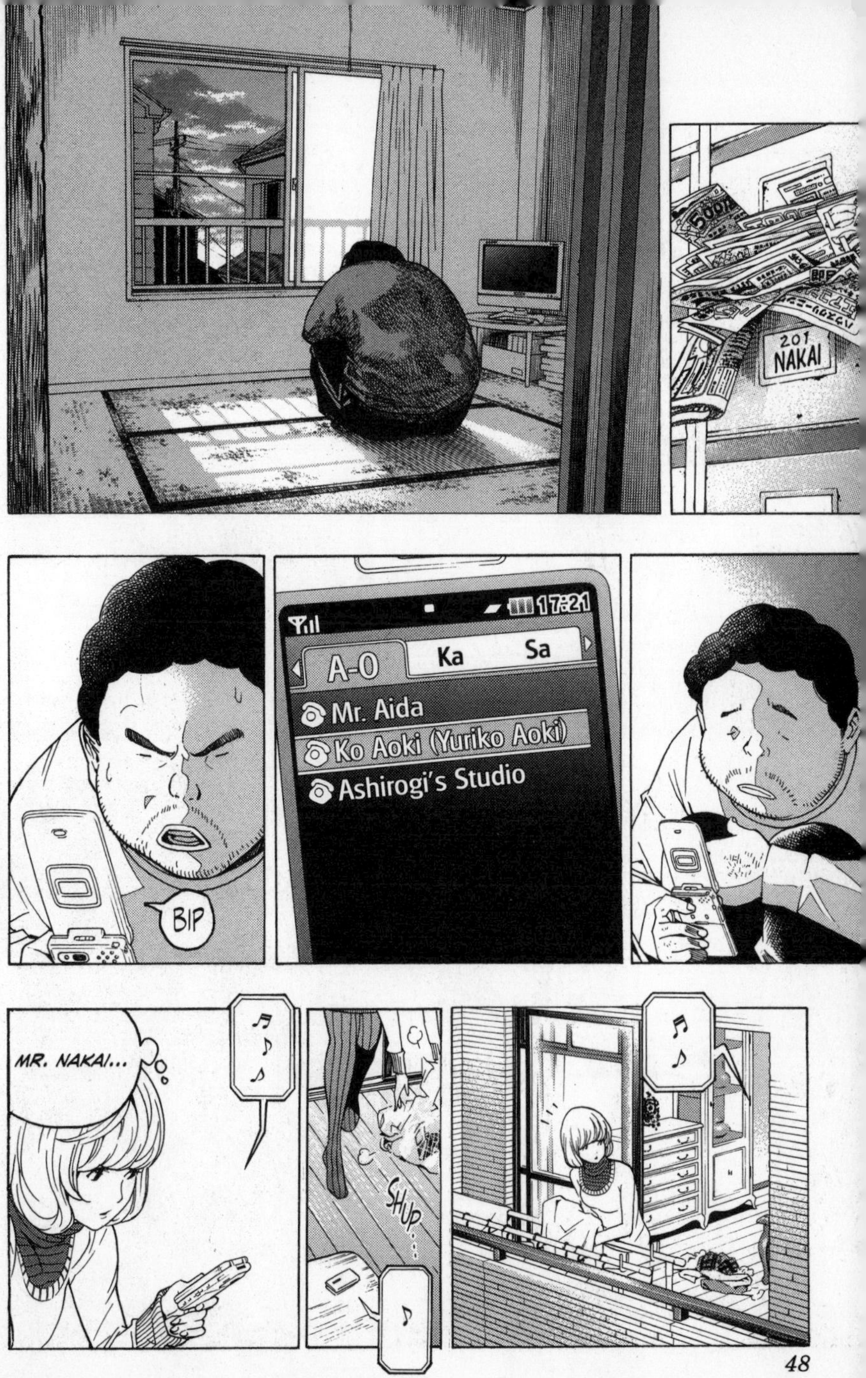
201
NAKAI
17:21
A-O
Ka
Sa
Mr. Aida
Ko Aoki (Yuriko Aoki)
Ashirogi's Studio
BIP
♪ ♪
SHUP...
♪
♪ ♪ ♪
MR. NAKAI...

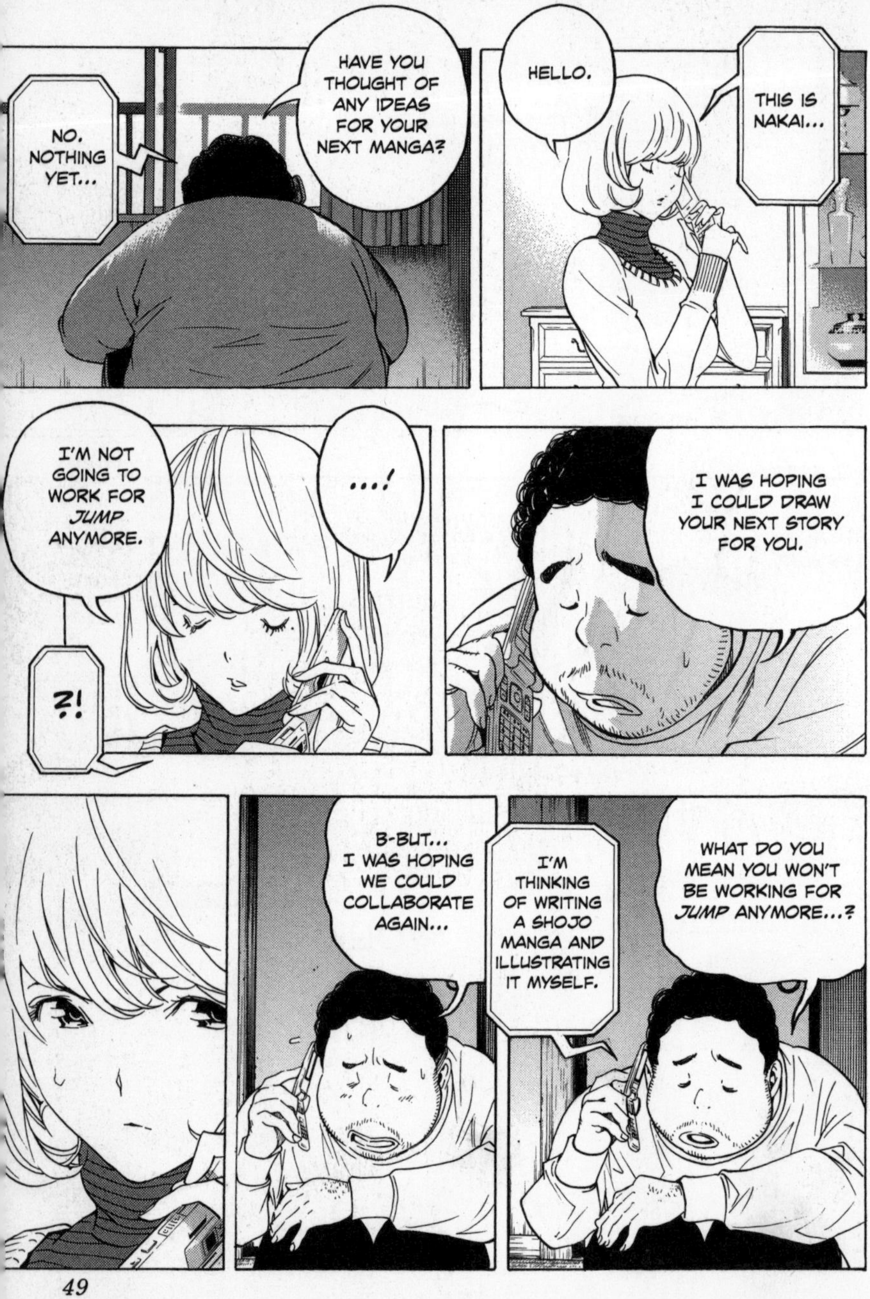
HELLO.
THIS IS NAKAI...
HAVE YOU THOUGHT OF ANY IDEAS FOR YOUR NEXT MANGA?
NO. NOTHING YET...
I WAS HOPING I COULD DRAW YOUR NEXT STORY FOR YOU.
...!
I'M NOT GOING TO WORK FOR *JUMP* ANYMORE.
?!
WHAT DO YOU MEAN YOU WON'T BE WORKING FOR *JUMP* ANYMORE...?
I'M THINKING OF WRITING A SHOJO MANGA AND ILLUSTRATING IT MYSELF.
B-BUT... I WAS HOPING WE COULD COLLABORATE AGAIN...

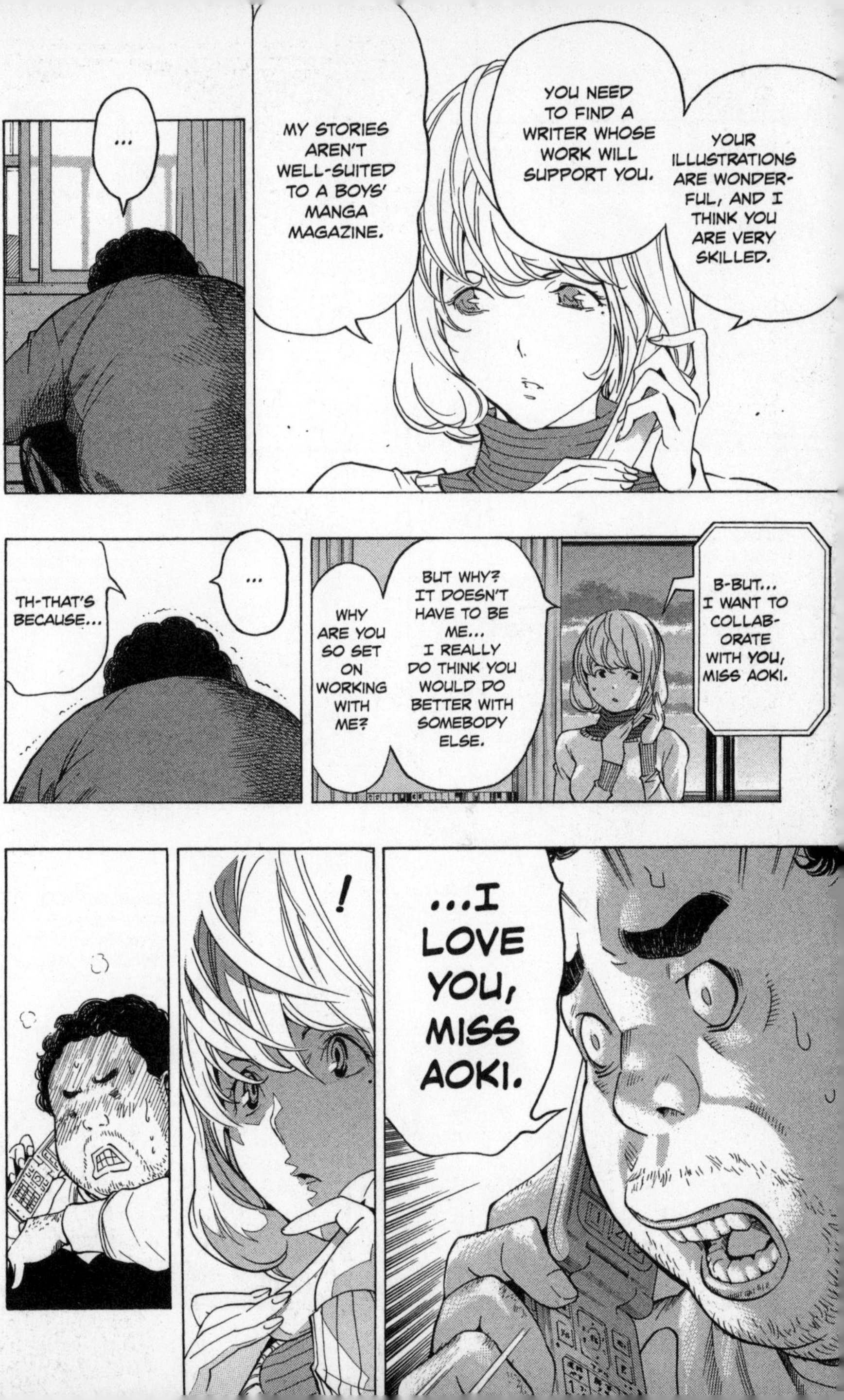
YOUR ILLUSTRATIONS ARE WONDERFUL, AND I THINK YOU ARE VERY SKILLED.
YOU NEED TO FIND A WRITER WHOSE WORK WILL SUPPORT YOU.
MY STORIES AREN'T WELL-SUITED TO A BOYS' MANGA MAGAZINE.
...
B-BUT... I WANT TO COLLABORATE WITH YOU, MISS AOKI.
BUT WHY? IT DOESN'T HAVE TO BE ME... I REALLY DO THINK YOU WOULD DO BETTER WITH SOMEBODY ELSE.
WHY ARE YOU SO SET ON WORKING WITH ME?
...
TH-THAT'S BECAUSE...
...I LOVE YOU, MISS AOKI.
!

READ THIS WAY

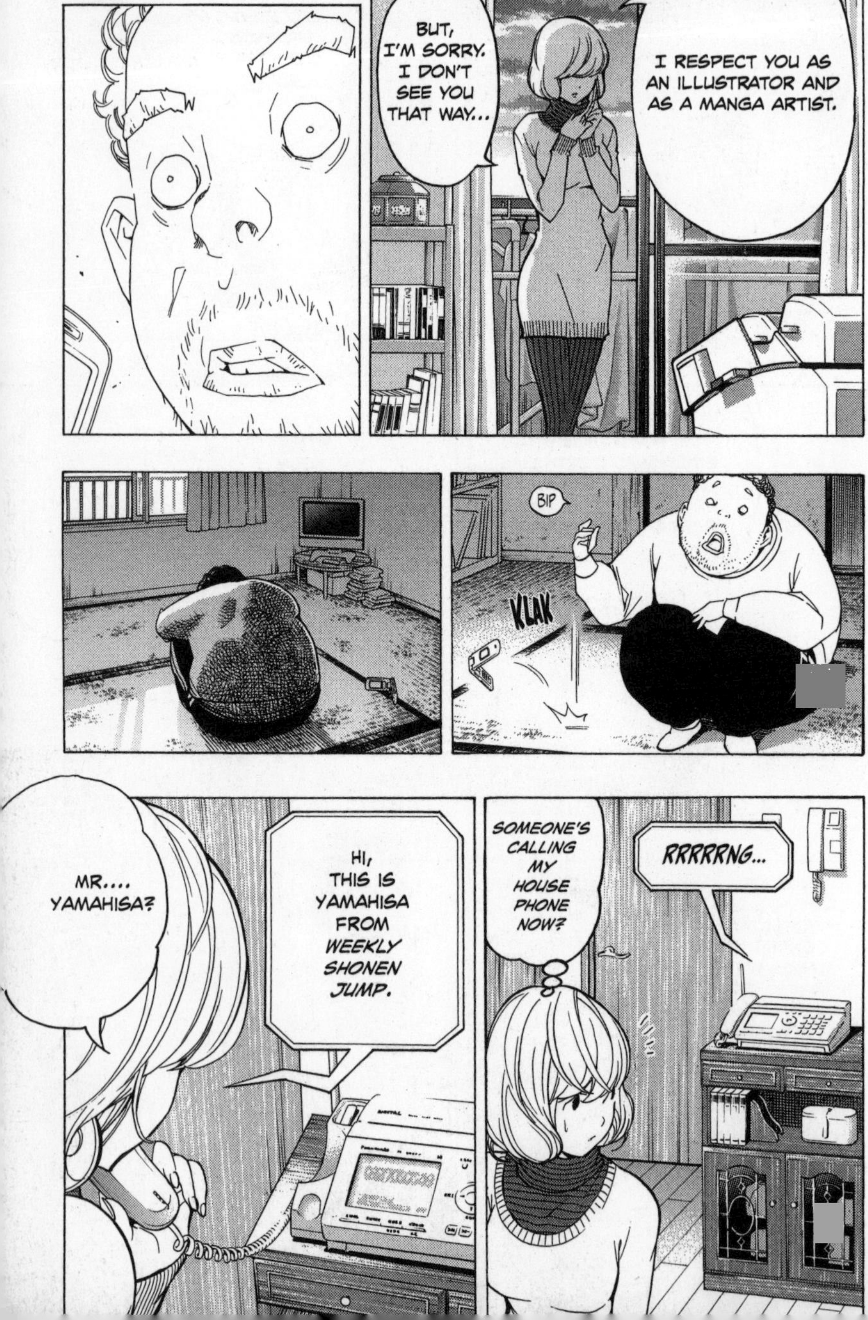
I RESPECT YOU AS AN ILLUSTRATOR AND AS A MANGA ARTIST.
BUT, I'M SORRY. I DON'T SEE YOU THAT WAY...
BIP
KLAK
RRRRRNG...
SOMEONE'S CALLING MY HOUSE PHONE NOW?
HI, THIS IS YAMAHISA FROM WEEKLY SHONEN JUMP.
MR.... YAMAHISA?

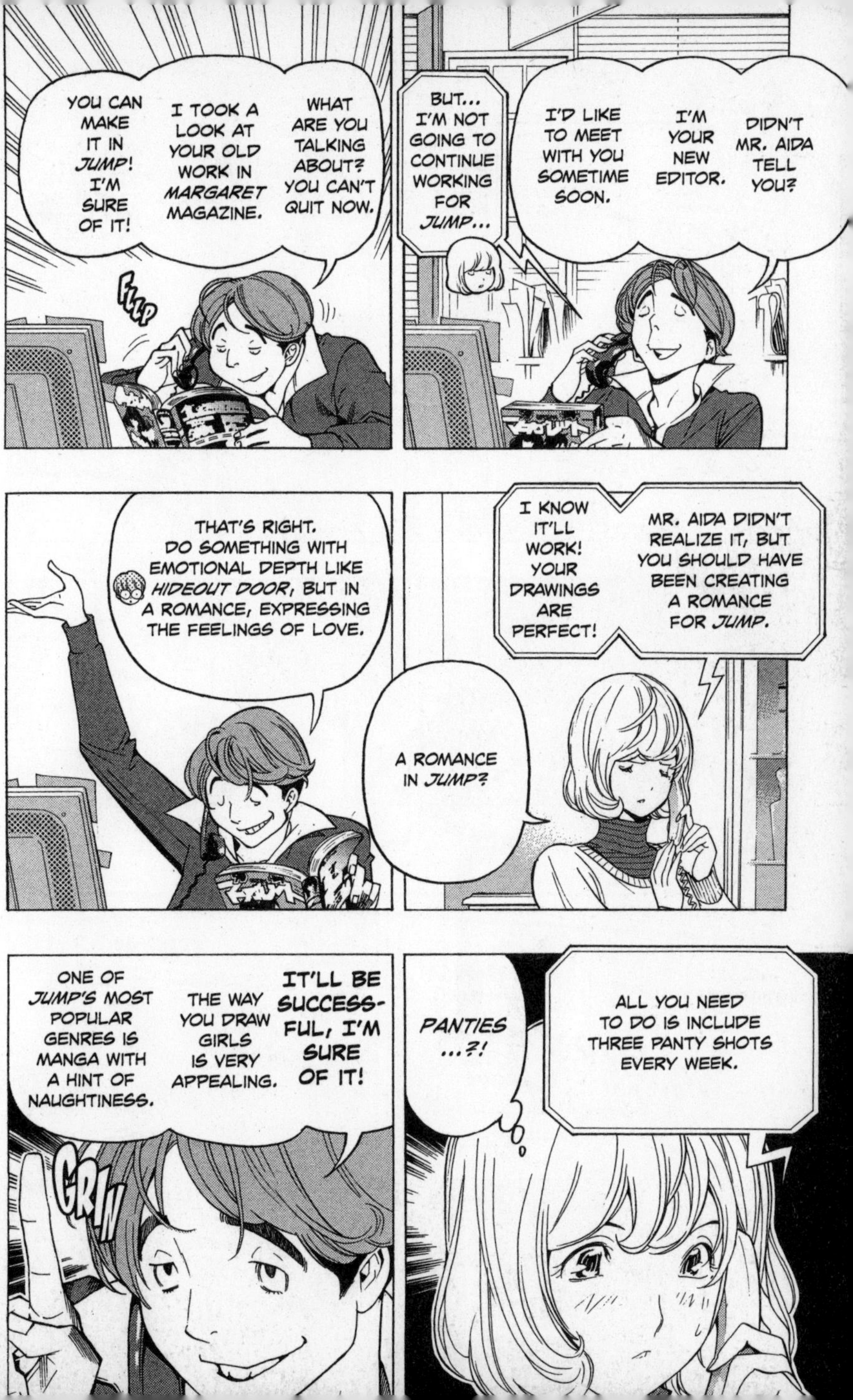
DIDN'T MR. AIDA TELL YOU?
I'M YOUR NEW EDITOR.
I'D LIKE TO MEET WITH YOU SOMETIME SOON.
BUT... I'M NOT GOING TO CONTINUE WORKING FOR *JUMP*...
WHAT ARE YOU TALKING ABOUT? YOU CAN'T QUIT NOW.
I TOOK A LOOK AT YOUR OLD WORK IN *MARGARET* MAGAZINE.
YOU CAN MAKE IT IN *JUMP*! I'M SURE OF IT!
FLIP
MR. AIDA DIDN'T REALIZE IT, BUT YOU SHOULD HAVE BEEN CREATING A ROMANCE FOR *JUMP*.
I KNOW IT'LL WORK! YOUR DRAWINGS ARE PERFECT!
A ROMANCE IN *JUMP*?
THAT'S RIGHT. DO SOMETHING WITH EMOTIONAL DEPTH LIKE *HIDEOUT DOOR*, BUT IN A ROMANCE, EXPRESSING THE FEELINGS OF LOVE.
ALL YOU NEED TO DO IS INCLUDE THREE PANTY SHOTS EVERY WEEK.
PANTIES ...?!
IT'LL BE SUCCESS-FUL, I'M SURE OF IT!
THE WAY YOU DRAW GIRLS IS VERY APPEALING.
ONE OF *JUMP'S* MOST POPULAR GENRES IS MANGA WITH A HINT OF NAUGHTINESS.
GRIN

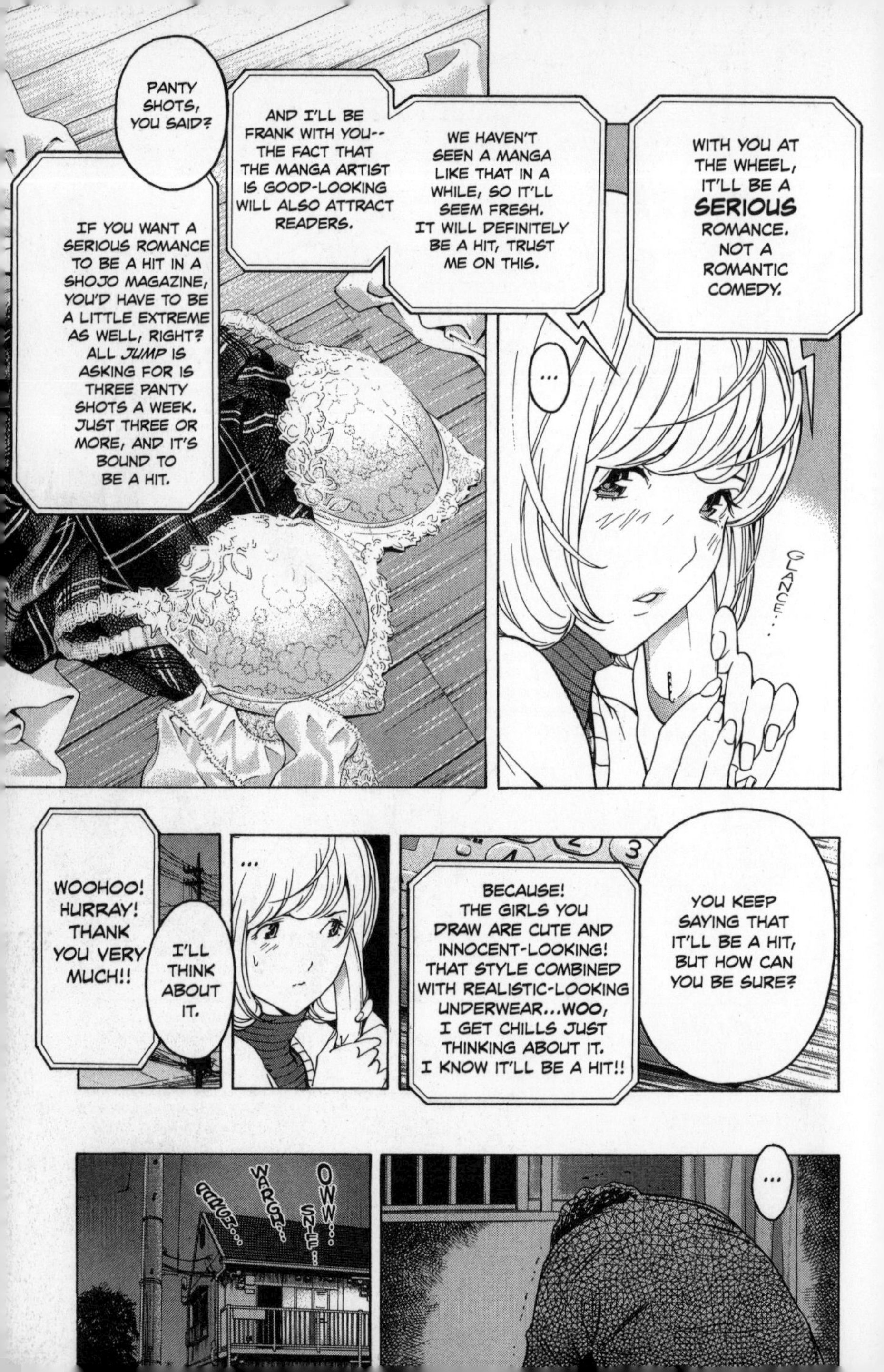
WITH YOU AT THE WHEEL, IT'LL BE A **SERIOUS** ROMANCE. NOT A ROMANTIC COMEDY.
WE HAVEN'T SEEN A MANGA LIKE THAT IN A WHILE, SO IT'LL SEEM FRESH. IT WILL DEFINITELY BE A HIT, TRUST ME ON THIS.
...
GLANCE...
AND I'LL BE FRANK WITH YOU-- THE FACT THAT THE MANGA ARTIST IS GOOD-LOOKING WILL ALSO ATTRACT READERS.
PANTY SHOTS, YOU SAID?
IF YOU WANT A SERIOUS ROMANCE TO BE A HIT IN A SHOJO MAGAZINE, YOU'D HAVE TO BE A LITTLE EXTREME AS WELL, RIGHT? ALL *JUMP* IS ASKING FOR IS THREE PANTY SHOTS A WEEK. JUST THREE OR MORE, AND IT'S BOUND TO BE A HIT.
YOU KEEP SAYING THAT IT'LL BE A HIT, BUT HOW CAN YOU BE SURE?
BECAUSE! THE GIRLS YOU DRAW ARE CUTE AND INNOCENT-LOOKING! THAT STYLE COMBINED WITH REALISTIC-LOOKING UNDERWEAR...WOO, I GET CHILLS JUST THINKING ABOUT IT. I KNOW IT'LL BE A HIT!!
...
I'LL THINK ABOUT IT.
WOOHOO! HURRAY! THANK YOU VERY MUCH!!
...
OWW...
SNIF...
WARGH...
UUUGH...

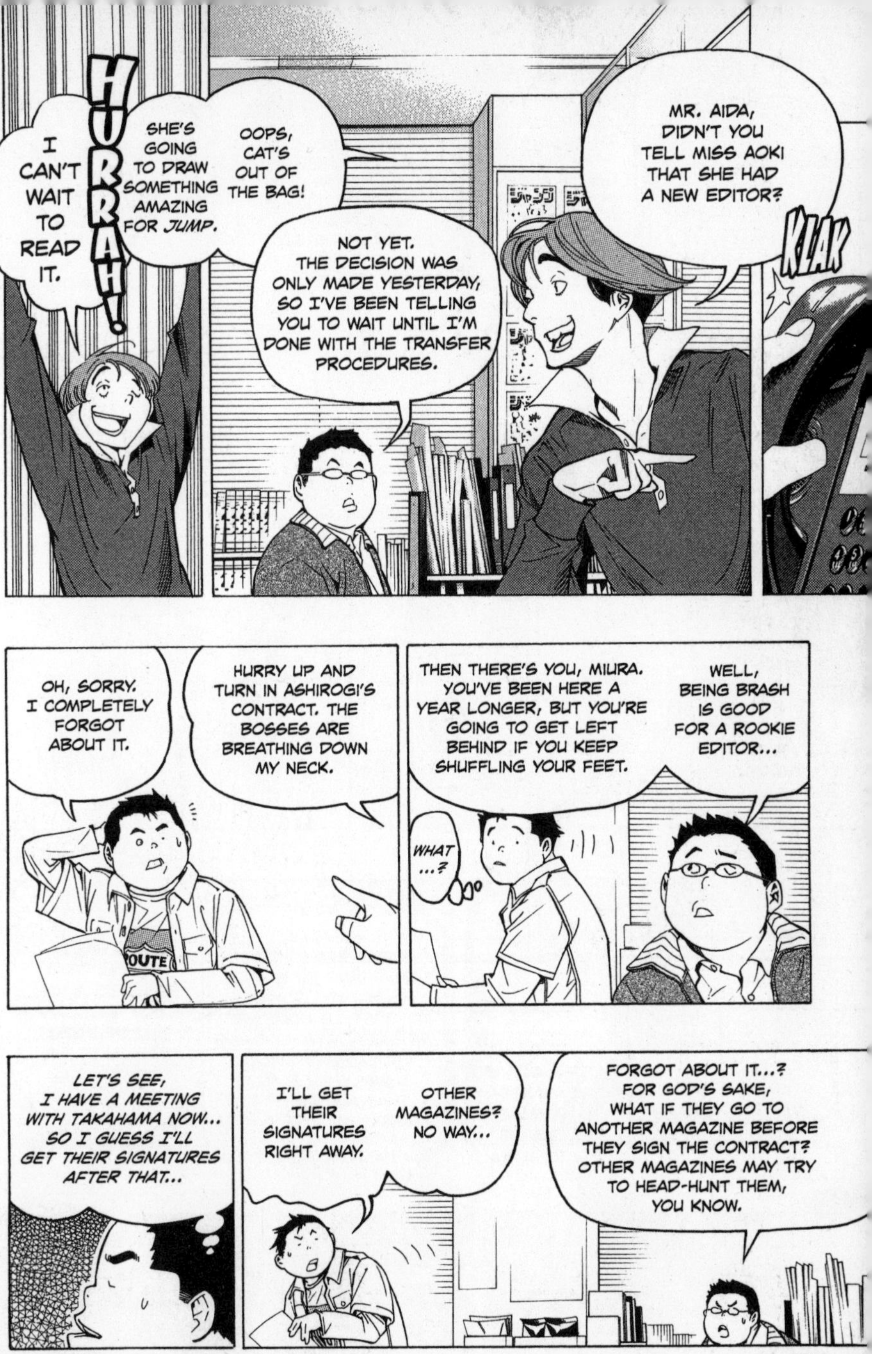
MR. AIDA, DIDN'T YOU TELL MISS AOKI THAT SHE HAD A NEW EDITOR?
KLAK
NOT YET. THE DECISION WAS ONLY MADE YESTERDAY, SO I'VE BEEN TELLING YOU TO WAIT UNTIL I'M DONE WITH THE TRANSFER PROCEDURES.
OOPS, CAT'S OUT OF THE BAG!
SHE'S GOING TO DRAW SOMETHING AMAZING FOR *JUMP*.
HURRAH!
I CAN'T WAIT TO READ IT.
WELL, BEING BRASH IS GOOD FOR A ROOKIE EDITOR...
THEN THERE'S YOU, MIURA. YOU'VE BEEN HERE A YEAR LONGER, BUT YOU'RE GOING TO GET LEFT BEHIND IF YOU KEEP SHUFFLING YOUR FEET.
WHAT...?
HURRY UP AND TURN IN ASHIROGI'S CONTRACT. THE BOSSES ARE BREATHING DOWN MY NECK.
OH, SORRY. I COMPLETELY FORGOT ABOUT IT.
FORGOT ABOUT IT...? FOR GOD'S SAKE, WHAT IF THEY GO TO ANOTHER MAGAZINE BEFORE THEY SIGN THE CONTRACT? OTHER MAGAZINES MAY TRY TO HEAD-HUNT THEM, YOU KNOW.
OTHER MAGAZINES? NO WAY...
I'LL GET THEIR SIGNATURES RIGHT AWAY.
LET'S SEE, I HAVE A MEETING WITH TAKAHAMA NOW... SO I GUESS I'LL GET THEIR SIGNATURES AFTER THAT...

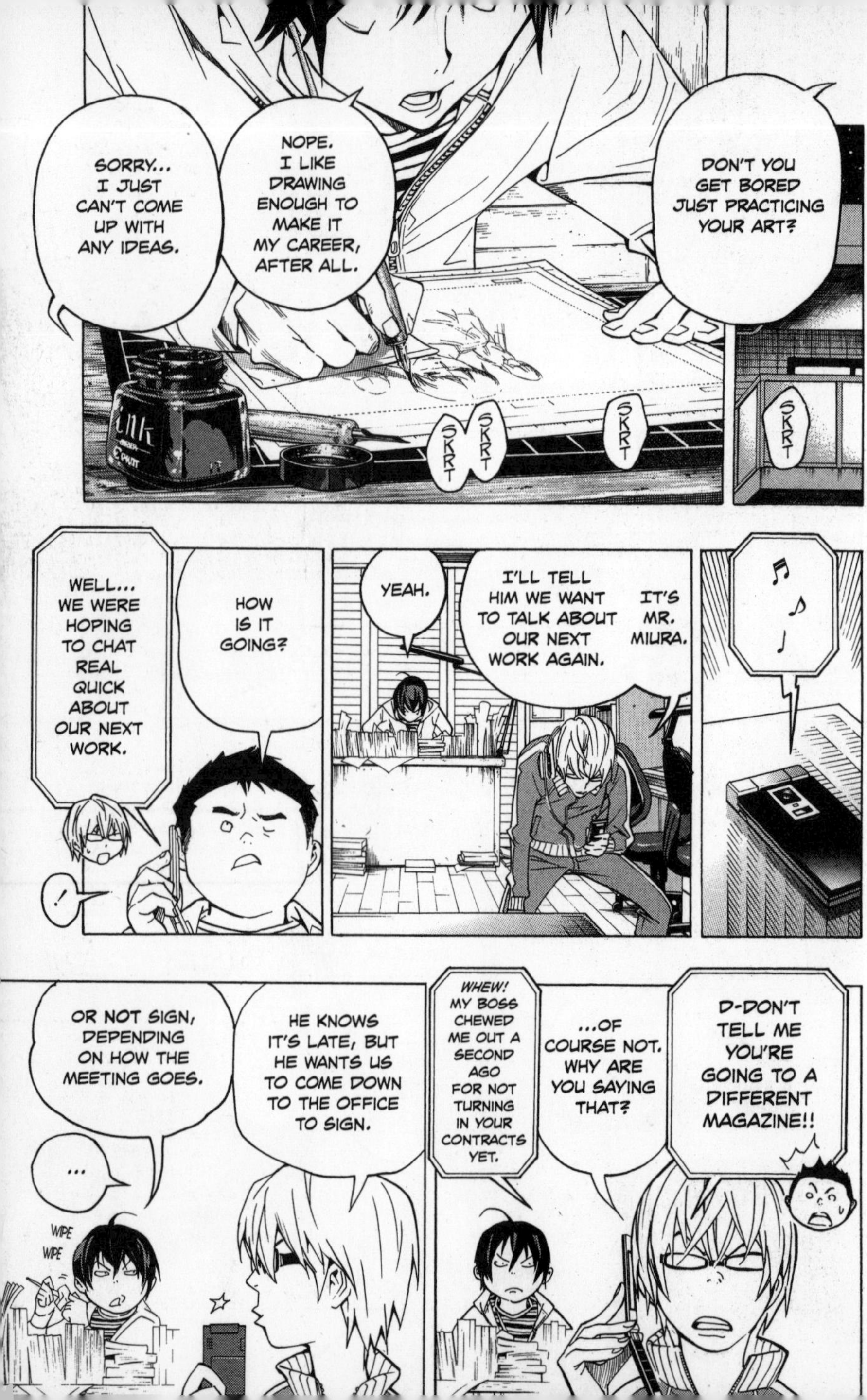
DON'T YOU GET BORED JUST PRACTICING YOUR ART?
SKRT
NOPE. I LIKE DRAWING ENOUGH TO MAKE IT MY CAREER, AFTER ALL.
SORRY... I JUST CAN'T COME UP WITH ANY IDEAS.
SKRT
SKRT
SKRT
IT'S MR. MIURA.
I'LL TELL HIM WE WANT TO TALK ABOUT OUR NEXT WORK AGAIN.
YEAH.
HOW IS IT GOING?
WELL... WE WERE HOPING TO CHAT REAL QUICK ABOUT OUR NEXT WORK.
!
D-DON'T TELL ME YOU'RE GOING TO A DIFFERENT MAGAZINE!!
...OF COURSE NOT. WHY ARE YOU SAYING THAT?
WHEW! MY BOSS CHEWED ME OUT A SECOND AGO FOR NOT TURNING IN YOUR CONTRACTS YET.
HE KNOWS IT'S LATE, BUT HE WANTS US TO COME DOWN TO THE OFFICE TO SIGN.
OR NOT SIGN, DEPENDING ON HOW THE MEETING GOES.
...
WIPE
WIPE

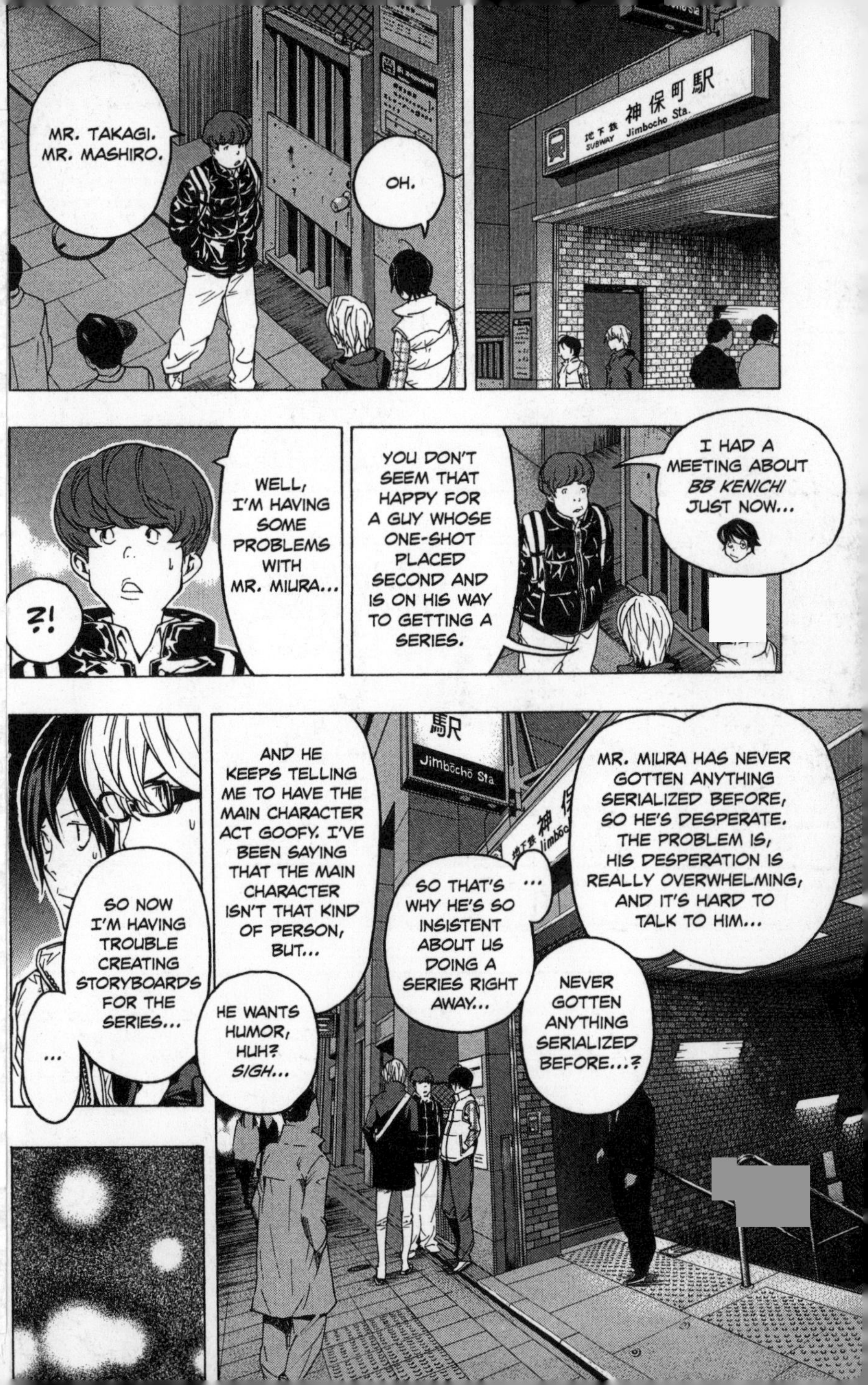
地下鉄 神保町駅
SUBWAY Jimbocho Sta.
MR. TAKAGI. MR. MASHIRO.
OH.
I HAD A MEETING ABOUT *BB KENICHI* JUST NOW...
YOU DON'T SEEM THAT HAPPY FOR A GUY WHOSE ONE-SHOT PLACED SECOND AND IS ON HIS WAY TO GETTING A SERIES.
WELL, I'M HAVING SOME PROBLEMS WITH MR. MIURA...
?!
駅
Jimbōchō Sta.
MR. MIURA HAS NEVER GOTTEN ANYTHING SERIALIZED BEFORE, SO HE'S DESPERATE. THE PROBLEM IS, HIS DESPERATION IS REALLY OVERWHELMING, AND IT'S HARD TO TALK TO HIM...
...
SO THAT'S WHY HE'S SO INSISTENT ABOUT US DOING A SERIES RIGHT AWAY...
NEVER GOTTEN ANYTHING SERIALIZED BEFORE...?
AND HE KEEPS TELLING ME TO HAVE THE MAIN CHARACTER ACT GOOFY. I'VE BEEN SAYING THAT THE MAIN CHARACTER ISN'T THAT KIND OF PERSON, BUT...
SO NOW I'M HAVING TROUBLE CREATING STORYBOARDS FOR THE SERIES...
...
HE WANTS HUMOR, HUH? *SIGH...*

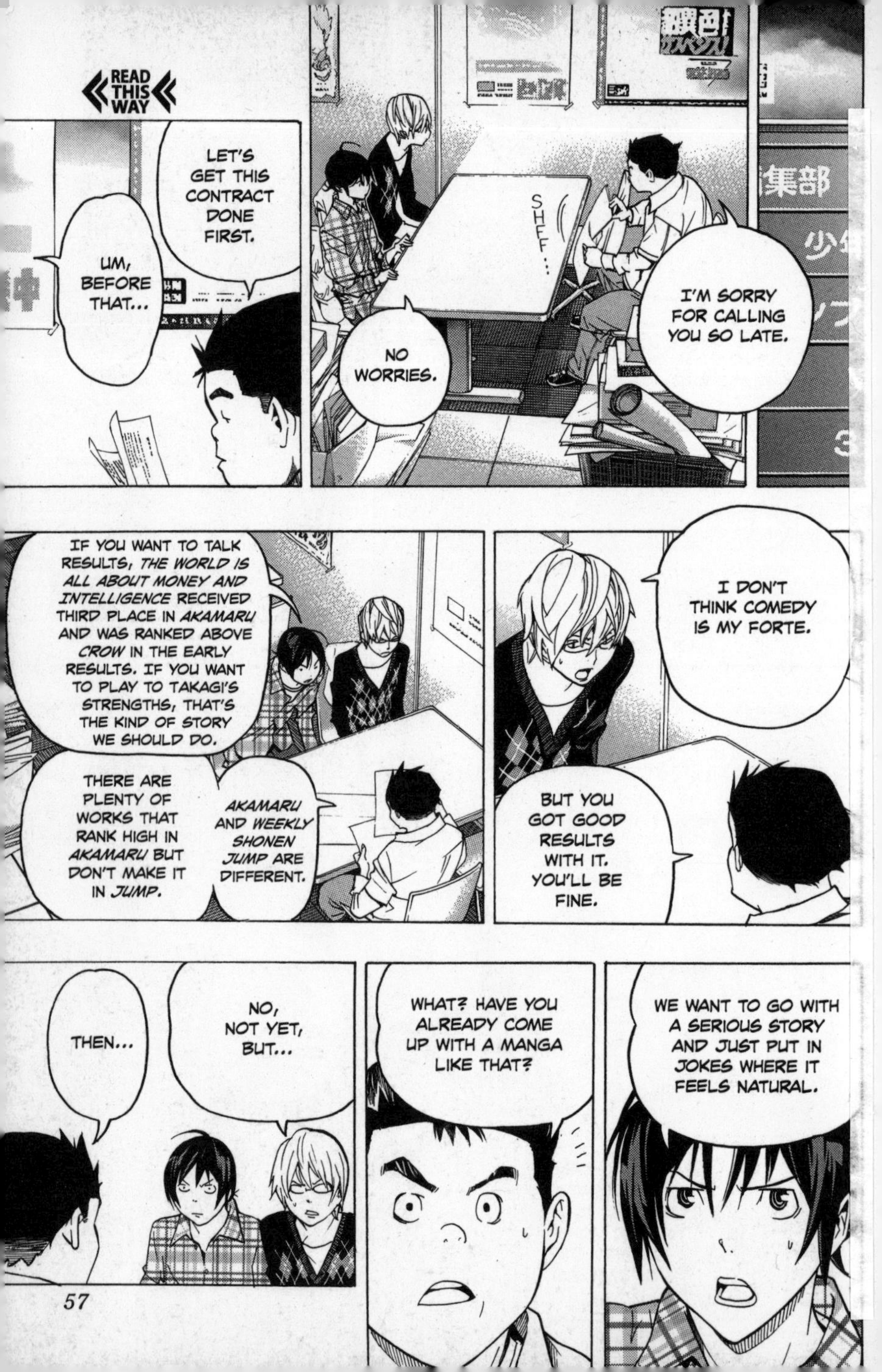
READ THIS WAY
I'M SORRY FOR CALLING YOU SO LATE.
SHFF...
NO WORRIES.
LET'S GET THIS CONTRACT DONE FIRST.
UM, BEFORE THAT...
I DON'T THINK COMEDY IS MY FORTE.
BUT YOU GOT GOOD RESULTS WITH IT. YOU'LL BE FINE.
IF YOU WANT TO TALK RESULTS, *THE WORLD IS ALL ABOUT MONEY AND INTELLIGENCE* RECEIVED THIRD PLACE IN *AKAMARU* AND WAS RANKED ABOVE *CROW* IN THE EARLY RESULTS. IF YOU WANT TO PLAY TO TAKAGI'S STRENGTHS, THAT'S THE KIND OF STORY WE SHOULD DO.
AKAMARU AND *WEEKLY SHONEN JUMP* ARE DIFFERENT.
THERE ARE PLENTY OF WORKS THAT RANK HIGH IN *AKAMARU* BUT DON'T MAKE IT IN *JUMP*.
WE WANT TO GO WITH A SERIOUS STORY AND JUST PUT IN JOKES WHERE IT FEELS NATURAL.
WHAT? HAVE YOU ALREADY COME UP WITH A MANGA LIKE THAT?
NO, NOT YET, BUT...
THEN...

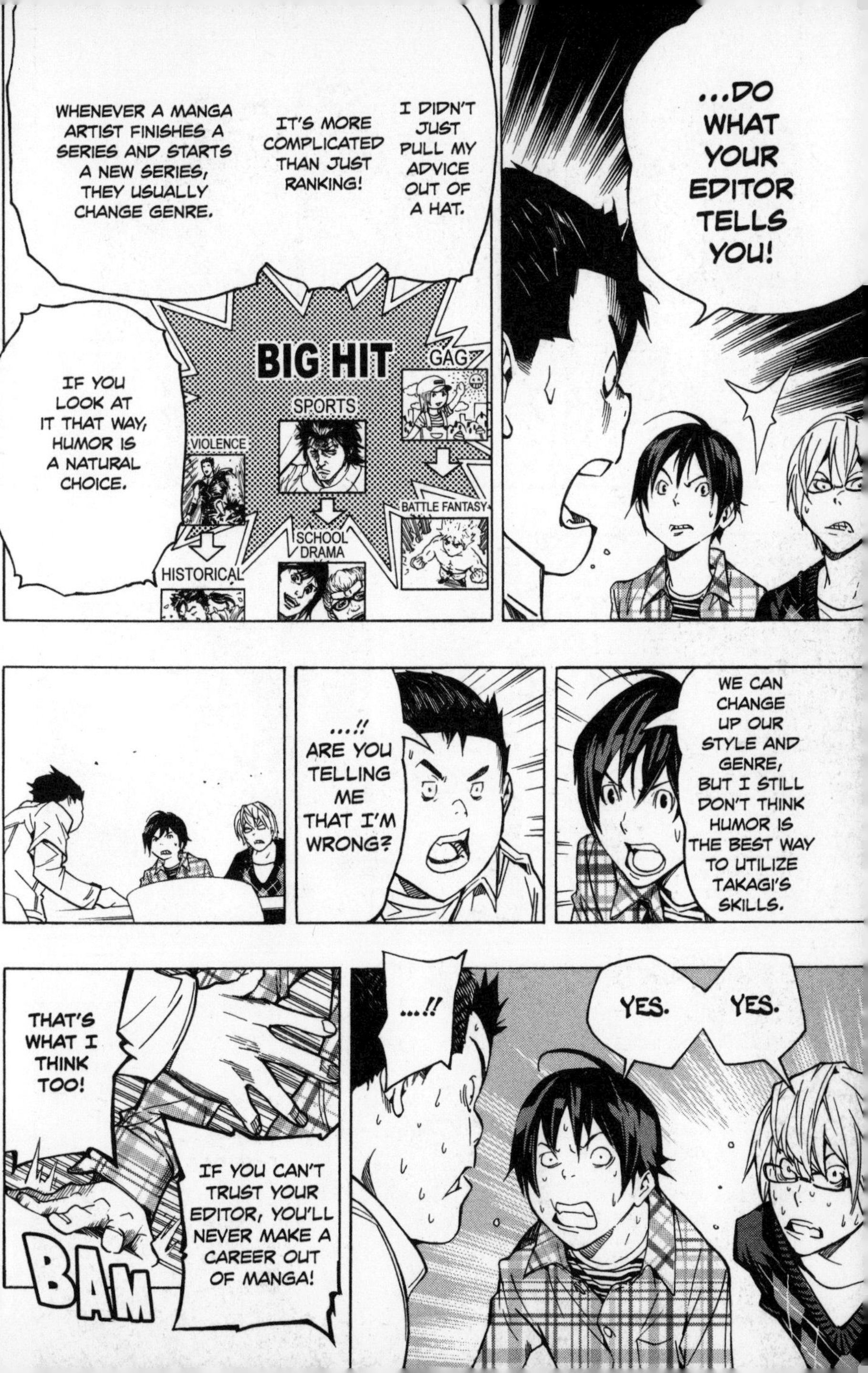
...DO WHAT YOUR EDITOR TELLS YOU!
I DIDN'T JUST PULL MY ADVICE OUT OF A HAT.
IT'S MORE COMPLICATED THAN JUST RANKING!
WHENEVER A MANGA ARTIST FINISHES A SERIES AND STARTS A NEW SERIES, THEY USUALLY CHANGE GENRE.
BIG HIT
GAG
SPORTS
VIOLENCE
BATTLE FANTASY
SCHOOL DRAMA
HISTORICAL
IF YOU LOOK AT IT THAT WAY, HUMOR IS A NATURAL CHOICE.
WE CAN CHANGE UP OUR STYLE AND GENRE, BUT I STILL DON'T THINK HUMOR IS THE BEST WAY TO UTILIZE TAKAGI'S SKILLS.
...!!
ARE YOU TELLING ME THAT I'M WRONG?
YES.
YES.
...!!
THAT'S WHAT I THINK TOO!
IF YOU CAN'T TRUST YOUR EDITOR, YOU'LL NEVER MAKE A CAREER OUT OF MANGA!
BAM

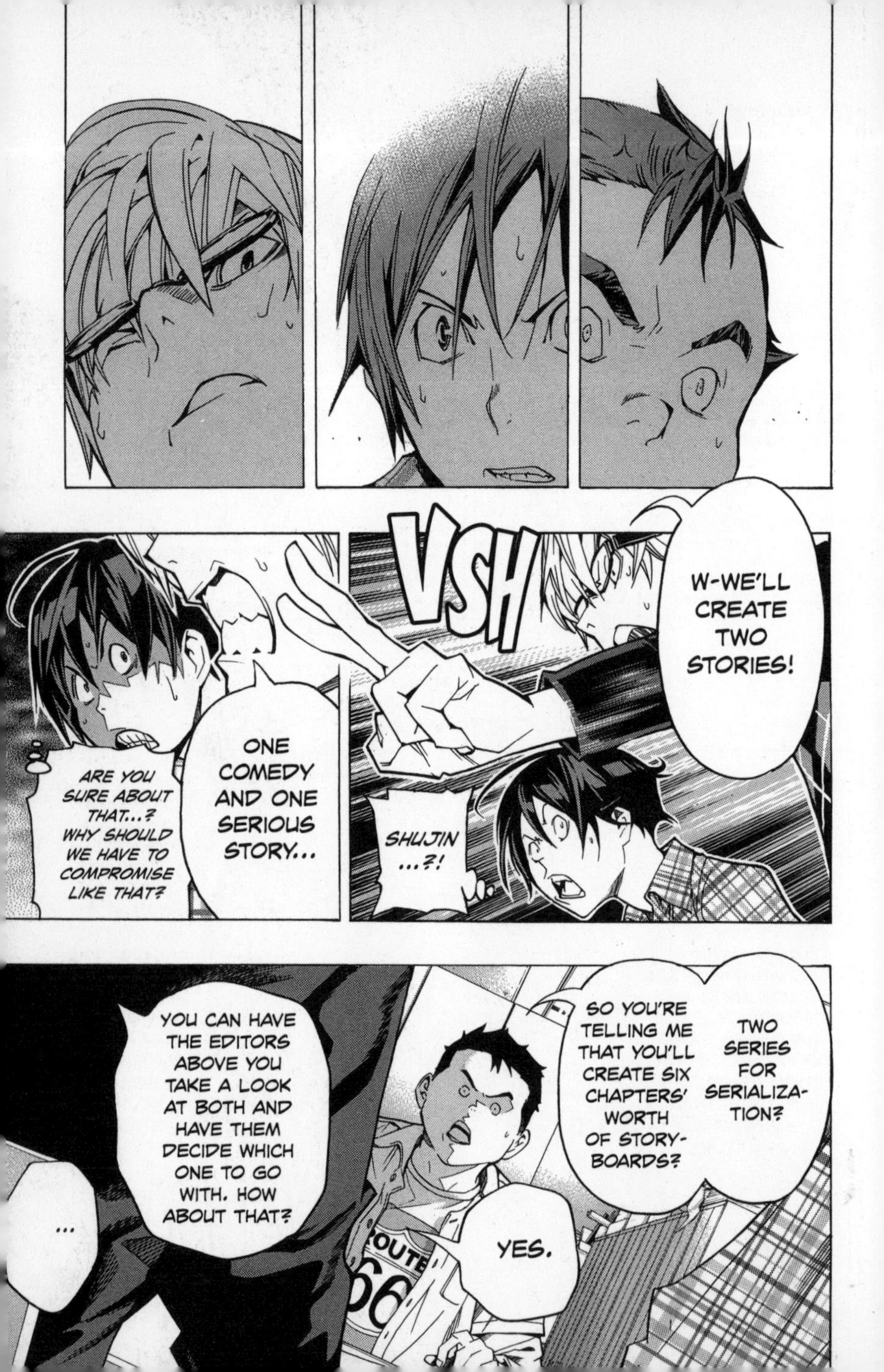
VSH
W-WE'LL CREATE TWO STORIES!
SHUJIN ...?!
ONE COMEDY AND ONE SERIOUS STORY...
ARE YOU SURE ABOUT THAT...? WHY SHOULD WE HAVE TO COMPROMISE LIKE THAT?
TWO SERIES FOR SERIALIZATION?
SO YOU'RE TELLING ME THAT YOU'LL CREATE SIX CHAPTERS' WORTH OF STORYBOARDS?
YES.
YOU CAN HAVE THE EDITORS ABOVE YOU TAKE A LOOK AT BOTH AND HAVE THEM DECIDE WHICH ONE TO GO WITH. HOW ABOUT THAT?
...
ROUTE 66

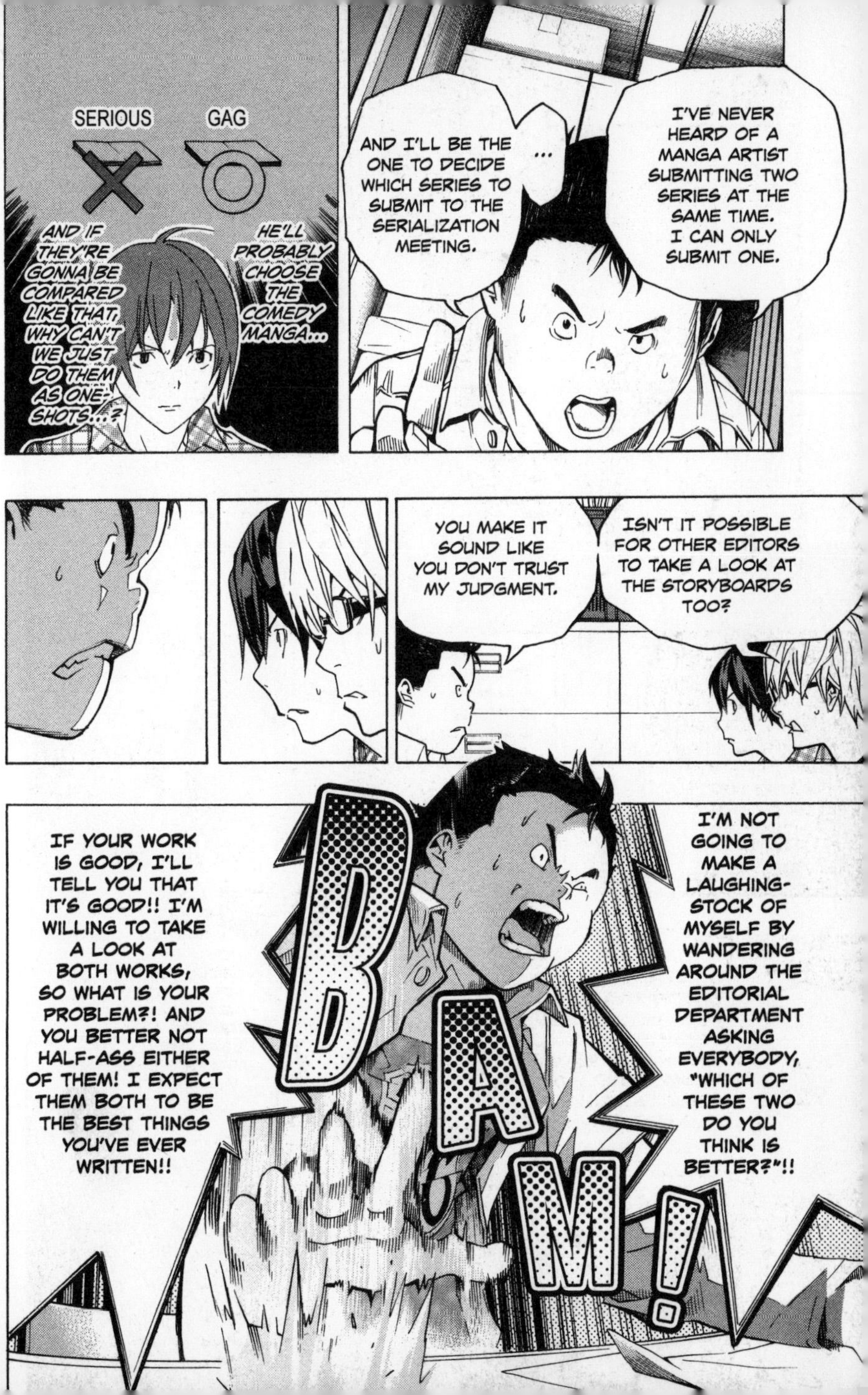
I'VE NEVER HEARD OF A MANGA ARTIST SUBMITTING TWO SERIES AT THE SAME TIME. I CAN ONLY SUBMIT ONE.
...
AND I'LL BE THE ONE TO DECIDE WHICH SERIES TO SUBMIT TO THE SERIALIZATION MEETING.
SERIOUS
GAG
HE'LL PROBABLY CHOOSE THE COMEDY MANGA...
AND IF THEY'RE GONNA BE COMPARED LIKE THAT, WHY CAN'T WE JUST DO THEM AS ONE-SHOTS...?
ISN'T IT POSSIBLE FOR OTHER EDITORS TO TAKE A LOOK AT THE STORYBOARDS TOO?
YOU MAKE IT SOUND LIKE YOU DON'T TRUST MY JUDGMENT.
I'M NOT GOING TO MAKE A LAUGHING-STOCK OF MYSELF BY WANDERING AROUND THE EDITORIAL DEPARTMENT ASKING EVERYBODY, "WHICH OF THESE TWO DO YOU THINK IS BETTER?"!!
BAM!
IF YOUR WORK IS GOOD, I'LL TELL YOU THAT IT'S GOOD!! I'M WILLING TO TAKE A LOOK AT BOTH WORKS, SO WHAT IS YOUR PROBLEM?! AND YOU BETTER NOT HALF-ASS EITHER OF THEM! I EXPECT THEM BOTH TO BE THE BEST THINGS YOU'VE EVER WRITTEN!!

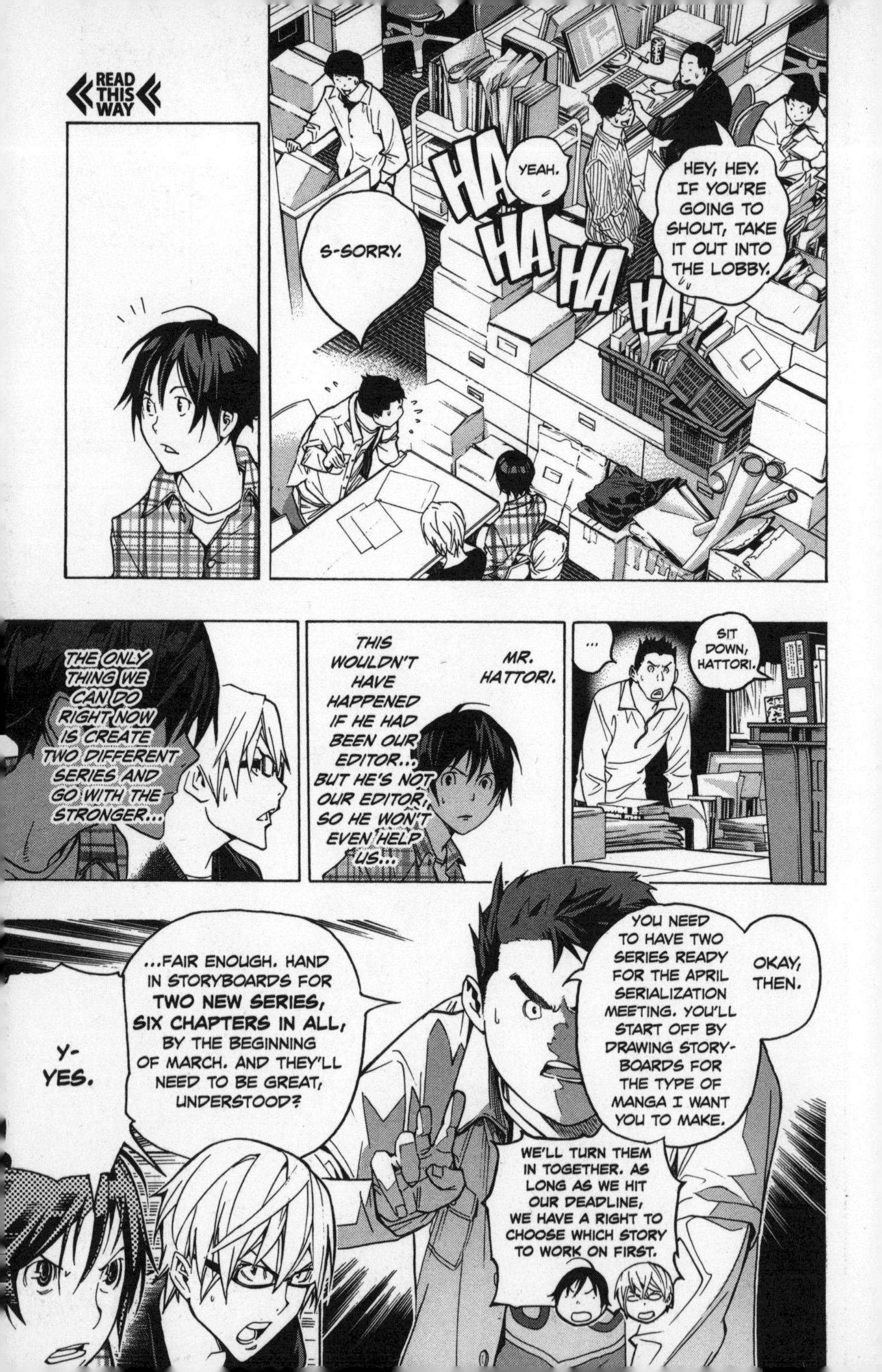
READ THIS WAY
HEY, HEY. IF YOU'RE GOING TO SHOUT, TAKE IT OUT INTO THE LOBBY.
YEAH.
HA HA HA HA
S-SORRY.
SIT DOWN, HATTORI.
...
MR. HATTORI.
THIS WOULDN'T HAVE HAPPENED IF HE HAD BEEN OUR EDITOR... BUT HE'S NOT OUR EDITOR, SO HE WON'T EVEN HELP US...
THE ONLY THING WE CAN DO RIGHT NOW IS CREATE TWO DIFFERENT SERIES AND GO WITH THE STRONGER...
OKAY, THEN.
YOU NEED TO HAVE TWO SERIES READY FOR THE APRIL SERIALIZATION MEETING. YOU'LL START OFF BY DRAWING STORY-BOARDS FOR THE TYPE OF MANGA I WANT YOU TO MAKE.
...FAIR ENOUGH. HAND IN STORYBOARDS FOR **TWO NEW SERIES, SIX CHAPTERS IN ALL,** BY THE BEGINNING OF MARCH. AND THEY'LL NEED TO BE GREAT, UNDERSTOOD?
Y-YES.
WE'LL TURN THEM IN TOGETHER. AS LONG AS WE HIT OUR DEADLINE, WE HAVE A RIGHT TO CHOOSE WHICH STORY TO WORK ON FIRST.

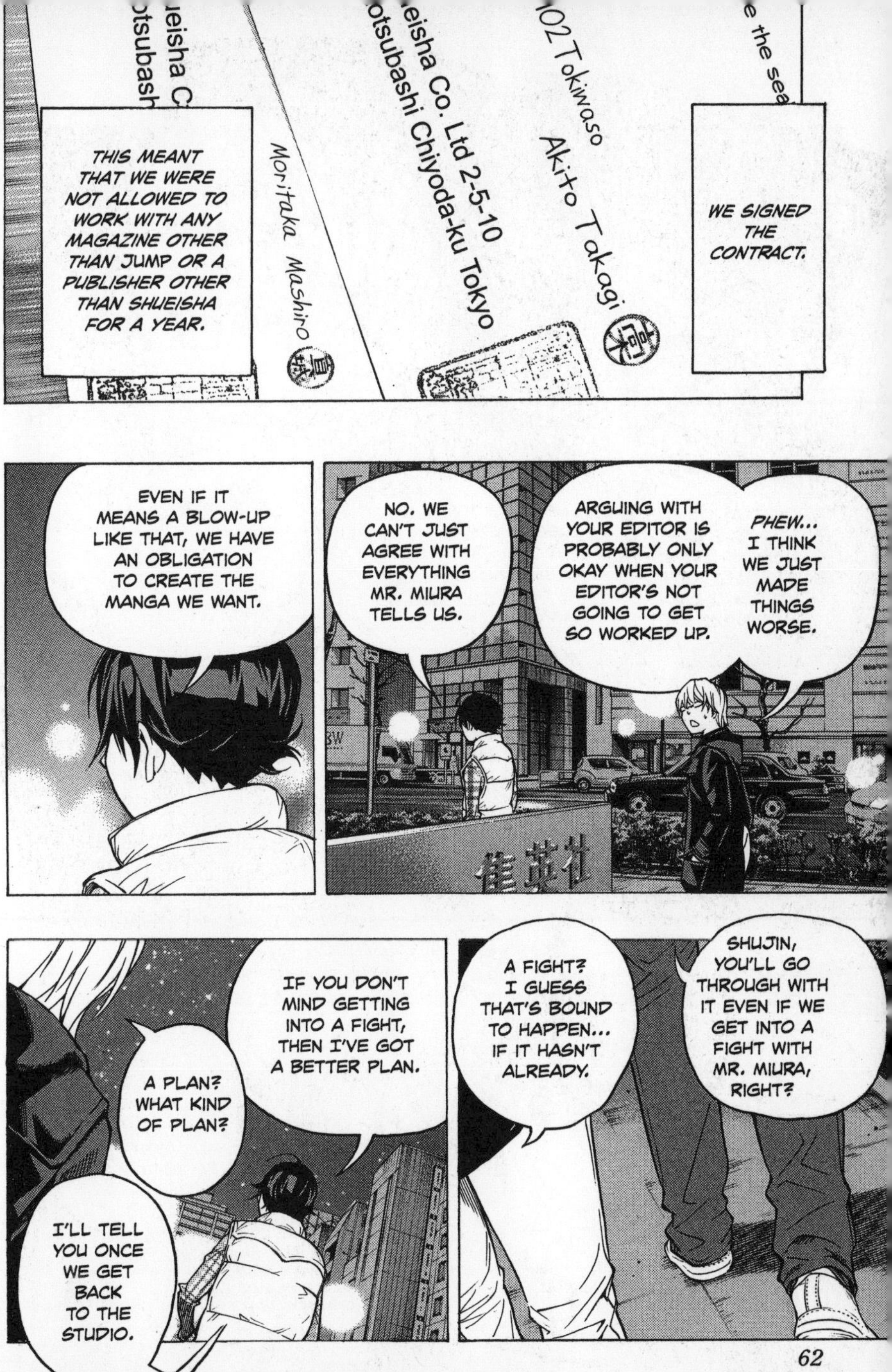
WE SIGNED THE CONTRACT.
e the sea
102 Tokiwaso Akito Takagi
eisha Co. Ltd 2-5-10
otsubashi Chiyoda-ku Tokyo
Moritaka Mashiro
ueisha C
otsubash
THIS MEANT THAT WE WERE NOT ALLOWED TO WORK WITH ANY MAGAZINE OTHER THAN JUMP OR A PUBLISHER OTHER THAN SHUEISHA FOR A YEAR.
PHEW... I THINK WE JUST MADE THINGS WORSE.
ARGUING WITH YOUR EDITOR IS PROBABLY ONLY OKAY WHEN YOUR EDITOR'S NOT GOING TO GET SO WORKED UP.
NO. WE CAN'T JUST AGREE WITH EVERYTHING MR. MIURA TELLS US.
EVEN IF IT MEANS A BLOW-UP LIKE THAT, WE HAVE AN OBLIGATION TO CREATE THE MANGA WE WANT.
SHUJIN, YOU'LL GO THROUGH WITH IT EVEN IF WE GET INTO A FIGHT WITH MR. MIURA, RIGHT?
A FIGHT? I GUESS THAT'S BOUND TO HAPPEN... IF IT HASN'T ALREADY.
IF YOU DON'T MIND GETTING INTO A FIGHT, THEN I'VE GOT A BETTER PLAN.
A PLAN? WHAT KIND OF PLAN?
I'LL TELL YOU ONCE WE GET BACK TO THE STUDIO.

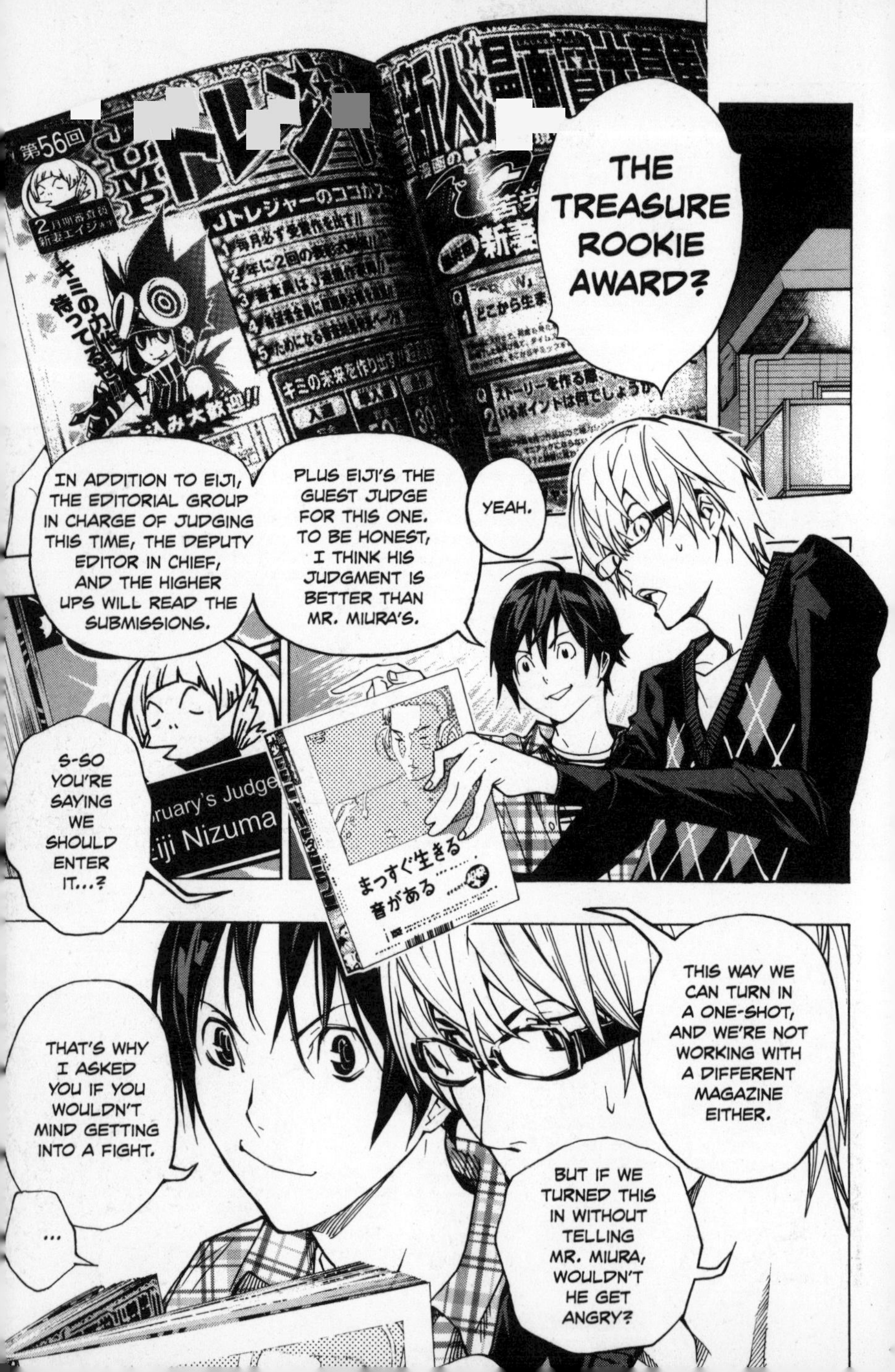
THE TREASURE ROOKIE AWARD?
YEAH.
PLUS EIJI'S THE GUEST JUDGE FOR THIS ONE. TO BE HONEST, I THINK HIS JUDGMENT IS BETTER THAN MR. MIURA'S.
IN ADDITION TO EIJI, THE EDITORIAL GROUP IN CHARGE OF JUDGING THIS TIME, THE DEPUTY EDITOR IN CHIEF, AND THE HIGHER UPS WILL READ THE SUBMISSIONS.
bruary's Judge
iji Nizuma
S-SO YOU'RE SAYING WE SHOULD ENTER IT...?
まっすぐ生きる音がある
THIS WAY WE CAN TURN IN A ONE-SHOT, AND WE'RE NOT WORKING WITH A DIFFERENT MAGAZINE EITHER.
BUT IF WE TURNED THIS IN WITHOUT TELLING MR. MIURA, WOULDN'T HE GET ANGRY?
THAT'S WHY I ASKED YOU IF YOU WOULDN'T MIND GETTING INTO A FIGHT.
...

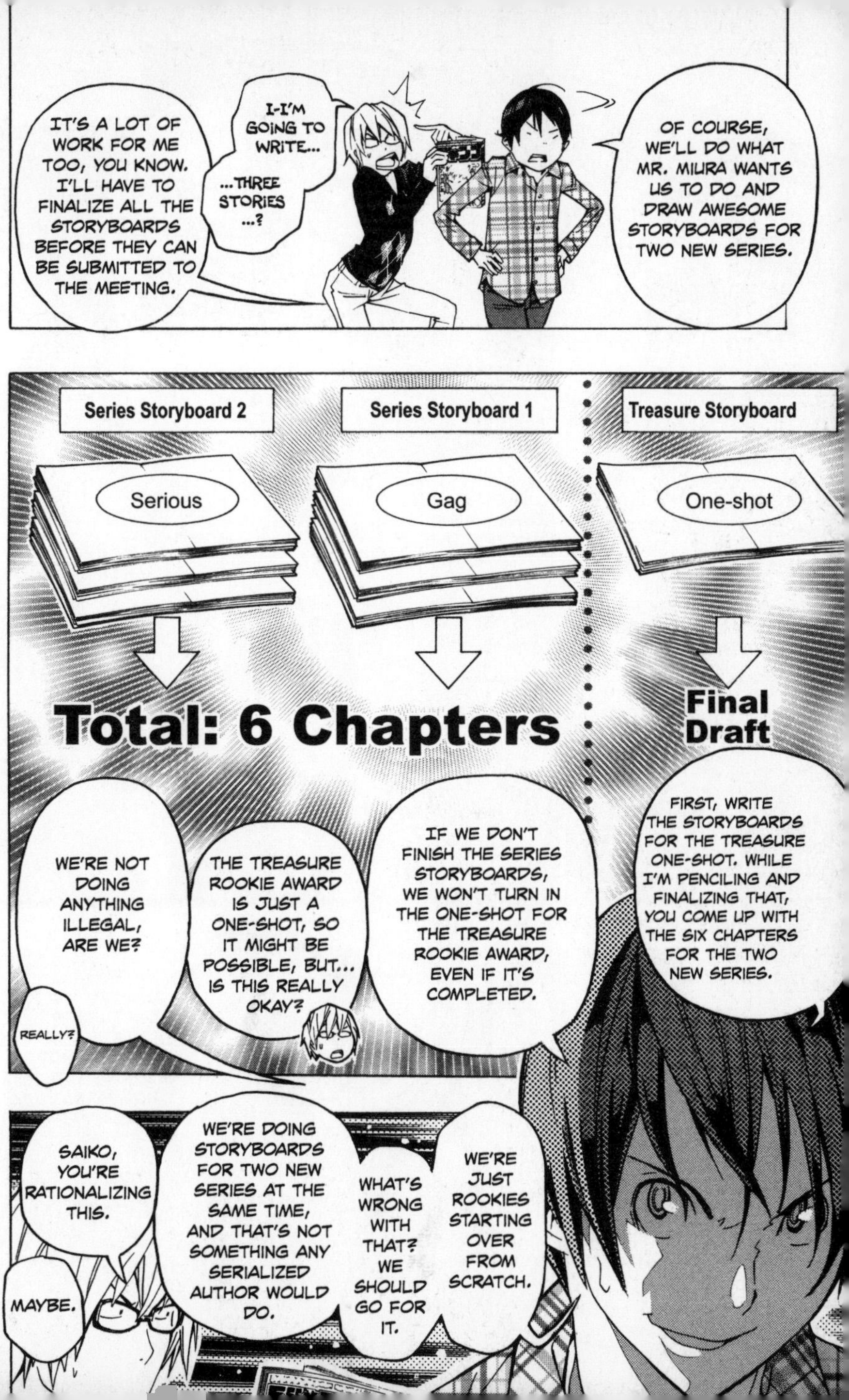

IT'S A LOT OF WORK FOR ME TOO, YOU KNOW. I'LL HAVE TO FINALIZE ALL THE STORYBOARDS BEFORE THEY CAN BE SUBMITTED TO THE MEETING.

I-I'M GOING TO WRITE...

...THREE STORIES...?

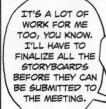

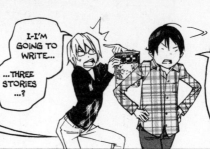

OF COURSE, WE'LL DO WHAT MR. MIURA WANTS US TO DO AND DRAW AWESOME STORYBOARDS FOR TWO NEW SERIES.

Series Storyboard 2	Series Storyboard 1	Treasure Storyboard
Serious	Gag	One-shot

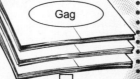

Total: 6 Chapters

Final Draft

WE'RE NOT DOING ANYTHING ILLEGAL, ARE WE?

REALLY?

THE TREASURE ROOKIE AWARD IS JUST A ONE-SHOT, SO IT MIGHT BE POSSIBLE, BUT... IS THIS REALLY OKAY?

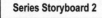

IF WE DON'T FINISH THE SERIES STORYBOARDS, WE WON'T TURN IN THE ONE-SHOT FOR THE TREASURE ROOKIE AWARD, EVEN IF IT'S COMPLETED.

FIRST, WRITE THE STORYBOARDS FOR THE TREASURE ONE-SHOT. WHILE I'M PENCILING AND FINALIZING THAT, YOU COME UP WITH THE SIX CHAPTERS FOR THE TWO NEW SERIES.

SAIKO, YOU'RE RATIONALIZING THIS.

MAYBE.

WE'RE DOING STORYBOARDS FOR TWO NEW SERIES AT THE SAME TIME, AND THAT'S NOT SOMETHING ANY SERIALIZED AUTHOR WOULD DO.

WHAT'S WRONG WITH THAT? WE SHOULD GO FOR IT.

WE'RE JUST ROOKIES STARTING OVER FROM SCRATCH.

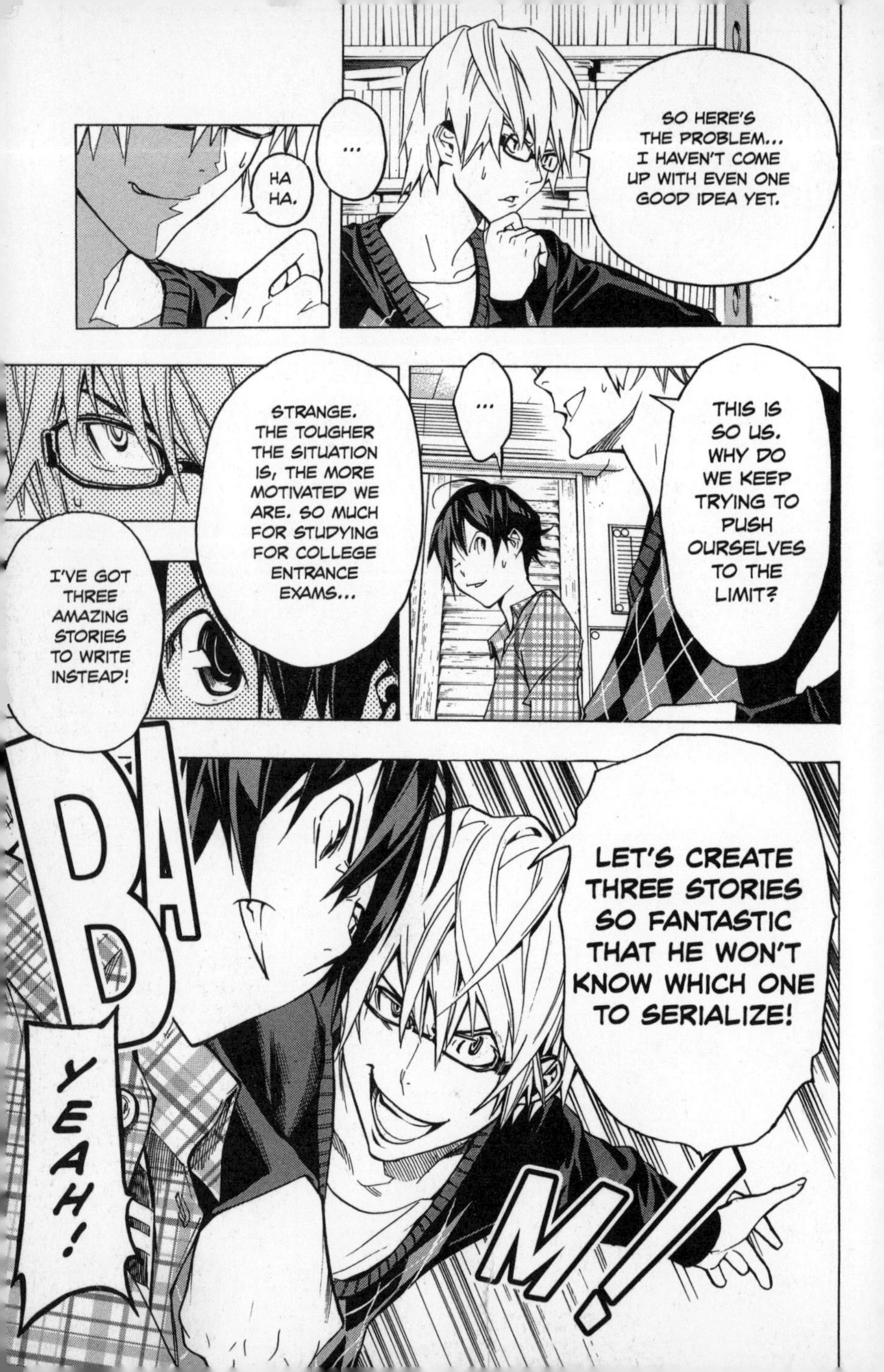
SO HERE'S THE PROBLEM... I HAVEN'T COME UP WITH EVEN ONE GOOD IDEA YET.
...
HA HA.
THIS IS SO US. WHY DO WE KEEP TRYING TO PUSH OURSELVES TO THE LIMIT?
...
STRANGE. THE TOUGHER THE SITUATION IS, THE MORE MOTIVATED WE ARE. SO MUCH FOR STUDYING FOR COLLEGE ENTRANCE EXAMS...
I'VE GOT THREE AMAZING STORIES TO WRITE INSTEAD!
LET'S CREATE THREE STORIES SO FANTASTIC THAT HE WON'T KNOW WHICH ONE TO SERIALIZE!
YEAH!

OHBA'S STORYBOARD

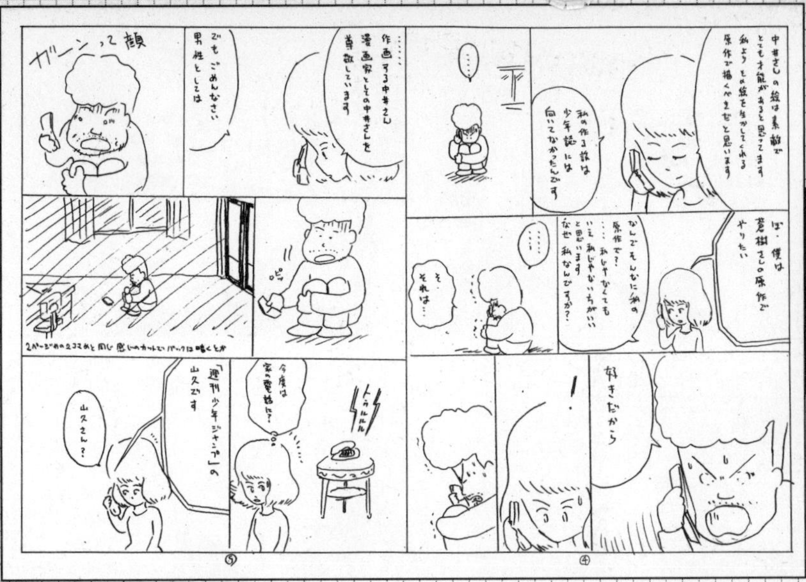
中井さんの絵は素敵でとても才能があると思ってます
私よりその絵を生かしてくれる原作で描くべきだと思います
……
私の作る話は少年誌には向いてなかったんです
ぼ・僕は蒼樹さんの原作でやりたい
なんでそんなに私の原作で？……私じゃなくてもいえ私じゃないちがいいと思います なぜ私なんですか？
……
そ、それは…
好きだから
！
④
……
作画する中井さん漫画家としての中井さんを尊敬しています
でもごめんなさい男性としては
ガーンって顔
ピッ
2ページめの2コマめと同じ感じのカットでバックは暗くとか
トゥルルル
今度は家の電話に？
「週刊少年ジャンプ」の山久です
山久さん？
⑤

OBATA'S STORYBOARD

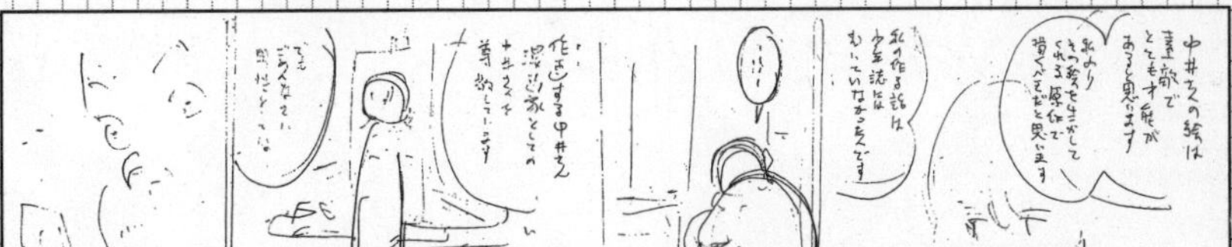
中井さんの絵は素敵でとても才能があると思います
私よりその絵を生かしてくれる原作で描くべきだと思います
私の作る話は少年誌にはむいていなかったんです
ぼ・僕は蒼樹さんの原作でやりたい
そ、それは…
蒼樹さんを好きだから
作画する中井さん漫画家としての中井さんを尊敬しています
でもごめんなさい男性としては
ポト
プルル
今度は家の電話
「週刊少年ジャンプ」の山久です

COMPLETE!

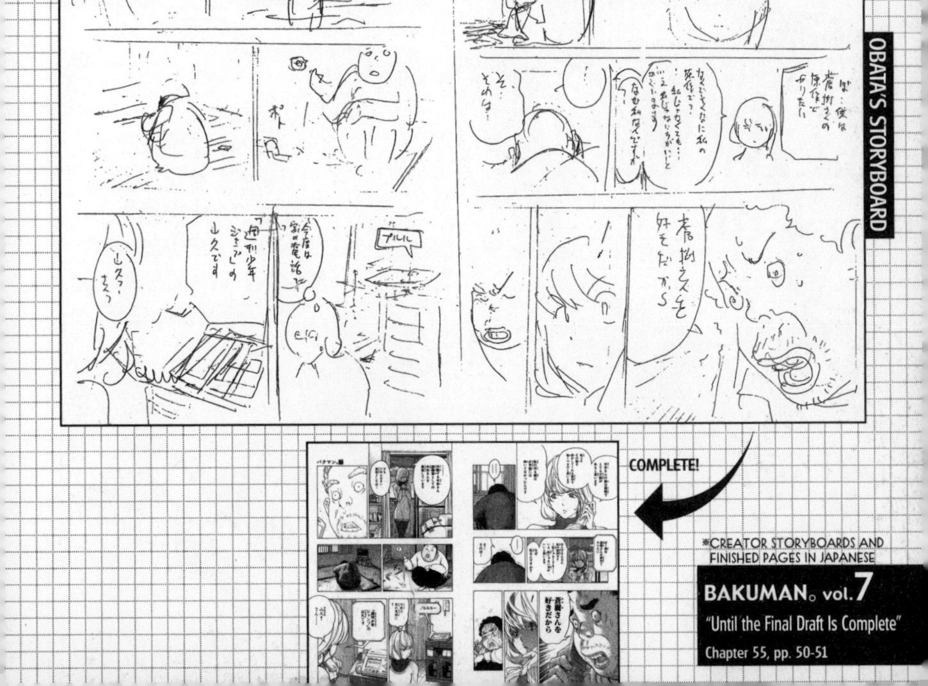

*CREATOR STORYBOARDS AND FINISHED PAGES IN JAPANESE

BAKUMAN。 vol.7

"Until the Final Draft Is Complete"

Chapter 55, pp. 50-51

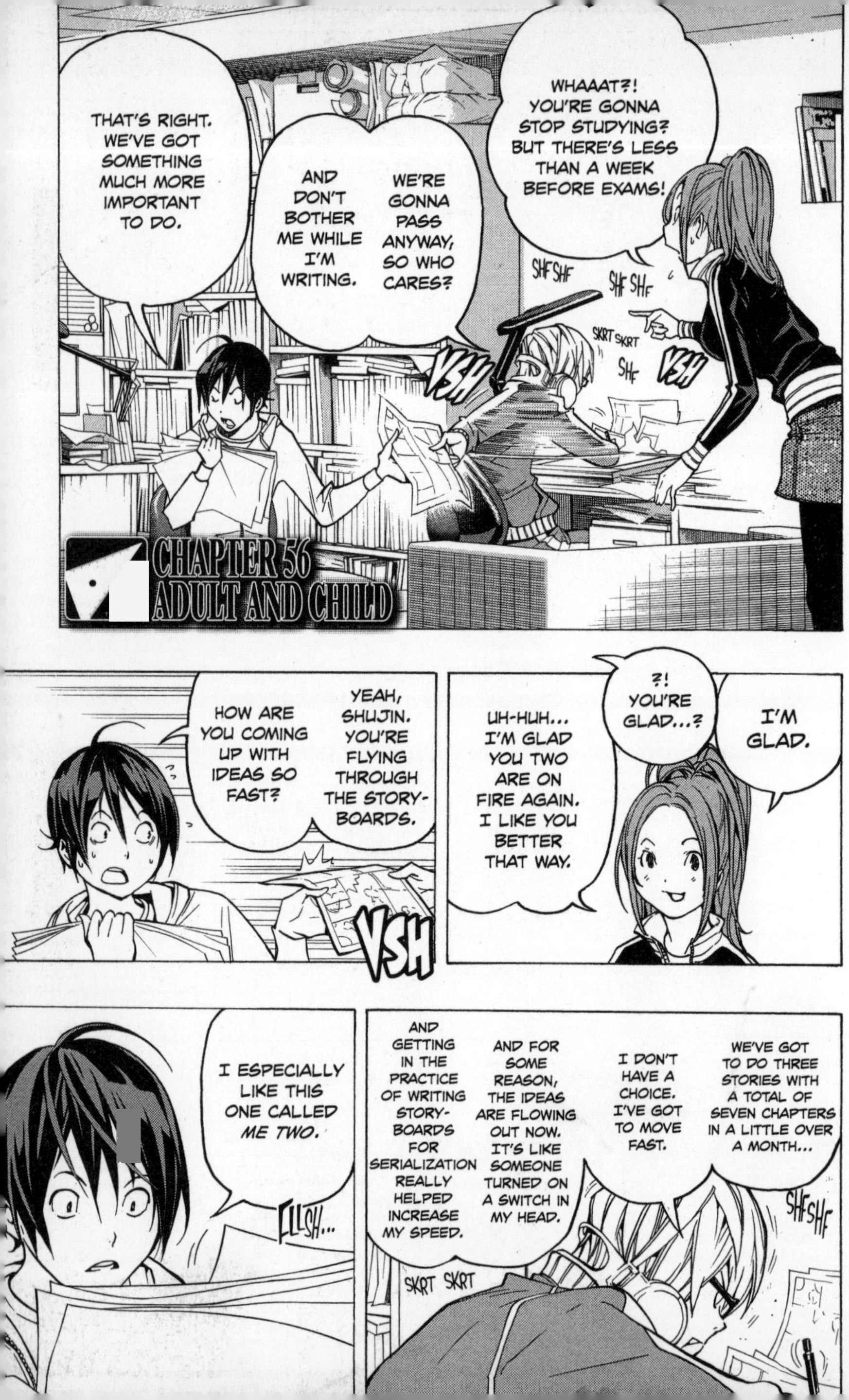
WHAAAT?! YOU'RE GONNA STOP STUDYING? BUT THERE'S LESS THAN A WEEK BEFORE EXAMS!
SHF SHF
SHF SHF
WE'RE GONNA PASS ANYWAY, SO WHO CARES?
AND DON'T BOTHER ME WHILE I'M WRITING.
THAT'S RIGHT. WE'VE GOT SOMETHING MUCH MORE IMPORTANT TO DO.
SKRT SKRT
SHF
VSH
VSH
CHAPTER 56
ADULT AND CHILD
I'M GLAD.
?! YOU'RE GLAD...?
UH-HUH... I'M GLAD YOU TWO ARE ON FIRE AGAIN. I LIKE YOU BETTER THAT WAY.
YEAH, SHUJIN. YOU'RE FLYING THROUGH THE STORY-BOARDS.
HOW ARE YOU COMING UP WITH IDEAS SO FAST?
VSH
WE'VE GOT TO DO THREE STORIES WITH A TOTAL OF SEVEN CHAPTERS IN A LITTLE OVER A MONTH...
I DON'T HAVE A CHOICE. I'VE GOT TO MOVE FAST.
AND FOR SOME REASON, THE IDEAS ARE FLOWING OUT NOW. IT'S LIKE SOMEONE TURNED ON A SWITCH IN MY HEAD.
AND GETTING IN THE PRACTICE OF WRITING STORY-BOARDS FOR SERIALIZATION REALLY HELPED INCREASE MY SPEED.
SHFSHF
SKRT SKRT
FLLSH...
I ESPECIALLY LIKE THIS ONE CALLED *ME TWO*.

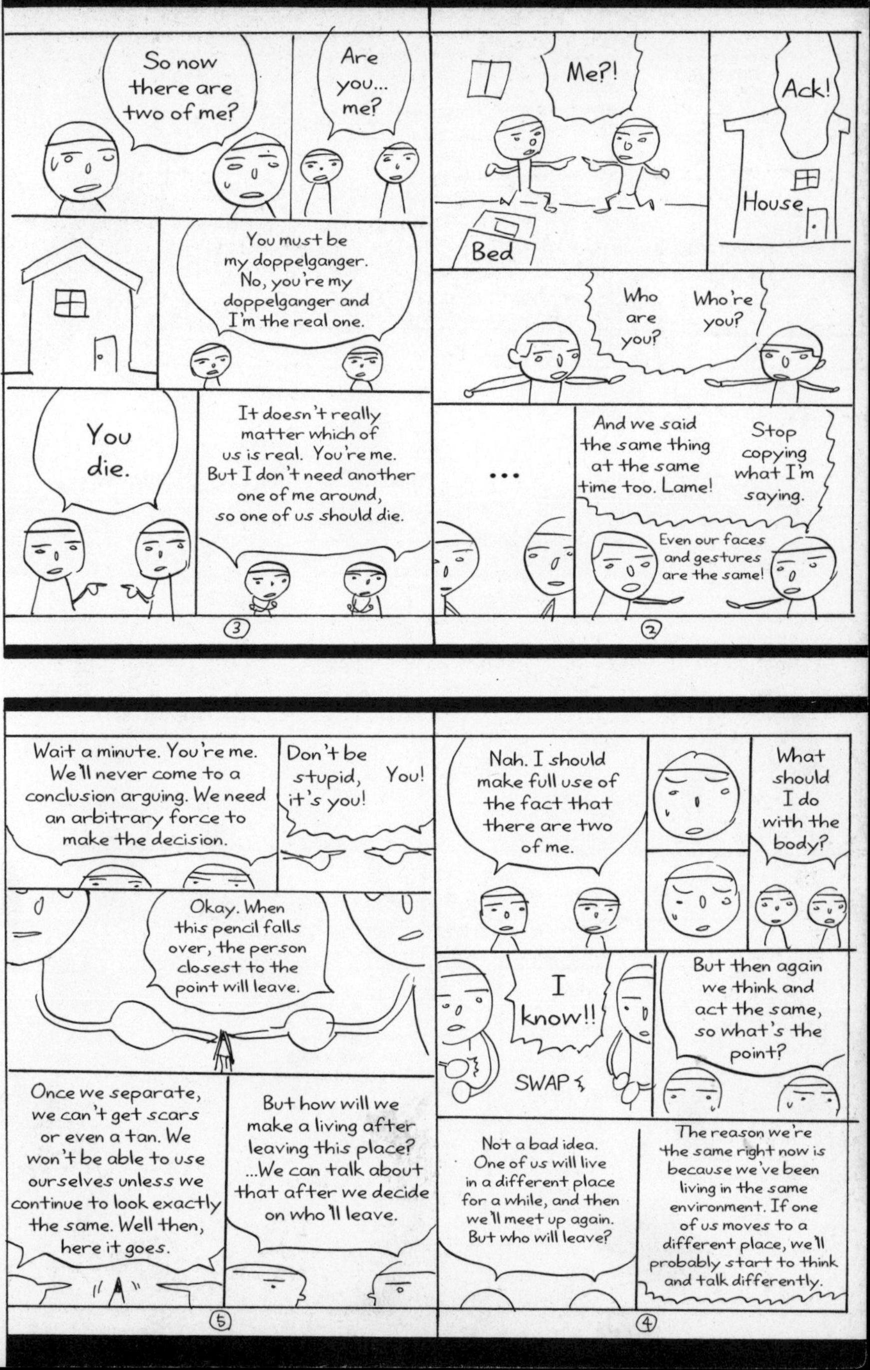
Ack!
House
Me?!
Bed
Who're you?
Who are you?
Stop copying what I'm saying.
And we said the same thing at the same time too. Lame!
Even our faces and gestures are the same!
...
②
Are you... me?
So now there are two of me?
You must be my doppelganger. No, you're my doppelganger and I'm the real one.
It doesn't really matter which of us is real. You're me. But I don't need another one of me around, so one of us should die.
You die.
③
What should I do with the body?
Nah. I should make full use of the fact that there are two of me.
But then again we think and act the same, so what's the point?
I know!!
SWAP
The reason we're the same right now is because we've been living in the same environment. If one of us moves to a different place, we'll probably start to think and talk differently.
Not a bad idea. One of us will live in a different place for a while, and then we'll meet up again. But who will leave?
④
You!
Don't be stupid, it's you!
Wait a minute. You're me. We'll never come to a conclusion arguing. We need an arbitrary force to make the decision.
Okay. When this pencil falls over, the person closest to the point will leave.
But how will we make a living after leaving this place? ...We can talk about that after we decide on who'll leave.
Once we separate, we can't get scars or even a tan. We won't be able to use ourselves unless we continue to look exactly the same. Well then, here it goes.
⑤

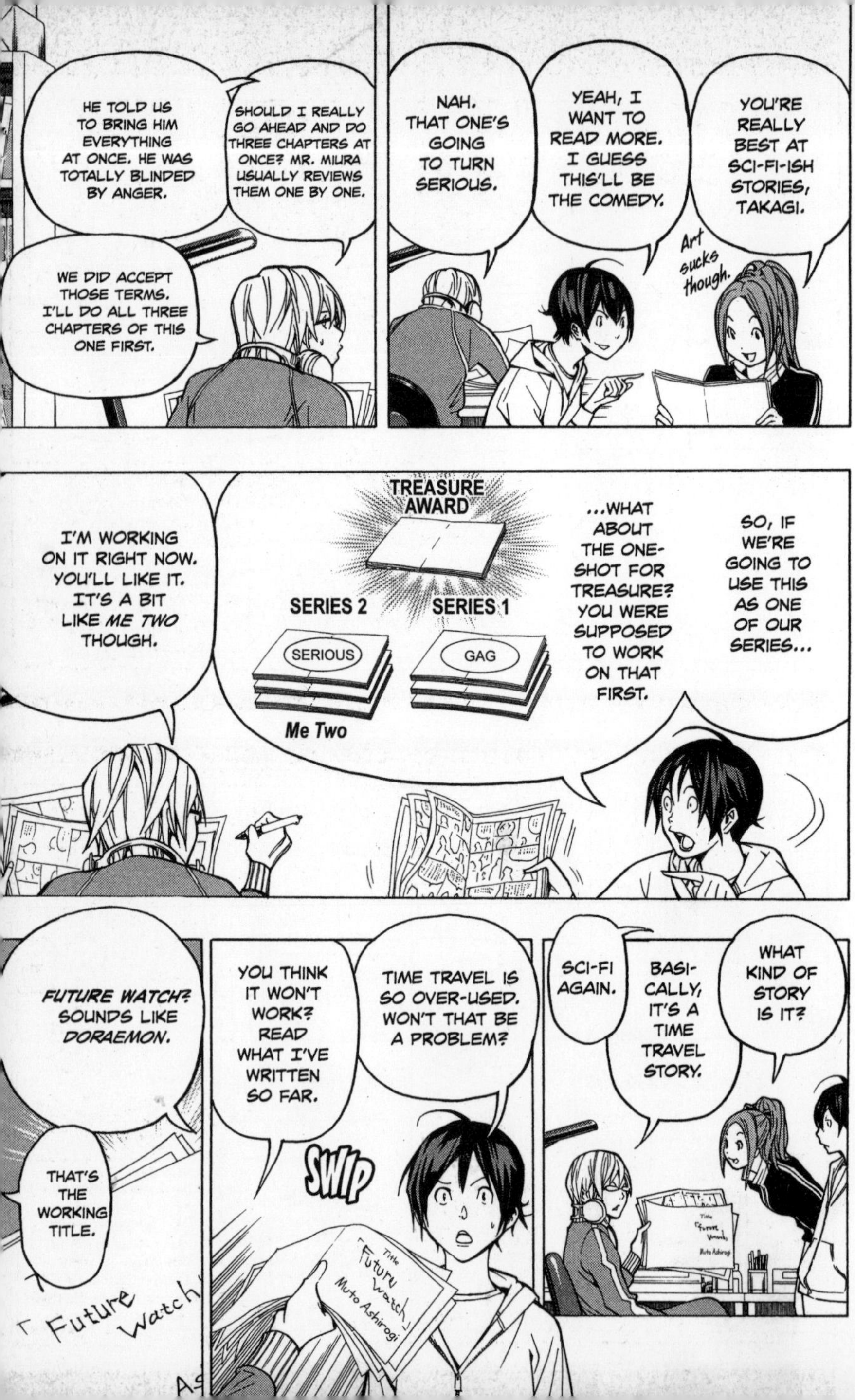
YOU'RE REALLY BEST AT SCI-FI-ISH STORIES, TAKAGI.
Art sucks though.
YEAH, I WANT TO READ MORE. I GUESS THIS'LL BE THE COMEDY.
NAH. THAT ONE'S GOING TO TURN SERIOUS.
SHOULD I REALLY GO AHEAD AND DO THREE CHAPTERS AT ONCE? MR. MIURA USUALLY REVIEWS THEM ONE BY ONE.
HE TOLD US TO BRING HIM EVERYTHING AT ONCE. HE WAS TOTALLY BLINDED BY ANGER.
WE DID ACCEPT THOSE TERMS. I'LL DO ALL THREE CHAPTERS OF THIS ONE FIRST.
SO, IF WE'RE GOING TO USE THIS AS ONE OF OUR SERIES...
...WHAT ABOUT THE ONE-SHOT FOR TREASURE? YOU WERE SUPPOSED TO WORK ON THAT FIRST.
TREASURE AWARD
SERIES 1
GAG
SERIES 2
SERIOUS
Me Two
I'M WORKING ON IT RIGHT NOW. YOU'LL LIKE IT. IT'S A BIT LIKE *ME TWO* THOUGH.
WHAT KIND OF STORY IS IT?
BASICALLY, IT'S A TIME TRAVEL STORY.
SCI-FI AGAIN.
TIME TRAVEL IS SO OVER-USED. WON'T THAT BE A PROBLEM?
YOU THINK IT WON'T WORK? READ WHAT I'VE WRITTEN SO FAR.
SWIP
Title 「Future Watch」 Muto Ashirogi
FUTURE WATCH? SOUNDS LIKE *DORAEMON*.
THAT'S THE WORKING TITLE.
「Future Watch

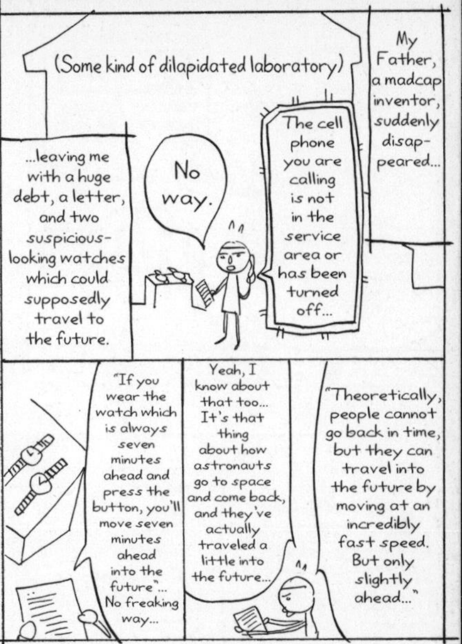
My Father, a madcap inventor, suddenly disappeared...
(Some kind of dilapidated laboratory)
The cell phone you are calling is not in the service area or has been turned off...
No way.
...leaving me with a huge debt, a letter, and two suspicious-looking watches which could supposedly travel to the future.
"Theoretically, people cannot go back in time, but they can travel into the future by moving at an incredibly fast speed. But only slightly ahead..."
Yeah, I know about that too... It's that thing about how astronauts go to space and come back, and they've actually traveled a little into the future...
"If you wear the watch which is always seven minutes ahead and press the button, you'll move seven minutes ahead into the future"... No freaking way...
②

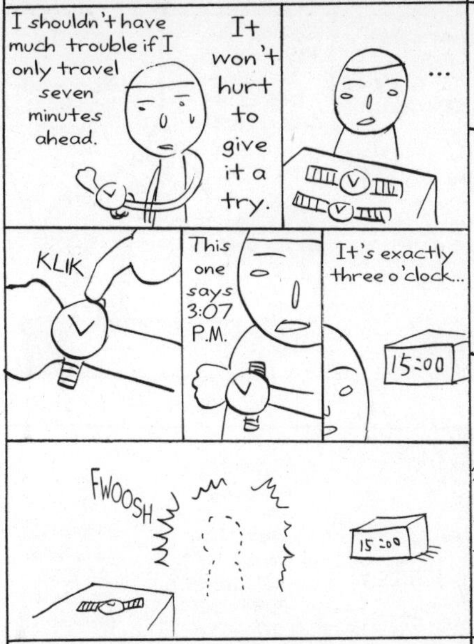
I shouldn't have much trouble if I only travel seven minutes ahead.
It won't hurt to give it a try.
...
It's exactly three o'clock...
15:00
This one says 3:07 P.M.
KLIK
FWOOSH
15:00
③

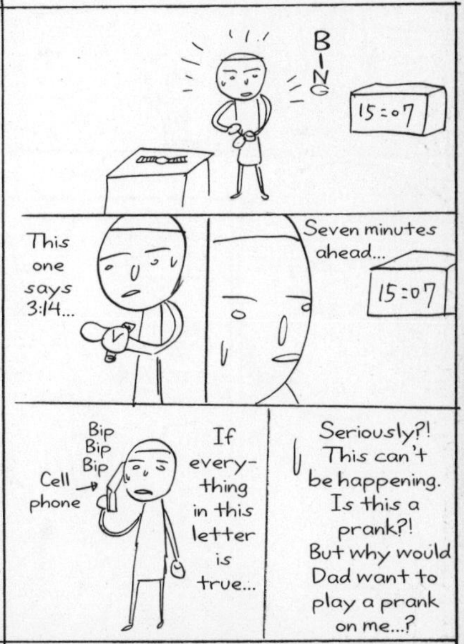
BING
15:07
Seven minutes ahead...
15:07
This one says 3:14...
Seriously?! This can't be happening. Is this a prank?! But why would Dad want to play a prank on me...?
If everything in this letter is true...
Bip Bip Bip
Cell phone
④

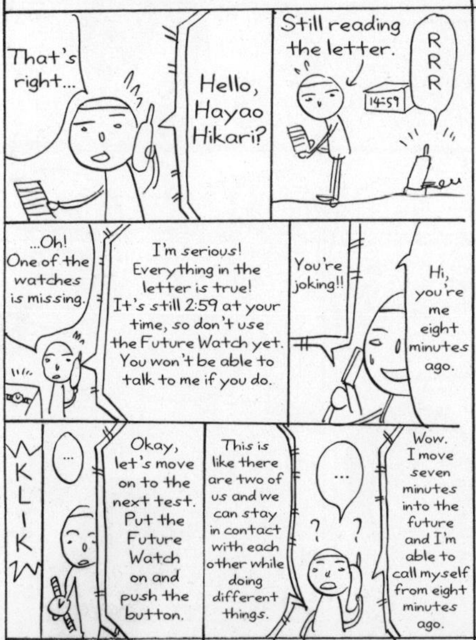
RRR
Still reading the letter.
14:59
Hello, Hayao Hikari?
That's right...
Hi, you're me eight minutes ago.
You're joking!!
I'm serious! Everything in the letter is true! It's still 2:59 at your time, so don't use the Future Watch yet. You won't be able to talk to me if you do.
...Oh! One of the watches is missing.
Wow. I move seven minutes into the future and I'm able to call myself from eight minutes ago.
...
? ?
This is like there are two of us and we can stay in contact with each other while doing different things.
Okay, let's move on to the next test. Put the Future Watch on and push the button.
...
KLIK
⑤

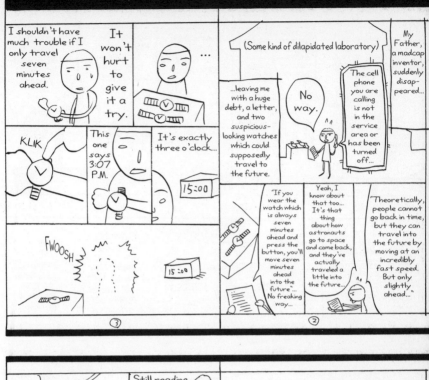

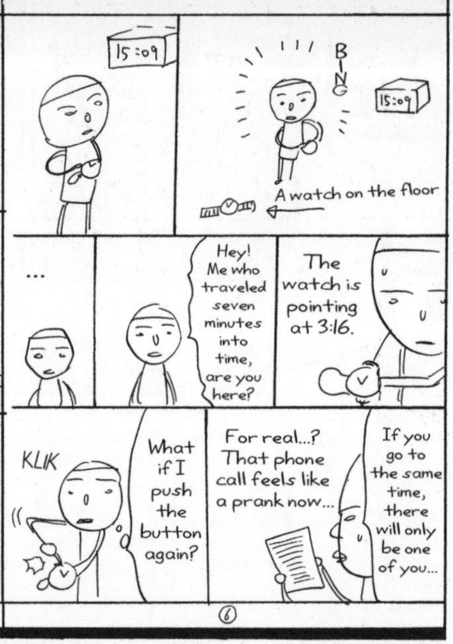
15:09
BING
A watch on the floor
15:09
The watch is pointing at 3:16.
Hey! Me who traveled seven minutes into time, are you here?
...
If you go to the same time, there will only be one of you...
For real...? That phone call feels like a prank now...
What if I push the button again?
KLIK
⑥

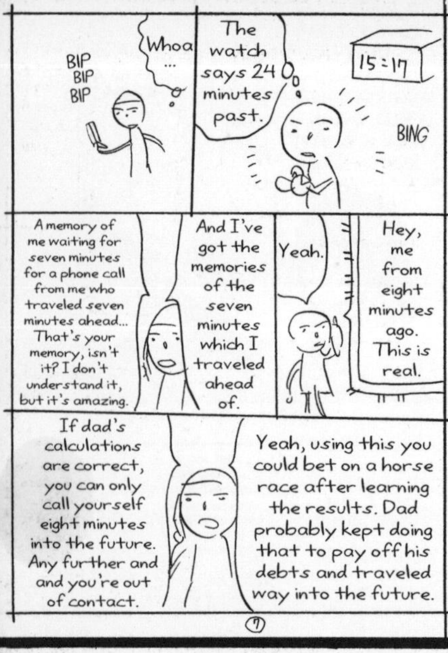
15:17
The watch says 24 minutes past.
BING
Whoa...
BIP BIP BIP
Hey, me from eight minutes ago. This is real.
Yeah.
And I've got the memories of the seven minutes which I traveled ahead of.
A memory of me waiting for seven minutes for a phone call from me who traveled seven minutes ahead... That's your memory, isn't it? I don't understand it, but it's amazing.
Yeah, using this you could bet on a horse race after learning the results. Dad probably kept doing that to pay off his debts and traveled way into the future.
If dad's calculations are correct, you can only call yourself eight minutes into the future. Any further and and you're out of contact.
⑦

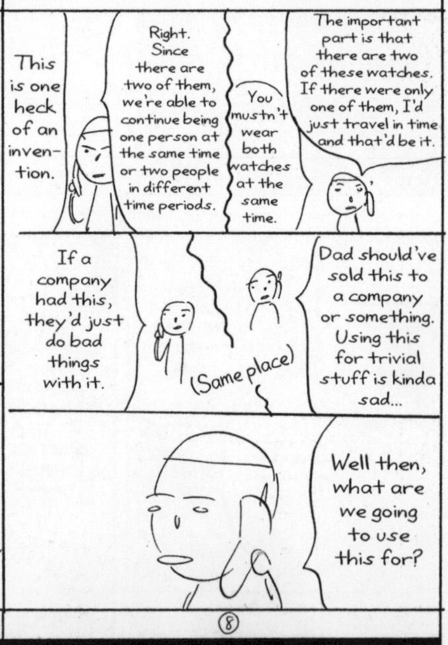
The important part is that there are two of these watches. If there were only one of them, I'd just travel in time and that'd be it.
You mustn't wear both watches at the same time.
Right. Since there are two of them, we're able to continue being one person at the same time or two people in different time periods.
This is one heck of an invention.
Dad should've sold this to a company or something. Using this for trivial stuff is kinda sad...
(Same place)
If a company had this, they'd just do bad things with it.
Well then, what are we going to use this for?
⑧

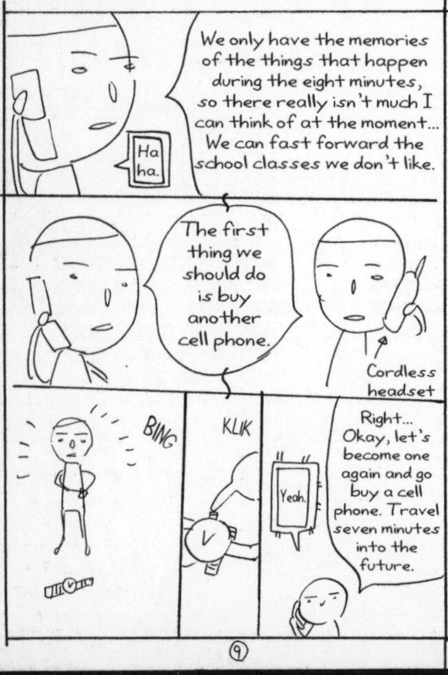
We only have the memories of the things that happen during the eight minutes, so there really isn't much I can think of at the moment... We can fast forward the school classes we don't like.
Ha ha.
Cordless headset
The first thing we should do is buy another cell phone.
Right... Okay, let's become one again and go buy a cell phone. Travel seven minutes into the future.
Yeah.
KLIK
BING
⑨

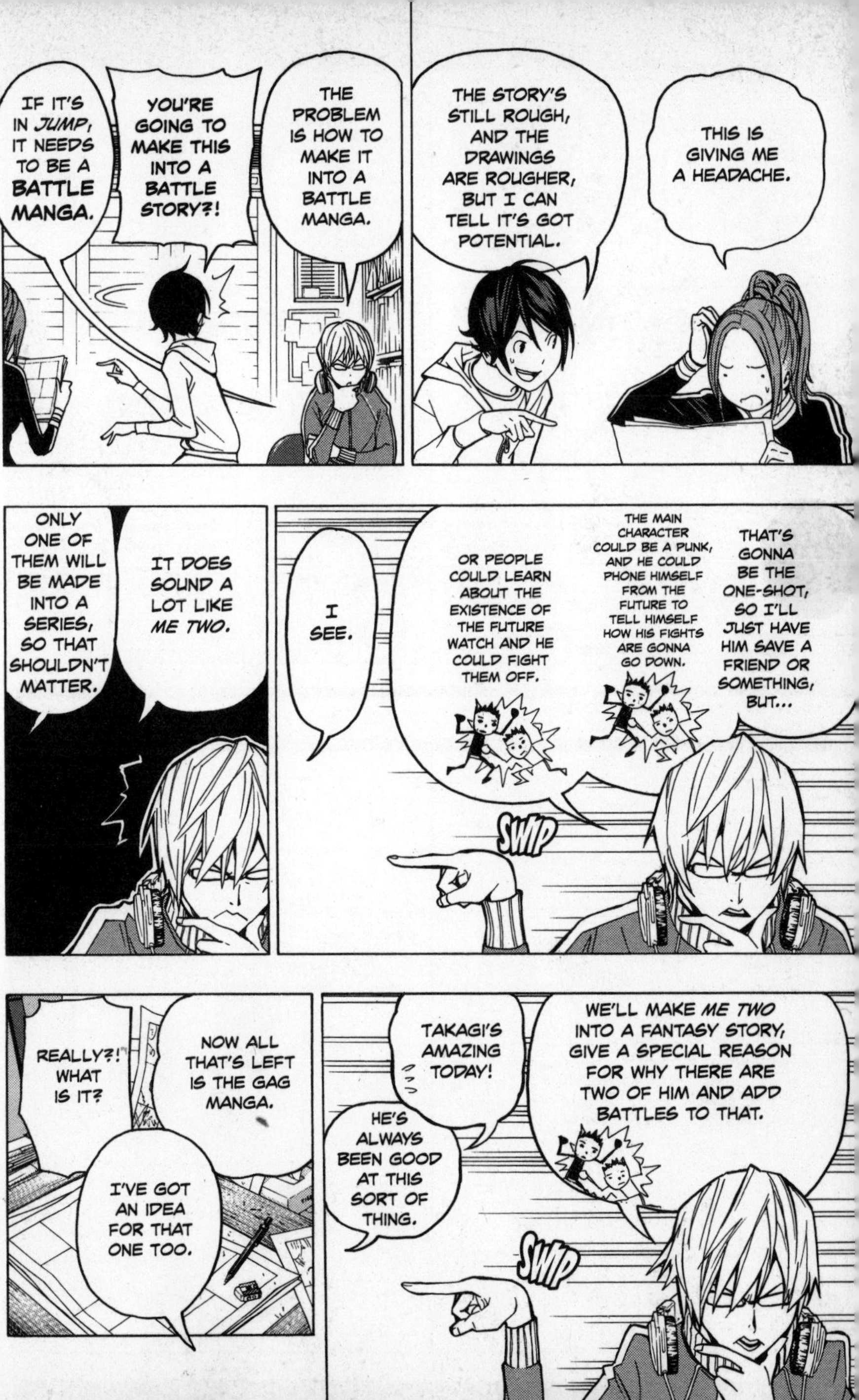
THIS IS GIVING ME A HEADACHE.
THE STORY'S STILL ROUGH, AND THE DRAWINGS ARE ROUGHER, BUT I CAN TELL IT'S GOT POTENTIAL.
THE PROBLEM IS HOW TO MAKE IT INTO A BATTLE MANGA.
YOU'RE GOING TO MAKE THIS INTO A BATTLE STORY?!
IF IT'S IN *JUMP*, IT NEEDS TO BE A **BATTLE MANGA.**
THAT'S GONNA BE THE ONE-SHOT, SO I'LL JUST HAVE HIM SAVE A FRIEND OR SOMETHING, BUT...
THE MAIN CHARACTER COULD BE A PUNK, AND HE COULD PHONE HIMSELF FROM THE FUTURE TO TELL HIMSELF HOW HIS FIGHTS ARE GONNA GO DOWN.
OR PEOPLE COULD LEARN ABOUT THE EXISTENCE OF THE FUTURE WATCH AND HE COULD FIGHT THEM OFF.
SWIP
I SEE.
IT DOES SOUND A LOT LIKE *ME TWO*.
ONLY ONE OF THEM WILL BE MADE INTO A SERIES, SO THAT SHOULDN'T MATTER.
WE'LL MAKE *ME TWO* INTO A FANTASY STORY, GIVE A SPECIAL REASON FOR WHY THERE ARE TWO OF HIM AND ADD BATTLES TO THAT.
SWIP
TAKAGI'S AMAZING TODAY!
HE'S ALWAYS BEEN GOOD AT THIS SORT OF THING.
NOW ALL THAT'S LEFT IS THE GAG MANGA.
REALLY?! WHAT IS IT?
I'VE GOT AN IDEA FOR THAT ONE TOO.

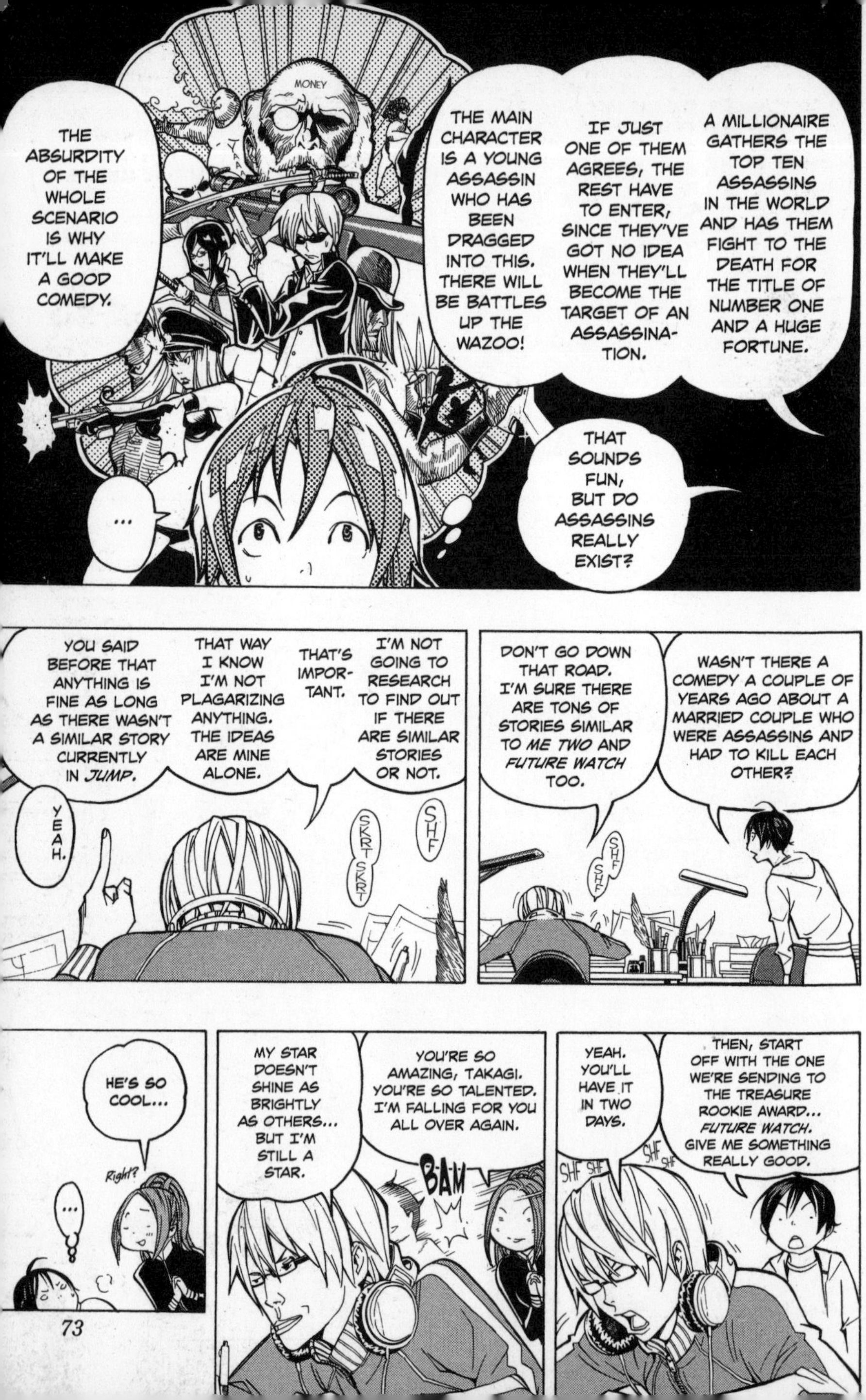
MONEY
A MILLIONAIRE GATHERS THE TOP TEN ASSASSINS IN THE WORLD AND HAS THEM FIGHT TO THE DEATH FOR THE TITLE OF NUMBER ONE AND A HUGE FORTUNE.
IF JUST ONE OF THEM AGREES, THE REST HAVE TO ENTER, SINCE THEY'VE GOT NO IDEA WHEN THEY'LL BECOME THE TARGET OF AN ASSASSINA-TION.
THE MAIN CHARACTER IS A YOUNG ASSASSIN WHO HAS BEEN DRAGGED INTO THIS. THERE WILL BE BATTLES UP THE WAZOO!
THE ABSURDITY OF THE WHOLE SCENARIO IS WHY IT'LL MAKE A GOOD COMEDY.
THAT SOUNDS FUN, BUT DO ASSASSINS REALLY EXIST?
...
WASN'T THERE A COMEDY A COUPLE OF YEARS AGO ABOUT A MARRIED COUPLE WHO WERE ASSASSINS AND HAD TO KILL EACH OTHER?
DON'T GO DOWN THAT ROAD. I'M SURE THERE ARE TONS OF STORIES SIMILAR TO *ME TWO* AND *FUTURE WATCH* TOO.
SHF SHF
I'M NOT GOING TO RESEARCH TO FIND OUT IF THERE ARE SIMILAR STORIES OR NOT.
THAT'S IMPOR-TANT.
THAT WAY I KNOW I'M NOT PLAGARIZING ANYTHING. THE IDEAS ARE MINE ALONE.
YOU SAID BEFORE THAT ANYTHING IS FINE AS LONG AS THERE WASN'T A SIMILAR STORY CURRENTLY IN *JUMP*.
SHF
SKRT SKRT
YEAH.
THEN, START OFF WITH THE ONE WE'RE SENDING TO THE TREASURE ROOKIE AWARD... *FUTURE WATCH*. GIVE ME SOMETHING REALLY GOOD.
YEAH. YOU'LL HAVE IT IN TWO DAYS.
SHF SHF SHF SHF
YOU'RE SO AMAZING, TAKAGI. YOU'RE SO TALENTED. I'M FALLING FOR YOU ALL OVER AGAIN.
MY STAR DOESN'T SHINE AS BRIGHTLY AS OTHERS... BUT I'M STILL A STAR.
BAM
HE'S SO COOL...
Right?
...

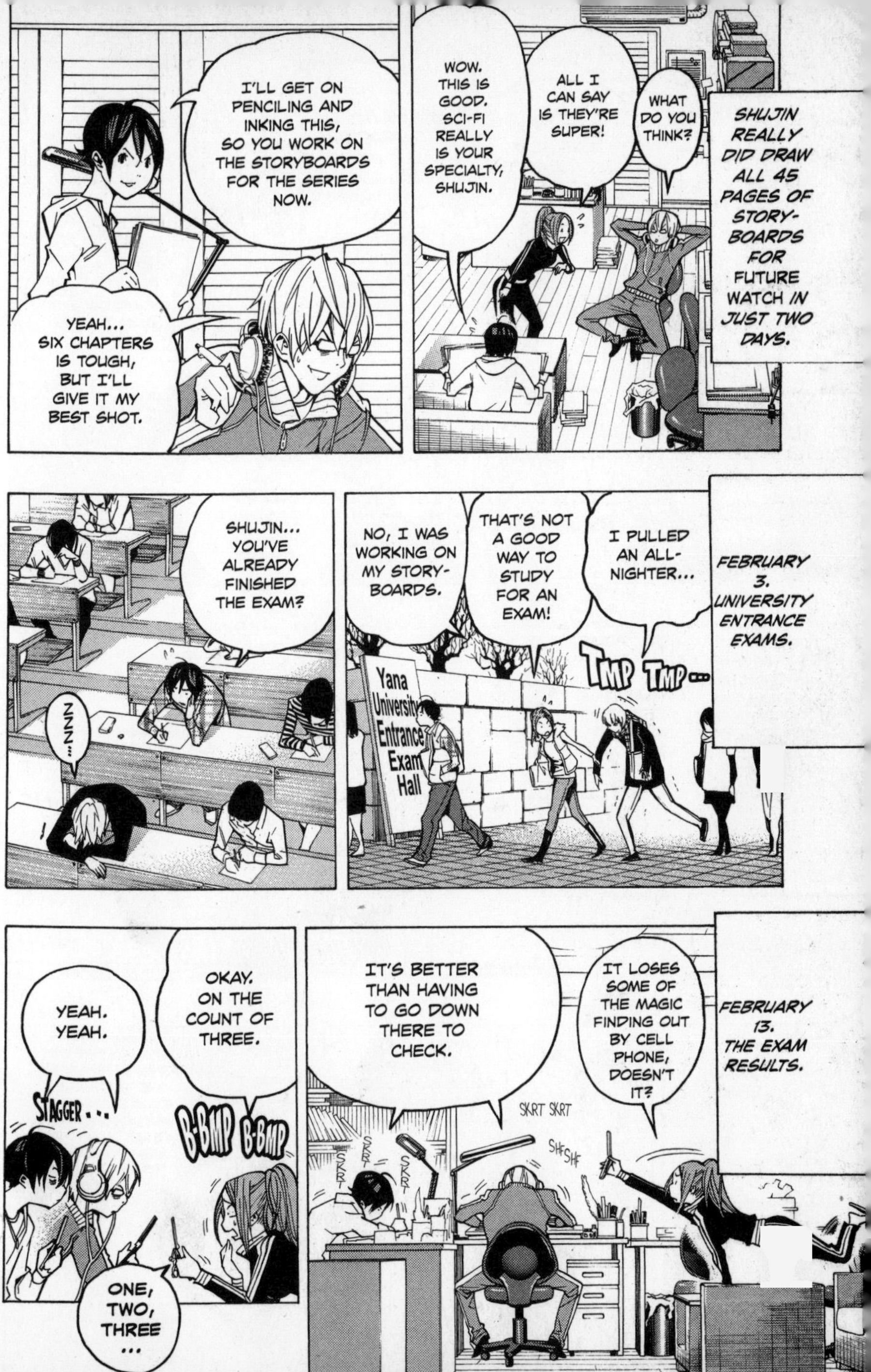
SHUJIN REALLY DID DRAW ALL 45 PAGES OF STORYBOARDS FOR FUTURE WATCH IN JUST TWO DAYS.
WHAT DO YOU THINK?
ALL I CAN SAY IS THEY'RE SUPER!
WOW. THIS IS GOOD. SCI-FI REALLY IS YOUR SPECIALTY, SHUJIN.
I'LL GET ON PENCILING AND INKING THIS, SO YOU WORK ON THE STORYBOARDS FOR THE SERIES NOW.
YEAH... SIX CHAPTERS IS TOUGH, BUT I'LL GIVE IT MY BEST SHOT.
FEBRUARY 3. UNIVERSITY ENTRANCE EXAMS.
TMP TMP...
I PULLED AN ALL-NIGHTER...
THAT'S NOT A GOOD WAY TO STUDY FOR AN EXAM!
NO, I WAS WORKING ON MY STORYBOARDS.
Yana University Entrance Exam Hall
SHUJIN... YOU'VE ALREADY FINISHED THE EXAM?
ZZZ...
FEBRUARY 13. THE EXAM RESULTS.
IT LOSES SOME OF THE MAGIC FINDING OUT BY CELL PHONE, DOESN'T IT?
SKRT SKRT
SHF SHF
IT'S BETTER THAN HAVING TO GO DOWN THERE TO CHECK.
SKRT SKRT
SKRT
OKAY. ON THE COUNT OF THREE.
B-BMP B-BMP
YEAH. YEAH.
STAGGER...
ONE, TWO, THREE...

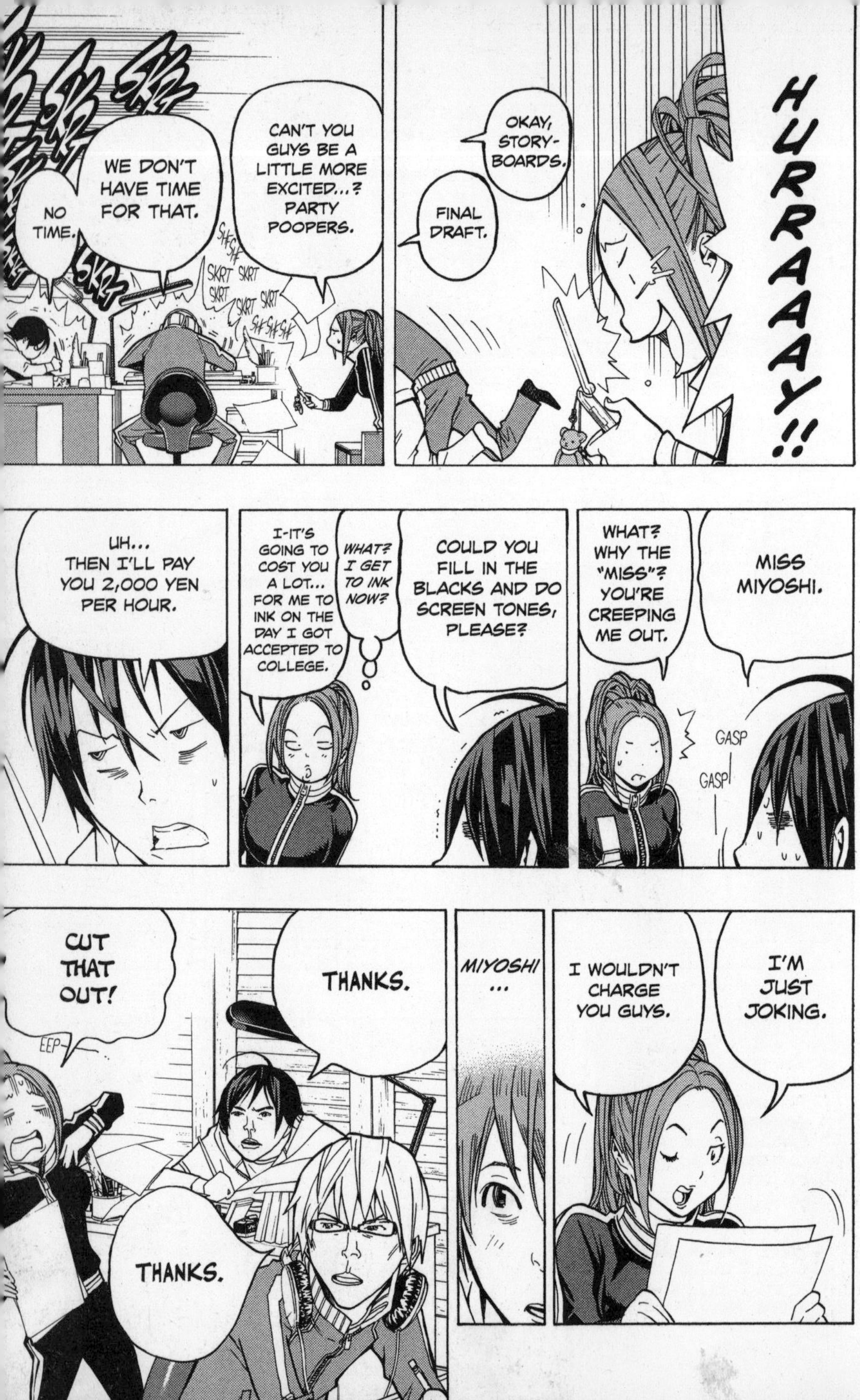
HURRAAAY!!
OKAY, STORYBOARDS.
FINAL DRAFT.
CAN'T YOU GUYS BE A LITTLE MORE EXCITED...? PARTY POOPERS.
WE DON'T HAVE TIME FOR THAT.
NO TIME.
SKRT SKRT SKRT SKRT SKRT
SHSHSH
MISS MIYOSHI.
GASP
GASP
WHAT? WHY THE "MISS"? YOU'RE CREEPING ME OUT.
COULD YOU FILL IN THE BLACKS AND DO SCREEN TONES, PLEASE?
WHAT? I GET TO INK NOW?
I-IT'S GOING TO COST YOU A LOT... FOR ME TO INK ON THE DAY I GOT ACCEPTED TO COLLEGE.
UH... THEN I'LL PAY YOU 2,000 YEN PER HOUR.
I'M JUST JOKING.
I WOULDN'T CHARGE YOU GUYS.
MIYOSHI...
THANKS.
THANKS.
CUT THAT OUT!
EEP

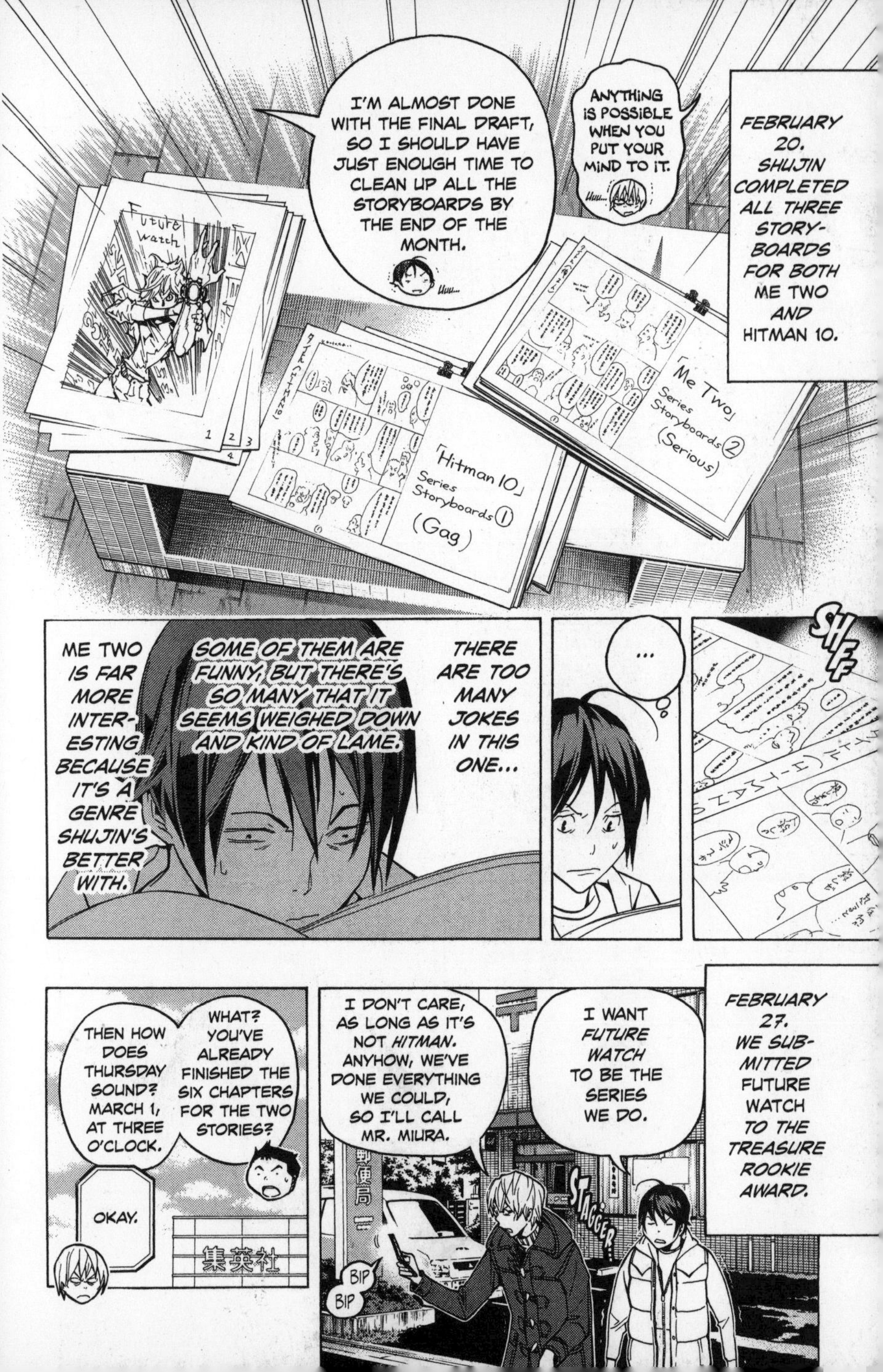
FEBRUARY 20. SHUJIN COMPLETED ALL THREE STORY-BOARDS FOR BOTH ME TWO AND HITMAN 10.
ANYTHING IS POSSIBLE WHEN YOU PUT YOUR MIND TO IT.
Uuu...
I'M ALMOST DONE WITH THE FINAL DRAFT, SO I SHOULD HAVE JUST ENOUGH TIME TO CLEAN UP ALL THE STORYBOARDS BY THE END OF THE MONTH.
Uuu...
「Me Two」 Series Storyboards ② (Serious)
「Hitman 10」 Series Storyboards ① (Gag)
Future watch
1 2 3 4
SHFF
...
THERE ARE TOO MANY JOKES IN THIS ONE...
SOME OF THEM ARE FUNNY, BUT THERE'S SO MANY THAT IT SEEMS WEIGHED DOWN AND KIND OF LAME.
ME TWO IS FAR MORE INTER-ESTING BECAUSE IT'S A GENRE SHUJIN'S BETTER WITH.
FEBRUARY 27. WE SUB-MITTED FUTURE WATCH TO THE TREASURE ROOKIE AWARD.
I WANT FUTURE WATCH TO BE THE SERIES WE DO.
I DON'T CARE, AS LONG AS IT'S NOT HITMAN. ANYHOW, WE'VE DONE EVERYTHING WE COULD, SO I'LL CALL MR. MIURA.
STAGGER
郵便局
BIP BIP
WHAT? YOU'VE ALREADY FINISHED THE SIX CHAPTERS FOR THE TWO STORIES?
THEN HOW DOES THURSDAY SOUND? MARCH 1, AT THREE O'CLOCK.
OKAY.
集英社

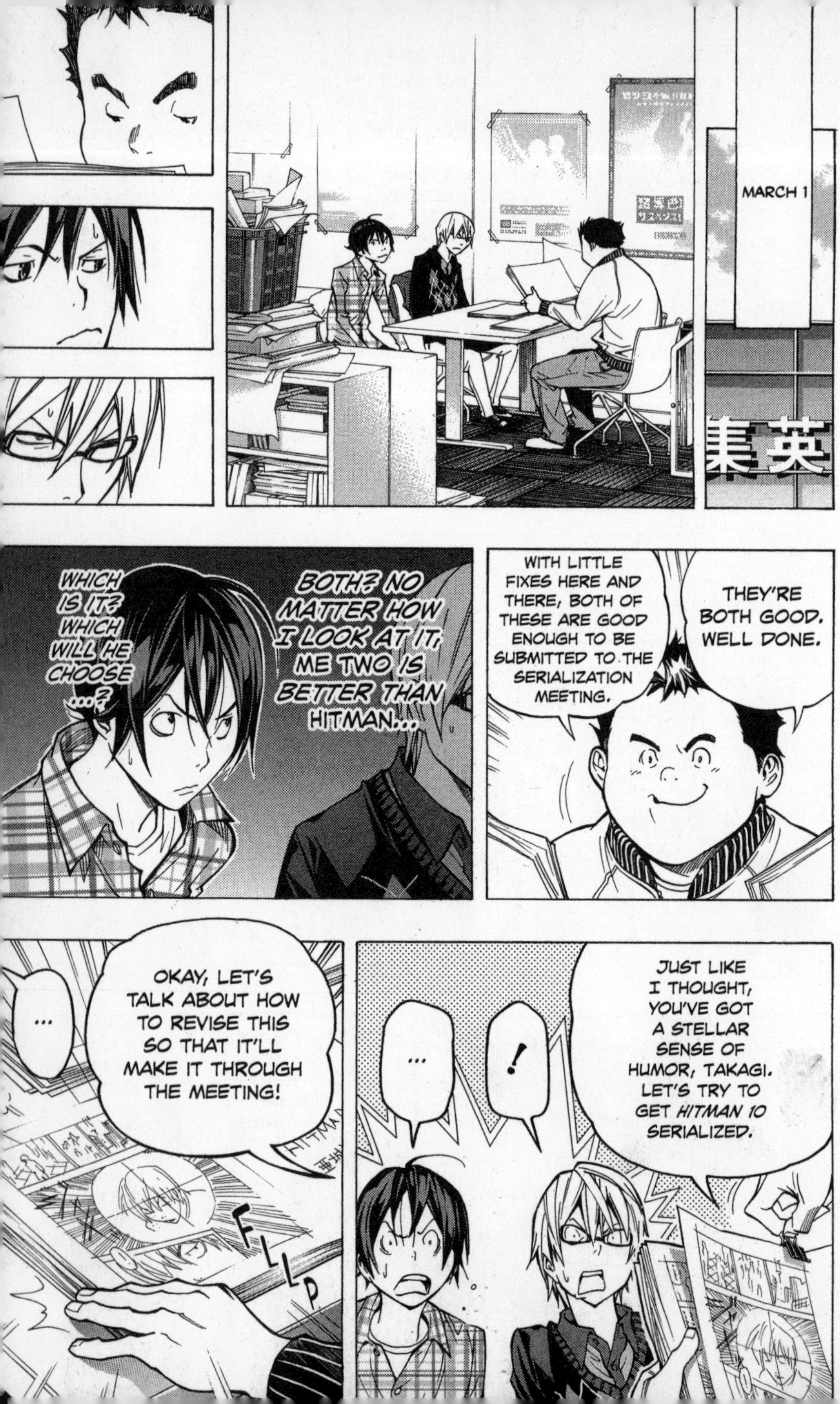

MARCH 1
集英
THEY'RE BOTH GOOD. WELL DONE.
WITH LITTLE FIXES HERE AND THERE, BOTH OF THESE ARE GOOD ENOUGH TO BE SUBMITTED TO THE SERIALIZATION MEETING.
BOTH? NO MATTER HOW I LOOK AT IT, ME TWO IS BETTER THAN HITMAN...
WHICH IS IT? WHICH WILL HE CHOOSE ...?
JUST LIKE I THOUGHT, YOU'VE GOT A STELLAR SENSE OF HUMOR, TAKAGI. LET'S TRY TO GET *HITMAN 10* SERIALIZED.
!
...
OKAY, LET'S TALK ABOUT HOW TO REVISE THIS SO THAT IT'LL MAKE IT THROUGH THE MEETING!
...
FLLP

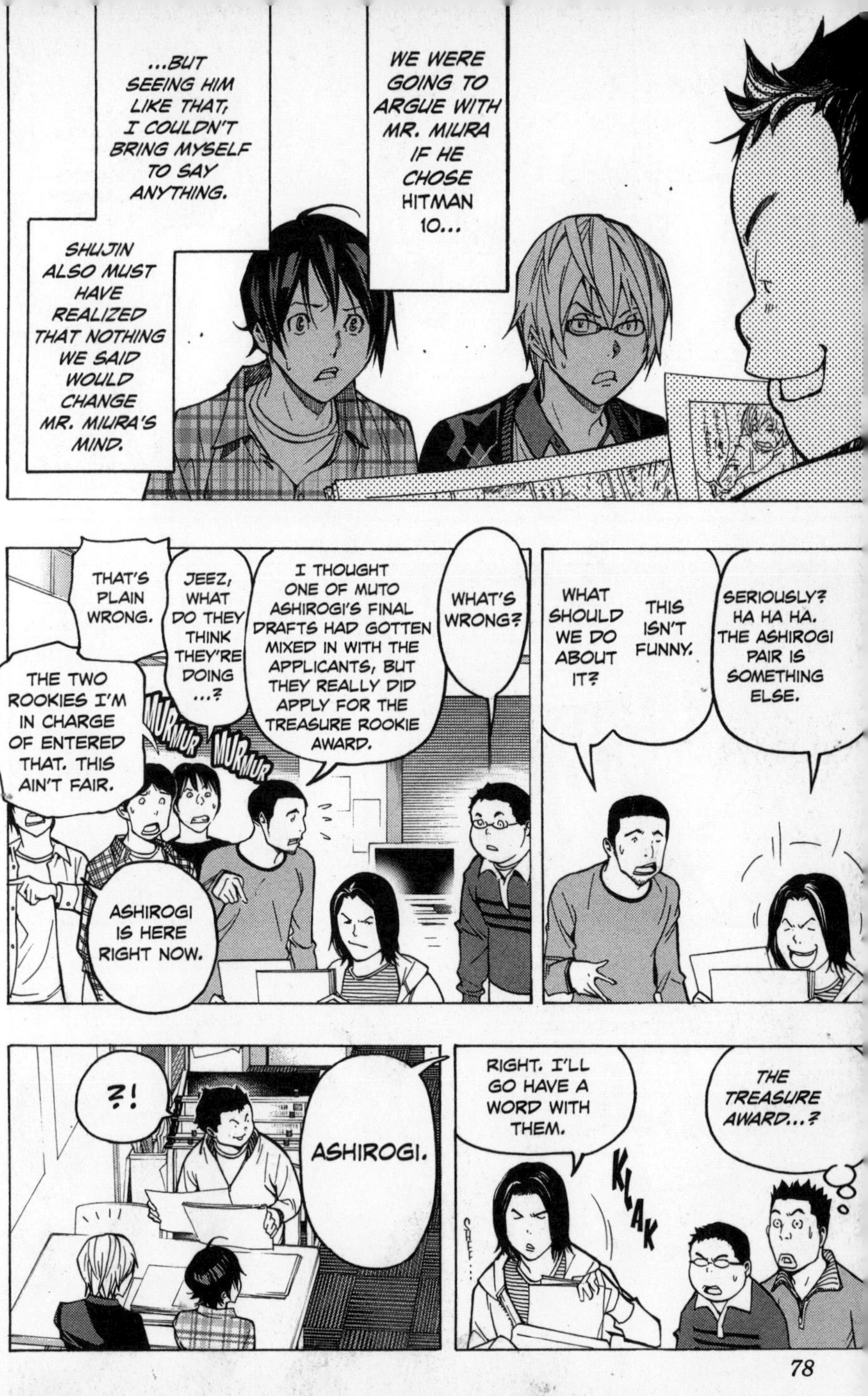
WE WERE GOING TO ARGUE WITH MR. MIURA IF HE CHOSE HITMAN 10...
...BUT SEEING HIM LIKE THAT, I COULDN'T BRING MYSELF TO SAY ANYTHING.
SHUJIN ALSO MUST HAVE REALIZED THAT NOTHING WE SAID WOULD CHANGE MR. MIURA'S MIND.
SERIOUSLY? HA HA HA. THE ASHIROGI PAIR IS SOMETHING ELSE.
THIS ISN'T FUNNY.
WHAT SHOULD WE DO ABOUT IT?
WHAT'S WRONG?
I THOUGHT ONE OF MUTO ASHIROGI'S FINAL DRAFTS HAD GOTTEN MIXED IN WITH THE APPLICANTS, BUT THEY REALLY DID APPLY FOR THE TREASURE ROOKIE AWARD.
JEEZ, WHAT DO THEY THINK THEY'RE DOING ...?
THAT'S PLAIN WRONG.
MURMUR MURMUR
THE TWO ROOKIES I'M IN CHARGE OF ENTERED THAT. THIS AIN'T FAIR.
ASHIROGI IS HERE RIGHT NOW.
THE TREASURE AWARD...?
RIGHT. I'LL GO HAVE A WORD WITH THEM.
KLAK
ASHIROGI.
?!

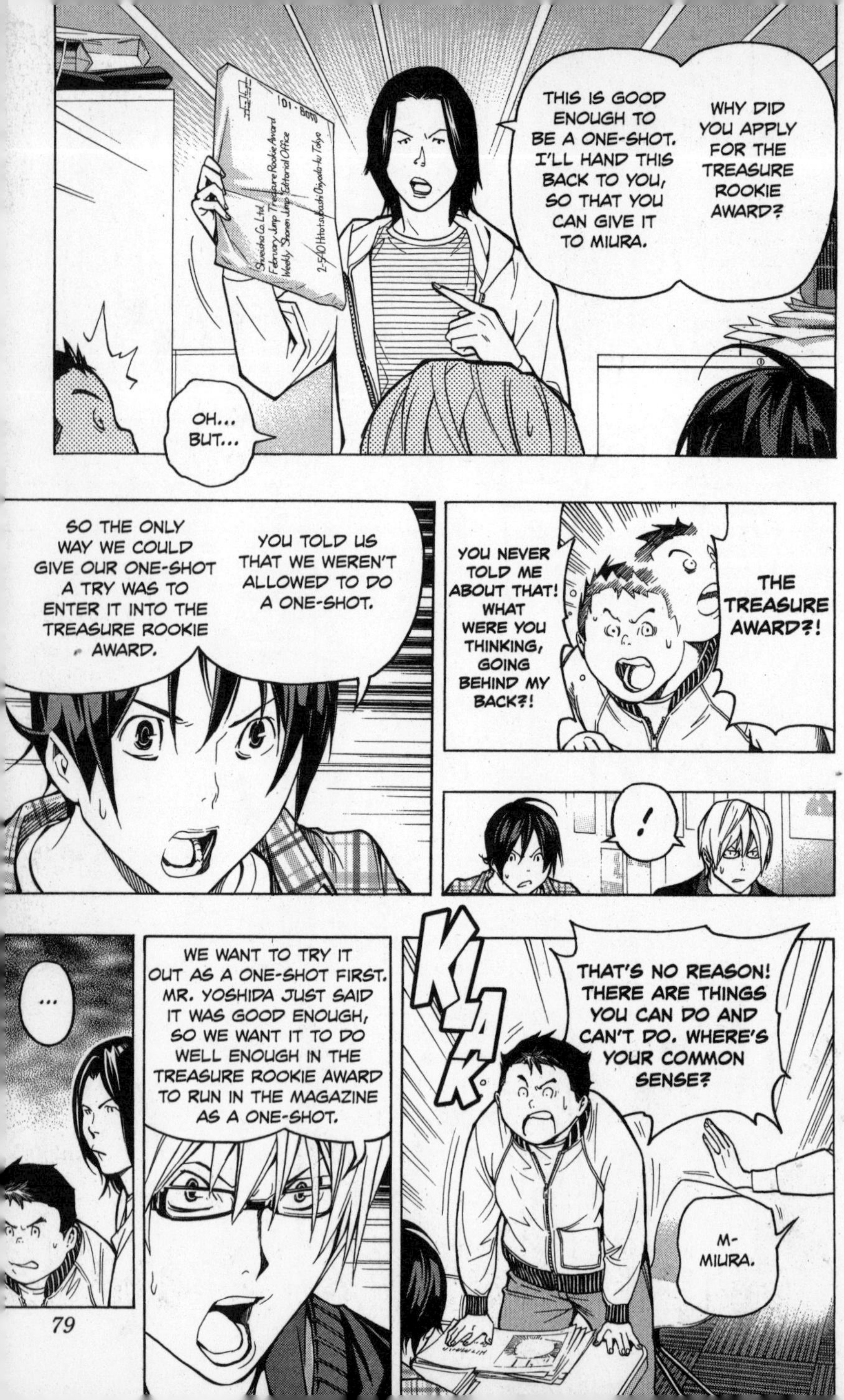
WHY DID YOU APPLY FOR THE TREASURE ROOKIE AWARD?
THIS IS GOOD ENOUGH TO BE A ONE-SHOT. I'LL HAND THIS BACK TO YOU, SO THAT YOU CAN GIVE IT TO MIURA.
101-8050
Shueisha Co. Ltd.
February Jump Treasure Rookie Award
Weekly Shonen Jump Editorial Office
2-5-10 Hitotsubashi Chiyoda-ku Tokyo
OH... BUT...
THE TREASURE AWARD?!
YOU NEVER TOLD ME ABOUT THAT! WHAT WERE YOU THINKING, GOING BEHIND MY BACK?!
!
YOU TOLD US THAT WE WEREN'T ALLOWED TO DO A ONE-SHOT.
SO THE ONLY WAY WE COULD GIVE OUR ONE-SHOT A TRY WAS TO ENTER IT INTO THE TREASURE ROOKIE AWARD.
KLAK
THAT'S NO REASON! THERE ARE THINGS YOU CAN DO AND CAN'T DO. WHERE'S YOUR COMMON SENSE?
M-MIURA.
WE WANT TO TRY IT OUT AS A ONE-SHOT FIRST. MR. YOSHIDA JUST SAID IT WAS GOOD ENOUGH, SO WE WANT IT TO DO WELL ENOUGH IN THE TREASURE ROOKIE AWARD TO RUN IN THE MAGAZINE AS A ONE-SHOT.
...

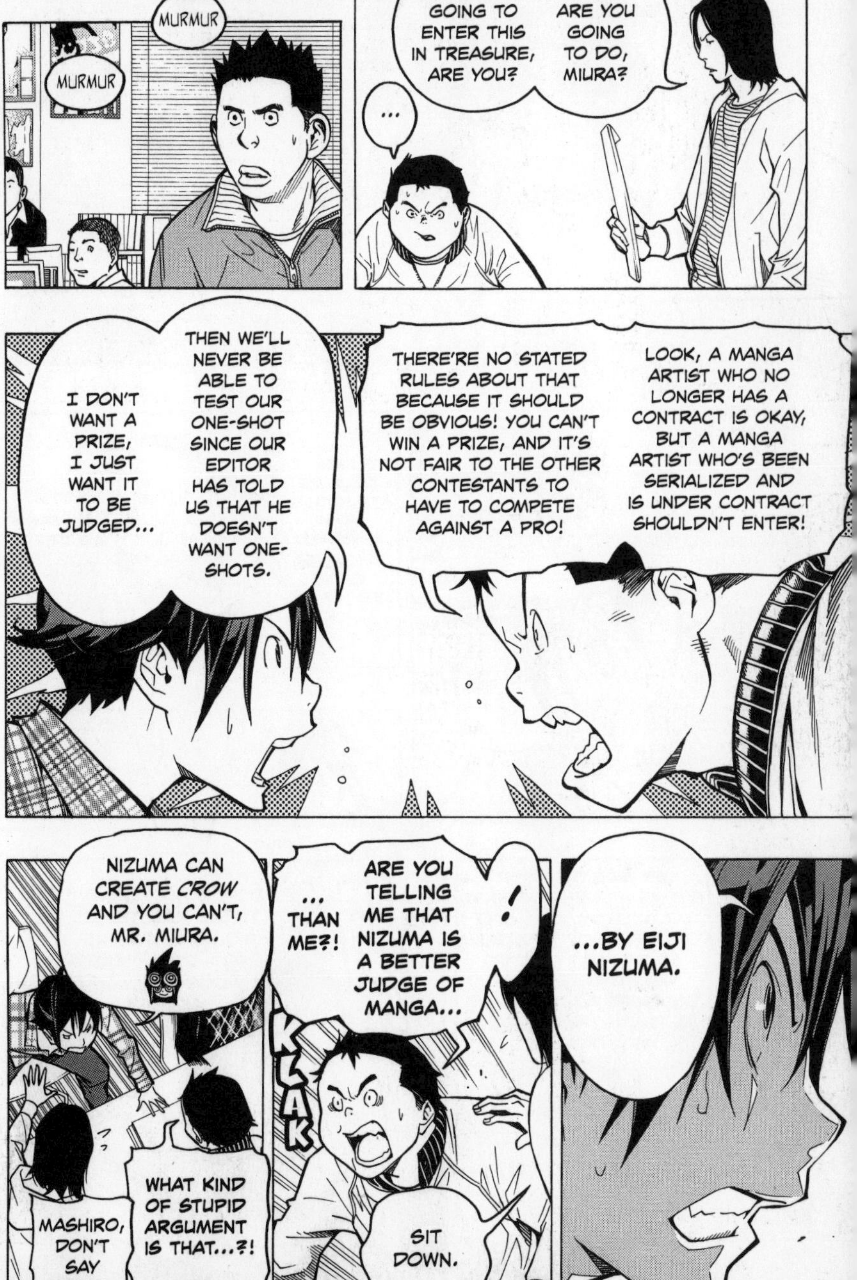
WHAT ARE YOU GOING TO DO, MIURA?
YOU'RE NOT GOING TO ENTER THIS IN TREASURE, ARE YOU?
...
MURMUR
MURMUR
LOOK, A MANGA ARTIST WHO NO LONGER HAS A CONTRACT IS OKAY, BUT A MANGA ARTIST WHO'S BEEN SERIALIZED AND IS UNDER CONTRACT SHOULDN'T ENTER!
THERE'RE NO STATED RULES ABOUT THAT BECAUSE IT SHOULD BE OBVIOUS! YOU CAN'T WIN A PRIZE, AND IT'S NOT FAIR TO THE OTHER CONTESTANTS TO HAVE TO COMPETE AGAINST A PRO!
THEN WE'LL NEVER BE ABLE TO TEST OUR ONE-SHOT SINCE OUR EDITOR HAS TOLD US THAT HE DOESN'T WANT ONE-SHOTS.
I DON'T WANT A PRIZE, I JUST WANT IT TO BE JUDGED...
...BY EIJI NIZUMA.
!
ARE YOU TELLING ME THAT NIZUMA IS A BETTER JUDGE OF MANGA...
... THAN ME?!
KLAK
SIT DOWN.
NIZUMA CAN CREATE *CROW* AND YOU CAN'T, MR. MIURA.
WHAT KIND OF STUPID ARGUMENT IS THAT...?!
MASHIRO, DON'T SAY THAT.

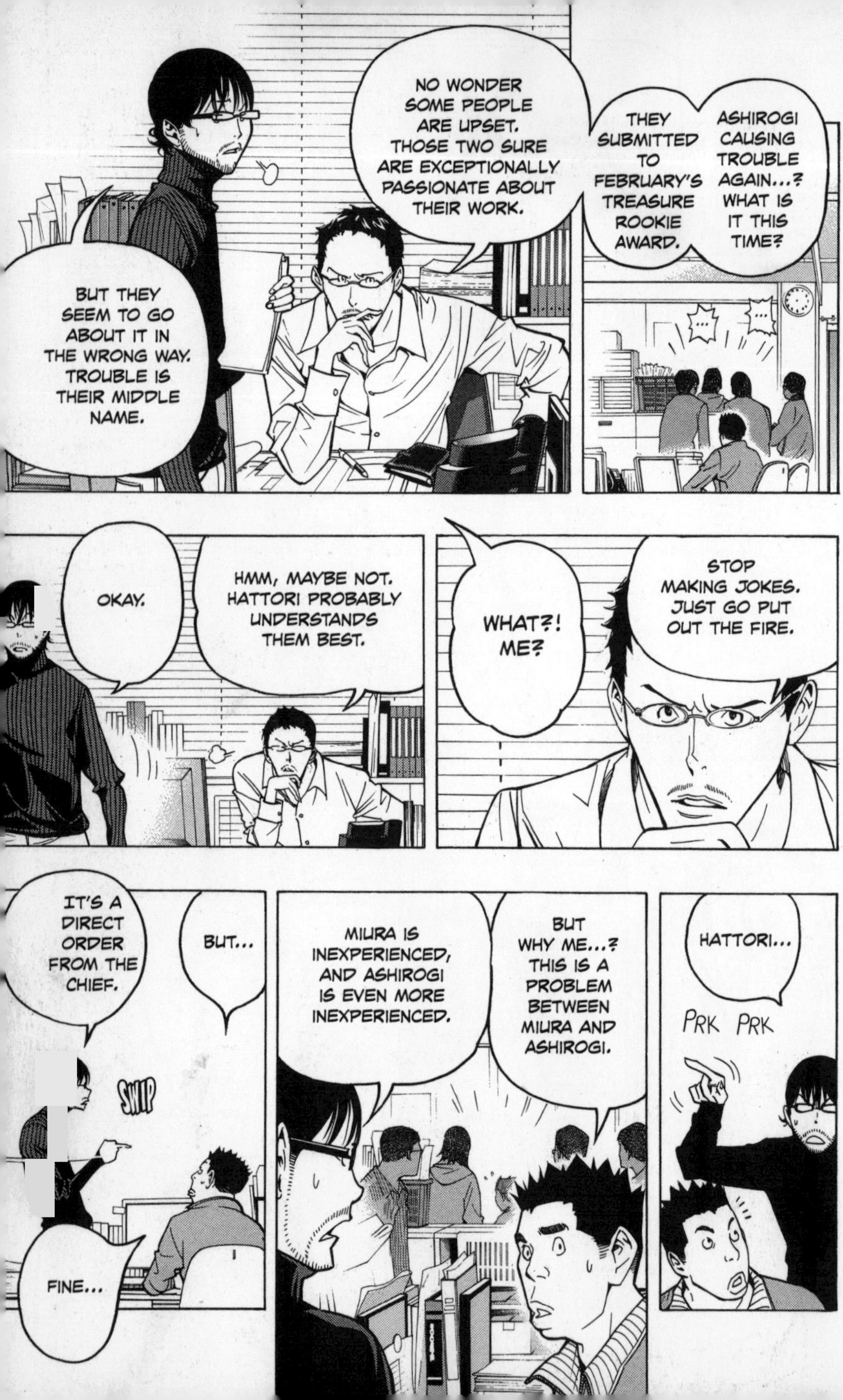
ASHIROGI CAUSING TROUBLE AGAIN...? WHAT IS IT THIS TIME?
THEY SUBMITTED TO FEBRUARY'S TREASURE ROOKIE AWARD.
...
...
NO WONDER SOME PEOPLE ARE UPSET. THOSE TWO SURE ARE EXCEPTIONALLY PASSIONATE ABOUT THEIR WORK.
BUT THEY SEEM TO GO ABOUT IT IN THE WRONG WAY. TROUBLE IS THEIR MIDDLE NAME.
STOP MAKING JOKES. JUST GO PUT OUT THE FIRE.
WHAT?! ME?
HMM, MAYBE NOT. HATTORI PROBABLY UNDERSTANDS THEM BEST.
OKAY.
HATTORI...
PRK PRK
BUT WHY ME...? THIS IS A PROBLEM BETWEEN MIURA AND ASHIROGI.
MIURA IS INEXPERIENCED, AND ASHIROGI IS EVEN MORE INEXPERIENCED.
BUT...
IT'S A DIRECT ORDER FROM THE CHIEF.
SWIP
FINE...

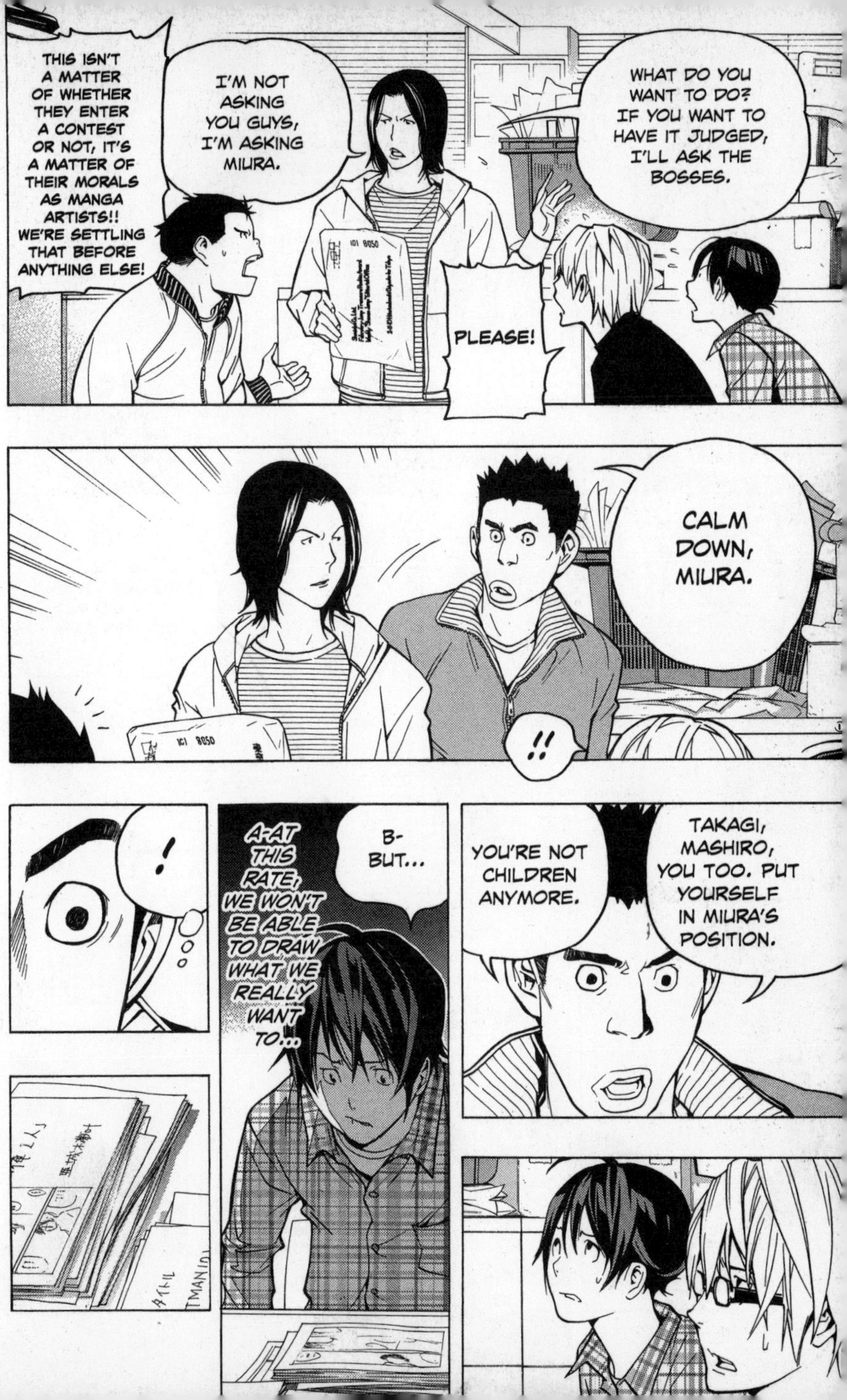
WHAT DO YOU WANT TO DO? IF YOU WANT TO HAVE IT JUDGED, I'LL ASK THE BOSSES.
I'M NOT ASKING YOU GUYS, I'M ASKING MIURA.
THIS ISN'T A MATTER OF WHETHER THEY ENTER A CONTEST OR NOT, IT'S A MATTER OF THEIR MORALS AS MANGA ARTISTS!! WE'RE SETTLING THAT BEFORE ANYTHING ELSE!
PLEASE!
CALM DOWN, MIURA.
!!
TAKAGI, MASHIRO, YOU TOO. PUT YOURSELF IN MIURA'S POSITION.
YOU'RE NOT CHILDREN ANYMORE.
B-BUT...
A-AT THIS RATE, WE WON'T BE ABLE TO DRAW WHAT WE REALLY WANT TO...
!

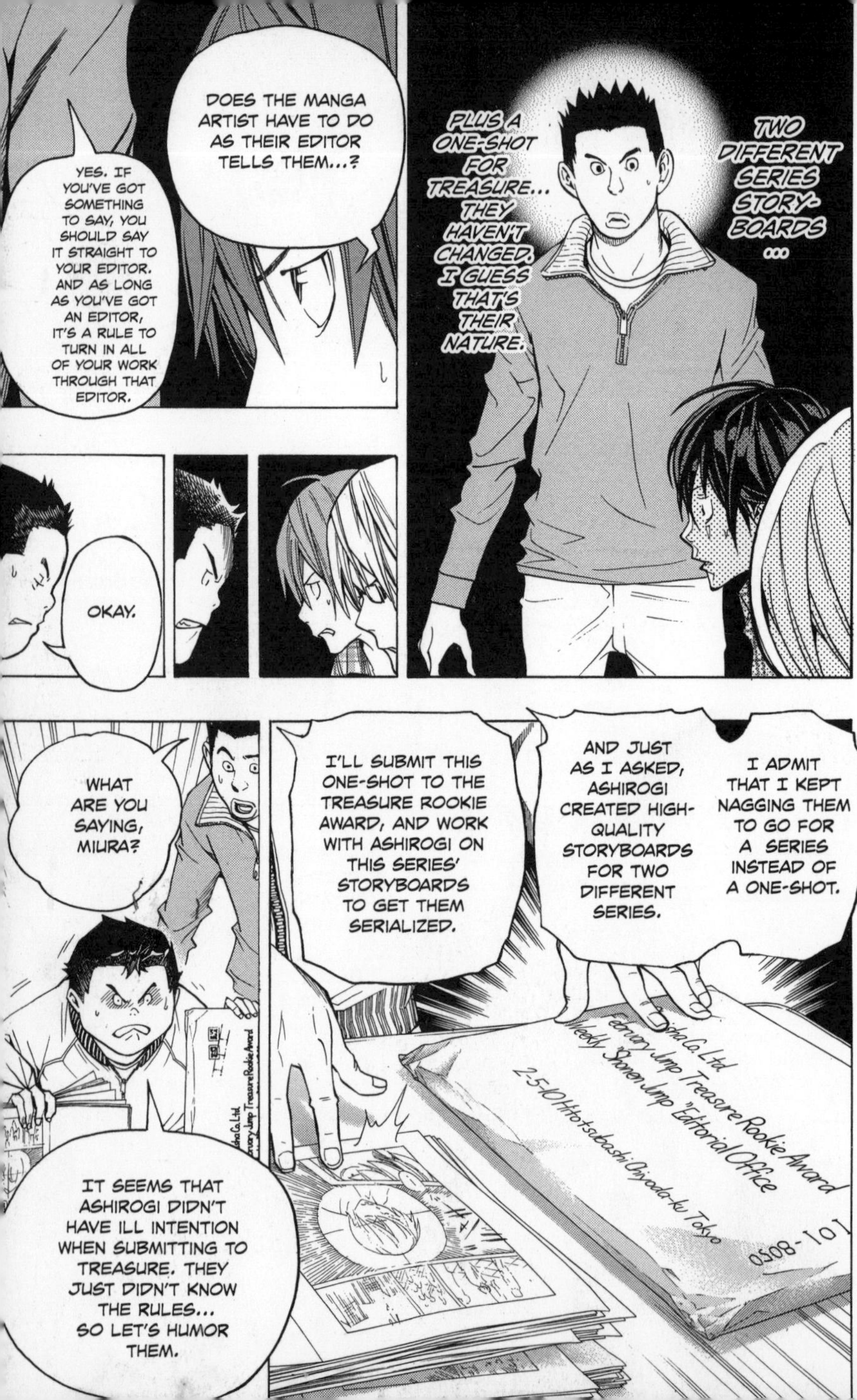
TWO DIFFERENT SERIES STORYBOARDS...
PLUS A ONE-SHOT FOR TREASURE... THEY HAVEN'T CHANGED. I GUESS THAT'S THEIR NATURE.
DOES THE MANGA ARTIST HAVE TO DO AS THEIR EDITOR TELLS THEM...?
YES. IF YOU'VE GOT SOMETHING TO SAY, YOU SHOULD SAY IT STRAIGHT TO YOUR EDITOR. AND AS LONG AS YOU'VE GOT AN EDITOR, IT'S A RULE TO TURN IN ALL OF YOUR WORK THROUGH THAT EDITOR.
OKAY.
I ADMIT THAT I KEPT NAGGING THEM TO GO FOR A SERIES INSTEAD OF A ONE-SHOT.
AND JUST AS I ASKED, ASHIROGI CREATED HIGH-QUALITY STORYBOARDS FOR TWO DIFFERENT SERIES.
I'LL SUBMIT THIS ONE-SHOT TO THE TREASURE ROOKIE AWARD, AND WORK WITH ASHIROGI ON THIS SERIES' STORYBOARDS TO GET THEM SERIALIZED.
February Jump Treasure Rookie Award
Shonen Jump Editorial Office
2-5-10 Hitotsubashi Chiyoda-ku Tokyo
101-8050
WHAT ARE YOU SAYING, MIURA?
IT SEEMS THAT ASHIROGI DIDN'T HAVE ILL INTENTION WHEN SUBMITTING TO TREASURE. THEY JUST DIDN'T KNOW THE RULES... SO LET'S HUMOR THEM.

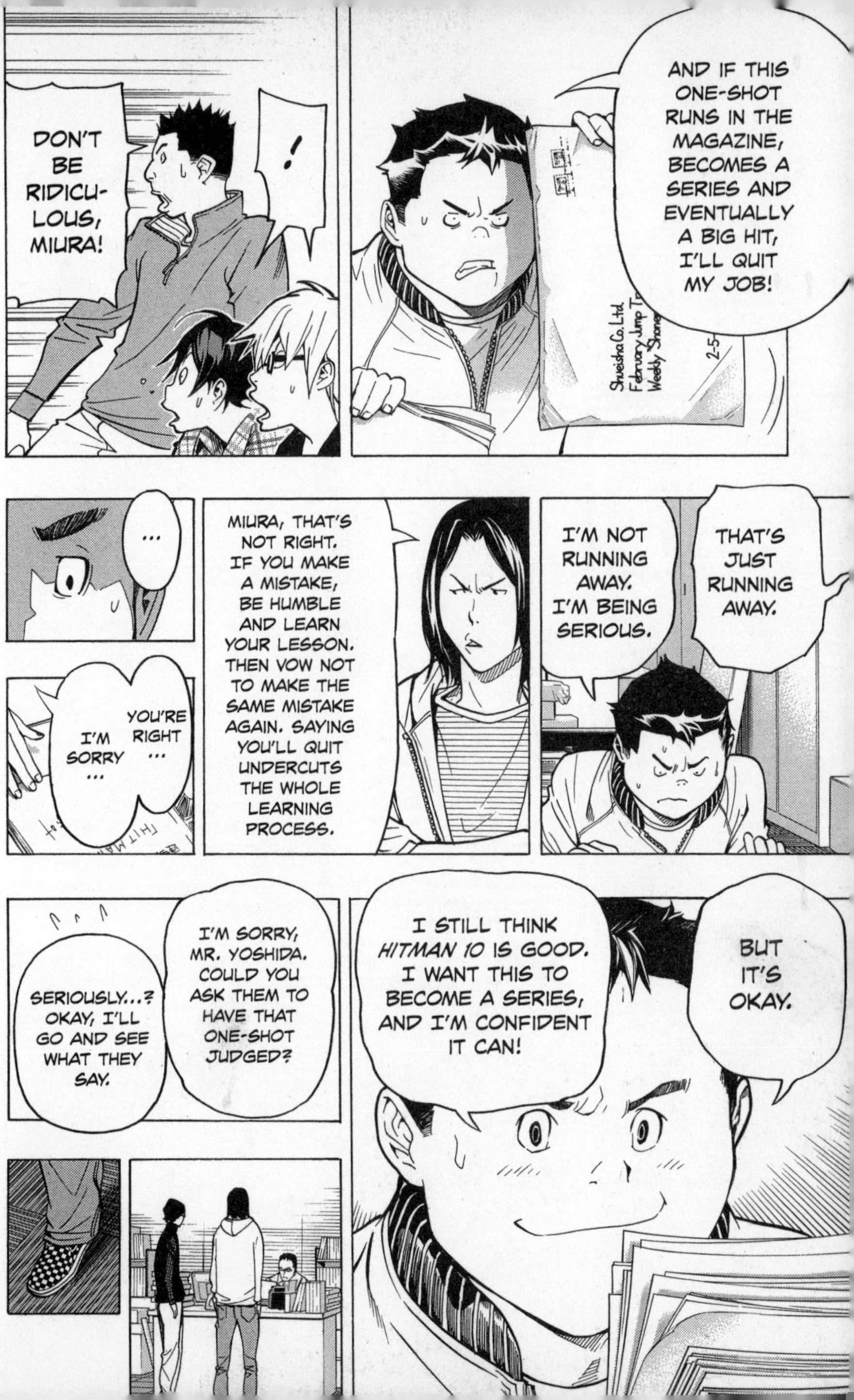
AND IF THIS ONE-SHOT RUNS IN THE MAGAZINE, BECOMES A SERIES AND EVENTUALLY A BIG HIT, I'LL QUIT MY JOB!
Shueisha Co. Ltd.
!
DON'T BE RIDICULOUS, MIURA!
THAT'S JUST RUNNING AWAY.
I'M NOT RUNNING AWAY. I'M BEING SERIOUS.
MIURA, THAT'S NOT RIGHT. IF YOU MAKE A MISTAKE, BE HUMBLE AND LEARN YOUR LESSON. THEN VOW NOT TO MAKE THE SAME MISTAKE AGAIN. SAYING YOU'LL QUIT UNDERCUTS THE WHOLE LEARNING PROCESS.
...
YOU'RE RIGHT...
I'M SORRY...
BUT IT'S OKAY.
I STILL THINK *HITMAN 10* IS GOOD. I WANT THIS TO BECOME A SERIES, AND I'M CONFIDENT IT CAN!
I'M SORRY, MR. YOSHIDA. COULD YOU ASK THEM TO HAVE THAT ONE-SHOT JUDGED?
SERIOUSLY...? OKAY, I'LL GO AND SEE WHAT THEY SAY.

PHEW—...
HERE'S WHAT THEY SAID...
FIRST OF ALL, ASHIROGI, DO NOT CAUSE ANY MORE PROBLEMS FOR US.
GOT IT?
YES...
WE'LL HAVE IT JUDGED, BUT YOU WON'T BE ELIGIBLE FOR A PRIZE. IF WE FEEL THAT THIS IS GOOD AS A ONE-SHOT...
...WE'LL RUN IT IN THE MAGAZINE.
BUT IF YOU TWO GET A SERIES WITH THE STORYBOARDS YOU TURN IN FOR APRIL'S SERIALIZATION MEETING, THIS ONE-SHOT WILL NOT RUN. IN OTHER WORDS, IF THIS ONE-SHOT IS GOING TO BE IN THE MAGAZINE, IT'LL BE AFTER THE MEETING.
SERIES
ONE-SHOT
ADDITIONALLY, IF WE THINK YOU SHORTCHANGED YOUR SERIES STORYBOARDS TO MAKE THE ONE-SHOT LOOK BETTER, WE WON'T RUN THE ONE-SHOT.
SERIES
ONE-SHOT
...
IN OTHER WORDS, DO YOUR BEST ON THE SERIES STORYBOARDS.
WE WILL!
YUP!
I CAN AGREE WITH THAT.

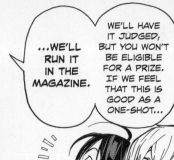

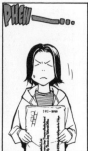

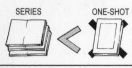

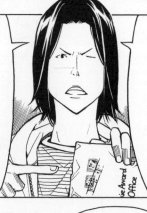

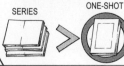

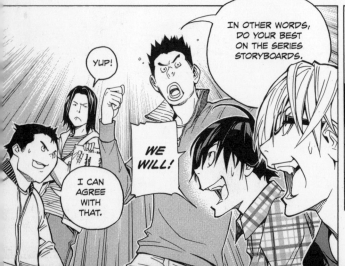

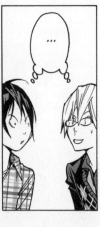

OHBA'S STORYBOARD

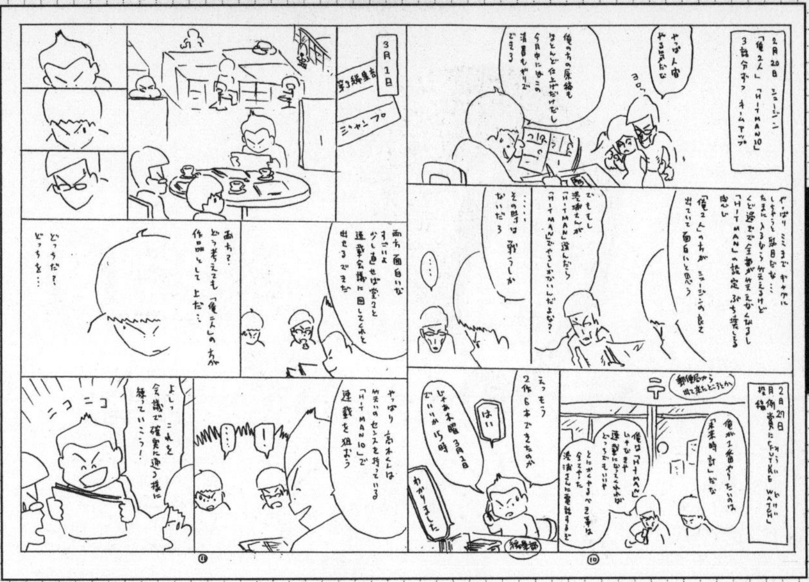

OBATA'S STORYBOARD

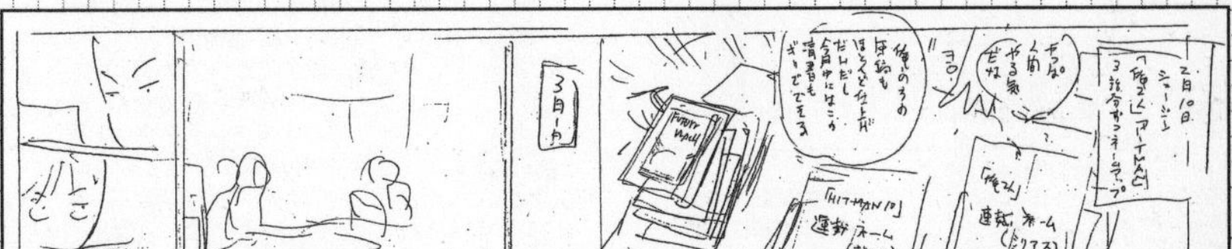

COMPLETE!

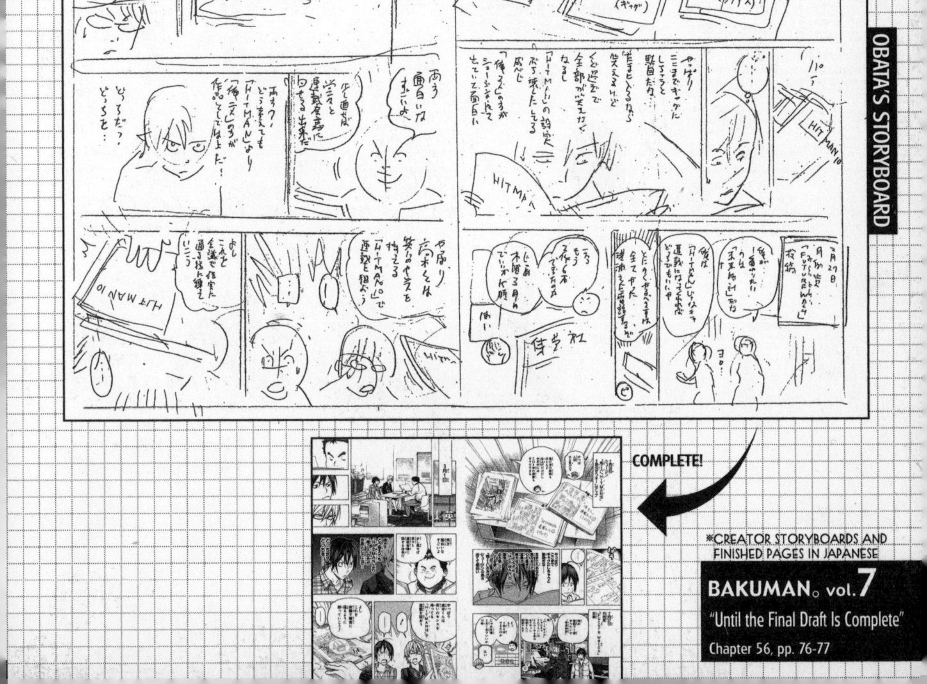

※CREATOR STORYBOARDS AND FINISHED PAGES IN JAPANESE

BAKUMAN。 vol. 7

"Until the Final Draft Is Complete"

Chapter 56, pp. 76-77

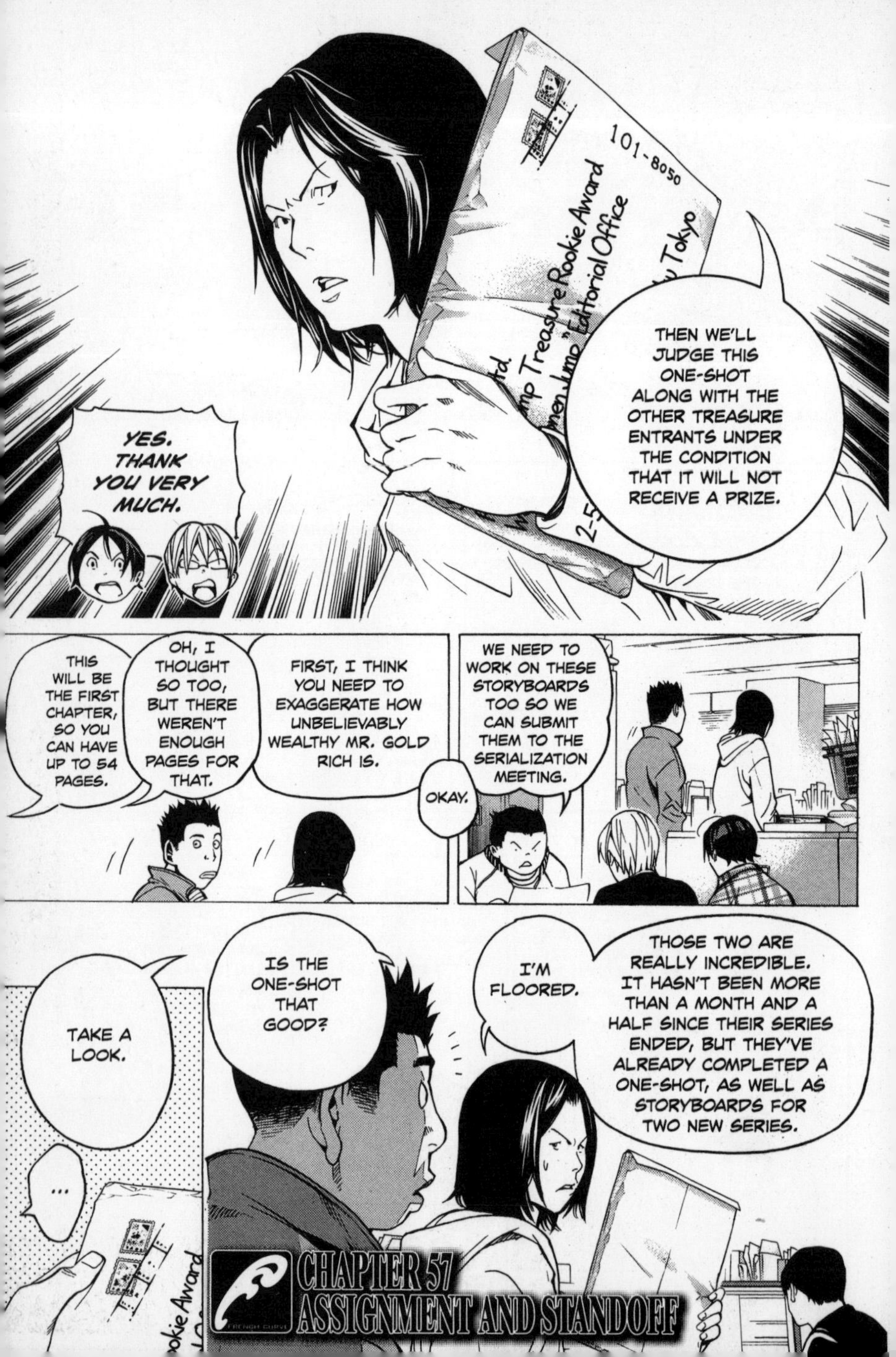
101-8050
THEN WE'LL JUDGE THIS ONE-SHOT ALONG WITH THE OTHER TREASURE ENTRANTS UNDER THE CONDITION THAT IT WILL NOT RECEIVE A PRIZE.
YES. THANK YOU VERY MUCH.
WE NEED TO WORK ON THESE STORYBOARDS TOO SO WE CAN SUBMIT THEM TO THE SERIALIZATION MEETING.
OKAY.
FIRST, I THINK YOU NEED TO EXAGGERATE HOW UNBELIEVABLY WEALTHY MR. GOLD RICH IS.
OH, I THOUGHT SO TOO, BUT THERE WEREN'T ENOUGH PAGES FOR THAT.
THIS WILL BE THE FIRST CHAPTER, SO YOU CAN HAVE UP TO 54 PAGES.
THOSE TWO ARE REALLY INCREDIBLE. IT HASN'T BEEN MORE THAN A MONTH AND A HALF SINCE THEIR SERIES ENDED, BUT THEY'VE ALREADY COMPLETED A ONE-SHOT, AS WELL AS STORYBOARDS FOR TWO NEW SERIES.
I'M FLOORED.
IS THE ONE-SHOT THAT GOOD?
TAKE A LOOK.
...
CHAPTER 57
ASSIGNMENT AND STANDOFF

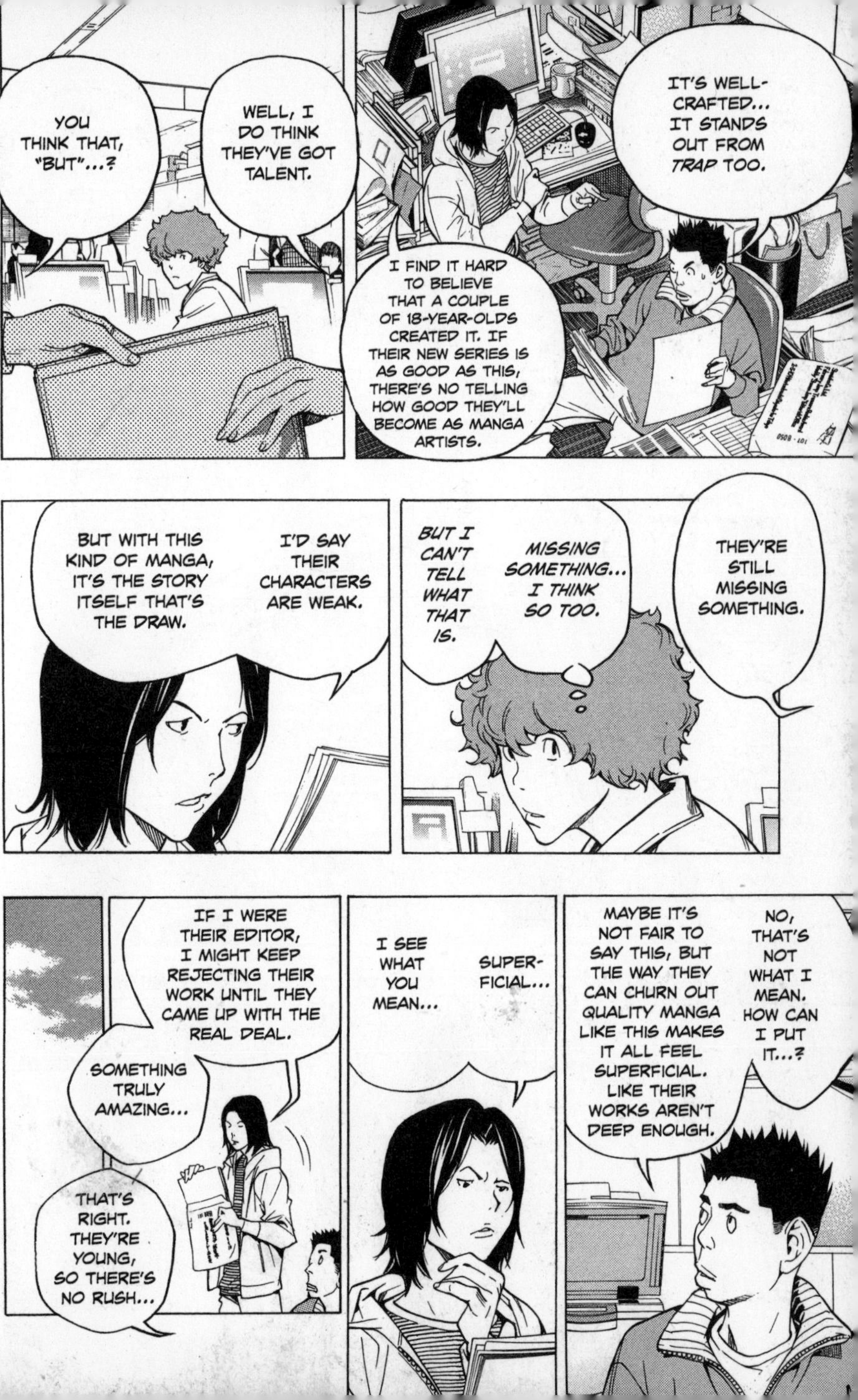
IT'S WELL-CRAFTED... IT STANDS OUT FROM *TRAP* TOO.
I FIND IT HARD TO BELIEVE THAT A COUPLE OF 18-YEAR-OLDS CREATED IT. IF THEIR NEW SERIES IS AS GOOD AS THIS, THERE'S NO TELLING HOW GOOD THEY'LL BECOME AS MANGA ARTISTS.
WELL, I DO THINK THEY'VE GOT TALENT.
YOU THINK THAT, "BUT"...?
THEY'RE STILL MISSING SOMETHING.
MISSING SOMETHING... I THINK SO TOO.
BUT I CAN'T TELL WHAT THAT IS.
I'D SAY THEIR CHARACTERS ARE WEAK.
BUT WITH THIS KIND OF MANGA, IT'S THE STORY ITSELF THAT'S THE DRAW.
NO, THAT'S NOT WHAT I MEAN. HOW CAN I PUT IT...?
MAYBE IT'S NOT FAIR TO SAY THIS, BUT THE WAY THEY CAN CHURN OUT QUALITY MANGA LIKE THIS MAKES IT ALL FEEL SUPERFICIAL. LIKE THEIR WORKS AREN'T DEEP ENOUGH.
SUPER-FICIAL...
I SEE WHAT YOU MEAN...
IF I WERE THEIR EDITOR, I MIGHT KEEP REJECTING THEIR WORK UNTIL THEY CAME UP WITH THE REAL DEAL.
SOMETHING TRULY AMAZING...
THAT'S RIGHT. THEY'RE YOUNG, SO THERE'S NO RUSH...

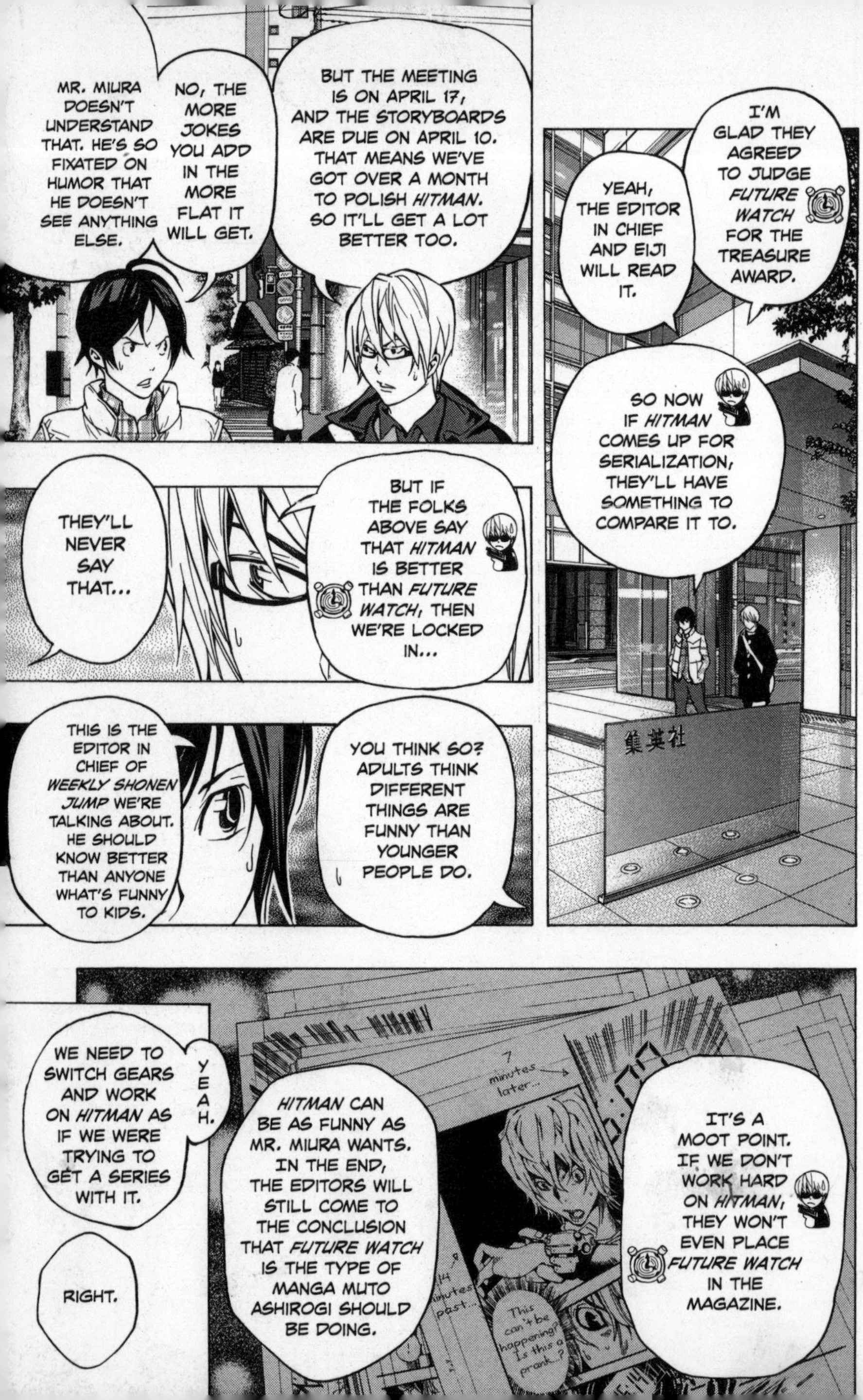
I'M GLAD THEY AGREED TO JUDGE *FUTURE WATCH* FOR THE TREASURE AWARD.
YEAH, THE EDITOR IN CHIEF AND EIJI WILL READ IT.
SO NOW IF *HITMAN* COMES UP FOR SERIALIZATION, THEY'LL HAVE SOMETHING TO COMPARE IT TO.
集英社
BUT THE MEETING IS ON APRIL 17, AND THE STORYBOARDS ARE DUE ON APRIL 10. THAT MEANS WE'VE GOT OVER A MONTH TO POLISH *HITMAN*. SO IT'LL GET A LOT BETTER TOO.
NO, THE MORE JOKES YOU ADD IN THE MORE FLAT IT WILL GET.
MR. MIURA DOESN'T UNDERSTAND THAT. HE'S SO FIXATED ON HUMOR THAT HE DOESN'T SEE ANYTHING ELSE.
BUT IF THE FOLKS ABOVE SAY THAT *HITMAN* IS BETTER THAN *FUTURE WATCH*, THEN WE'RE LOCKED IN...
THEY'LL NEVER SAY THAT...
YOU THINK SO? ADULTS THINK DIFFERENT THINGS ARE FUNNY THAN YOUNGER PEOPLE DO.
THIS IS THE EDITOR IN CHIEF OF *WEEKLY SHONEN JUMP* WE'RE TALKING ABOUT. HE SHOULD KNOW BETTER THAN ANYONE WHAT'S FUNNY TO KIDS.
IT'S A MOOT POINT. IF WE DON'T WORK HARD ON *HITMAN*, THEY WON'T EVEN PLACE *FUTURE WATCH* IN THE MAGAZINE.
7 minutes later...
This can't be happening? Is this a prank..?
14 minutes past...
HITMAN CAN BE AS FUNNY AS MR. MIURA WANTS. IN THE END, THE EDITORS WILL STILL COME TO THE CONCLUSION THAT *FUTURE WATCH* IS THE TYPE OF MANGA MUTO ASHIROGI SHOULD BE DOING.
YEAH.
WE NEED TO SWITCH GEARS AND WORK ON *HITMAN* AS IF WE WERE TRYING TO GET A SERIES WITH IT.
RIGHT.

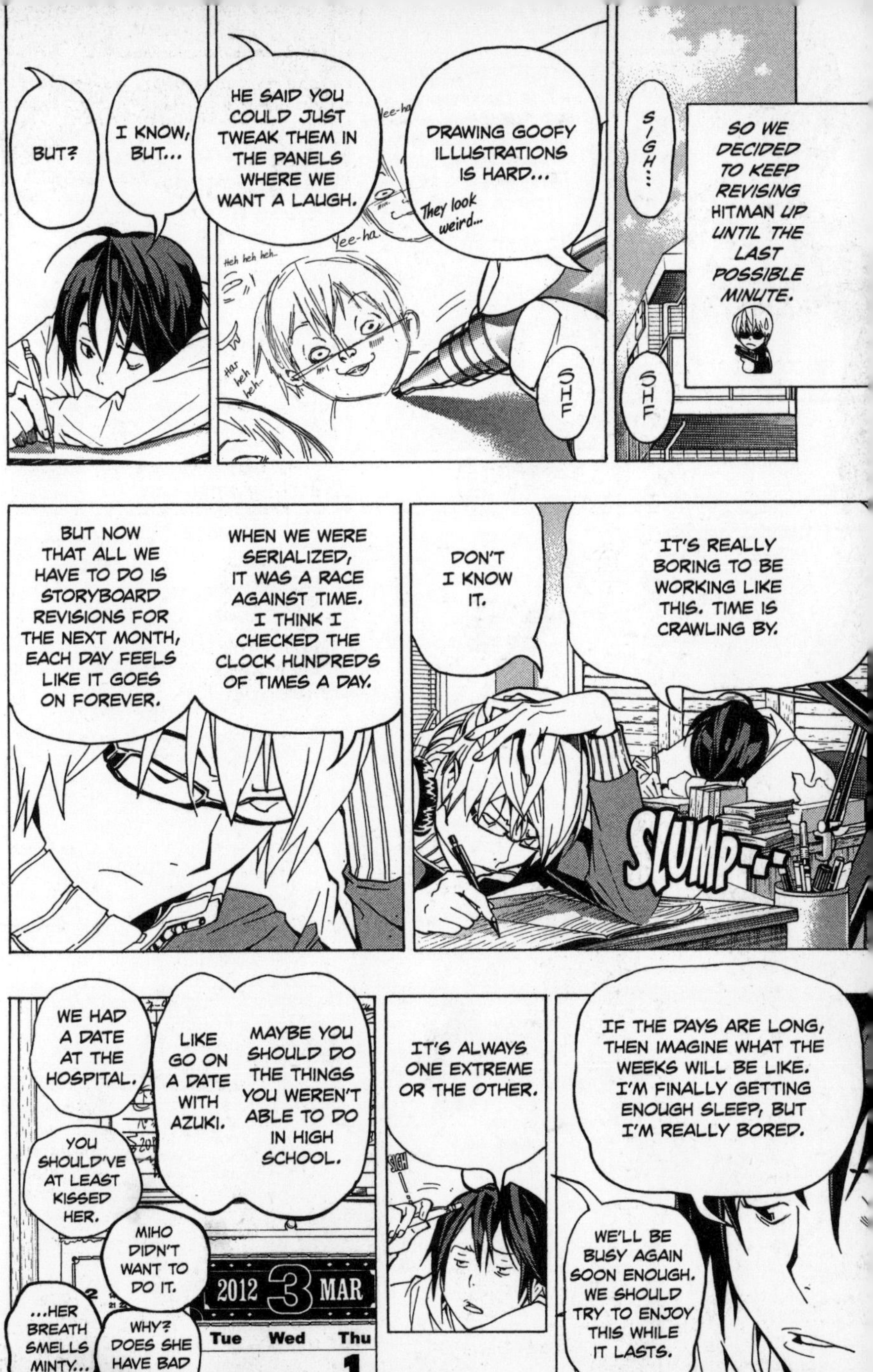

SO WE DECIDED TO KEEP REVISING HITMAN UP UNTIL THE LAST POSSIBLE MINUTE.
SIGH...
SHF
DRAWING GOOFY ILLUSTRATIONS IS HARD...
HE SAID YOU COULD JUST TWEAK THEM IN THE PANELS WHERE WE WANT A LAUGH.
Yee-ha
They look weird...
Yee-ha
Heh heh heh..
Har heh heh..
SHF
I KNOW, BUT...
BUT?
IT'S REALLY BORING TO BE WORKING LIKE THIS. TIME IS CRAWLING BY.
DON'T I KNOW IT.
SLUMP...
WHEN WE WERE SERIALIZED, IT WAS A RACE AGAINST TIME. I THINK I CHECKED THE CLOCK HUNDREDS OF TIMES A DAY.
BUT NOW THAT ALL WE HAVE TO DO IS STORYBOARD REVISIONS FOR THE NEXT MONTH, EACH DAY FEELS LIKE IT GOES ON FOREVER.
IF THE DAYS ARE LONG, THEN IMAGINE WHAT THE WEEKS WILL BE LIKE. I'M FINALLY GETTING ENOUGH SLEEP, BUT I'M REALLY BORED.
WE'LL BE BUSY AGAIN SOON ENOUGH. WE SHOULD TRY TO ENJOY THIS WHILE IT LASTS.
IT'S ALWAYS ONE EXTREME OR THE OTHER.
SIGH
MAYBE YOU SHOULD DO THE THINGS YOU WEREN'T ABLE TO DO IN HIGH SCHOOL.
LIKE GO ON A DATE WITH AZUKI.
WE HAD A DATE AT THE HOSPITAL.
YOU SHOULD'VE AT LEAST KISSED HER.
MIHO DIDN'T WANT TO DO IT.
WHY? DOES SHE HAVE BAD BREATH?
...HER BREATH SMELLS MINTY...
2012 3 MAR
Tue Wed Thu
1

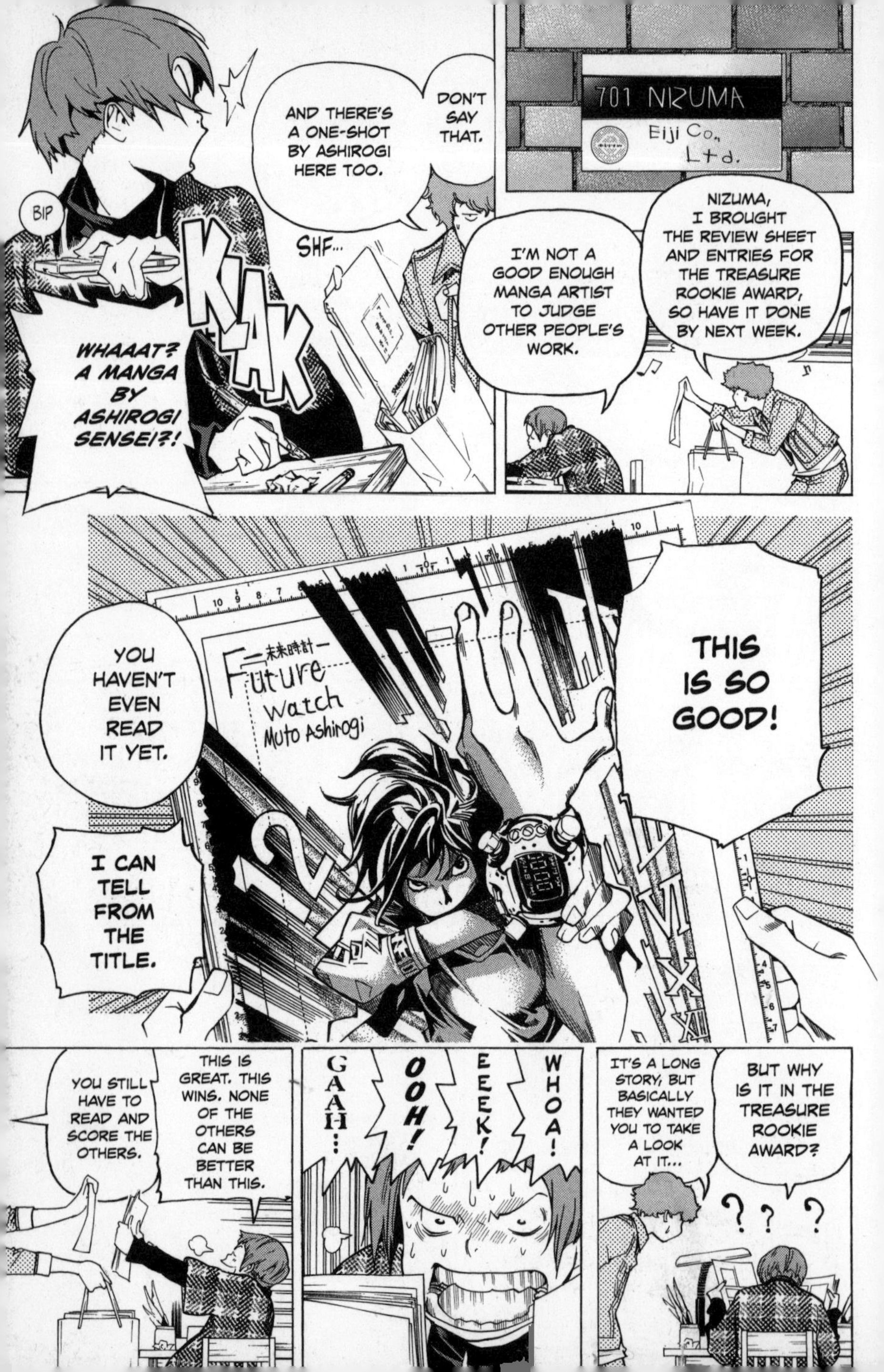
701 NIZUMA
Eiji Co., Ltd.
NIZUMA, I BROUGHT THE REVIEW SHEET AND ENTRIES FOR THE TREASURE ROOKIE AWARD, SO HAVE IT DONE BY NEXT WEEK.
I'M NOT A GOOD ENOUGH MANGA ARTIST TO JUDGE OTHER PEOPLE'S WORK.
DON'T SAY THAT.
AND THERE'S A ONE-SHOT BY ASHIROGI HERE TOO.
SHF...
BIP
KLAK
WHAAAT? A MANGA BY ASHIROGI SENSEI?!
THIS IS SO GOOD!
—未来時計—
Future Watch
Muto Ashirogi
YOU HAVEN'T EVEN READ IT YET.
I CAN TELL FROM THE TITLE.
BUT WHY IS IT IN THE TREASURE ROOKIE AWARD?
IT'S A LONG STORY, BUT BASICALLY THEY WANTED YOU TO TAKE A LOOK AT IT...
? ? ?
WHOA!
EEEK!
OOH!
GAAH...
THIS IS GREAT. THIS WINS. NONE OF THE OTHERS CAN BE BETTER THAN THIS.
YOU STILL HAVE TO READ AND SCORE THE OTHERS.

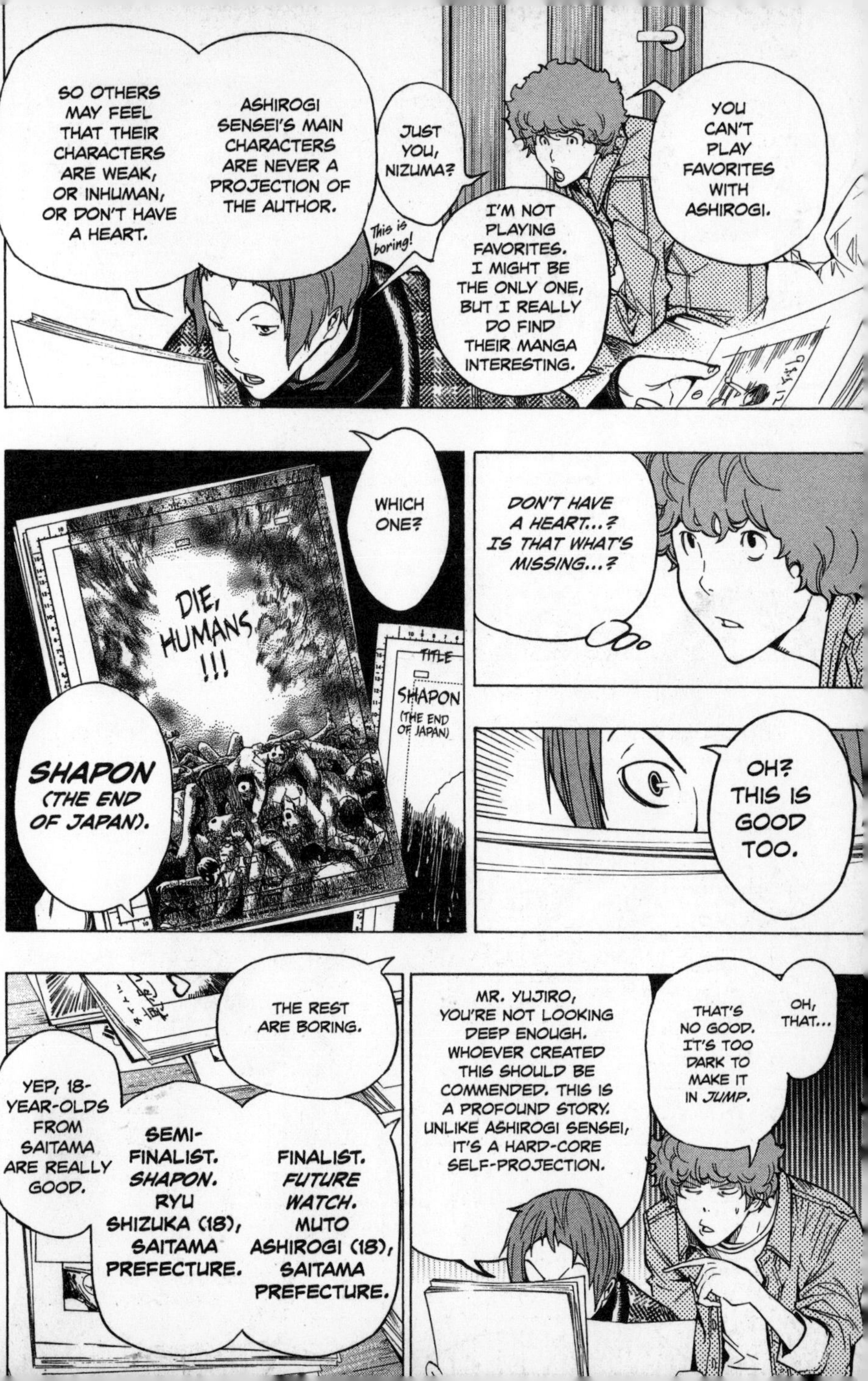
YOU CAN'T PLAY FAVORITES WITH ASHIROGI.
I'M NOT PLAYING FAVORITES. I MIGHT BE THE ONLY ONE, BUT I REALLY DO FIND THEIR MANGA INTERESTING.
JUST YOU, NIZUMA?
This is boring!
ASHIROGI SENSEI'S MAIN CHARACTERS ARE NEVER A PROJECTION OF THE AUTHOR.
SO OTHERS MAY FEEL THAT THEIR CHARACTERS ARE WEAK, OR INHUMAN, OR DON'T HAVE A HEART.
DON'T HAVE A HEART...? IS THAT WHAT'S MISSING...?
OH? THIS IS GOOD TOO.
WHICH ONE?
DIE, HUMANS !!!
TITLE
SHAPON (THE END OF JAPAN)
SHAPON (THE END OF JAPAN).
OH, THAT...
THAT'S NO GOOD. IT'S TOO DARK TO MAKE IT IN JUMP.
MR. YUJIRO, YOU'RE NOT LOOKING DEEP ENOUGH. WHOEVER CREATED THIS SHOULD BE COMMENDED. THIS IS A PROFOUND STORY. UNLIKE ASHIROGI SENSEI, IT'S A HARD-CORE SELF-PROJECTION.
THE REST ARE BORING.
FINALIST. FUTURE WATCH. MUTO ASHIROGI (18), SAITAMA PREFECTURE.
SEMI-FINALIST. SHAPON. RYU SHIZUKA (18), SAITAMA PREFECTURE.
YEP, 18-YEAR-OLDS FROM SAITAMA ARE REALLY GOOD.

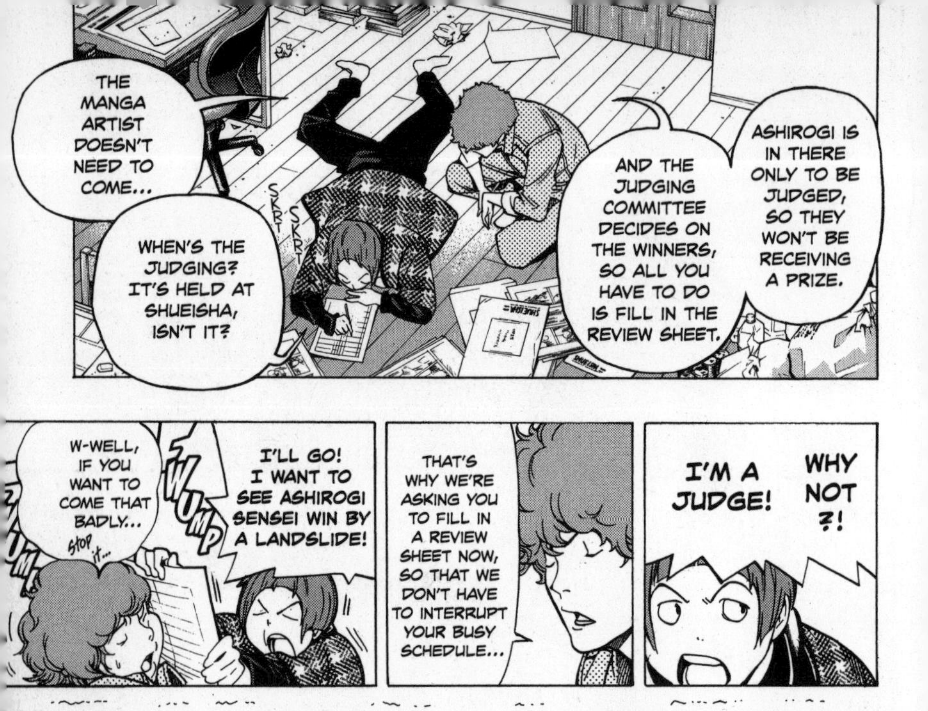
ASHIROGI IS IN THERE ONLY TO BE JUDGED, SO THEY WON'T BE RECEIVING A PRIZE.
AND THE JUDGING COMMITTEE DECIDES ON THE WINNERS, SO ALL YOU HAVE TO DO IS FILL IN THE REVIEW SHEET.
THE MANGA ARTIST DOESN'T NEED TO COME...
SKRT SKRT
WHEN'S THE JUDGING? IT'S HELD AT SHUEISHA, ISN'T IT?
WHY NOT ?!
I'M A JUDGE!
THAT'S WHY WE'RE ASKING YOU TO FILL IN A REVIEW SHEET NOW, SO THAT WE DON'T HAVE TO INTERRUPT YOUR BUSY SCHEDULE...
I'LL GO! I WANT TO SEE ASHIROGI SENSEI WIN BY A LANDSLIDE!
WUMP
W-WELL, IF YOU WANT TO COME THAT BADLY...
STOP IT...

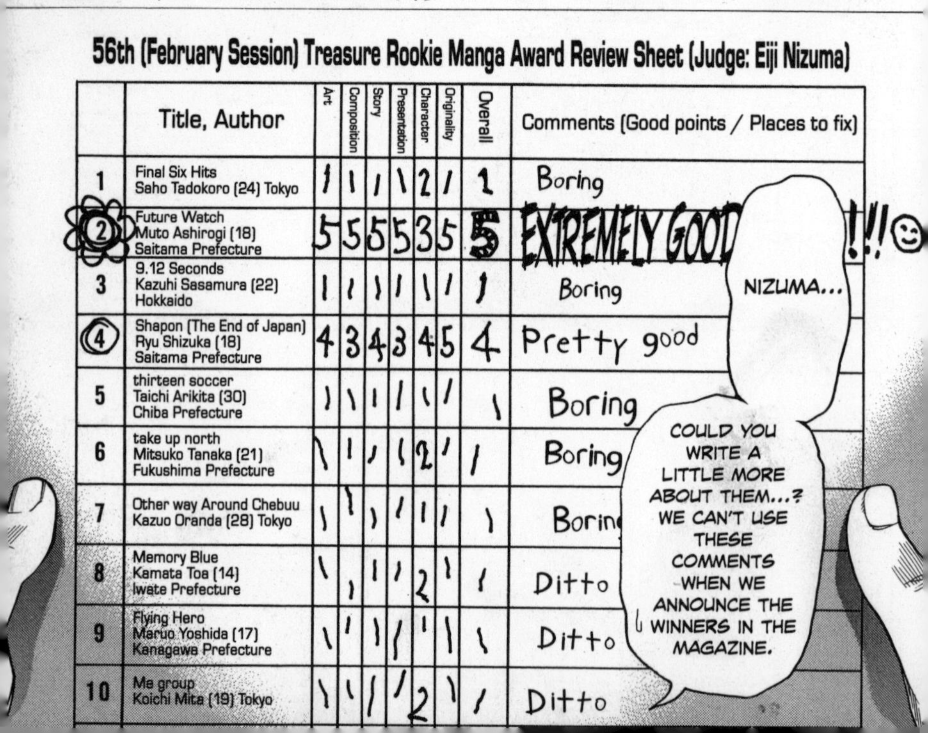

56th (February Session) Treasure Rookie Manga Award Review Sheet (Judge: Eiji Nizuma)

	Title, Author	Art	Composition	Story	Presentation	Character	Originality	Overall	Comments (Good points / Places to fix)
1	Final Six Hits Saho Tadokoro (24) Tokyo	1	1	1	1	2	1	1	Boring
2	Future Watch Muto Ashirogi (18) Saitama Prefecture	5	5	5	5	3	5	5	EXTREMELY GOOD !!! ☺
3	9.12 Seconds Kazuhi Sasamura (22) Hokkaido	1	1	1	1	1	1	1	Boring
4	Shapon (The End of Japan) Ryu Shizuka (18) Saitama Prefecture	4	3	4	3	4	5	4	Pretty good
5	thirteen soccer Taichi Arikita (30) Chiba Prefecture	1	1	1	1	1	1	1	Boring
6	take up north Mitsuko Tanaka (21) Fukushima Prefecture	1	1	1	1	2	1	1	Boring
7	Other way Around Chebuu Kazuo Oranda (28) Tokyo	1	1	1	1	1	1	1	Borin
8	Memory Blue Kamata Toa (14) Iwate Prefecture	1	1	1	1	2	1	1	Ditto
9	Flying Hero Maruo Yoshida (17) Kanagawa Prefecture	1	1	1	1	1	1	1	Ditto
10	Me group Koichi Mita (19) Tokyo	1	1	1	1	2	1	1	Ditto

NIZUMA...
COULD YOU WRITE A LITTLE MORE ABOUT THEM...? WE CAN'T USE THESE COMMENTS WHEN WE ANNOUNCE THE WINNERS IN THE MAGAZINE.

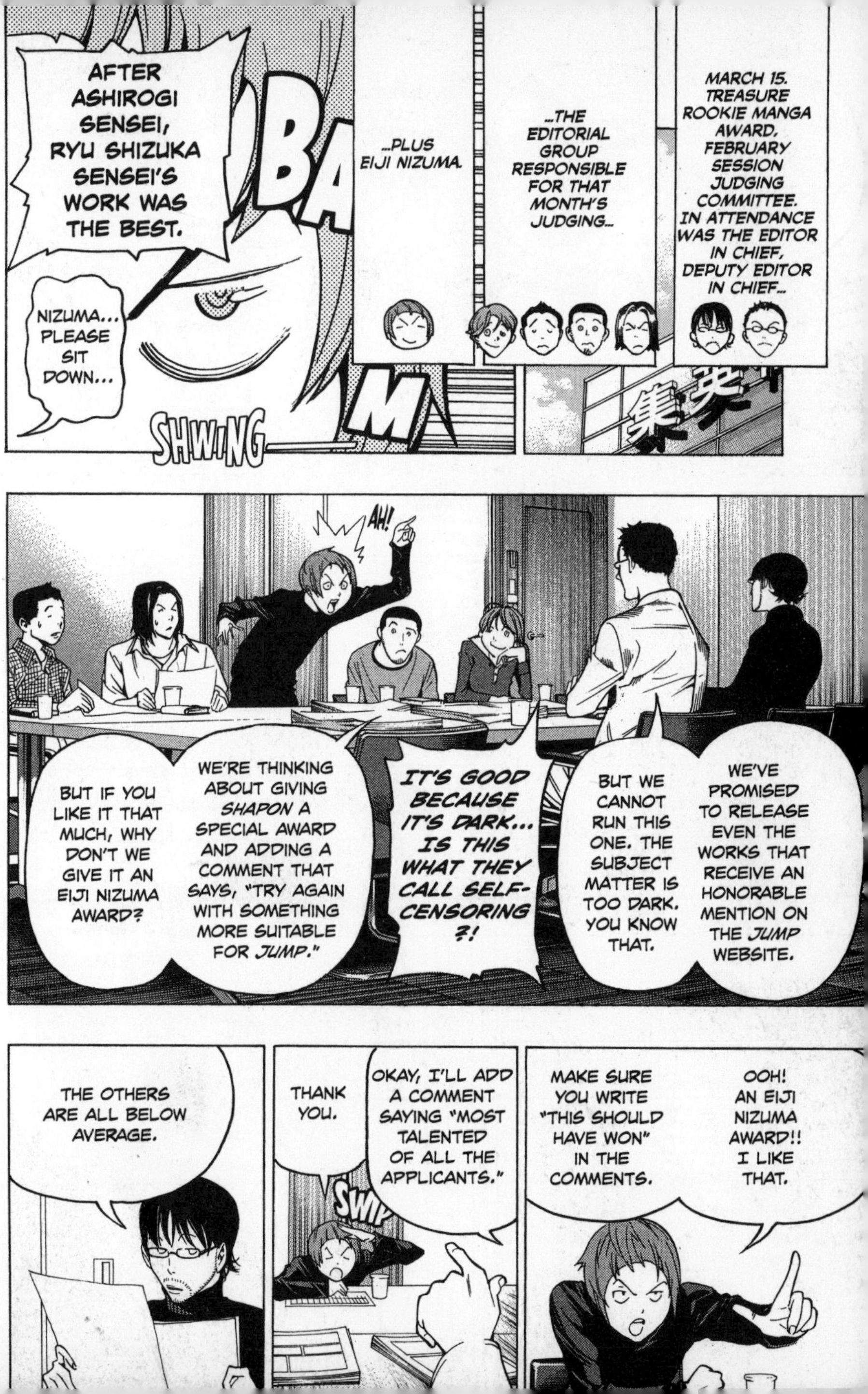
MARCH 15. TREASURE ROOKIE MANGA AWARD, FEBRUARY SESSION JUDGING COMMITTEE. IN ATTENDANCE WAS THE EDITOR IN CHIEF, DEPUTY EDITOR IN CHIEF...
集英
...THE EDITORIAL GROUP RESPONSIBLE FOR THAT MONTH'S JUDGING...
...PLUS EIJI NIZUMA.
BAM
AFTER ASHIROGI SENSEI, RYU SHIZUKA SENSEI'S WORK WAS THE BEST.
NIZUMA... PLEASE SIT DOWN...
SHWING
AH!
WE'VE PROMISED TO RELEASE EVEN THE WORKS THAT RECEIVE AN HONORABLE MENTION ON THE *JUMP* WEBSITE.
BUT WE CANNOT RUN THIS ONE. THE SUBJECT MATTER IS TOO DARK. YOU KNOW THAT.
IT'S GOOD BECAUSE IT'S DARK... IS THIS WHAT THEY CALL SELF-CENSORING?!
WE'RE THINKING ABOUT GIVING *SHAPON* A SPECIAL AWARD AND ADDING A COMMENT THAT SAYS, "TRY AGAIN WITH SOMETHING MORE SUITABLE FOR *JUMP*."
BUT IF YOU LIKE IT THAT MUCH, WHY DON'T WE GIVE IT AN EIJI NIZUMA AWARD?
OOH! AN EIJI NIZUMA AWARD!! I LIKE THAT.
MAKE SURE YOU WRITE "THIS SHOULD HAVE WON" IN THE COMMENTS.
OKAY, I'LL ADD A COMMENT SAYING "MOST TALENTED OF ALL THE APPLICANTS."
SWIP
THANK YOU.
THE OTHERS ARE ALL BELOW AVERAGE.

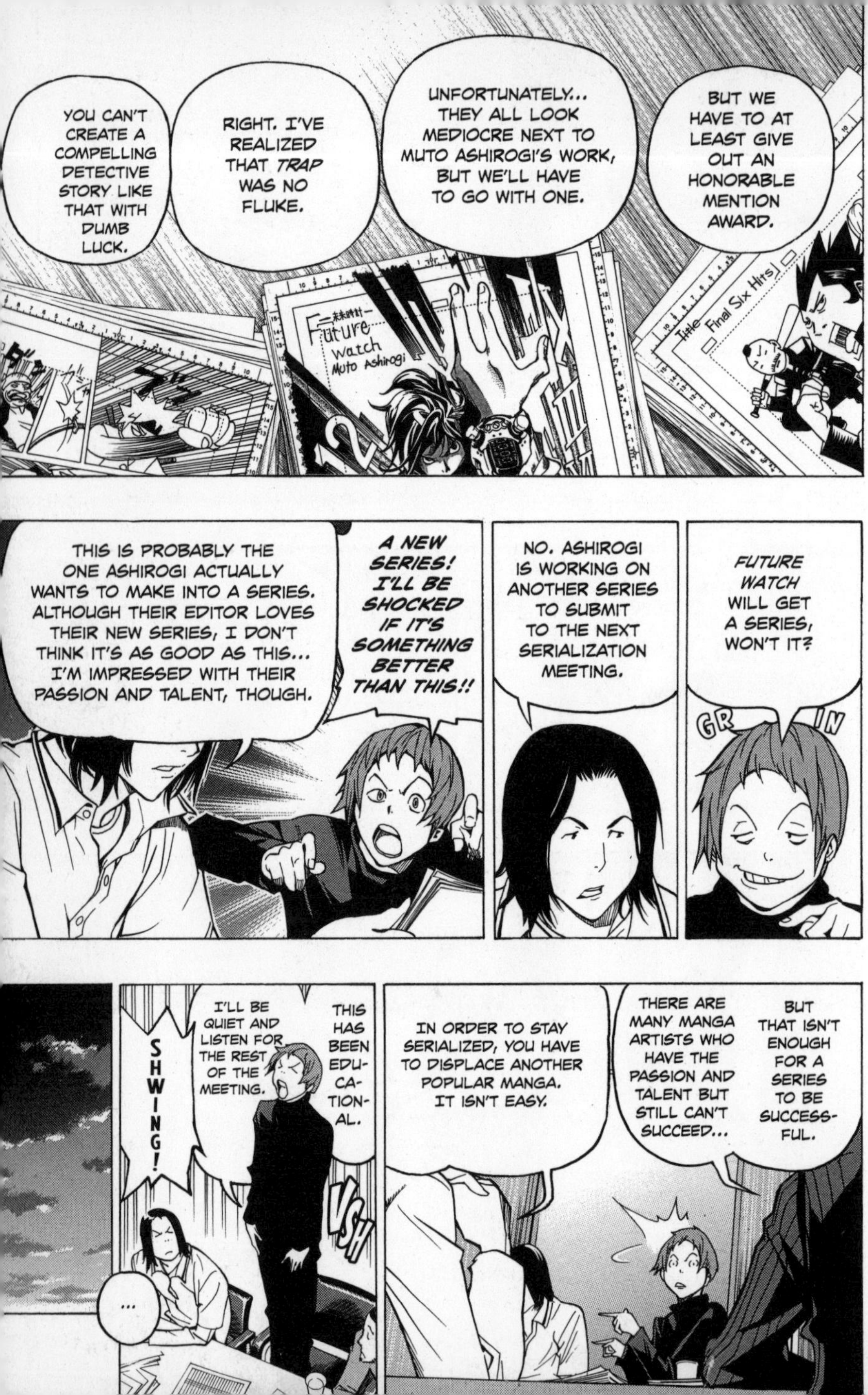
BUT WE HAVE TO AT LEAST GIVE OUT AN HONORABLE MENTION AWARD.
UNFORTUNATELY... THEY ALL LOOK MEDIOCRE NEXT TO MUTO ASHIROGI'S WORK, BUT WE'LL HAVE TO GO WITH ONE.
RIGHT. I'VE REALIZED THAT *TRAP* WAS NO FLUKE.
YOU CAN'T CREATE A COMPELLING DETECTIVE STORY LIKE THAT WITH DUMB LUCK.
Title Final Six Hits
Future Watch
Muto Ashirogi
FUTURE WATCH WILL GET A SERIES, WON'T IT?
GRIN
NO. ASHIROGI IS WORKING ON ANOTHER SERIES TO SUBMIT TO THE NEXT SERIALIZATION MEETING.
A NEW SERIES! I'LL BE SHOCKED IF IT'S SOMETHING BETTER THAN THIS!!
THIS IS PROBABLY THE ONE ASHIROGI ACTUALLY WANTS TO MAKE INTO A SERIES. ALTHOUGH THEIR EDITOR LOVES THEIR NEW SERIES, I DON'T THINK IT'S AS GOOD AS THIS... I'M IMPRESSED WITH THEIR PASSION AND TALENT, THOUGH.
BUT THAT ISN'T ENOUGH FOR A SERIES TO BE SUCCESSFUL.
THERE ARE MANY MANGA ARTISTS WHO HAVE THE PASSION AND TALENT BUT STILL CAN'T SUCCEED...
IN ORDER TO STAY SERIALIZED, YOU HAVE TO DISPLACE ANOTHER POPULAR MANGA. IT ISN'T EASY.
THIS HAS BEEN EDUCATIONAL.
I'LL BE QUIET AND LISTEN FOR THE REST OF THE MEETING.
SHWING!
VSH
...

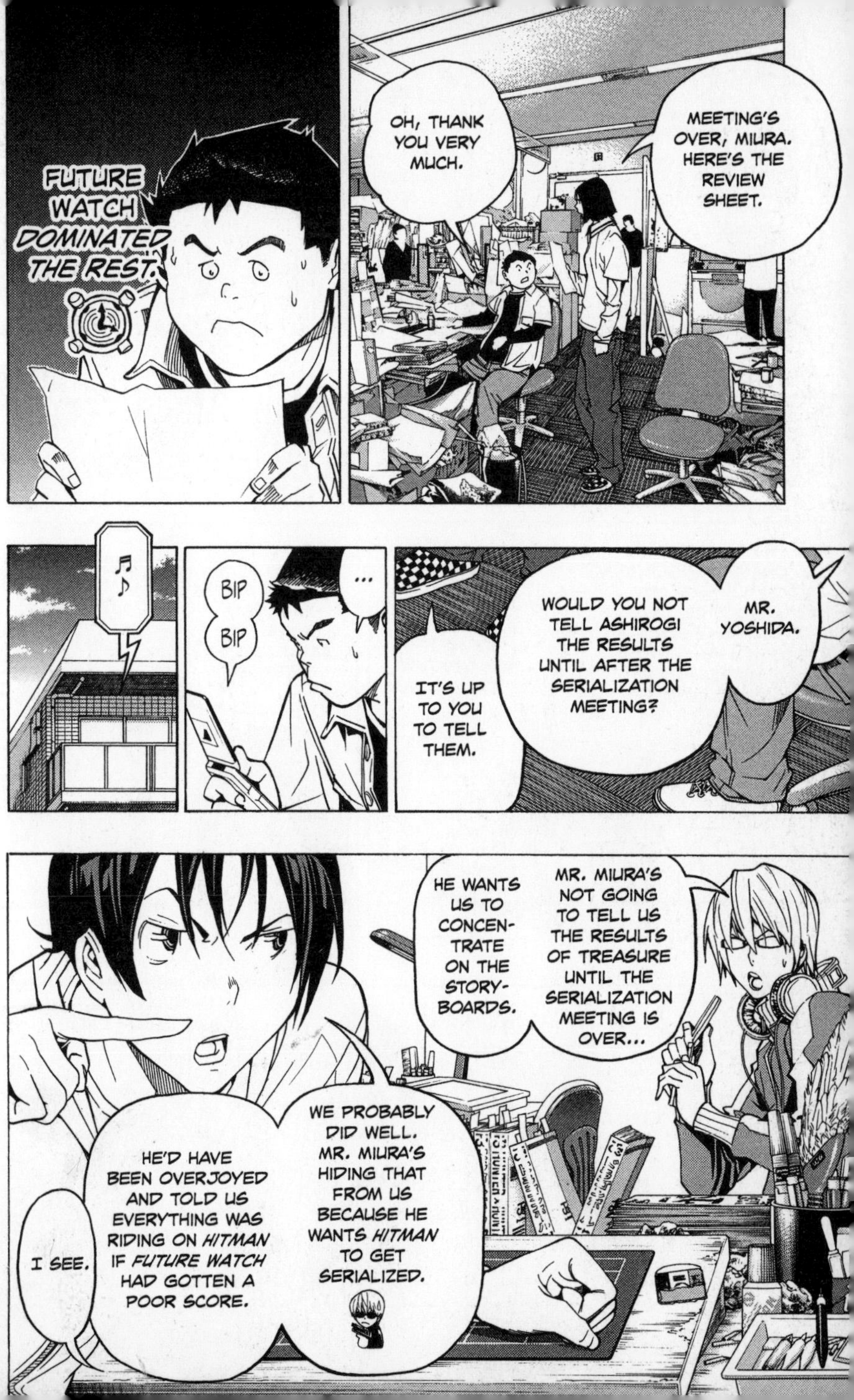
MEETING'S OVER, MIURA. HERE'S THE REVIEW SHEET.
OH, THANK YOU VERY MUCH.
FUTURE WATCH DOMINATED THE REST.
MR. YOSHIDA.
WOULD YOU NOT TELL ASHIROGI THE RESULTS UNTIL AFTER THE SERIALIZATION MEETING?
IT'S UP TO YOU TO TELL THEM.
...
BIP
BIP
♫ ♪
MR. MIURA'S NOT GOING TO TELL US THE RESULTS OF TREASURE UNTIL THE SERIALIZATION MEETING IS OVER...
HE WANTS US TO CONCEN-TRATE ON THE STORY-BOARDS.
WE PROBABLY DID WELL. MR. MIURA'S HIDING THAT FROM US BECAUSE HE WANTS *HITMAN* TO GET SERIALIZED.
HE'D HAVE BEEN OVERJOYED AND TOLD US EVERYTHING WAS RIDING ON *HITMAN* IF *FUTURE WATCH* HAD GOTTEN A POOR SCORE.
I SEE.

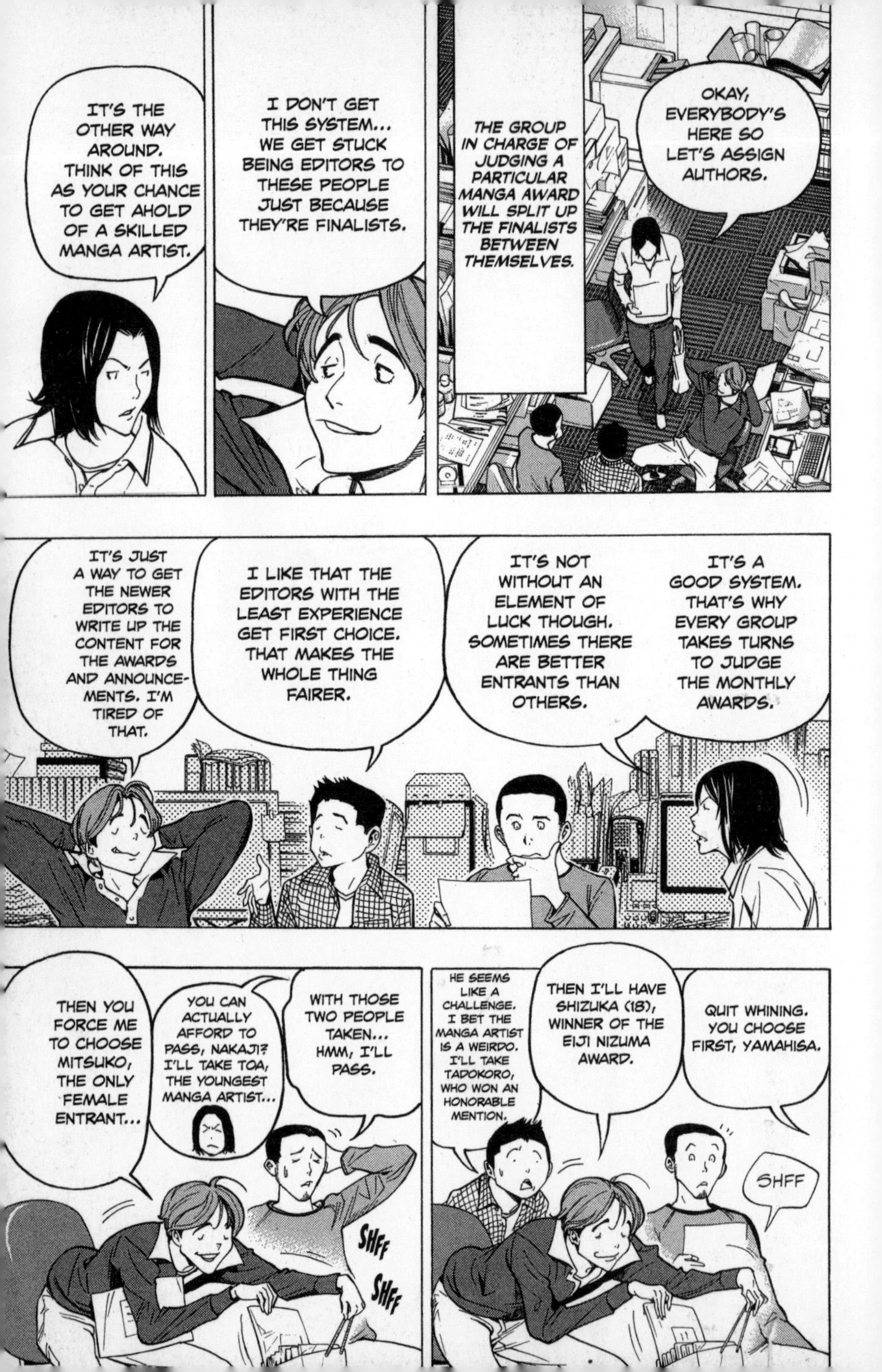
OKAY, EVERYBODY'S HERE SO LET'S ASSIGN AUTHORS.
THE GROUP IN CHARGE OF JUDGING A PARTICULAR MANGA AWARD WILL SPLIT UP THE FINALISTS BETWEEN THEMSELVES.
I DON'T GET THIS SYSTEM... WE GET STUCK BEING EDITORS TO THESE PEOPLE JUST BECAUSE THEY'RE FINALISTS.
IT'S THE OTHER WAY AROUND. THINK OF THIS AS YOUR CHANCE TO GET AHOLD OF A SKILLED MANGA ARTIST.
IT'S A GOOD SYSTEM. THAT'S WHY EVERY GROUP TAKES TURNS TO JUDGE THE MONTHLY AWARDS.
IT'S NOT WITHOUT AN ELEMENT OF LUCK THOUGH. SOMETIMES THERE ARE BETTER ENTRANTS THAN OTHERS.
I LIKE THAT THE EDITORS WITH THE LEAST EXPERIENCE GET FIRST CHOICE. THAT MAKES THE WHOLE THING FAIRER.
IT'S JUST A WAY TO GET THE NEWER EDITORS TO WRITE UP THE CONTENT FOR THE AWARDS AND ANNOUNCEMENTS. I'M TIRED OF THAT.
QUIT WHINING. YOU CHOOSE FIRST, YAMAHISA.
SHFF
THEN I'LL HAVE SHIZUKA (18), WINNER OF THE EIJI NIZUMA AWARD.
HE SEEMS LIKE A CHALLENGE. I BET THE MANGA ARTIST IS A WEIRDO. I'LL TAKE TADOKORO, WHO WON AN HONORABLE MENTION.
WITH THOSE TWO PEOPLE TAKEN... HMM, I'LL PASS.
YOU CAN ACTUALLY AFFORD TO PASS, NAKAJI? I'LL TAKE TOA, THE YOUNGEST MANGA ARTIST...
THEN YOU FORCE ME TO CHOOSE MITSUKO, THE ONLY FEMALE ENTRANT...
SHFF
SHFF

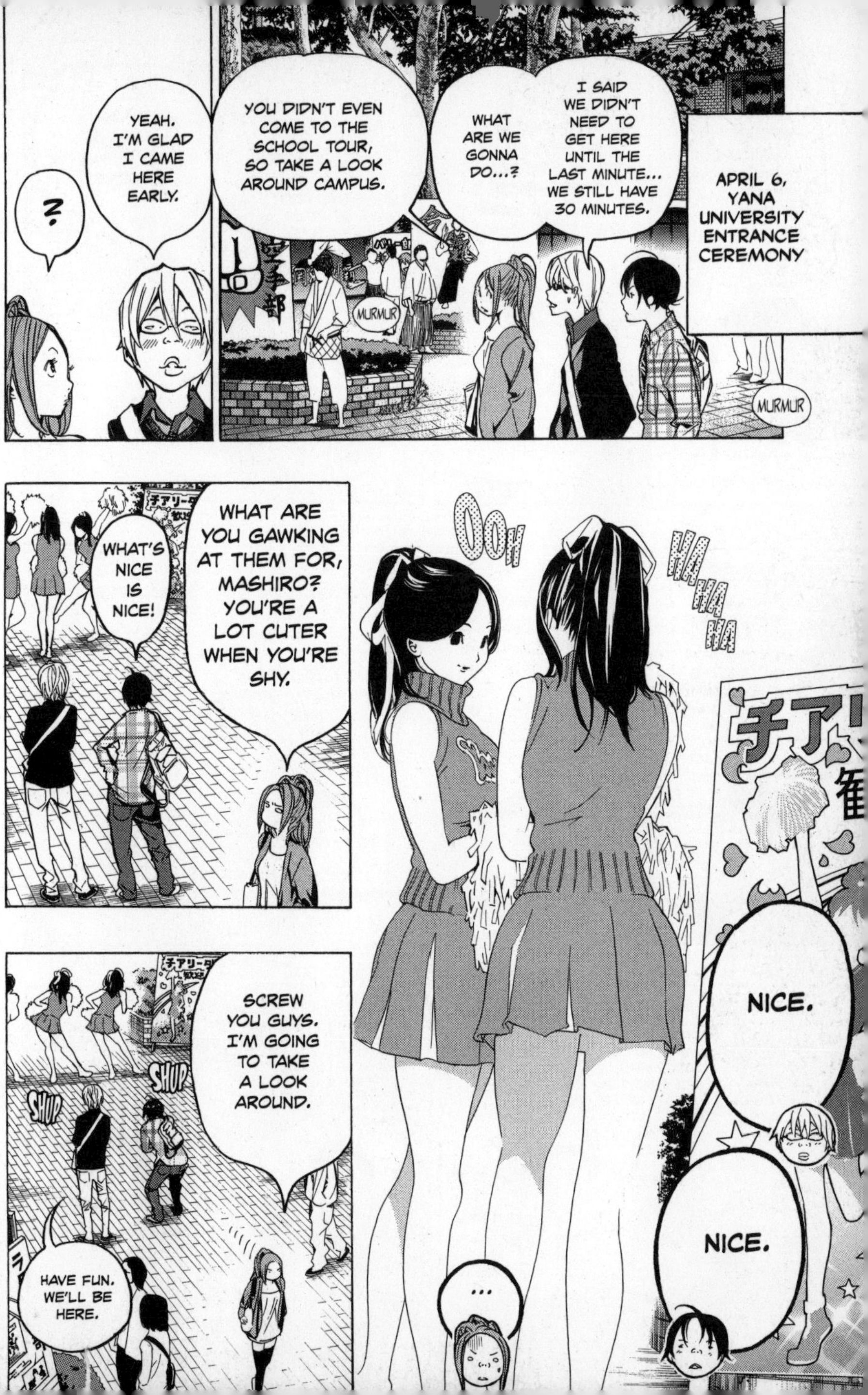
APRIL 6, YANA UNIVERSITY ENTRANCE CEREMONY
MURMUR
I SAID WE DIDN'T NEED TO GET HERE UNTIL THE LAST MINUTE... WE STILL HAVE 30 MINUTES.
WHAT ARE WE GONNA DO...?
YOU DIDN'T EVEN COME TO THE SCHOOL TOUR, SO TAKE A LOOK AROUND CAMPUS.
MURMUR
YEAH. I'M GLAD I CAME HERE EARLY.
?
OOH
HA HA HA
NICE.
NICE.
...
WHAT ARE YOU GAWKING AT THEM FOR, MASHIRO? YOU'RE A LOT CUTER WHEN YOU'RE SHY.
WHAT'S NICE IS NICE!
SCREW YOU GUYS. I'M GOING TO TAKE A LOOK AROUND.
SHUP
SHUP
HAVE FUN. WE'LL BE HERE.

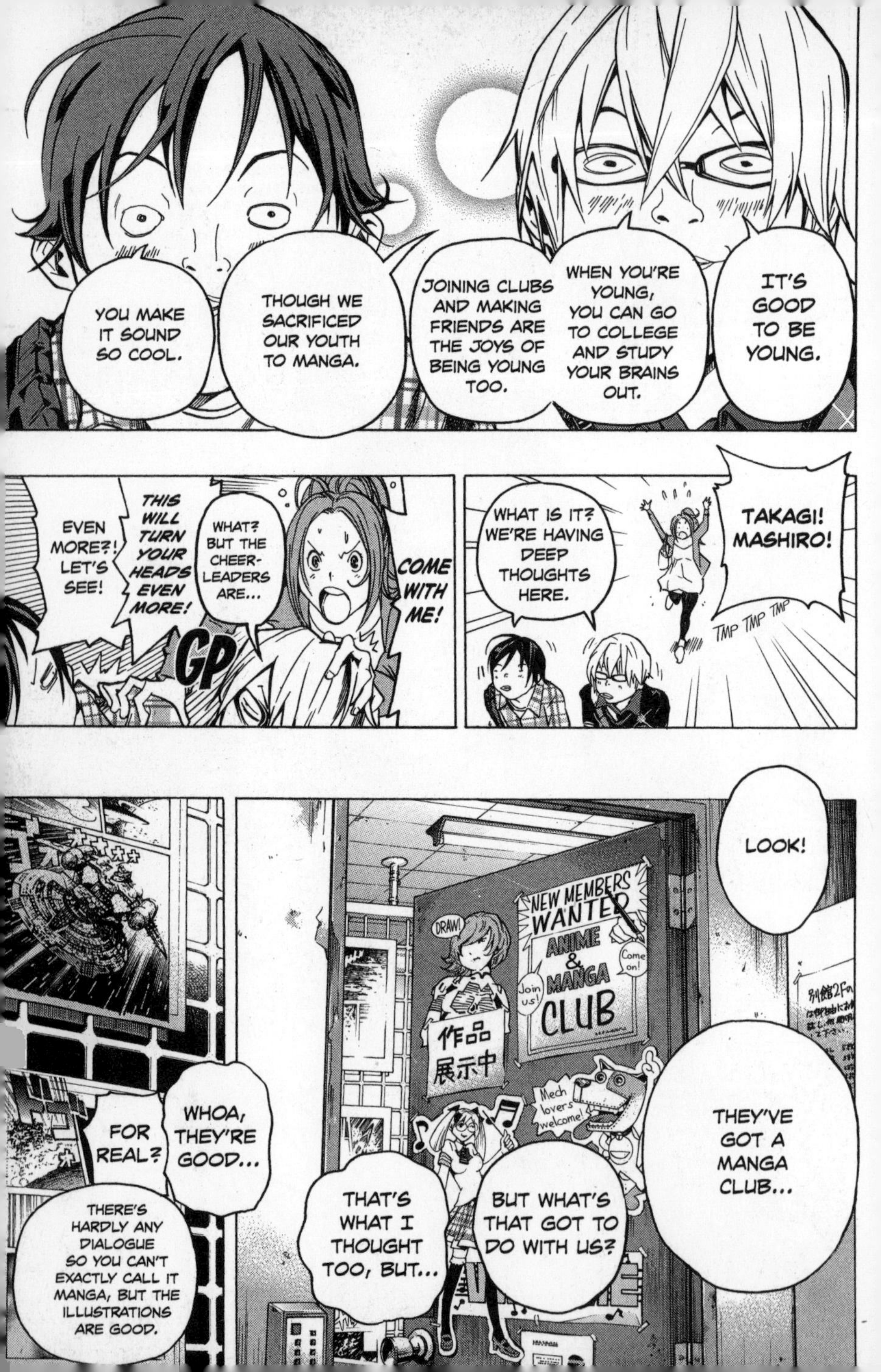
IT'S GOOD TO BE YOUNG.
WHEN YOU'RE YOUNG, YOU CAN GO TO COLLEGE AND STUDY YOUR BRAINS OUT.
JOINING CLUBS AND MAKING FRIENDS ARE THE JOYS OF BEING YOUNG TOO.
THOUGH WE SACRIFICED OUR YOUTH TO MANGA.
YOU MAKE IT SOUND SO COOL.
TAKAGI! MASHIRO!
TMP TMP TMP
WHAT IS IT? WE'RE HAVING DEEP THOUGHTS HERE.
COME WITH ME!
WHAT? BUT THE CHEER-LEADERS ARE...
THIS WILL TURN YOUR HEADS EVEN MORE!
GP
EVEN MORE?! LET'S SEE!
LOOK!
NEW MEMBERS WANTED
ANIME & MANGA CLUB
Come on!
Join us!
DRAW!
作品展示中
Mech lovers welcome!
THEY'VE GOT A MANGA CLUB...
BUT WHAT'S THAT GOT TO DO WITH US?
THAT'S WHAT I THOUGHT TOO, BUT...
WHOA, THEY'RE GOOD...
FOR REAL?
THERE'S HARDLY ANY DIALOGUE SO YOU CAN'T EXACTLY CALL IT MANGA, BUT THE ILLUSTRATIONS ARE GOOD.

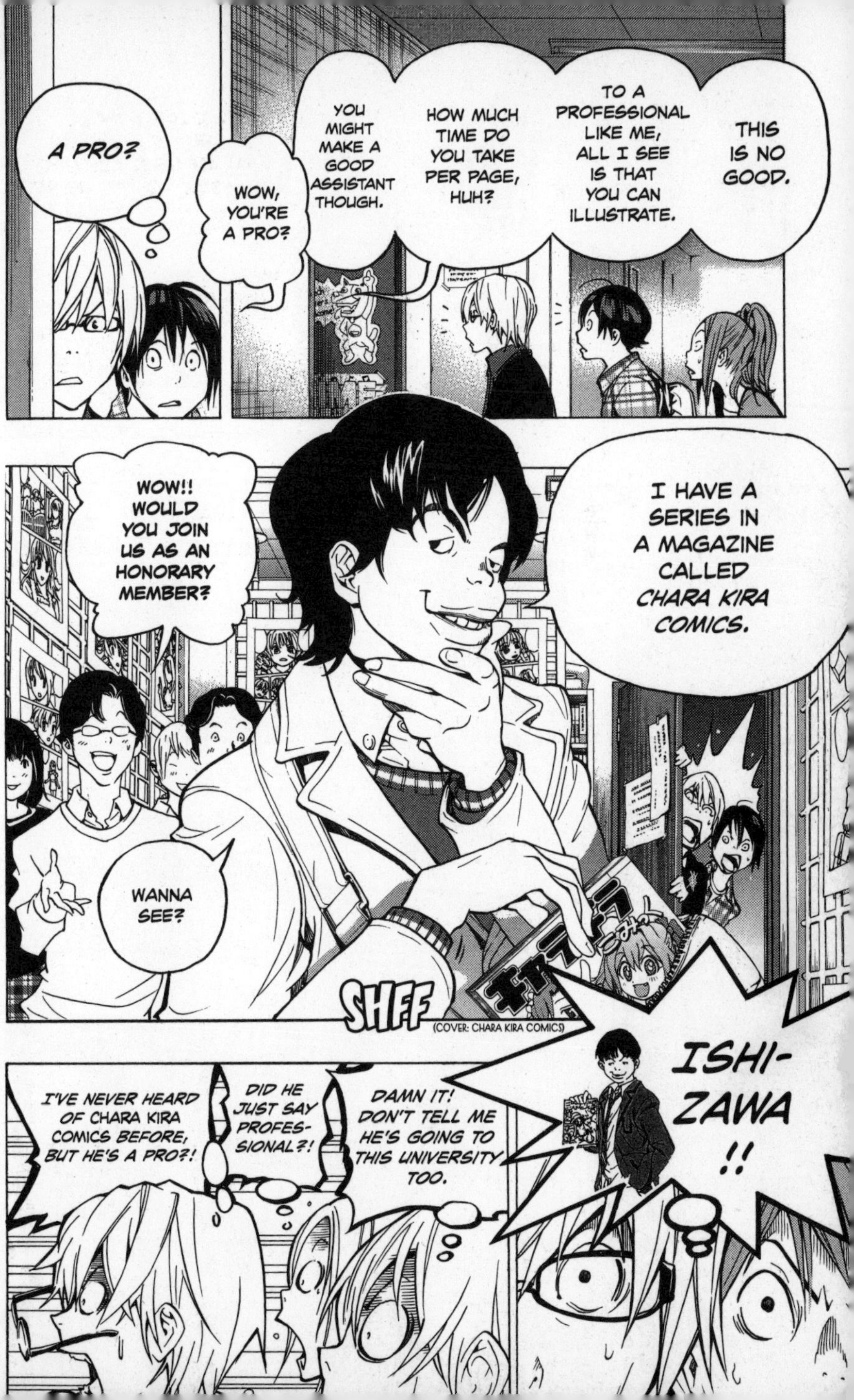
THIS IS NO GOOD.
TO A PROFESSIONAL LIKE ME, ALL I SEE IS THAT YOU CAN ILLUSTRATE.
HOW MUCH TIME DO YOU TAKE PER PAGE, HUH?
YOU MIGHT MAKE A GOOD ASSISTANT THOUGH.
WOW, YOU'RE A PRO?
A PRO?
I HAVE A SERIES IN A MAGAZINE CALLED CHARA KIRA COMICS.
WOW!! WOULD YOU JOIN US AS AN HONORARY MEMBER?
WANNA SEE?
SHFF
(COVER: CHARA KIRA COMICS)
ISHI-ZAWA !!
DAMN IT! DON'T TELL ME HE'S GOING TO THIS UNIVERSITY TOO.
DID HE JUST SAY PROFES-SIONAL?!
I'VE NEVER HEARD OF CHARA KIRA COMICS BEFORE, BUT HE'S A PRO?!

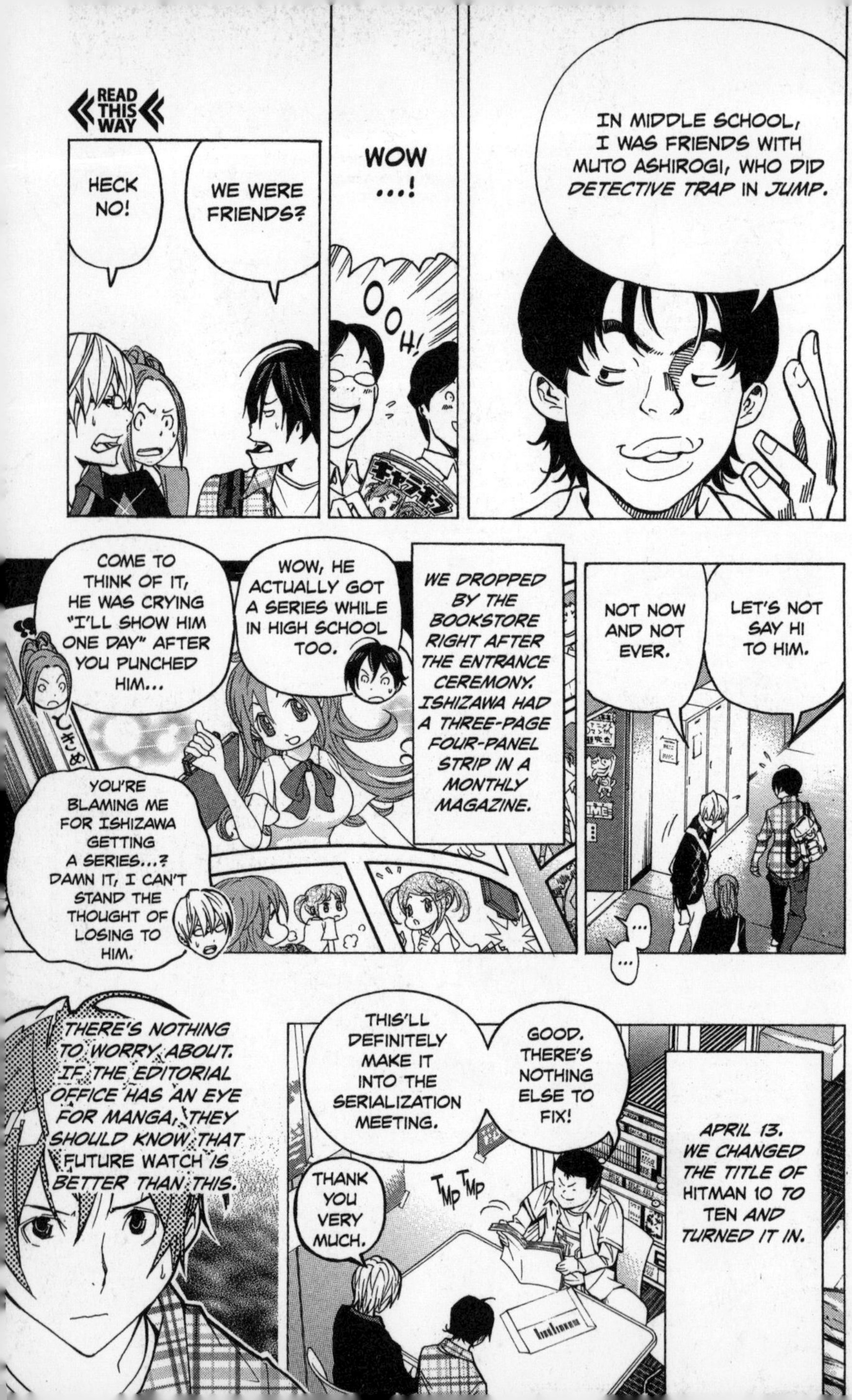
READ THIS WAY
IN MIDDLE SCHOOL, I WAS FRIENDS WITH MUTO ASHIROGI, WHO DID *DETECTIVE TRAP* IN *JUMP*.
WOW ...!
OOH!
WE WERE FRIENDS?
HECK NO!
LET'S NOT SAY HI TO HIM.
NOT NOW AND NOT EVER.
...
...
WE DROPPED BY THE BOOKSTORE RIGHT AFTER THE ENTRANCE CEREMONY. ISHIZAWA HAD A THREE-PAGE FOUR-PANEL STRIP IN A MONTHLY MAGAZINE.
WOW, HE ACTUALLY GOT A SERIES WHILE IN HIGH SCHOOL TOO.
COME TO THINK OF IT, HE WAS CRYING "I'LL SHOW HIM ONE DAY" AFTER YOU PUNCHED HIM...
YOU'RE BLAMING ME FOR ISHIZAWA GETTING A SERIES...? DAMN IT, I CAN'T STAND THE THOUGHT OF LOSING TO HIM.
APRIL 13. WE CHANGED THE TITLE OF HITMAN 10 TO TEN AND TURNED IT IN.
GOOD. THERE'S NOTHING ELSE TO FIX!
THIS'LL DEFINITELY MAKE IT INTO THE SERIALIZATION MEETING.
TMP TMP
THANK YOU VERY MUCH.
THERE'S NOTHING TO WORRY ABOUT. IF THE EDITORIAL OFFICE HAS AN EYE FOR MANGA, THEY SHOULD KNOW THAT FUTURE WATCH IS BETTER THAN THIS.

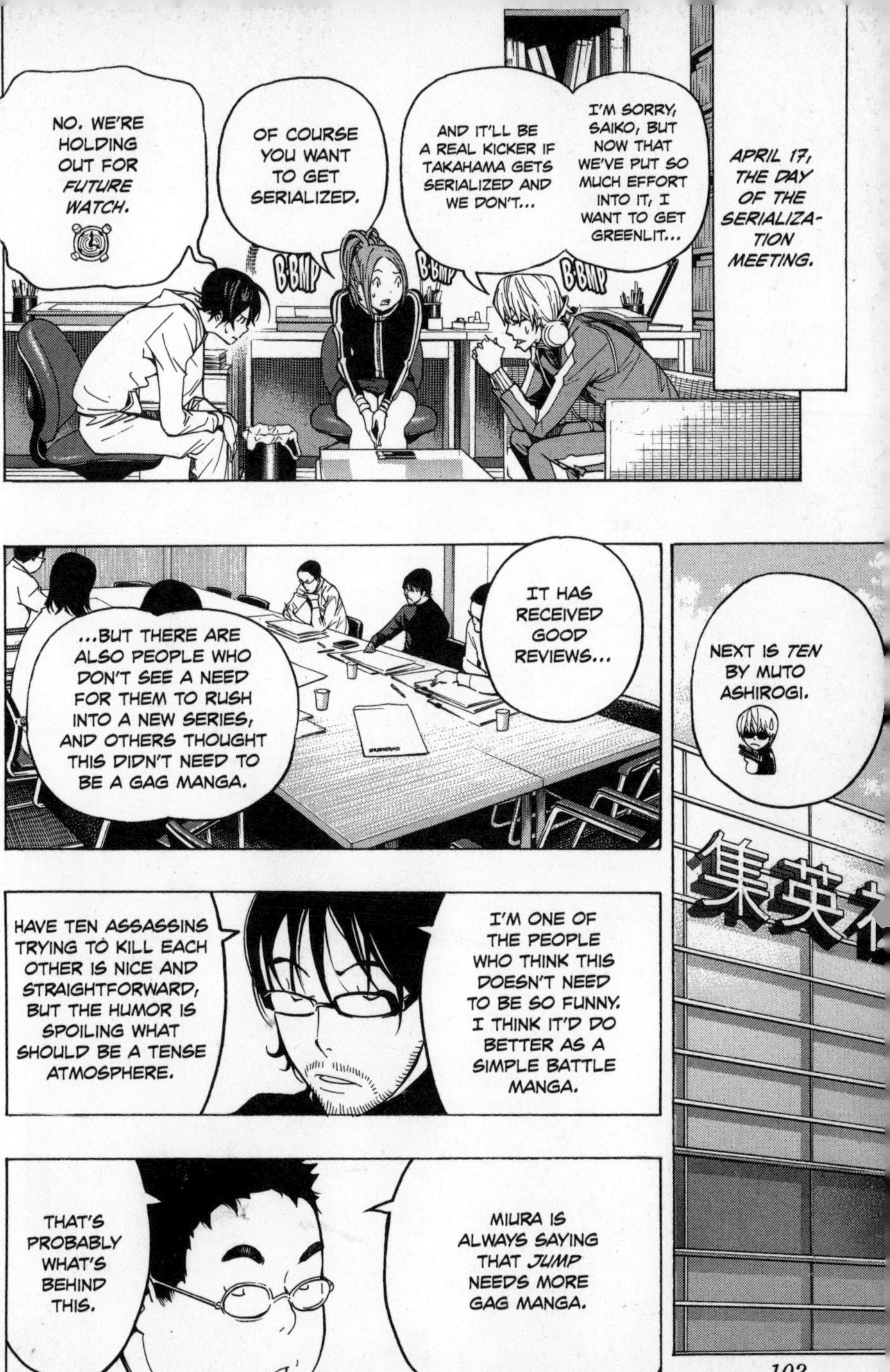
APRIL 17, THE DAY OF THE SERIALIZATION MEETING.
I'M SORRY, SAIKO, BUT NOW THAT WE'VE PUT SO MUCH EFFORT INTO IT, I WANT TO GET GREENLIT...
B-BMP
AND IT'LL BE A REAL KICKER IF TAKAHAMA GETS SERIALIZED AND WE DON'T...
B-BMP
OF COURSE YOU WANT TO GET SERIALIZED.
B-BMP
NO. WE'RE HOLDING OUT FOR *FUTURE WATCH*.
NEXT IS *TEN* BY MUTO ASHIROGI.
集英
IT HAS RECEIVED GOOD REVIEWS...
...BUT THERE ARE ALSO PEOPLE WHO DON'T SEE A NEED FOR THEM TO RUSH INTO A NEW SERIES, AND OTHERS THOUGHT THIS DIDN'T NEED TO BE A GAG MANGA.
I'M ONE OF THE PEOPLE WHO THINK THIS DOESN'T NEED TO BE SO FUNNY. I THINK IT'D DO BETTER AS A SIMPLE BATTLE MANGA.
HAVE TEN ASSASSINS TRYING TO KILL EACH OTHER IS NICE AND STRAIGHTFORWARD, BUT THE HUMOR IS SPOILING WHAT SHOULD BE A TENSE ATMOSPHERE.
MIURA IS ALWAYS SAYING THAT *JUMP* NEEDS MORE GAG MANGA.
THAT'S PROBABLY WHAT'S BEHIND THIS.

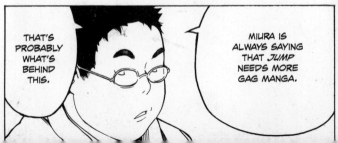

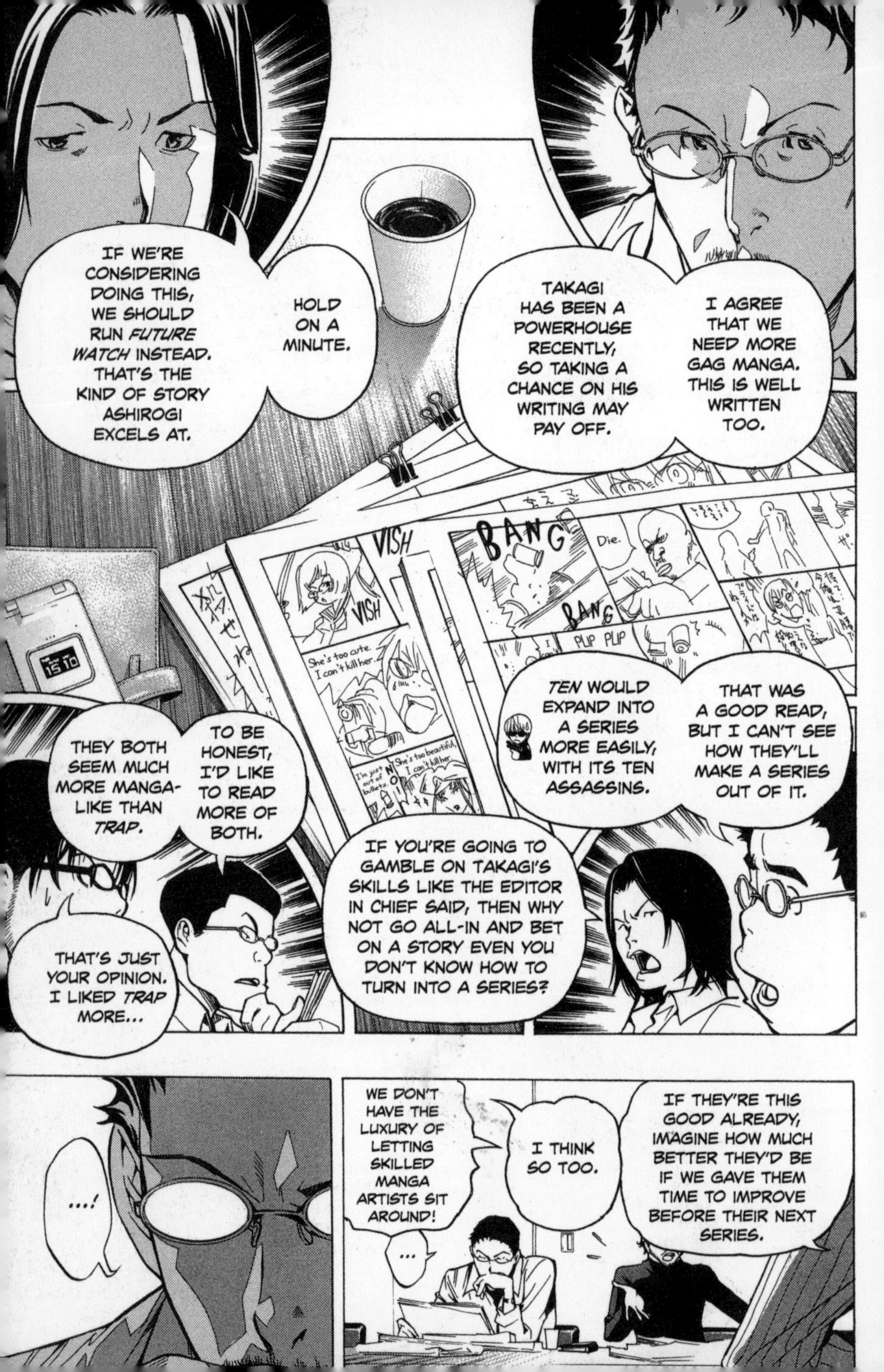
I AGREE THAT WE NEED MORE GAG MANGA. THIS IS WELL WRITTEN TOO.
TAKAGI HAS BEEN A POWERHOUSE RECENTLY, SO TAKING A CHANCE ON HIS WRITING MAY PAY OFF.
HOLD ON A MINUTE.
IF WE'RE CONSIDERING DOING THIS, WE SHOULD RUN *FUTURE WATCH* INSTEAD. THAT'S THE KIND OF STORY ASHIROGI EXCELS AT.
BANG
Die.
BANG
PLIP PLIP
VISH
VISH
She's too cute. I can't kill her.
She's too beautiful, I can't kill her.
I'm just out of bullets.
THAT WAS A GOOD READ, BUT I CAN'T SEE HOW THEY'LL MAKE A SERIES OUT OF IT.
TEN WOULD EXPAND INTO A SERIES MORE EASILY, WITH ITS TEN ASSASSINS.
TO BE HONEST, I'D LIKE TO READ MORE OF BOTH.
THEY BOTH SEEM MUCH MORE MANGA-LIKE THAN *TRAP*.
IF YOU'RE GOING TO GAMBLE ON TAKAGI'S SKILLS LIKE THE EDITOR IN CHIEF SAID, THEN WHY NOT GO ALL-IN AND BET ON A STORY EVEN YOU DON'T KNOW HOW TO TURN INTO A SERIES?
THAT'S JUST YOUR OPINION. I LIKED *TRAP* MORE...
IF THEY'RE THIS GOOD ALREADY, IMAGINE HOW MUCH BETTER THEY'D BE IF WE GAVE THEM TIME TO IMPROVE BEFORE THEIR NEXT SERIES.
I THINK SO TOO.
WE DON'T HAVE THE LUXURY OF LETTING SKILLED MANGA ARTISTS SIT AROUND!
...
...!

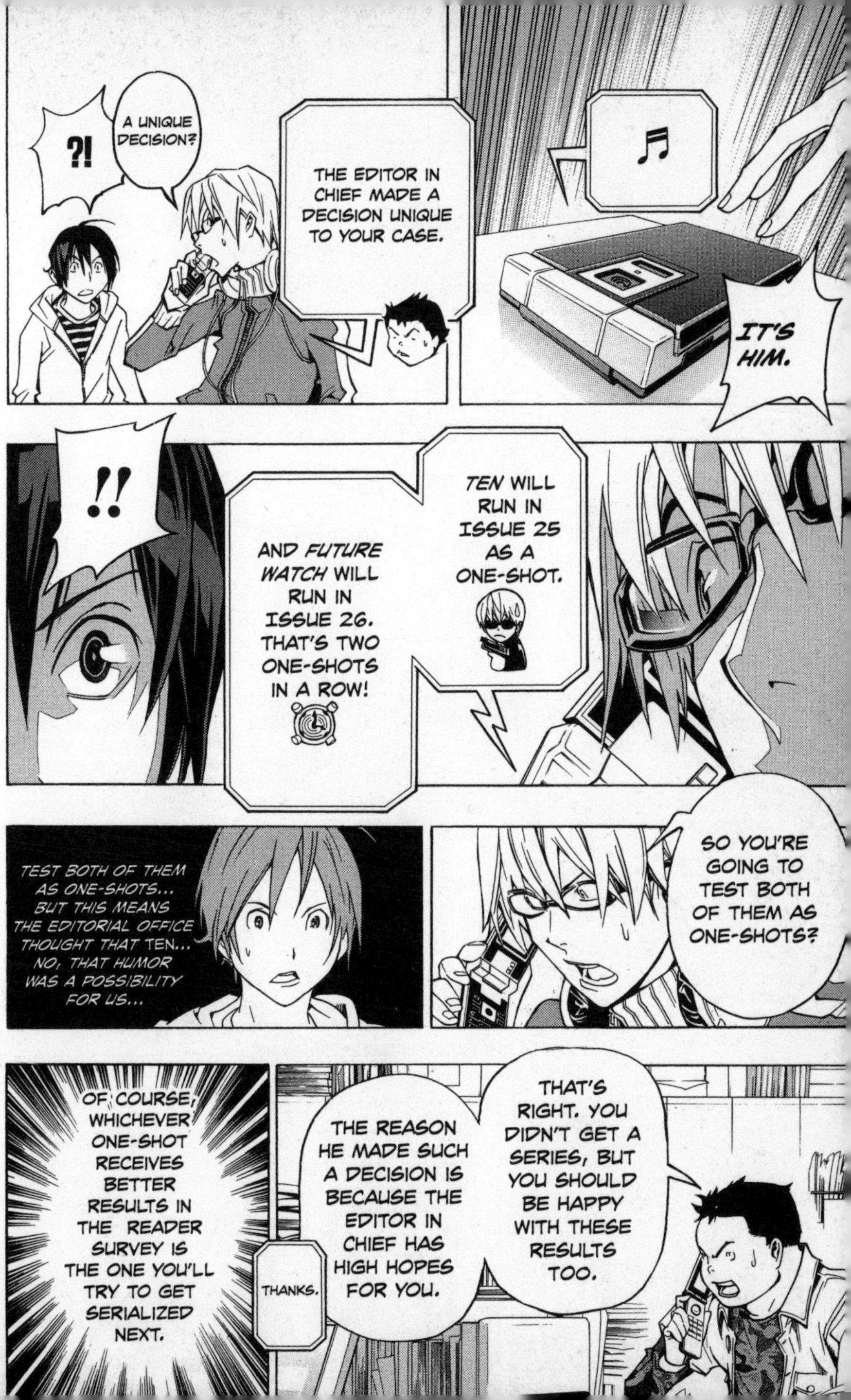
♪
IT'S HIM.
THE EDITOR IN CHIEF MADE A DECISION UNIQUE TO YOUR CASE.
A UNIQUE DECISION?
?!
TEN WILL RUN IN ISSUE 25 AS A ONE-SHOT.
AND *FUTURE WATCH* WILL RUN IN ISSUE 26. THAT'S TWO ONE-SHOTS IN A ROW!
!!
SO YOU'RE GOING TO TEST BOTH OF THEM AS ONE-SHOTS?
TEST BOTH OF THEM AS ONE-SHOTS... BUT THIS MEANS THE EDITORIAL OFFICE THOUGHT THAT TEN... NO, THAT HUMOR WAS A POSSIBILITY FOR US...
THAT'S RIGHT. YOU DIDN'T GET A SERIES, BUT YOU SHOULD BE HAPPY WITH THESE RESULTS TOO.
THE REASON HE MADE SUCH A DECISION IS BECAUSE THE EDITOR IN CHIEF HAS HIGH HOPES FOR YOU.
THANKS.
OF COURSE, WHICHEVER ONE-SHOT RECEIVES BETTER RESULTS IN THE READER SURVEY IS THE ONE YOU'LL TRY TO GET SERIALIZED NEXT.

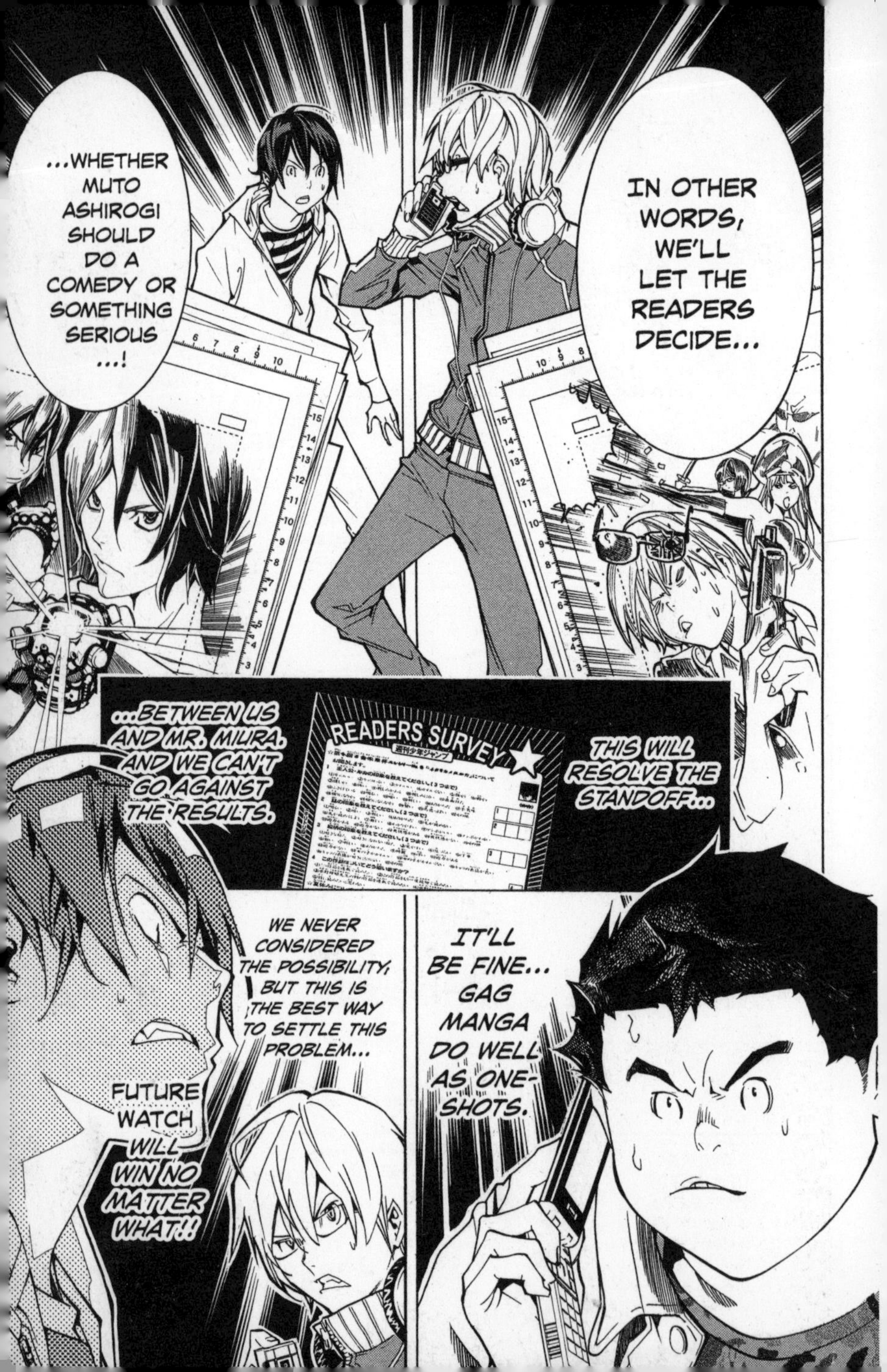
IN OTHER WORDS, WE'LL LET THE READERS DECIDE...
...WHETHER MUTO ASHIROGI SHOULD DO A COMEDY OR SOMETHING SERIOUS...!
THIS WILL RESOLVE THE STANDOFF...
READERS SURVEY
...BETWEEN US AND MR. MIURA. AND WE CAN'T GO AGAINST THE RESULTS.
IT'LL BE FINE... GAG MANGA DO WELL AS ONE-SHOTS.
WE NEVER CONSIDERED THE POSSIBILITY, BUT THIS IS THE BEST WAY TO SETTLE THIS PROBLEM...
FUTURE WATCH WILL WIN NO MATTER WHAT!!

OHBA'S STORYBOARD

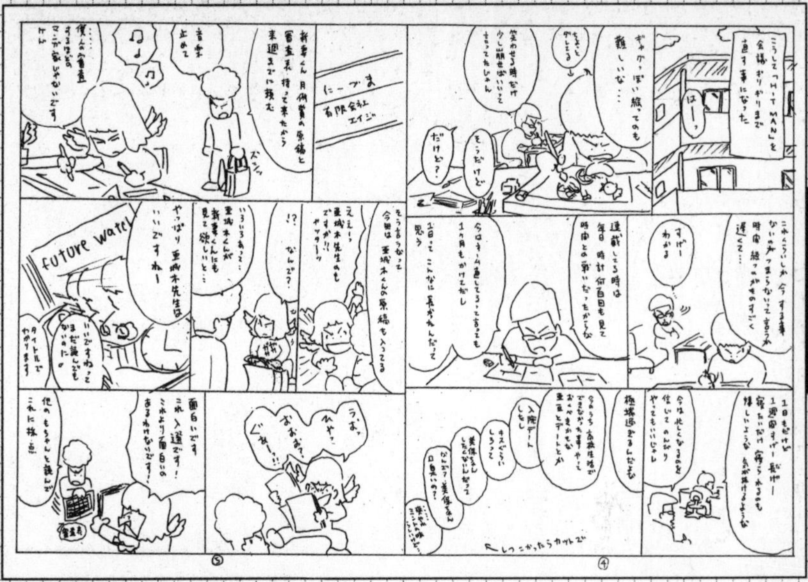

こうして「HIT MAN」を会議ギリギリまで直す事になった
はーっ
ギャグっぽい絵ってのも難しいな…
笑わせる時だけクレ崩せばいいって言ってたじゃん
そうだけど
だけど？
これくらいしか今する事ないのがつまらないって言うか時間経つのがものすごく遅くて…
すげーわかる
連載してる時は毎日時計何百回も見て時間との戦いだったからな
今ネーム直してるっつっても1ヶ月もかけてだし
1日ってこんなに長かったんだって思う
今は忙しくなるのを信じてのんびりやってもいいじゃん
極端過ぎるんだよな
入院デートしたし
にーづま
有限会社エイジ
新妻くん 月例賞の原稿と審査表持って来たから来週までに頼む
音楽止めて
そう言うなって今回は亜城木くんの原稿も入ってる
えぇー 亜城木先生のもですか!! ヤッターッ
!? なんで？
やっぱり亜城木先生はいいですねー
Future Water
タイトルでわかります
面白いです これ入選です! これより面白いのあるわけないです!
他のもちゃんと読んでこれに採点
審査表

OBATA'S STORYBOARD

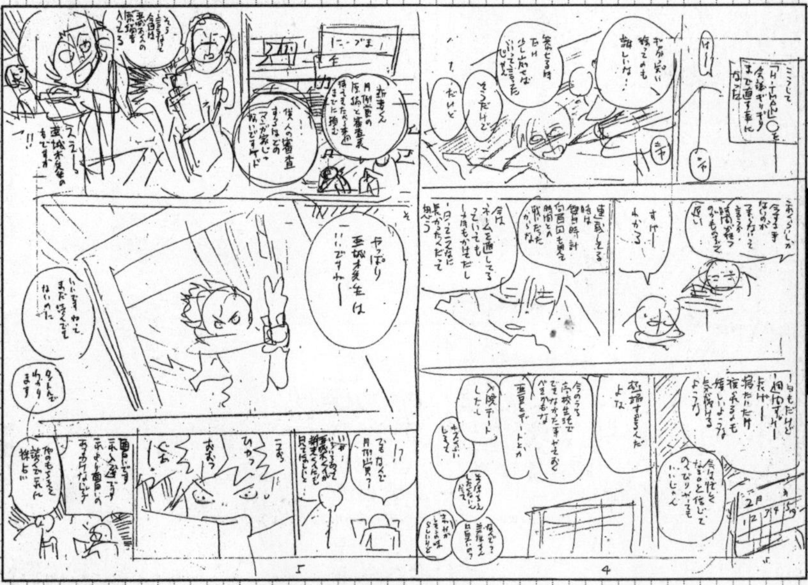

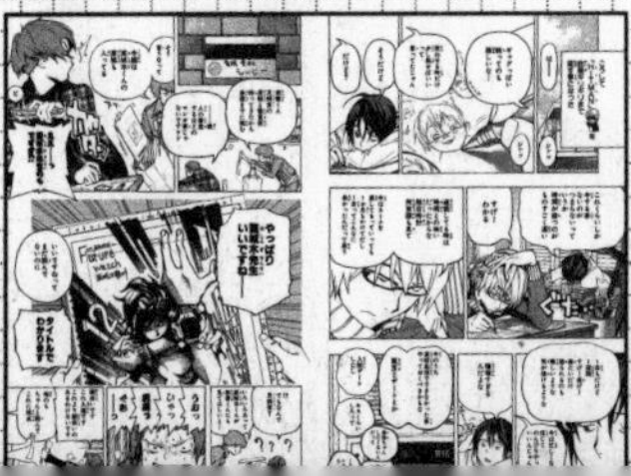

COMPLETE!

※CREATOR STORYBOARDS AND FINISHED PAGES IN JAPANESE

BAKUMAN。vol.7

"Until the Final Draft Is Complete"

Chapter 57, pp. 90-91

FIRST-EVER *BAKUMAN* "MANGA" POPULARITY CONTEST RESULTS!!!

6692 VOTES RECEIVED!!

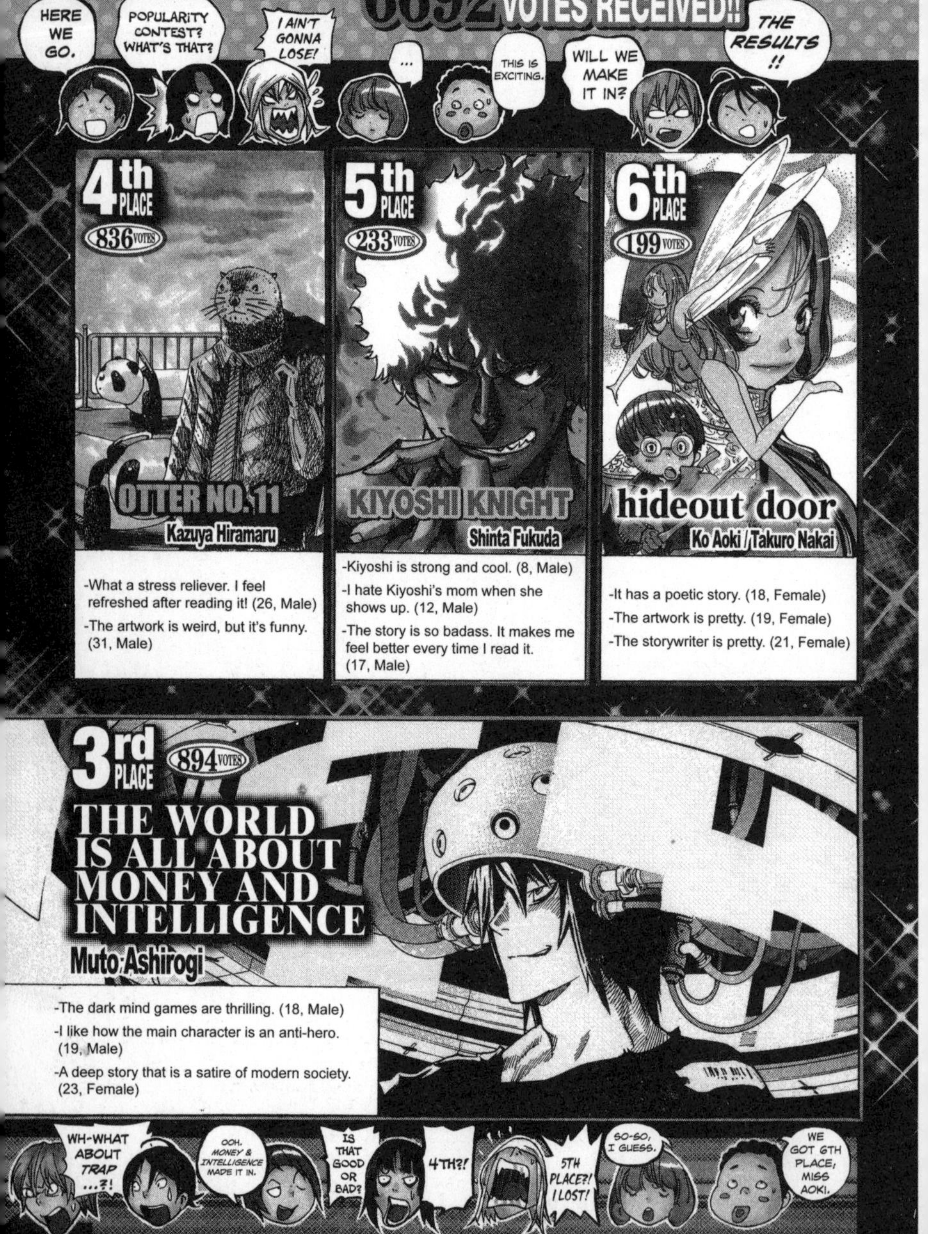
THE RESULTS !!
WILL WE MAKE IT IN?
THIS IS EXCITING.
...
I AIN'T GONNA LOSE!
POPULARITY CONTEST? WHAT'S THAT?
HERE WE GO.
4th PLACE
836 VOTES
OTTER NO. 11
Kazuya Hiramaru
-What a stress reliever. I feel refreshed after reading it! (26, Male)
-The artwork is weird, but it's funny. (31, Male)
5th PLACE
233 VOTES
KIYOSHI KNIGHT
Shinta Fukuda
-Kiyoshi is strong and cool. (8, Male)
-I hate Kiyoshi's mom when she shows up. (12, Male)
-The story is so badass. It makes me feel better every time I read it. (17, Male)
6th PLACE
199 VOTES
hideout door
Ko Aoki / Takuro Nakai
-It has a poetic story. (18, Female)
-The artwork is pretty. (19, Female)
-The storywriter is pretty. (21, Female)
3rd PLACE
894 VOTES
THE WORLD IS ALL ABOUT MONEY AND INTELLIGENCE
Muto Ashirogi
-The dark mind games are thrilling. (18, Male)
-I like how the main character is an anti-hero. (19, Male)
-A deep story that is a satire of modern society. (23, Female)
WE GOT 6TH PLACE, MISS AOKI.
SO-SO, I GUESS.
5TH PLACE?! I LOST!
4TH?!
IS THAT GOOD OR BAD?
OOH. MONEY & INTELLIGENCE MADE IT IN.
WH-WHAT ABOUT TRAP ...?!

CHAPTER 58 SINGLE AND DOUBLE DIGITS

※ Results of the popularity contest held in Jump Issue 39, 2009. Skip three pages ahead to see all the nominated works.

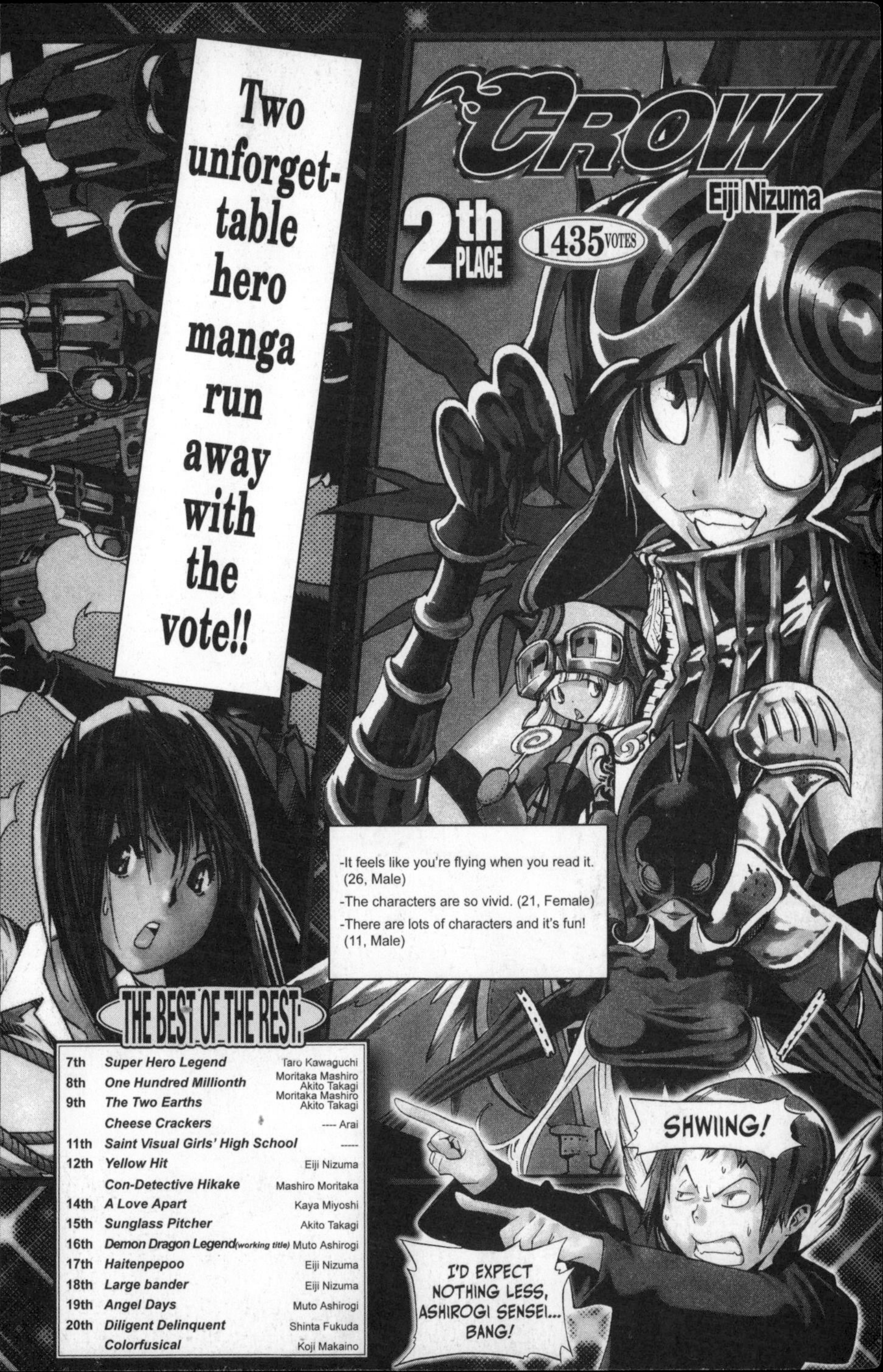
Two unforgettable hero manga run away with the vote!!
CROW
Eiji Nizuma
2th PLACE
1435 VOTES
-It feels like you're flying when you read it. (26, Male)
-The characters are so vivid. (21, Female)
-There are lots of characters and it's fun! (11, Male)
SHWIING!
I'D EXPECT NOTHING LESS, ASHIROGI SENSEI... BANG!
THE BEST OF THE REST:
7th Super Hero Legend Taro Kawaguchi
8th One Hundred Millionth Moritaka Mashiro Akito Takagi
9th The Two Earths Moritaka Mashiro Akito Takagi
Cheese Crackers ---- Arai
11th Saint Visual Girls' High School -----
12th Yellow Hit Eiji Nizuma
Con-Detective Hikake Mashiro Moritaka
14th A Love Apart Kaya Miyoshi
15th Sunglass Pitcher Akito Takagi
16th Demon Dragon Legend (working title) Muto Ashirogi
17th Haitenpepoo Eiji Nizuma
18th Large bander Eiji Nizuma
19th Angel Days Muto Ashirogi
20th Diligent Delinquent Shinta Fukuda
Colorfusical Koji Makaino

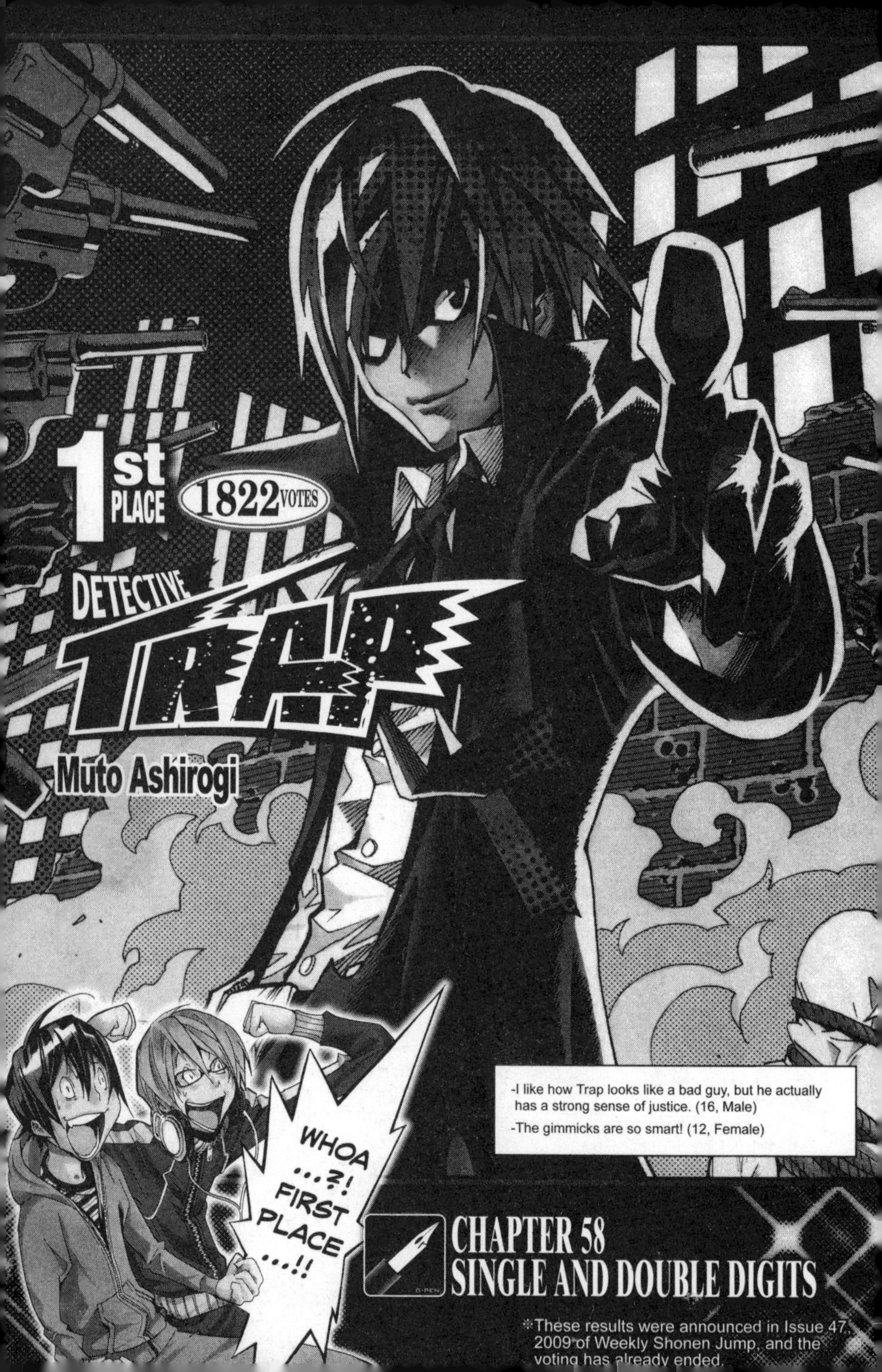
1st PLACE
1822 VOTES
DETECTIVE TRAP
Muto Ashirogi
-I like how Trap looks like a bad guy, but he actually has a strong sense of justice. (16, Male)
-The gimmicks are so smart! (12, Female)
WHOA ...?! FIRST PLACE ...!!
CHAPTER 58
SINGLE AND DOUBLE DIGITS
G-PEN
※These results were announced in Issue 47, 2009 of Weekly Shonen Jump, and the voting has already ended.

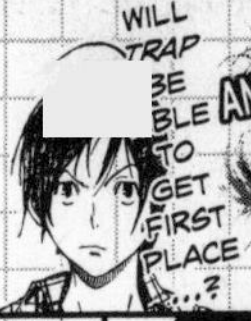

WILL TRAP BE ABLE TO GET FIRST PLACE...?

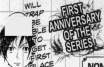

FIRST ANNIVERSARY OF THE SERIES

FIRST-EVER *BAKUMAN* "MANGA" POPULARITY CONTEST!!

Which manga do want to read most?!

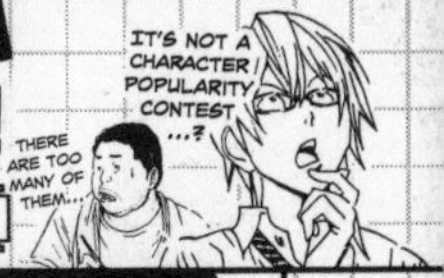

IT'S NOT A CHARACTER POPULARITY CONTEST...?
THERE ARE TOO MANY OF THEM...

NOMINEES BELOW. THIRTY GEMS(?!) TO CHOOSE FROM!!

No. 1 *Super Hero Legend* Taro Kawaguchi
Moritaka Mashiro's uncle, Nobuhiro Mashiro's, biggest hit. It became a hugely popular anime!!

No. 2 *Happy Ranger* Taro Kawaguchi
Taro Kawaguchi's first published work!! It ran in a magazine similar to *Shonen Jump*.

No. 3 *Large bander* Eiji Nizuma
Eiji Nizuma won the semi-final prize in the Tezuka Award at 15 years old with this work. It ran in *Jump* too!!

No. 4 *The Two Earths* Moritaka Mashiro, Akito Takagi
The working title was *Double Earth*. The first piece of work the two completed and took to Shueisha!!

No. 5 *Sunglass Pitcher* Akito Takagi
A sports manga Akito brainstormed. It was so over-the-top that it caught the eye!!

No. 6 *The Camera and the Hare* Akito Takagi
One of the relatively okay stories which Akito brainstormed while coming up with ideas for the Tezuka Award!!

No. 7 *One Hundred Millionth* Moritaka Mashiro, Akito Takagi
A finalist for the Tezuka Award. This was the first time their artwork made it into *Jump*. The story received a 4 out of 5.

No. 8 *Haitenpepoo* Eiji Nizuma
The big prize winner when Eiji received both Final and Semi-Final prize for the Tezuka Award. The prize money was two million yen!!

No. 9 *Dogamiberon* Eiji Nizuma
The semi-final prize winner when Eiji received both finalist and semi-finalist awards for the Tezuka Award. The prize was one million yen!!

No. 10 *The World Is All About Money and Intelligence* Muto Ashirogi
The memorable debut work of Muto Ashirogi as manga artists!! Received third place in the *Akamaru* surveys.

No. 11 *Crow* Eiji Nizuma
Serialized in *Jump* after receiving first place in Akamaru!! It is now a huge hit!!

No. 12 *Yellow Hit* Eiji Nizuma
This was supposed to become Eiji Nizuma's first series... but was not used due to protestation by the artist!!

No. 13 *Demon Dragon Legend* (working title) Muto Ashirogi
Muto Ashirogi's attempt at mainstream manga, a story in which the hero fights against demon dragons!!

No. 14 *Saint Visual Girls' High School* ?
A series running in *Young Three*. It became a late-night anime where Azuki made her debut as a voice actress!!

No. 15 *Angel Days* Muto Ashirogi
The tentative title was *My Angel*. The storyboard was turned into the Gold Future Cup but it didn't even make it into *Akamaru*.

No. 16 *Diligent Delinquent* Shinta Fukuda
A manga about a bad kid. It went up against *The World is All About Money and Intelligence* in *Akamaru* and lost.

No. 17 *Overconfidence Hero Super-Confidence Man* Moritaka Mashiro
A "stupid" piece of work that Moritaka drew in his notebook back in elementary school.

No. 18 *The Shadiest Man In The World* Moritaka Mashiro
An old work by Moritaka in which people compete to see how shady they are. The Shady Detective appears in it.

No. 19 *Con-Detective Hikake* Moritaka Mashiro
The work *Trap* is based on. Moritaka's favorite character stars in it.

No. 20 *Invisible Detective Skeleton* Muto Ashirogi (Akito Takagi)
An idea for a detective story which Akito wrote while Moritaka was trying to create a detective manga.

No. 21 *Detective Trap* Muto Ashirogi
Muto Ashirogi's first series in *Jump*!! But it was put on hiatus just when it was starting to get popular...

No. 22 *Kiyoshi Knight* Shinta Fukuda
A manga about a delinquent that became serialized after tying for the Gold Future Cup.

No. 23 *hideout door* Ko Aoki, Takuro Nakai
A fantasy manga that competed against *Trap* for the Gold Future Cup and later at the serialization meeting.

No. 24 *Colorfusical* Koji Makaino
A piece of work that could not win the popularity of the everyday readers even though it entered the Gold Future Cup.

No. 25 *Tank Top* ---- Orihara
Uchida is the editor. It was submitted to a serialization meeting but the editors decided to send it back for revision.

No. 26 *Cheese Crackers* ---- Arai
A series that started at the same time as *Trap*. Nicknamed "Chee-Crack." But it was soon canceled...

No. 27 *Otter No. 11* Kazuya Hiramaru
A striking work starring a humanoid otter. It turned out to be popular and became Ashirogi's rival.

No. 28 *Taracone* ----
Supposedly Hattori is the editor for this and *One Piece*...

No. 29 *+β [Plus Beta]* ---- Ibaraki
A series that started at the same time as Ashirogi and Hiramaru's series. The first chapter was ranked at 5th place.

No. 30 *Chain gold* ---- Takano
Brought to an end at the same serialization meeting as *Chee-Crack* when the editors decided to make Fukuda's work into a series.

BONUS *A Love Apart* Kaya Miyoshi
The pretty popular(?) cell-phone novel Miyoshi wrote. Akito helped a lot on it.

Maybe this will influence the direction of the manga?! We're waiting for realistic comments from our readers!!

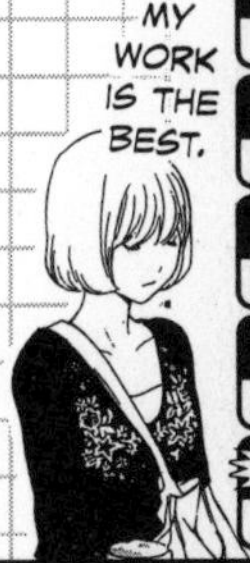

MY WORK IS THE BEST.

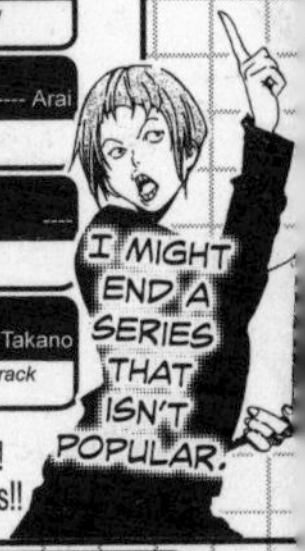

I MIGHT END A SERIES THAT ISN'T POPULAR.

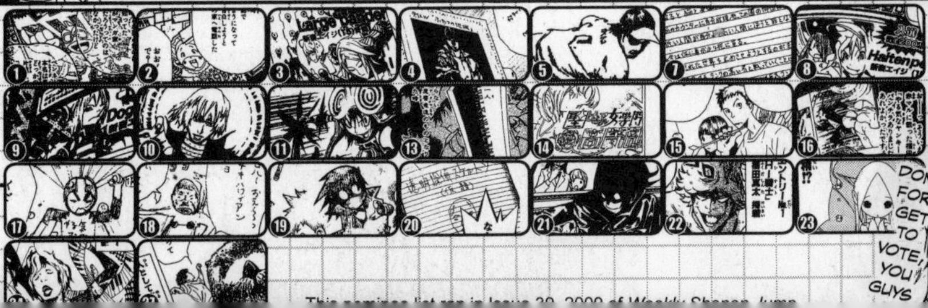

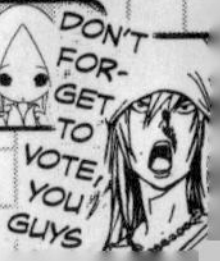

DON'T FORGET TO VOTE, YOU GUYS

This nominee list ran in issue 30, 2009 of *Weekly Shonen Jump*.

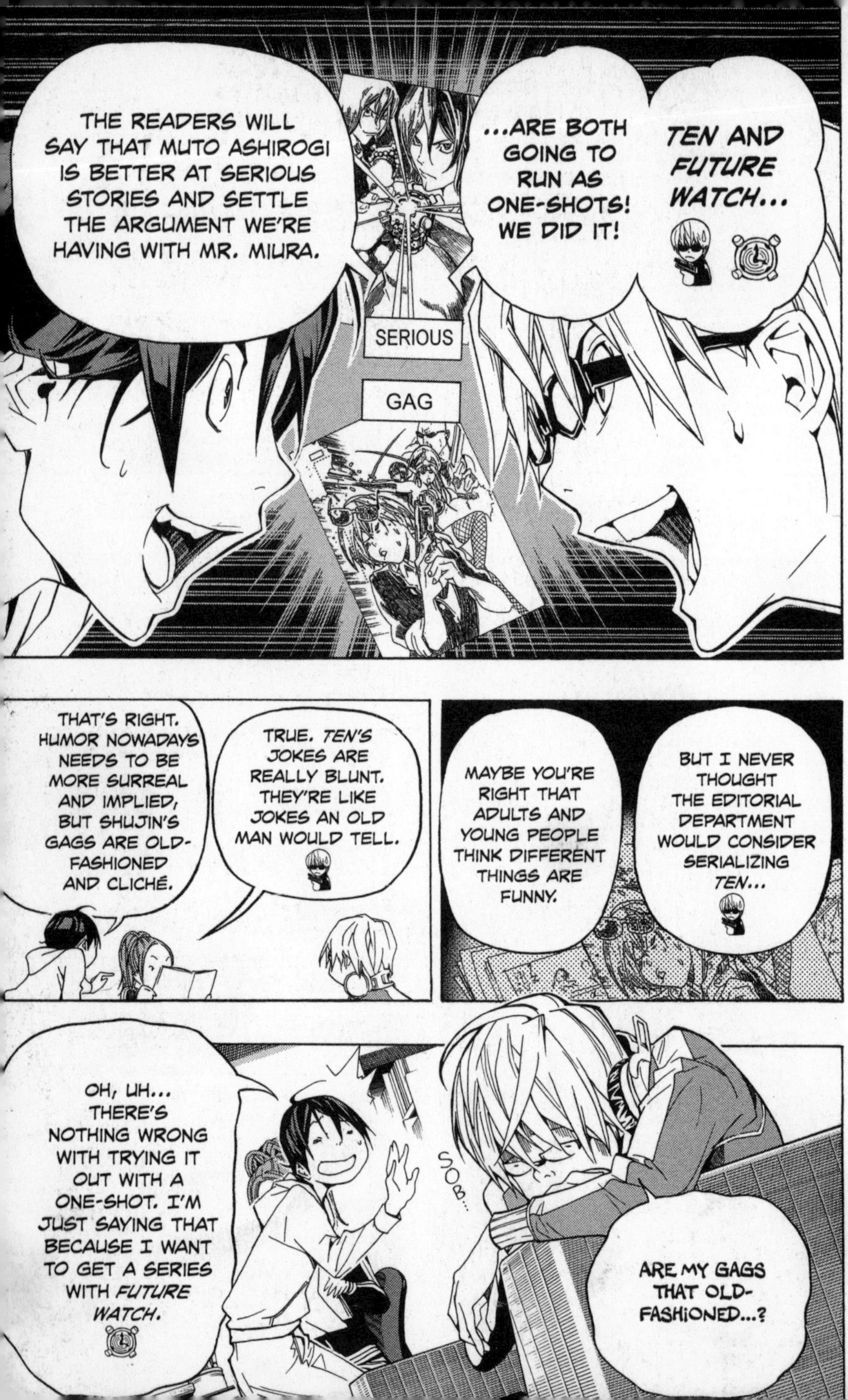
TEN AND FUTURE WATCH...
...ARE BOTH GOING TO RUN AS ONE-SHOTS! WE DID IT!
THE READERS WILL SAY THAT MUTO ASHIROGI IS BETTER AT SERIOUS STORIES AND SETTLE THE ARGUMENT WE'RE HAVING WITH MR. MIURA.
SERIOUS
GAG
BUT I NEVER THOUGHT THE EDITORIAL DEPARTMENT WOULD CONSIDER SERIALIZING TEN...
MAYBE YOU'RE RIGHT THAT ADULTS AND YOUNG PEOPLE THINK DIFFERENT THINGS ARE FUNNY.
TRUE. TEN'S JOKES ARE REALLY BLUNT. THEY'RE LIKE JOKES AN OLD MAN WOULD TELL.
THAT'S RIGHT. HUMOR NOWADAYS NEEDS TO BE MORE SURREAL AND IMPLIED, BUT SHUJIN'S GAGS ARE OLD-FASHIONED AND CLICHÉ.
ARE MY GAGS THAT OLD-FASHIONED...?
SOB...
OH, UH... THERE'S NOTHING WRONG WITH TRYING IT OUT WITH A ONE-SHOT. I'M JUST SAYING THAT BECAUSE I WANT TO GET A SERIES WITH FUTURE WATCH.

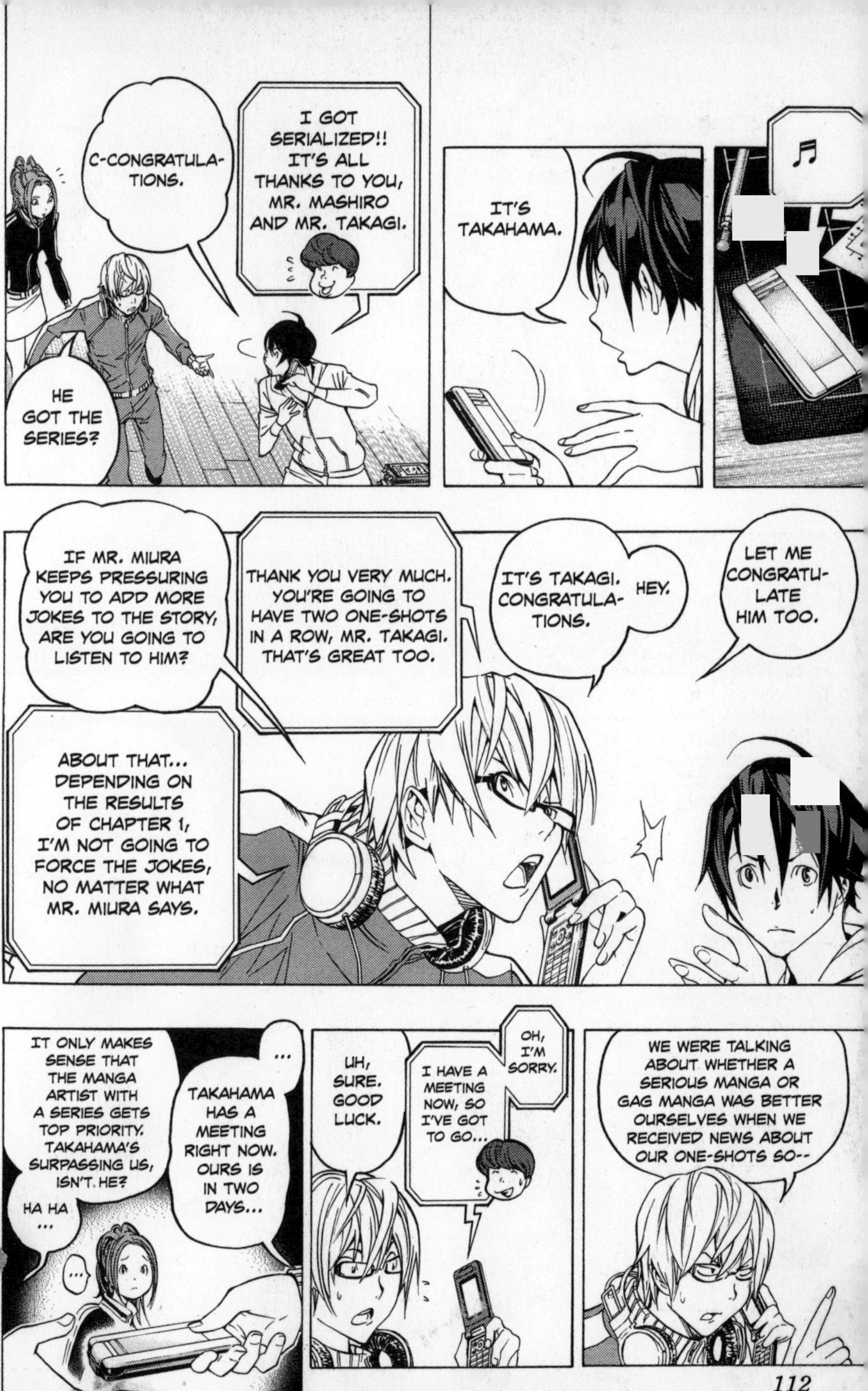
♪
IT'S TAKAHAMA.
I GOT SERIALIZED!! IT'S ALL THANKS TO YOU, MR. MASHIRO AND MR. TAKAGI.
C-CONGRATULA-TIONS.
HE GOT THE SERIES?
LET ME CONGRATU-LATE HIM TOO.
HEY.
IT'S TAKAGI. CONGRATULA-TIONS.
THANK YOU VERY MUCH. YOU'RE GOING TO HAVE TWO ONE-SHOTS IN A ROW, MR. TAKAGI. THAT'S GREAT TOO.
IF MR. MIURA KEEPS PRESSURING YOU TO ADD MORE JOKES TO THE STORY, ARE YOU GOING TO LISTEN TO HIM?
ABOUT THAT... DEPENDING ON THE RESULTS OF CHAPTER 1, I'M NOT GOING TO FORCE THE JOKES, NO MATTER WHAT MR. MIURA SAYS.
WE WERE TALKING ABOUT WHETHER A SERIOUS MANGA OR GAG MANGA WAS BETTER OURSELVES WHEN WE RECEIVED NEWS ABOUT OUR ONE-SHOTS SO--
OH, I'M SORRY.
I HAVE A MEETING NOW, SO I'VE GOT TO GO...
UH, SURE. GOOD LUCK.
...
TAKAHAMA HAS A MEETING RIGHT NOW. OURS IS IN TWO DAYS...
IT ONLY MAKES SENSE THAT THE MANGA ARTIST WITH A SERIES GETS TOP PRIORITY. TAKAHAMA'S SURPASSING US, ISN'T HE?
HA HA ...
...

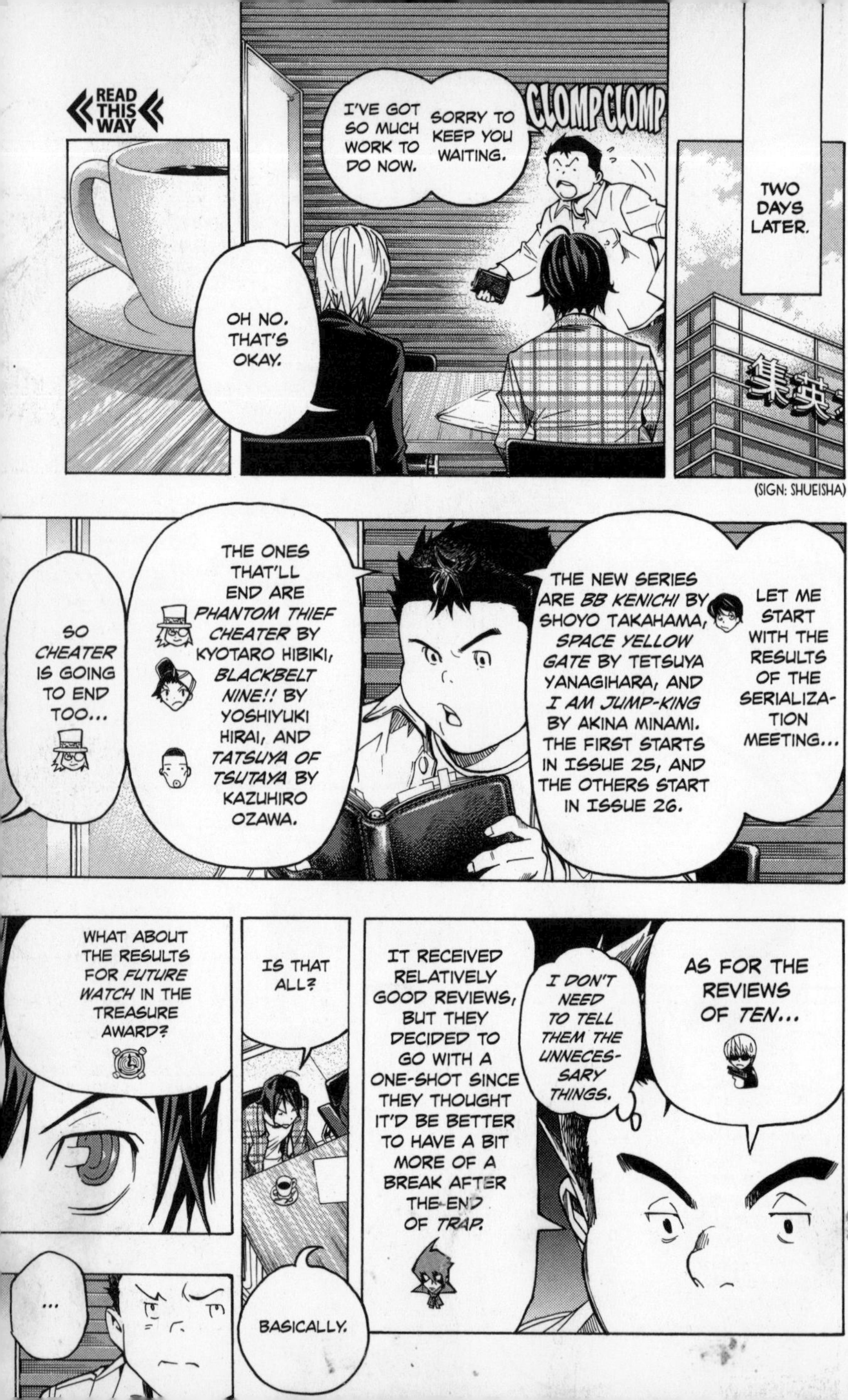
READ THIS WAY
TWO DAYS LATER.
(SIGN: SHUEISHA)
CLOMPCLOMP
SORRY TO KEEP YOU WAITING.
I'VE GOT SO MUCH WORK TO DO NOW.
OH NO. THAT'S OKAY.
LET ME START WITH THE RESULTS OF THE SERIALIZATION MEETING...
THE NEW SERIES ARE *BB KENICHI* BY SHOYO TAKAHAMA, *SPACE YELLOW GATE* BY TETSUYA YANAGIHARA, AND *I AM JUMP-KING* BY AKINA MINAMI. THE FIRST STARTS IN ISSUE 25, AND THE OTHERS START IN ISSUE 26.
THE ONES THAT'LL END ARE *PHANTOM THIEF CHEATER* BY KYOTARO HIBIKI, *BLACKBELT NINE!!* BY YOSHIYUKI HIRAI, AND *TATSUYA OF TSUTAYA* BY KAZUHIRO OZAWA.
SO *CHEATER* IS GOING TO END TOO...
AS FOR THE REVIEWS OF *TEN*...
I DON'T NEED TO TELL THEM THE UNNECESSARY THINGS.
IT RECEIVED RELATIVELY GOOD REVIEWS, BUT THEY DECIDED TO GO WITH A ONE-SHOT SINCE THEY THOUGHT IT'D BE BETTER TO HAVE A BIT MORE OF A BREAK AFTER THE END OF *TRAP*.
IS THAT ALL?
BASICALLY.
WHAT ABOUT THE RESULTS FOR *FUTURE WATCH* IN THE TREASURE AWARD?
...

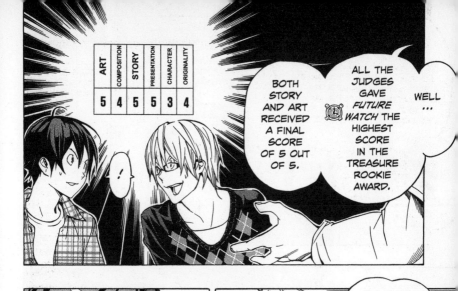

ART	COMPOSITION	STORY	PRESENTATION	CHARACTER	ORIGINALITY
5	4	5	5	3	4

WELL...

ALL THE JUDGES GAVE *FUTURE WATCH* THE HIGHEST SCORE IN THE TREASURE ROOKIE AWARD.

BOTH STORY AND ART RECEIVED A FINAL SCORE OF 5 OUT OF 5.

NOT THE CHARACTERS...

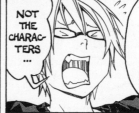

BUT IT RECEIVED 3 OUT OF 5 FOR THE CHARACTERS. THAT'S YOUR WEAKNESS.

RIGHT...

BUT YOU SHOULD EXPECT NOTHING LESS IN COMPARISON TO A BUNCH OF ROOKIES.

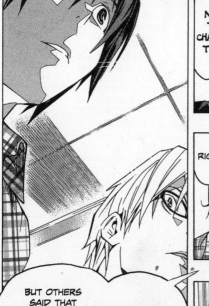

BUT OTHERS SAID THAT *FUTURE WATCH* WOULD BE BETTER THAN *TEN* AND THAT'S WHY THE EDITOR IN CHIEF DECIDED TO TRY BOTH OF THEM AS ONE-SHOTS.

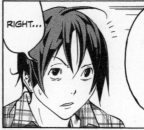

THERE WERE PEOPLE WHO SAID *TEN* SHOULD BE MADE INTO A SERIES.

?!

I MIGHT AS WELL TELL YOU EVERYTHING.

...

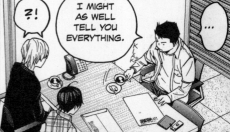

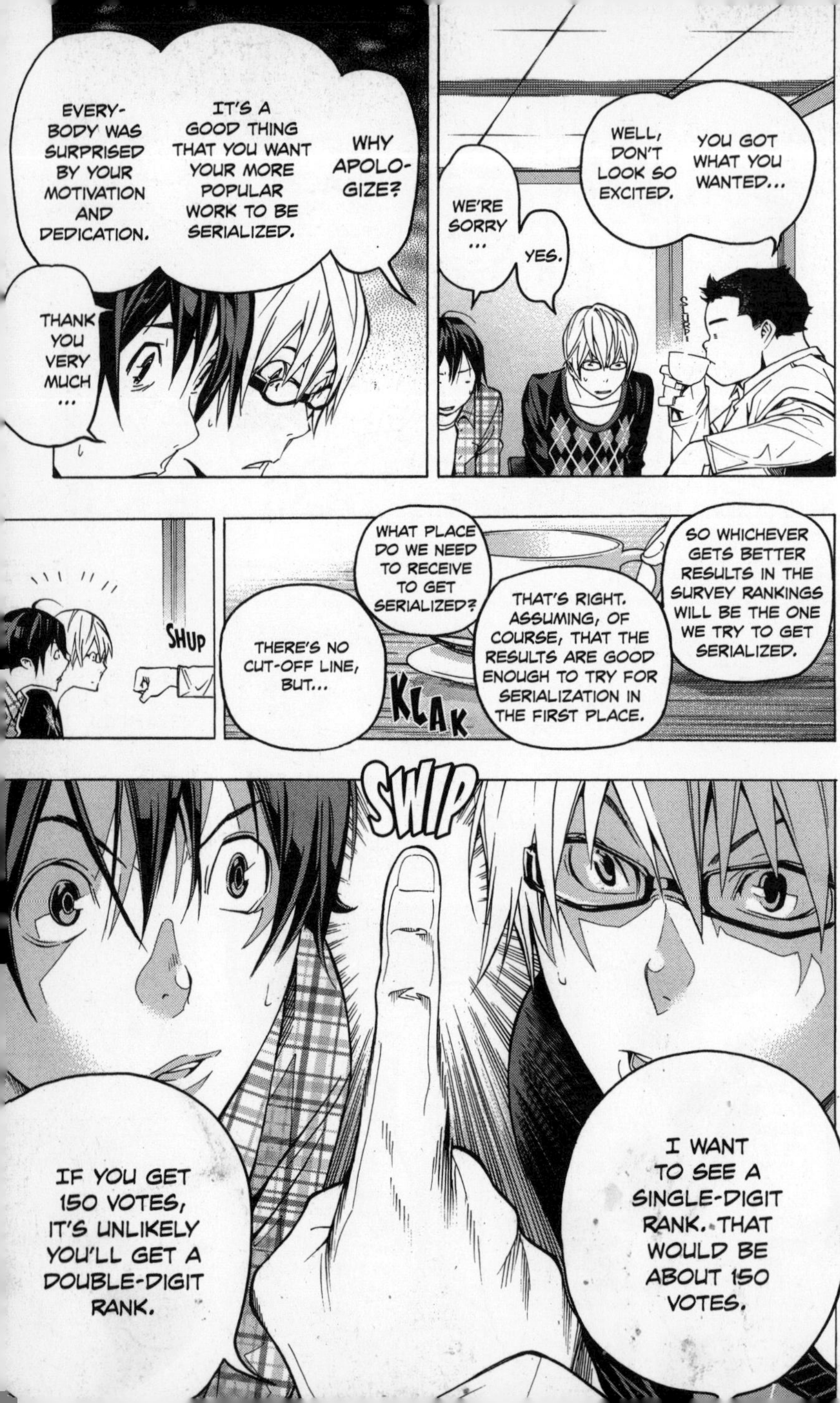
YOU GOT WHAT YOU WANTED...
WELL, DON'T LOOK SO EXCITED.
YES.
WE'RE SORRY...
WHY APOLOGIZE?
IT'S A GOOD THING THAT YOU WANT YOUR MORE POPULAR WORK TO BE SERIALIZED.
EVERYBODY WAS SURPRISED BY YOUR MOTIVATION AND DEDICATION.
THANK YOU VERY MUCH...
SO WHICHEVER GETS BETTER RESULTS IN THE SURVEY RANKINGS WILL BE THE ONE WE TRY TO GET SERIALIZED.
THAT'S RIGHT. ASSUMING, OF COURSE, THAT THE RESULTS ARE GOOD ENOUGH TO TRY FOR SERIALIZATION IN THE FIRST PLACE.
WHAT PLACE DO WE NEED TO RECEIVE TO GET SERIALIZED?
KLAK
THERE'S NO CUT-OFF LINE, BUT...
SHUP
SWIP
I WANT TO SEE A SINGLE-DIGIT RANK. THAT WOULD BE ABOUT 150 VOTES.
IF YOU GET 150 VOTES, IT'S UNLIKELY YOU'LL GET A DOUBLE-DIGIT RANK.

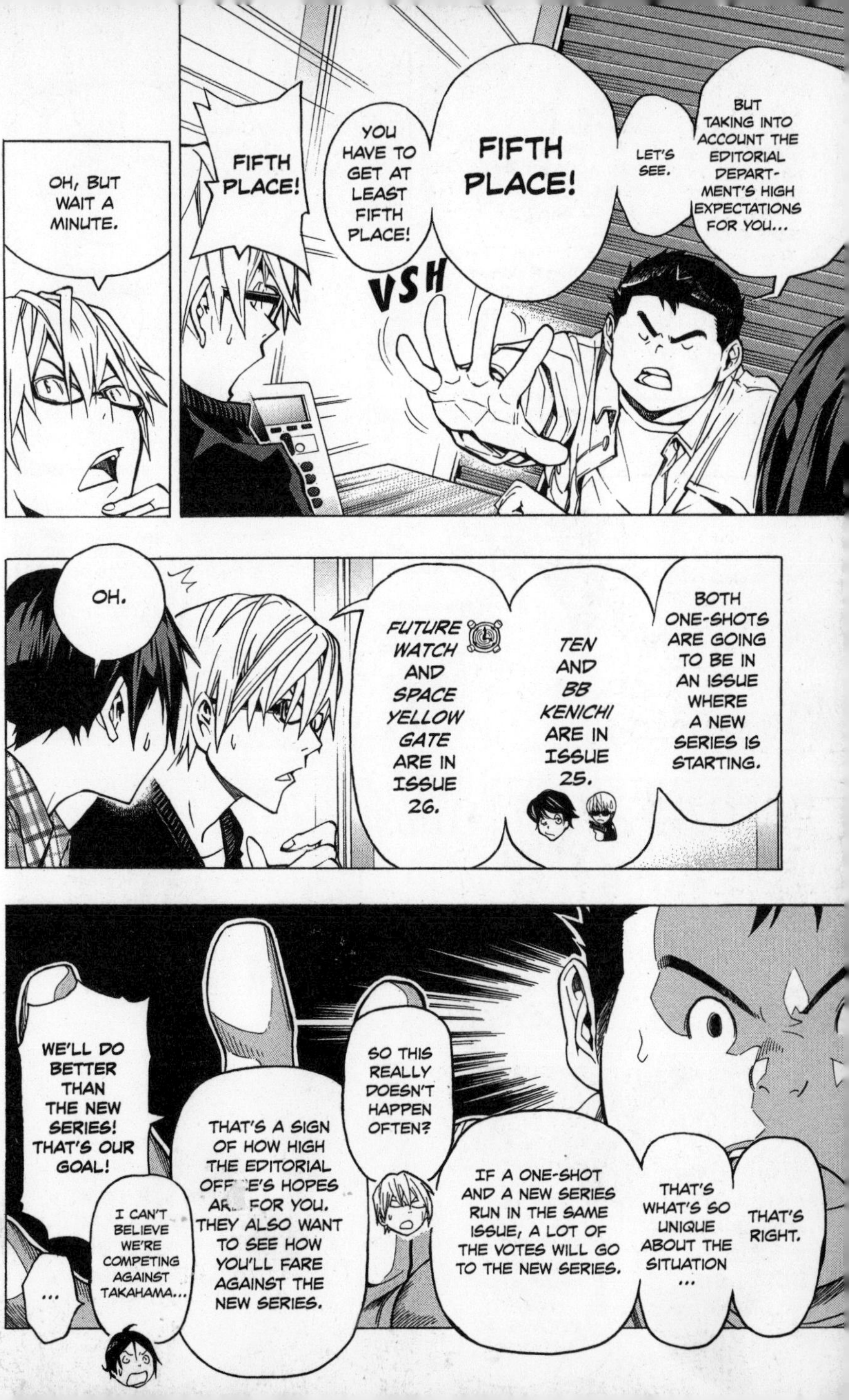
BUT TAKING INTO ACCOUNT THE EDITORIAL DEPARTMENT'S HIGH EXPECTATIONS FOR YOU...
LET'S SEE.
FIFTH PLACE!
YOU HAVE TO GET AT LEAST FIFTH PLACE!
VSH
FIFTH PLACE!
OH, BUT WAIT A MINUTE.
BOTH ONE-SHOTS ARE GOING TO BE IN AN ISSUE WHERE A NEW SERIES IS STARTING.
TEN AND BB KENICHI ARE IN ISSUE 25.
FUTURE WATCH AND SPACE YELLOW GATE ARE IN ISSUE 26.
OH.
THAT'S RIGHT.
THAT'S WHAT'S SO UNIQUE ABOUT THE SITUATION ...
IF A ONE-SHOT AND A NEW SERIES RUN IN THE SAME ISSUE, A LOT OF THE VOTES WILL GO TO THE NEW SERIES.
SO THIS REALLY DOESN'T HAPPEN OFTEN?
THAT'S A SIGN OF HOW HIGH THE EDITORIAL OFFICE'S HOPES ARE FOR YOU. THEY ALSO WANT TO SEE HOW YOU'LL FARE AGAINST THE NEW SERIES.
WE'LL DO BETTER THAN THE NEW SERIES! THAT'S OUR GOAL!
I CAN'T BELIEVE WE'RE COMPETING AGAINST TAKAHAMA...
...

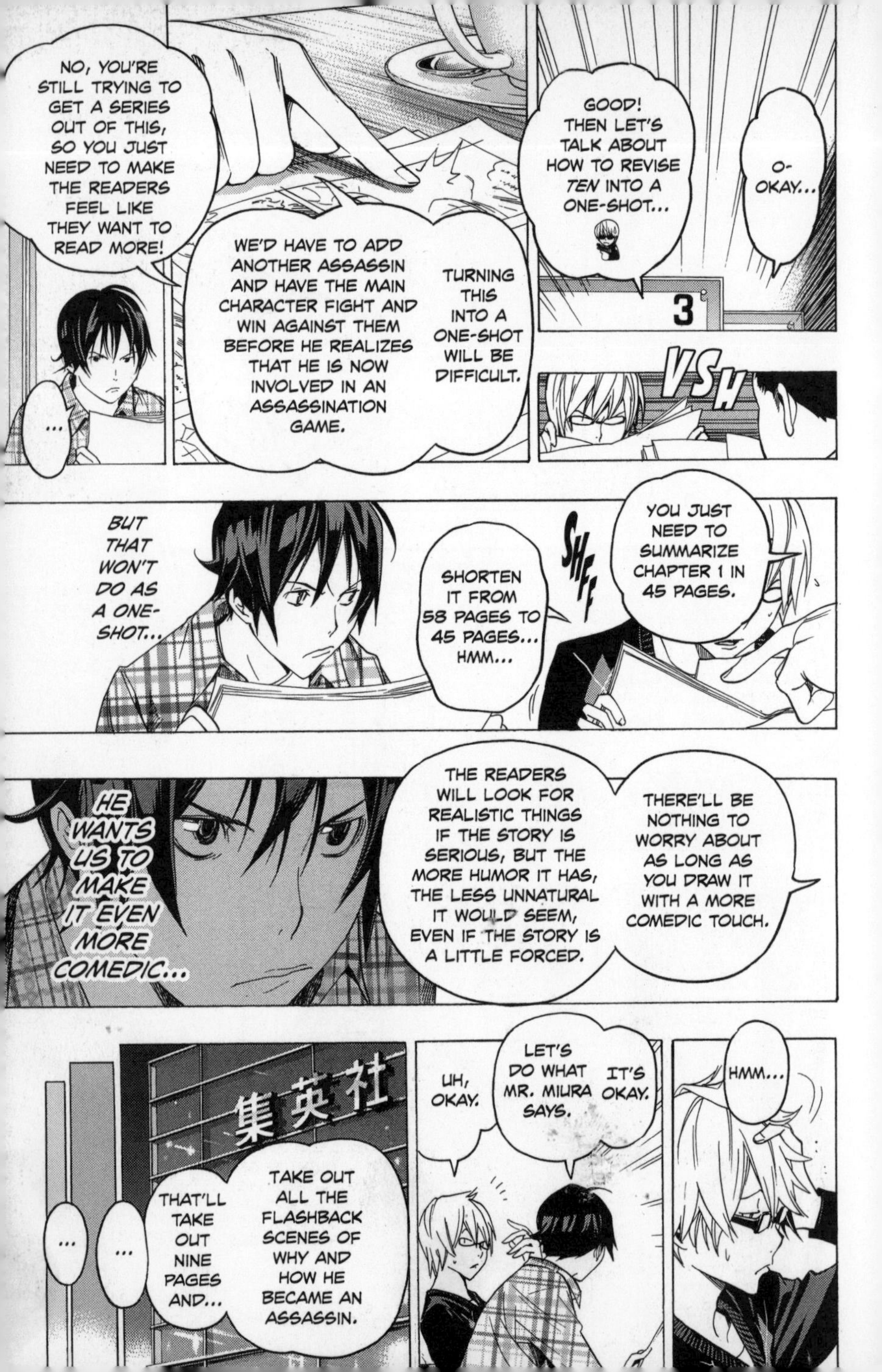
GOOD! THEN LET'S TALK ABOUT HOW TO REVISE *TEN* INTO A ONE-SHOT...
O-OKAY...
3
VSH
TURNING THIS INTO A ONE-SHOT WILL BE DIFFICULT.
WE'D HAVE TO ADD ANOTHER ASSASSIN AND HAVE THE MAIN CHARACTER FIGHT AND WIN AGAINST THEM BEFORE HE REALIZES THAT HE IS NOW INVOLVED IN AN ASSASSINATION GAME.
NO, YOU'RE STILL TRYING TO GET A SERIES OUT OF THIS, SO YOU JUST NEED TO MAKE THE READERS FEEL LIKE THEY WANT TO READ MORE!
...
YOU JUST NEED TO SUMMARIZE CHAPTER 1 IN 45 PAGES.
SHFF
SHORTEN IT FROM 58 PAGES TO 45 PAGES... HMM...
BUT THAT WON'T DO AS A ONE-SHOT...
THERE'LL BE NOTHING TO WORRY ABOUT AS LONG AS YOU DRAW IT WITH A MORE COMEDIC TOUCH.
THE READERS WILL LOOK FOR REALISTIC THINGS IF THE STORY IS SERIOUS, BUT THE MORE HUMOR IT HAS, THE LESS UNNATURAL IT WOULD SEEM, EVEN IF THE STORY IS A LITTLE FORCED.
HE WANTS US TO MAKE IT EVEN MORE COMEDIC...
HMM...
IT'S OKAY.
LET'S DO WHAT MR. MIURA SAYS.
UH, OKAY.
集英社
TAKE OUT ALL THE FLASHBACK SCENES OF WHY AND HOW HE BECAME AN ASSASSIN.
THAT'LL TAKE OUT NINE PAGES AND...
...
...

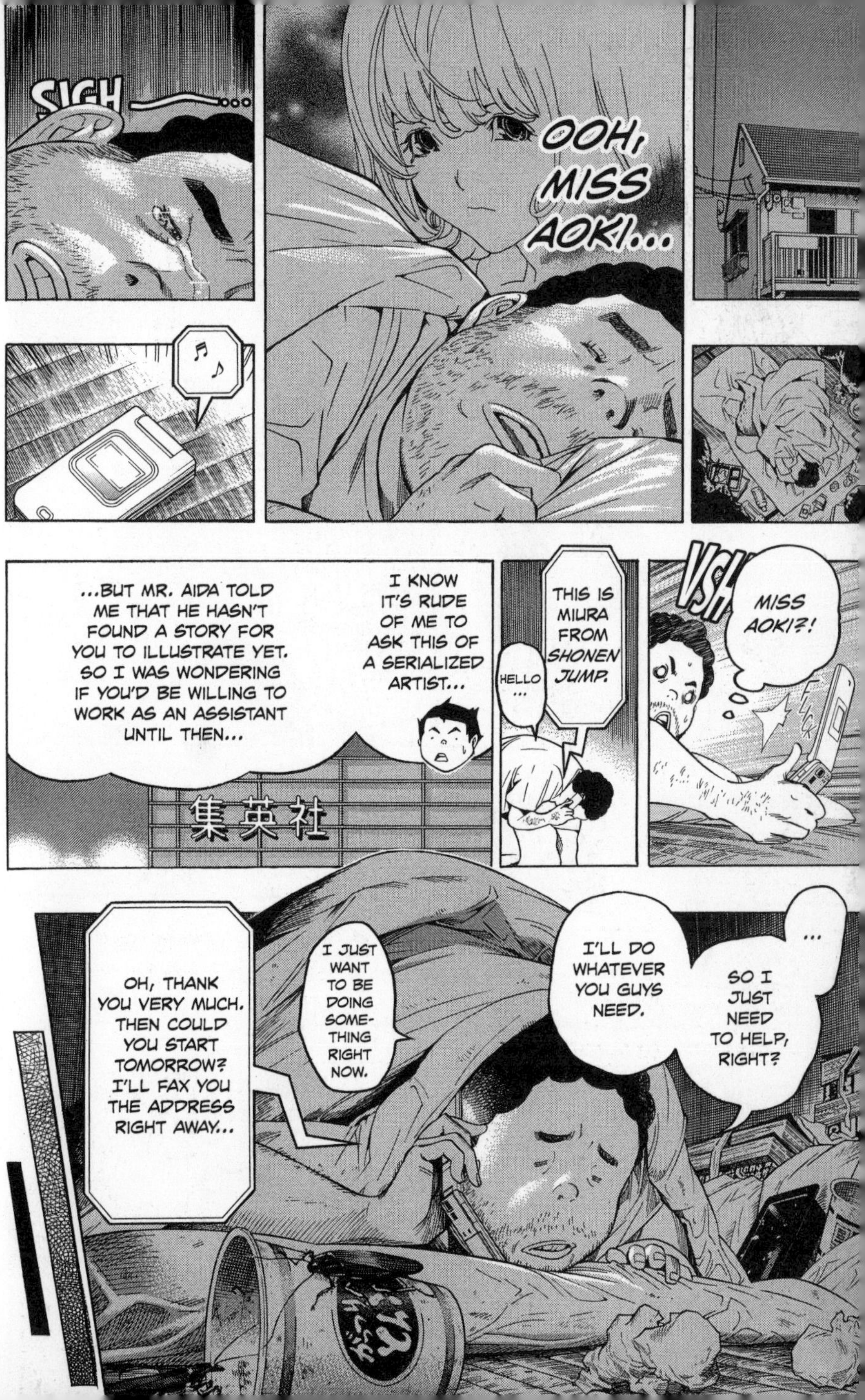
OOH, MISS AOKI...
SIGH—...
♪ ♪
VSH
MISS AOKI?!
FLICK
THIS IS MIURA FROM SHONEN JUMP.
HELLO...
I KNOW IT'S RUDE OF ME TO ASK THIS OF A SERIALIZED ARTIST...
...BUT MR. AIDA TOLD ME THAT HE HASN'T FOUND A STORY FOR YOU TO ILLUSTRATE YET. SO I WAS WONDERING IF YOU'D BE WILLING TO WORK AS AN ASSISTANT UNTIL THEN...
集英社
...
SO I JUST NEED TO HELP, RIGHT?
I'LL DO WHATEVER YOU GUYS NEED.
I JUST WANT TO BE DOING SOME-THING RIGHT NOW.
OH, THANK YOU VERY MUCH. THEN COULD YOU START TOMORROW? I'LL FAX YOU THE ADDRESS RIGHT AWAY...

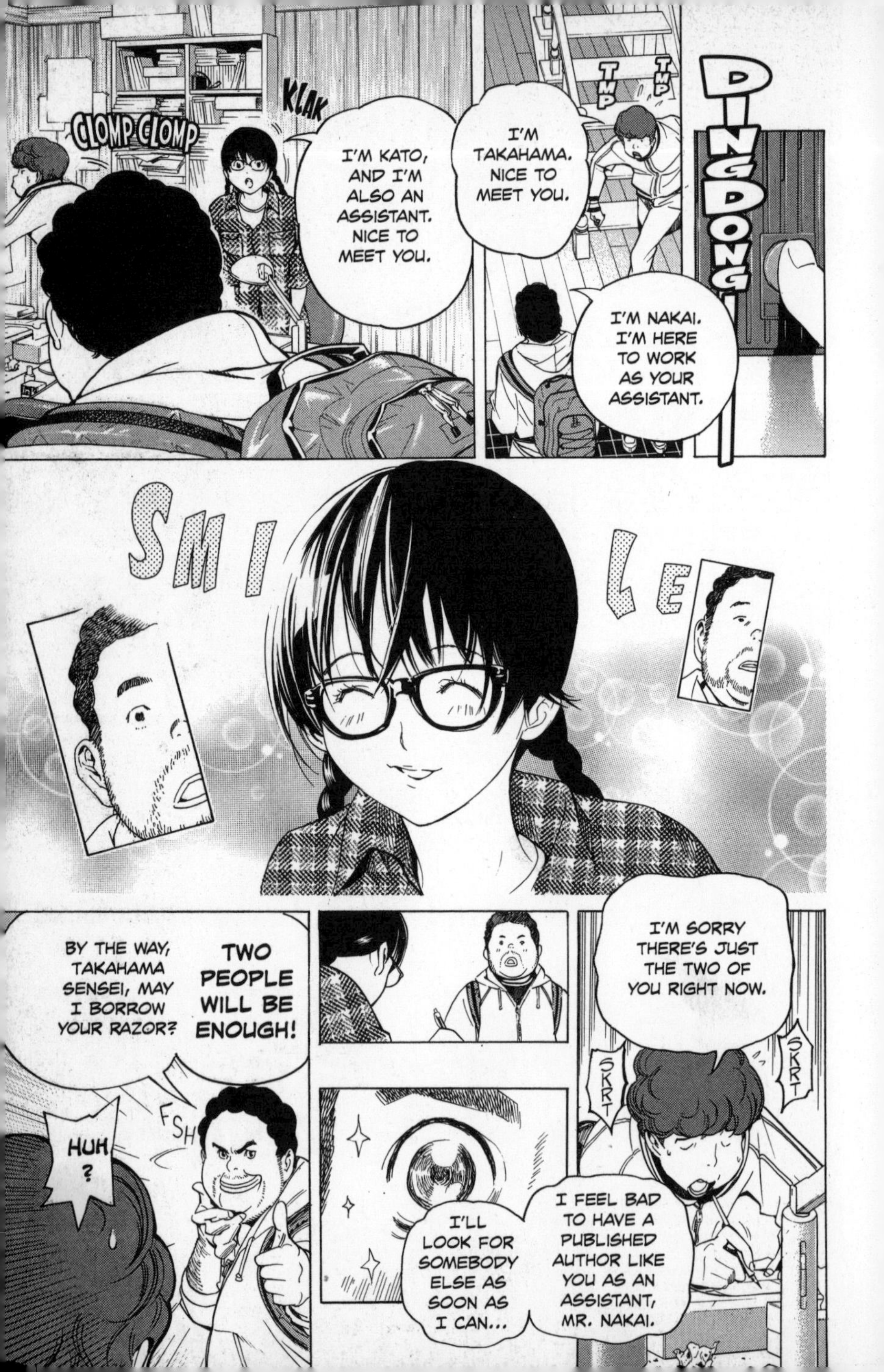
DINGDONG
TMP TMP
I'M TAKAHAMA. NICE TO MEET YOU.
I'M NAKAI. I'M HERE TO WORK AS YOUR ASSISTANT.
KLAK
I'M KATO, AND I'M ALSO AN ASSISTANT. NICE TO MEET YOU.
CLOMP CLOMP
SMILE
I'M SORRY THERE'S JUST THE TWO OF YOU RIGHT NOW.
SKRT
SKRT
I FEEL BAD TO HAVE A PUBLISHED AUTHOR LIKE YOU AS AN ASSISTANT, MR. NAKAI.
I'LL LOOK FOR SOMEBODY ELSE AS SOON AS I CAN...
TWO PEOPLE WILL BE ENOUGH!
BY THE WAY, TAKAHAMA SENSEI, MAY I BORROW YOUR RAZOR?
FSH
HUH?

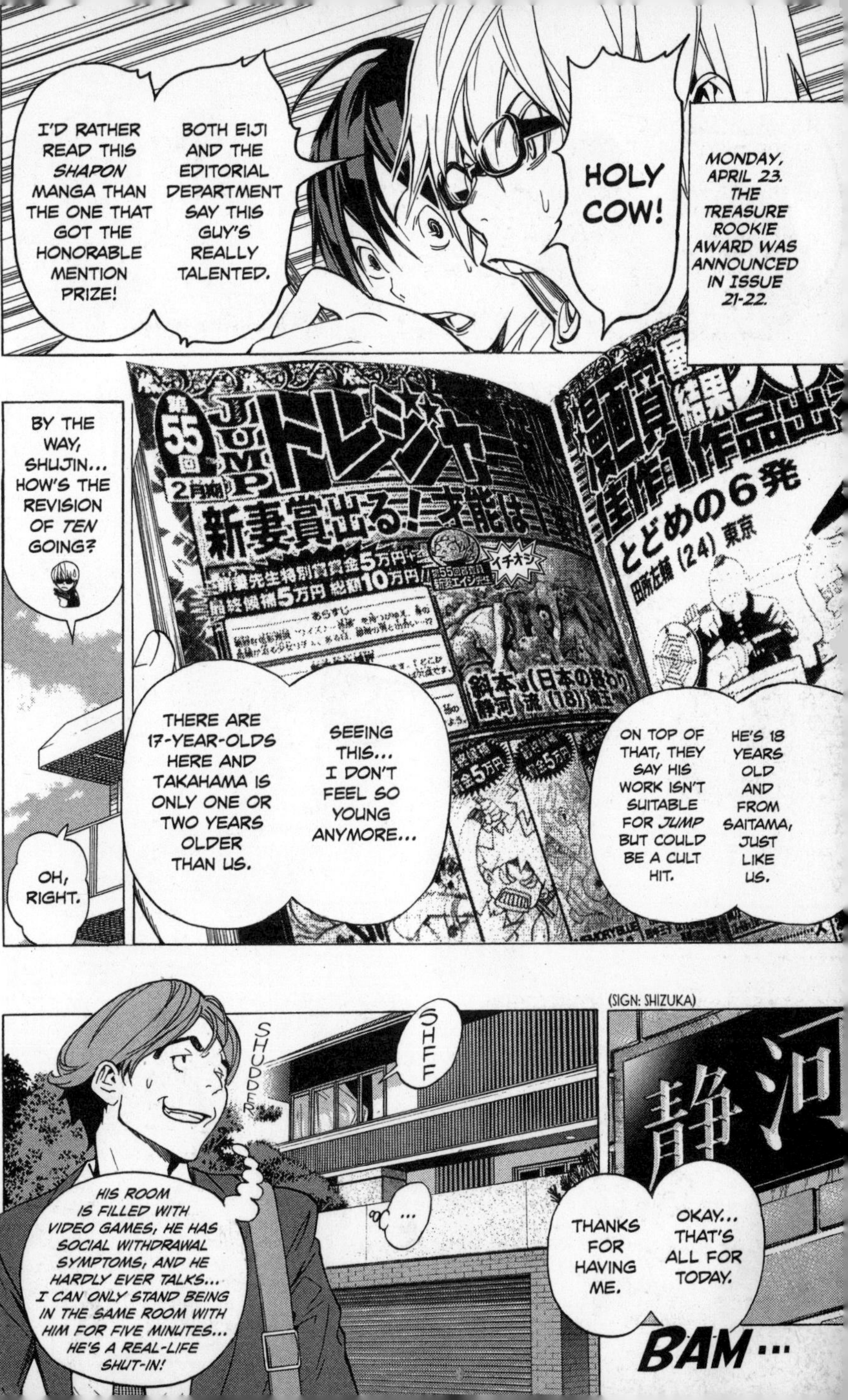
MONDAY, APRIL 23. THE TREASURE ROOKIE AWARD WAS ANNOUNCED IN ISSUE 21-22.
HOLY COW!
BOTH EIJI AND THE EDITORIAL DEPARTMENT SAY THIS GUY'S REALLY TALENTED.
I'D RATHER READ THIS *SHAPON* MANGA THAN THE ONE THAT GOT THE HONORABLE MENTION PRIZE!
トレジャー
新妻賞出る！
とどめの6発
HE'S 18 YEARS OLD AND FROM SAITAMA, JUST LIKE US.
ON TOP OF THAT, THEY SAY HIS WORK ISN'T SUITABLE FOR *JUMP* BUT COULD BE A CULT HIT.
SEEING THIS... I DON'T FEEL SO YOUNG ANYMORE...
THERE ARE 17-YEAR-OLDS HERE AND TAKAHAMA IS ONLY ONE OR TWO YEARS OLDER THAN US.
BY THE WAY, SHUJIN... HOW'S THE REVISION OF *TEN* GOING?
OH, RIGHT.
(SIGN: SHIZUKA)
静河
BAM...
OKAY... THAT'S ALL FOR TODAY.
THANKS FOR HAVING ME.
...
SHFF
SHUDDER
HIS ROOM IS FILLED WITH VIDEO GAMES, HE HAS SOCIAL WITHDRAWAL SYMPTOMS, AND HE HARDLY EVER TALKS... I CAN ONLY STAND BEING IN THE SAME ROOM WITH HIM FOR FIVE MINUTES... HE'S A REAL-LIFE SHUT-IN!

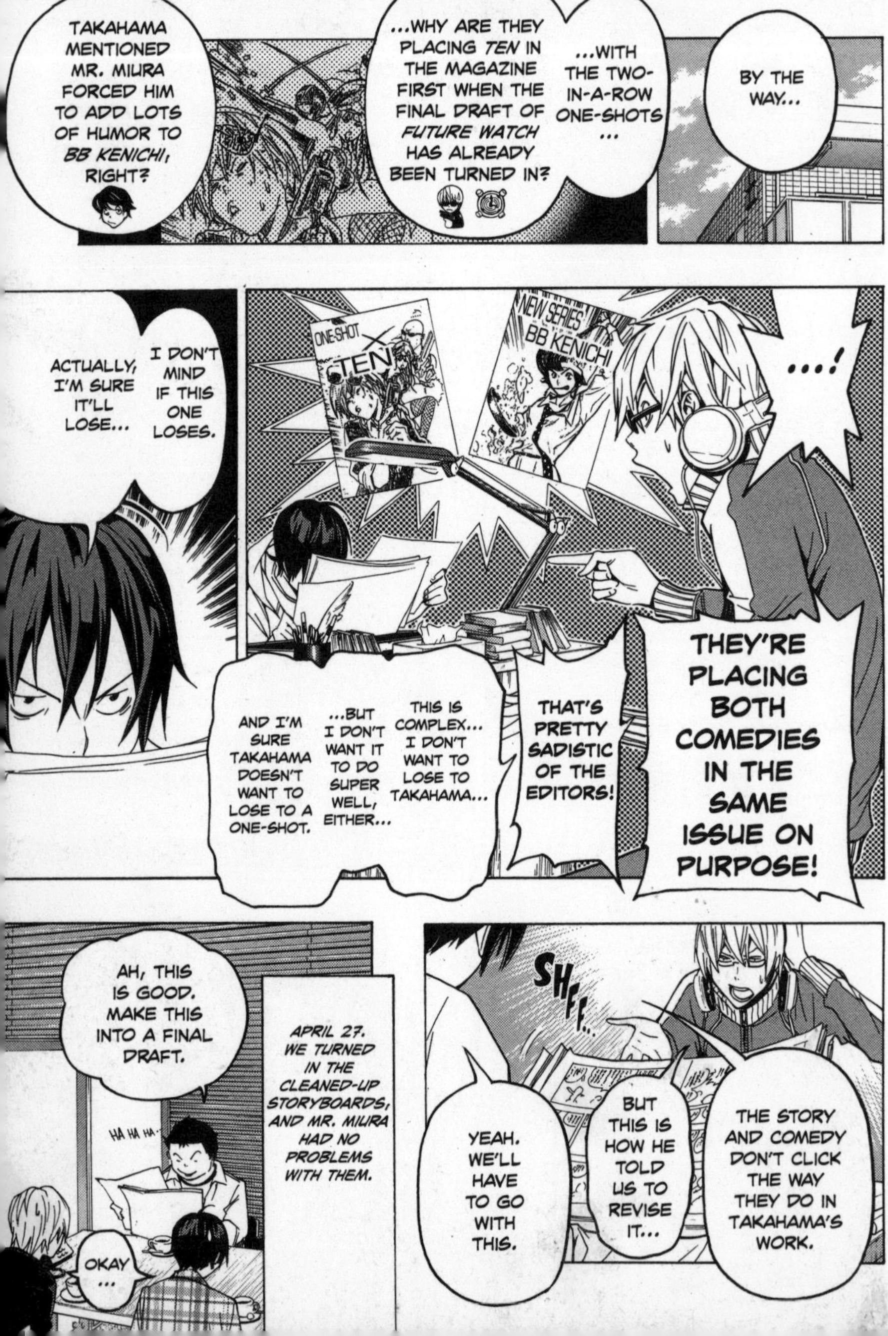
BY THE WAY...
...WITH THE TWO-IN-A-ROW ONE-SHOTS...
...WHY ARE THEY PLACING *TEN* IN THE MAGAZINE FIRST WHEN THE FINAL DRAFT OF *FUTURE WATCH* HAS ALREADY BEEN TURNED IN?
TAKAHAMA MENTIONED MR. MIURA FORCED HIM TO ADD LOTS OF HUMOR TO *BB KENICHI*, RIGHT?
...!
NEW SERIES BB KENICHI
ONE-SHOT TEN
THEY'RE PLACING BOTH COMEDIES IN THE SAME ISSUE ON PURPOSE!
THAT'S PRETTY SADISTIC OF THE EDITORS!
THIS IS COMPLEX... I DON'T WANT TO LOSE TO TAKAHAMA...
...BUT I DON'T WANT IT TO DO SUPER WELL, EITHER...
AND I'M SURE TAKAHAMA DOESN'T WANT TO LOSE TO A ONE-SHOT.
I DON'T MIND IF THIS ONE LOSES.
ACTUALLY, I'M SURE IT'LL LOSE...
SHFF...
THE STORY AND COMEDY DON'T CLICK THE WAY THEY DO IN TAKAHAMA'S WORK.
BUT THIS IS HOW HE TOLD US TO REVISE IT...
YEAH. WE'LL HAVE TO GO WITH THIS.
APRIL 27. WE TURNED IN THE CLEANED-UP STORYBOARDS, AND MR. MIURA HAD NO PROBLEMS WITH THEM.
AH, THIS IS GOOD. MAKE THIS INTO A FINAL DRAFT.
HA HA HA
OKAY...

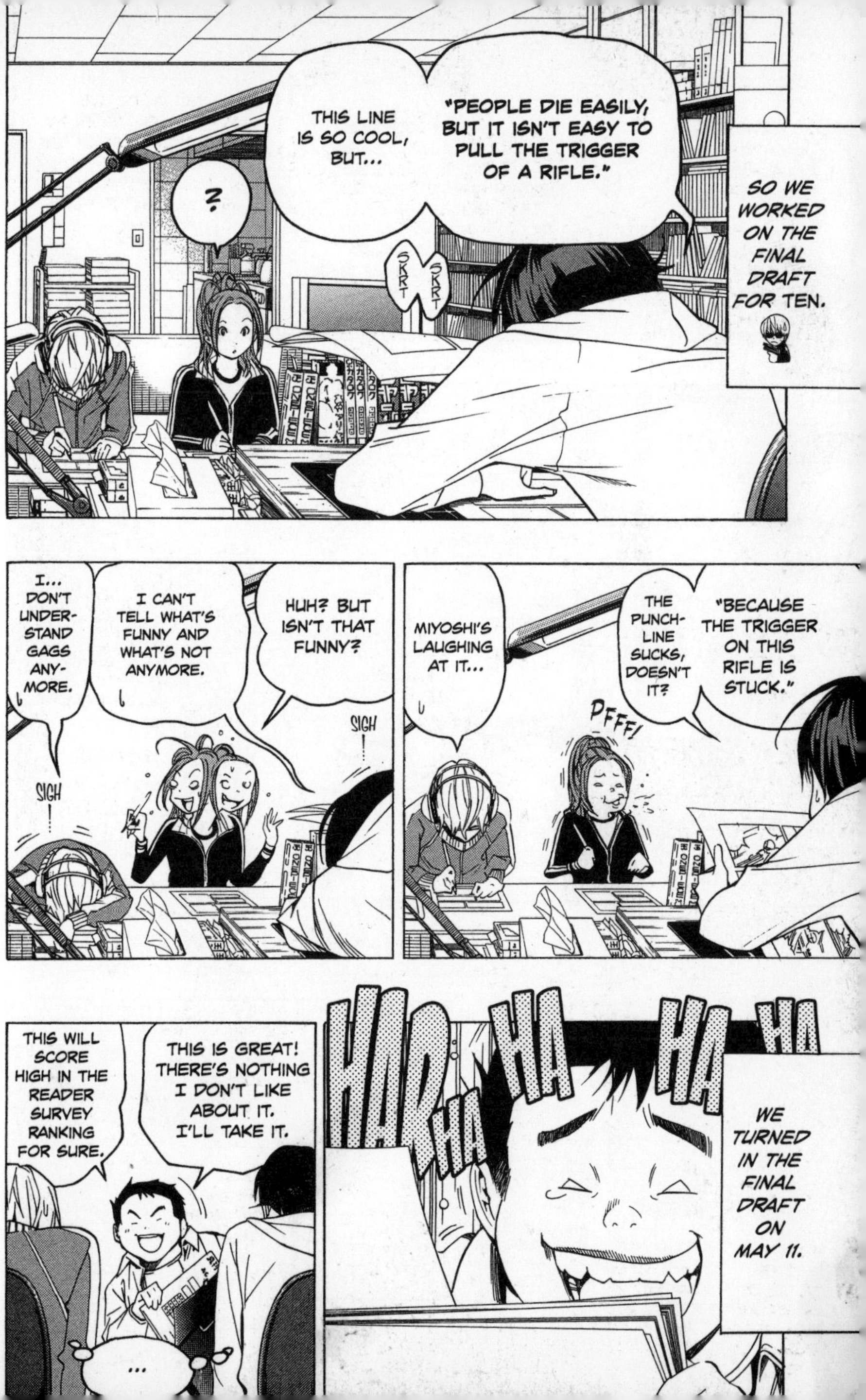
SO WE WORKED ON THE FINAL DRAFT FOR TEN.
"PEOPLE DIE EASILY, BUT IT ISN'T EASY TO PULL THE TRIGGER OF A RIFLE."
THIS LINE IS SO COOL, BUT...
?
SKRT SKRT
"BECAUSE THE TRIGGER ON THIS RIFLE IS STUCK."
THE PUNCHLINE SUCKS, DOESN'T IT?
PFFF!
MIYOSHI'S LAUGHING AT IT...
HUH? BUT ISN'T THAT FUNNY?
SIGH
I CAN'T TELL WHAT'S FUNNY AND WHAT'S NOT ANYMORE.
I... DON'T UNDERSTAND GAGS ANYMORE.
SIGH
WE TURNED IN THE FINAL DRAFT ON MAY 11.
HA HA HA HA HA HA
THIS IS GREAT! THERE'S NOTHING I DON'T LIKE ABOUT IT. I'LL TAKE IT.
THIS WILL SCORE HIGH IN THE READER SURVEY RANKING FOR SURE.
...

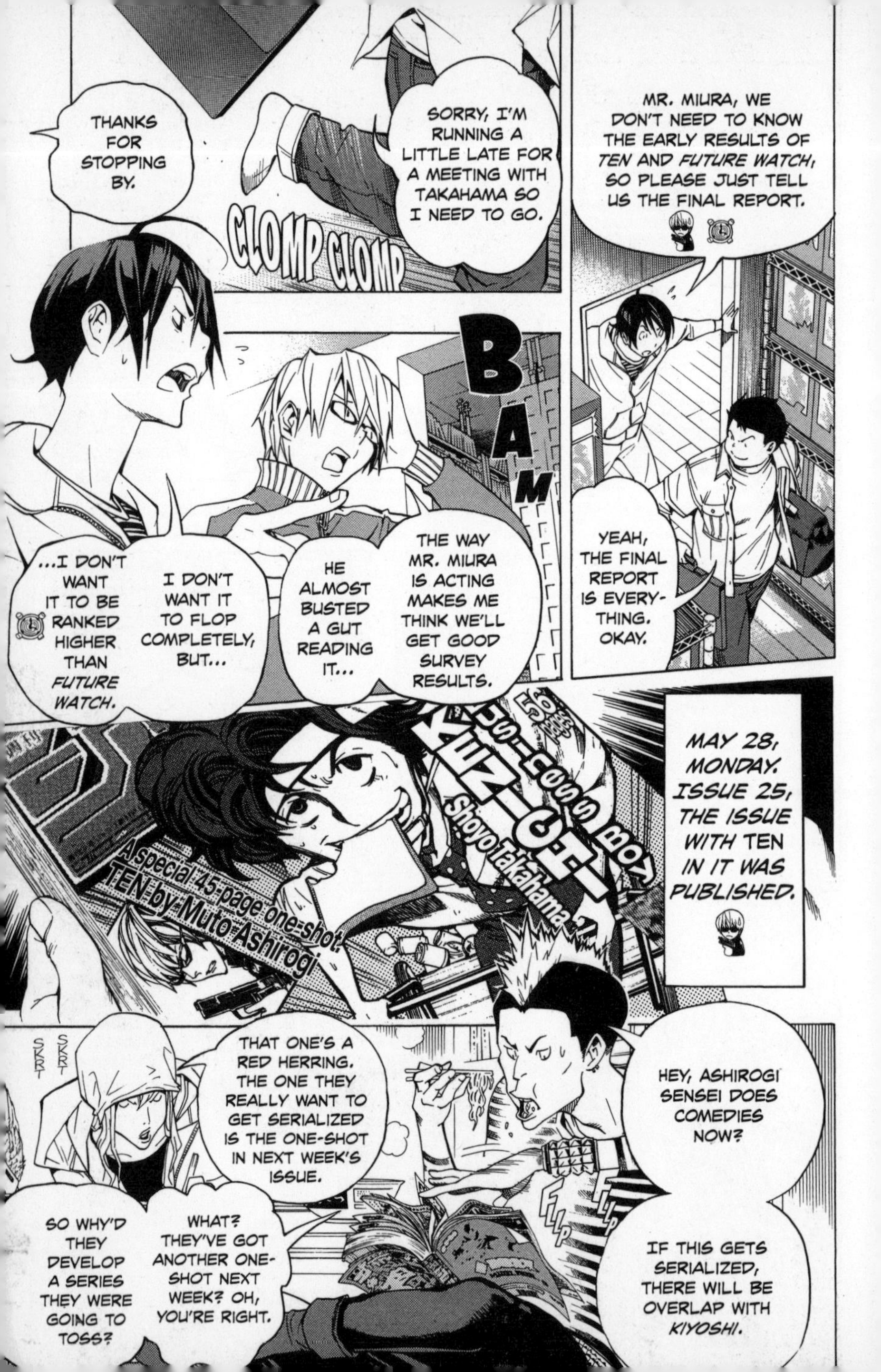
MR. MIURA, WE DON'T NEED TO KNOW THE EARLY RESULTS OF *TEN* AND *FUTURE WATCH*, SO PLEASE JUST TELL US THE FINAL REPORT.
YEAH, THE FINAL REPORT IS EVERYTHING. OKAY.
SORRY, I'M RUNNING A LITTLE LATE FOR A MEETING WITH TAKAHAMA SO I NEED TO GO.
CLOMP CLOMP
THANKS FOR STOPPING BY.
BAM
THE WAY MR. MIURA IS ACTING MAKES ME THINK WE'LL GET GOOD SURVEY RESULTS.
HE ALMOST BUSTED A GUT READING IT...
I DON'T WANT IT TO FLOP COMPLETELY, BUT...
...I DON'T WANT IT TO BE RANKED HIGHER THAN *FUTURE WATCH*.
MAY 28, MONDAY. ISSUE 25, THE ISSUE WITH TEN *IN IT WAS PUBLISHED.*
Shoyo Takahama
A special 45-page one-shot, TEN by Muto Ashirogi
HEY, ASHIROGI SENSEI DOES COMEDIES NOW?
THAT ONE'S A RED HERRING. THE ONE THEY REALLY WANT TO GET SERIALIZED IS THE ONE-SHOT IN NEXT WEEK'S ISSUE.
SKRT SKRT
FLIP FLIP
IF THIS GETS SERIALIZED, THERE WILL BE OVERLAP WITH *KIYOSHI*.
WHAT? THEY'VE GOT ANOTHER ONE-SHOT NEXT WEEK? OH, YOU'RE RIGHT.
SO WHY'D THEY DEVELOP A SERIES THEY WERE GOING TO TOSS?

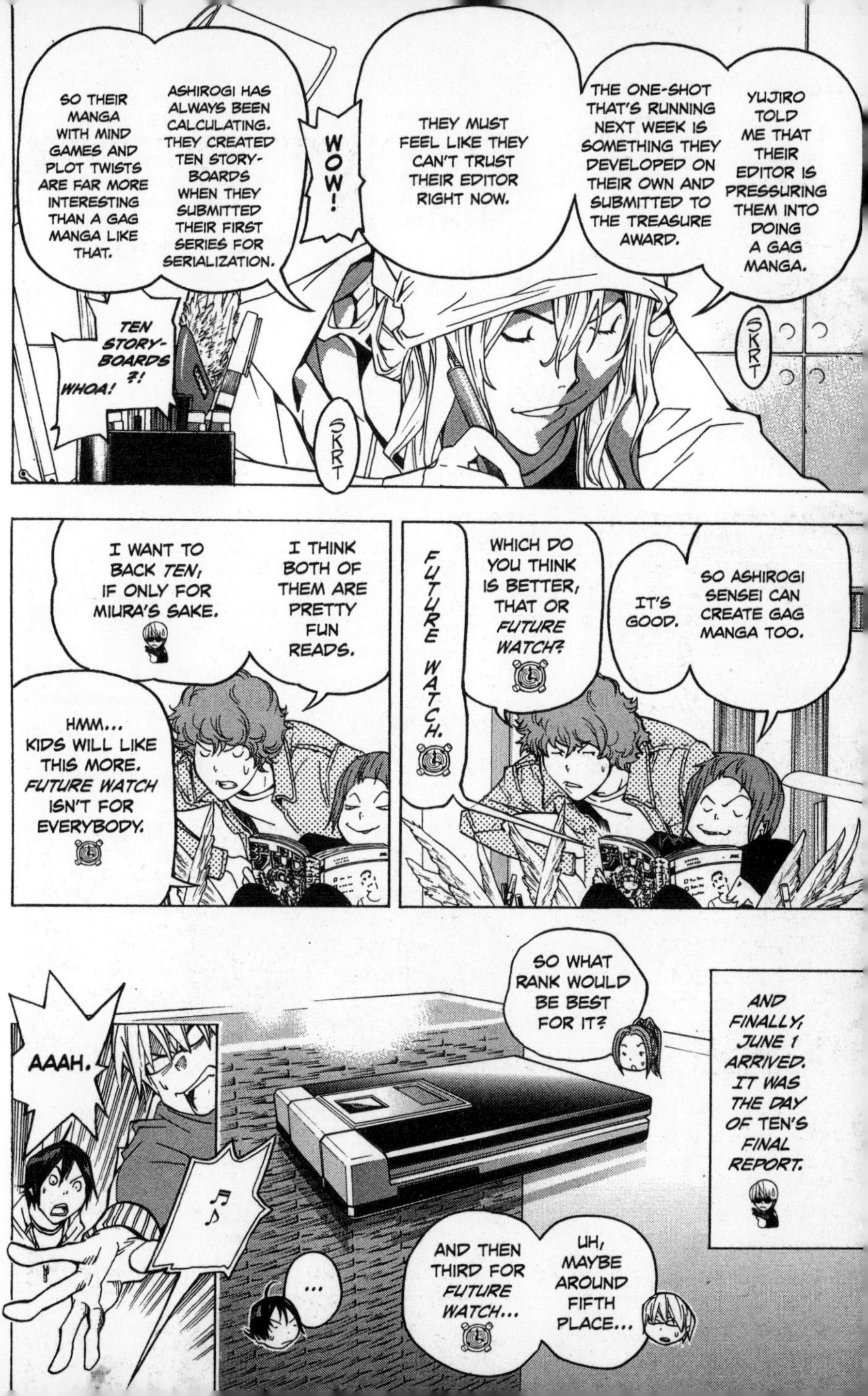
YUJIRO TOLD ME THAT THEIR EDITOR IS PRESSURING THEM INTO DOING A GAG MANGA.
THE ONE-SHOT THAT'S RUNNING NEXT WEEK IS SOMETHING THEY DEVELOPED ON THEIR OWN AND SUBMITTED TO THE TREASURE AWARD.
SKRT
THEY MUST FEEL LIKE THEY CAN'T TRUST THEIR EDITOR RIGHT NOW.
WOW!
ASHIROGI HAS ALWAYS BEEN CALCULATING. THEY CREATED TEN STORY-BOARDS WHEN THEY SUBMITTED THEIR FIRST SERIES FOR SERIALIZATION.
SO THEIR MANGA WITH MIND GAMES AND PLOT TWISTS ARE FAR MORE INTERESTING THAN A GAG MANGA LIKE THAT.
SKRT
TEN STORY-BOARDS?!
WHOA!
SO ASHIROGI SENSEI CAN CREATE GAG MANGA TOO.
IT'S GOOD.
WHICH DO YOU THINK IS BETTER, THAT OR *FUTURE WATCH*?
FUTURE WATCH.
I THINK BOTH OF THEM ARE PRETTY FUN READS.
I WANT TO BACK *TEN*, IF ONLY FOR MIURA'S SAKE.
HMM... KIDS WILL LIKE THIS MORE. *FUTURE WATCH* ISN'T FOR EVERYBODY.
AND FINALLY, JUNE 1 ARRIVED. IT WAS THE DAY OF TEN'S FINAL REPORT.
SO WHAT RANK WOULD BE BEST FOR IT?
UH, MAYBE AROUND FIFTH PLACE...
AND THEN THIRD FOR *FUTURE WATCH*...
...
AAAH.

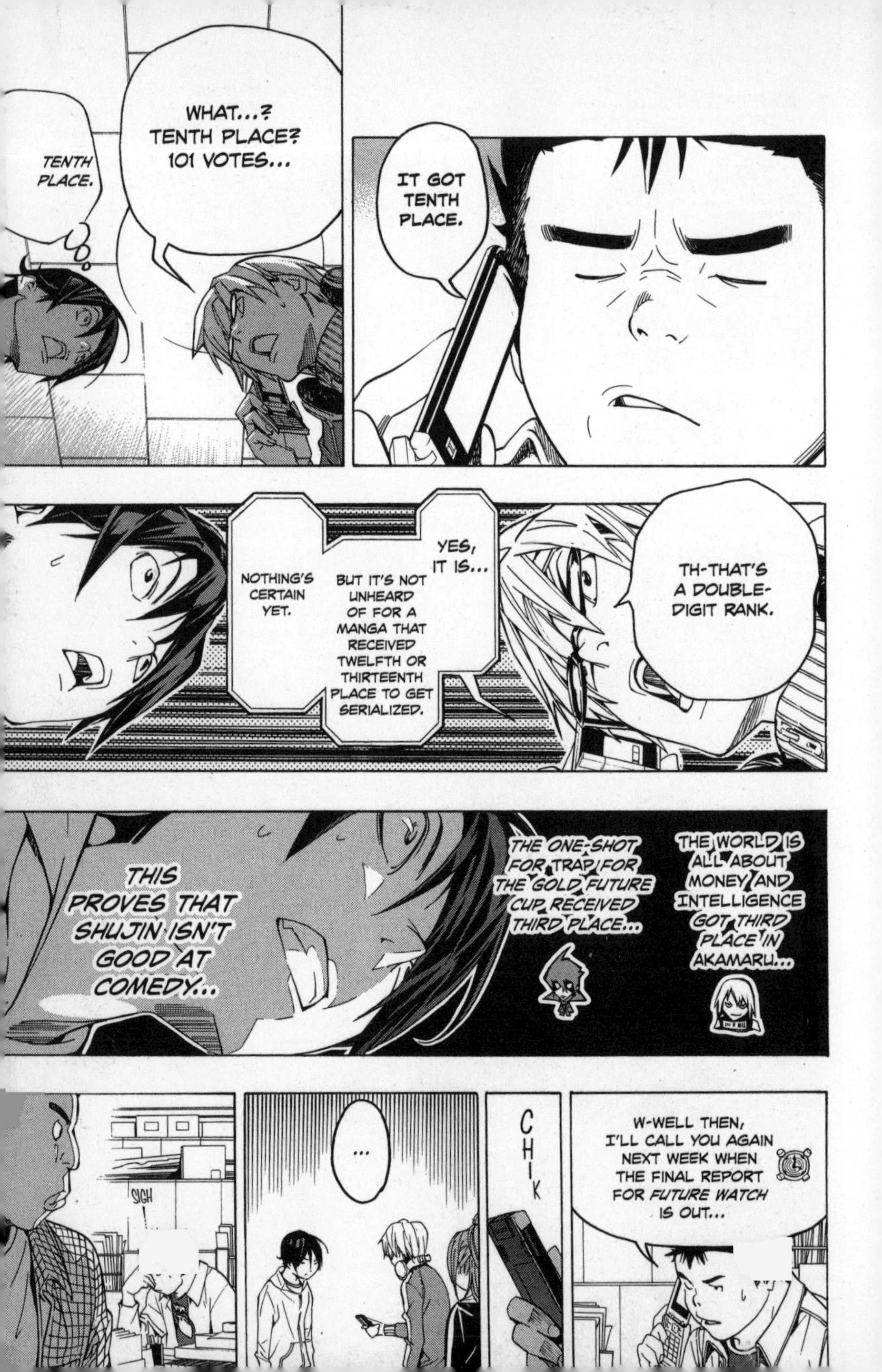
IT GOT TENTH PLACE.
WHAT...? TENTH PLACE? 101 VOTES...
TENTH PLACE.
TH-THAT'S A DOUBLE-DIGIT RANK.
YES, IT IS...
BUT IT'S NOT UNHEARD OF FOR A MANGA THAT RECEIVED TWELFTH OR THIRTEENTH PLACE TO GET SERIALIZED.
NOTHING'S CERTAIN YET.
THE WORLD IS ALL ABOUT MONEY AND INTELLIGENCE GOT THIRD PLACE IN AKAMARU...
THE ONE-SHOT FOR TRAP FOR THE GOLD FUTURE CUP RECEIVED THIRD PLACE...
THIS PROVES THAT SHUJIN ISN'T GOOD AT COMEDY...
W-WELL THEN, I'LL CALL YOU AGAIN NEXT WEEK WHEN THE FINAL REPORT FOR FUTURE WATCH IS OUT...
CHIK
...
SIGH

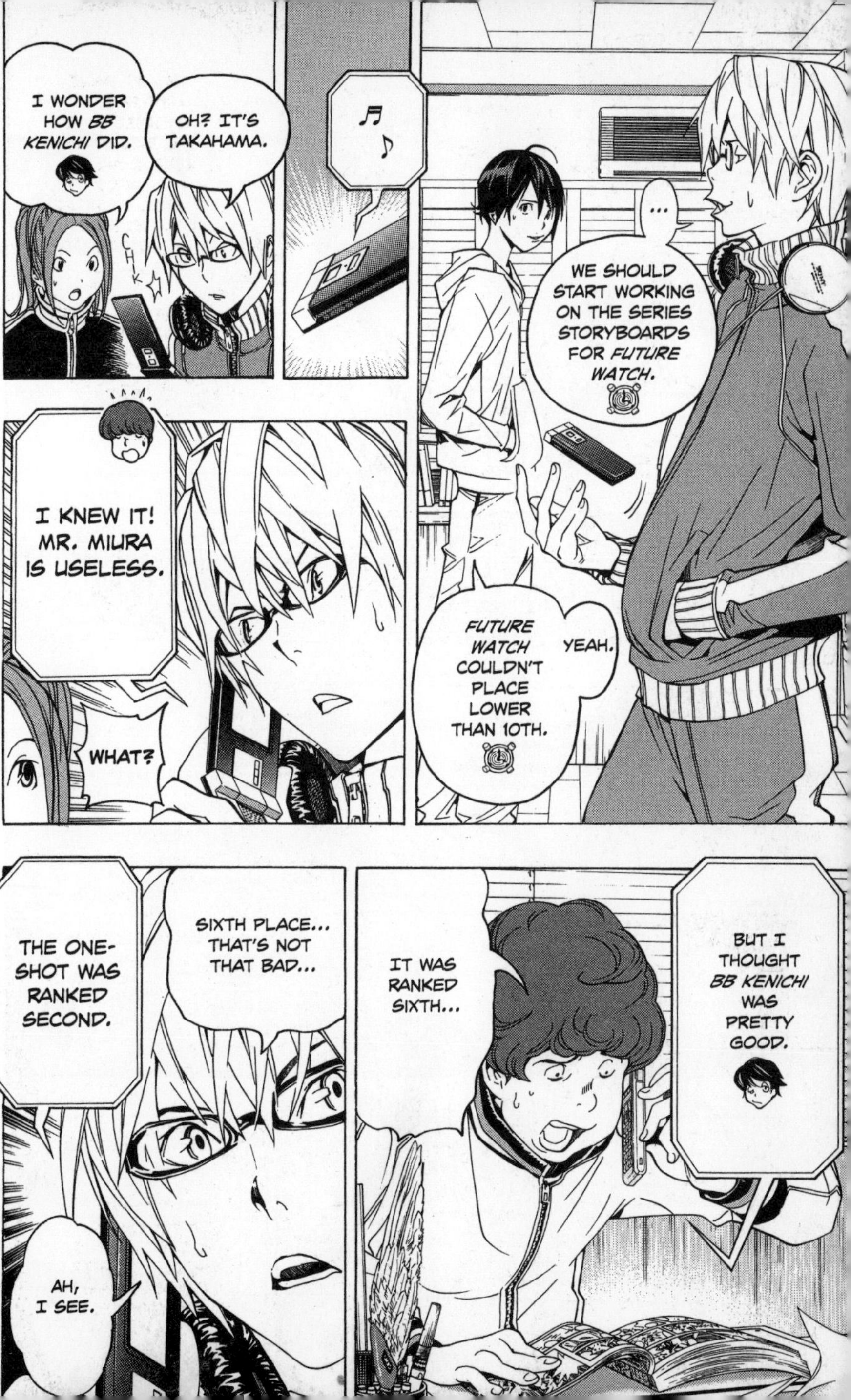
...
WE SHOULD START WORKING ON THE SERIES STORYBOARDS FOR *FUTURE WATCH.*
YEAH.
FUTURE WATCH COULDN'T PLACE LOWER THAN 10TH.
♬ ♪
OH? IT'S TAKAHAMA.
CHIK
I WONDER HOW *BB KENICHI* DID.
I KNEW IT! MR. MIURA IS USELESS.
WHAT?
BUT I THOUGHT *BB KENICHI* WAS PRETTY GOOD.
IT WAS RANKED SIXTH...
SIXTH PLACE... THAT'S NOT THAT BAD...
THE ONE-SHOT WAS RANKED SECOND.
AH, I SEE.

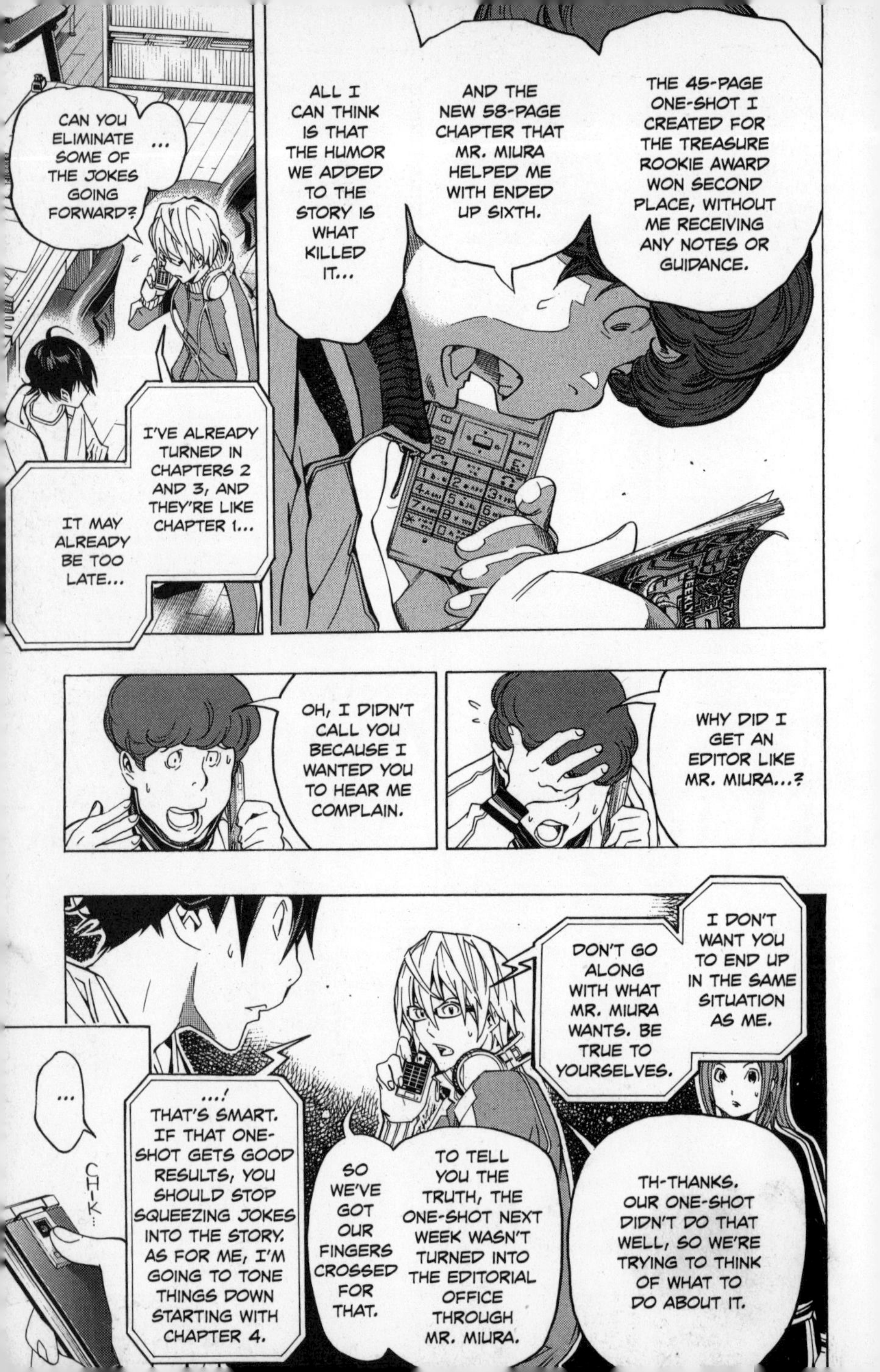
THE 45-PAGE ONE-SHOT I CREATED FOR THE TREASURE ROOKIE AWARD WON SECOND PLACE, WITHOUT ME RECEIVING ANY NOTES OR GUIDANCE.
AND THE NEW 58-PAGE CHAPTER THAT MR. MIURA HELPED ME WITH ENDED UP SIXTH.
ALL I CAN THINK IS THAT THE HUMOR WE ADDED TO THE STORY IS WHAT KILLED IT...
CAN YOU ELIMINATE SOME OF THE JOKES GOING FORWARD?
...
I'VE ALREADY TURNED IN CHAPTERS 2 AND 3, AND THEY'RE LIKE CHAPTER 1...
IT MAY ALREADY BE TOO LATE...
WHY DID I GET AN EDITOR LIKE MR. MIURA...?
OH, I DIDN'T CALL YOU BECAUSE I WANTED YOU TO HEAR ME COMPLAIN.
I DON'T WANT YOU TO END UP IN THE SAME SITUATION AS ME.
DON'T GO ALONG WITH WHAT MR. MIURA WANTS. BE TRUE TO YOURSELVES.
TH-THANKS. OUR ONE-SHOT DIDN'T DO THAT WELL, SO WE'RE TRYING TO THINK OF WHAT TO DO ABOUT IT.
TO TELL YOU THE TRUTH, THE ONE-SHOT NEXT WEEK WASN'T TURNED INTO THE EDITORIAL OFFICE THROUGH MR. MIURA.
SO WE'VE GOT OUR FINGERS CROSSED FOR THAT.
...! THAT'S SMART. IF THAT ONE-SHOT GETS GOOD RESULTS, YOU SHOULD STOP SQUEEZING JOKES INTO THE STORY. AS FOR ME, I'M GOING TO TONE THINGS DOWN STARTING WITH CHAPTER 4.
...
CHIK...

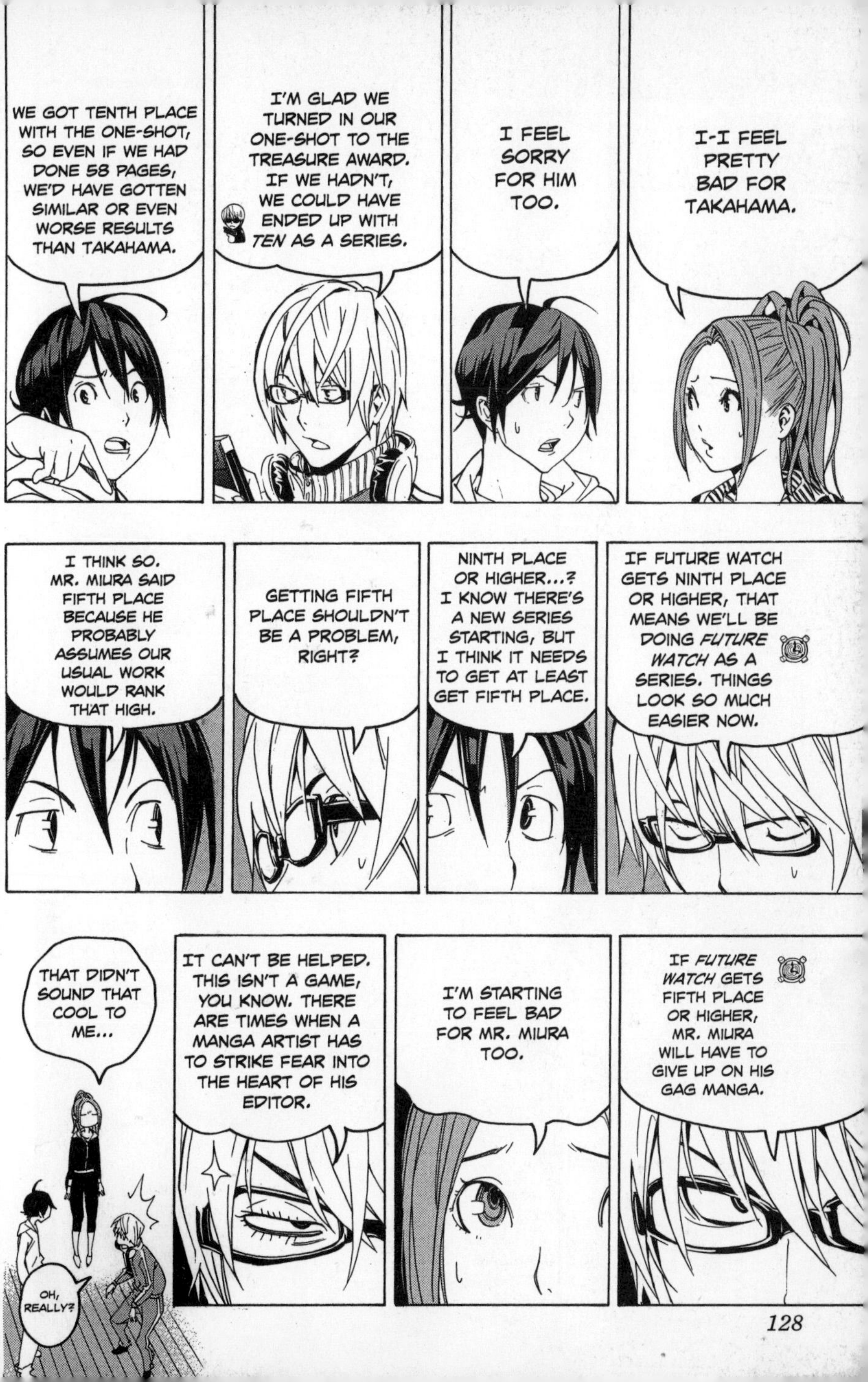
I-I FEEL PRETTY BAD FOR TAKAHAMA.
I FEEL SORRY FOR HIM TOO.
I'M GLAD WE TURNED IN OUR ONE-SHOT TO THE TREASURE AWARD. IF WE HADN'T, WE COULD HAVE ENDED UP WITH *TEN* AS A SERIES.
WE GOT TENTH PLACE WITH THE ONE-SHOT, SO EVEN IF WE HAD DONE 58 PAGES, WE'D HAVE GOTTEN SIMILAR OR EVEN WORSE RESULTS THAN TAKAHAMA.
IF FUTURE WATCH GETS NINTH PLACE OR HIGHER, THAT MEANS WE'LL BE DOING *FUTURE WATCH* AS A SERIES. THINGS LOOK SO MUCH EASIER NOW.
NINTH PLACE OR HIGHER...? I KNOW THERE'S A NEW SERIES STARTING, BUT I THINK IT NEEDS TO GET AT LEAST GET FIFTH PLACE.
GETTING FIFTH PLACE SHOULDN'T BE A PROBLEM, RIGHT?
I THINK SO. MR. MIURA SAID FIFTH PLACE BECAUSE HE PROBABLY ASSUMES OUR USUAL WORK WOULD RANK THAT HIGH.
IF *FUTURE WATCH* GETS FIFTH PLACE OR HIGHER, MR. MIURA WILL HAVE TO GIVE UP ON HIS GAG MANGA.
I'M STARTING TO FEEL BAD FOR MR. MIURA TOO.
IT CAN'T BE HELPED. THIS ISN'T A GAME, YOU KNOW. THERE ARE TIMES WHEN A MANGA ARTIST HAS TO STRIKE FEAR INTO THE HEART OF HIS EDITOR.
THAT DIDN'T SOUND THAT COOL TO ME...
OH, REALLY?

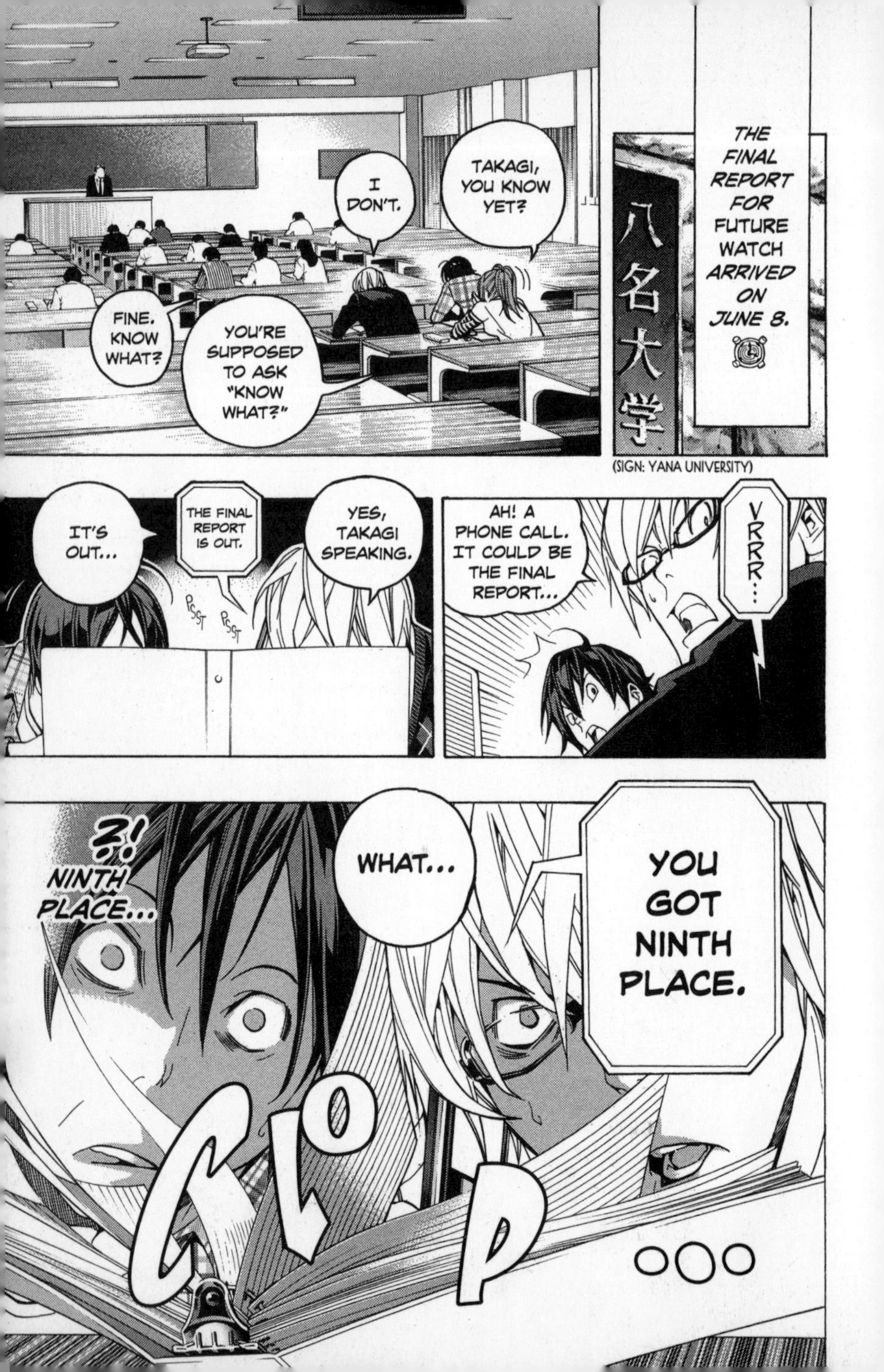
THE FINAL REPORT FOR FUTURE WATCH ARRIVED ON JUNE 8.
八名大学
(SIGN: YANA UNIVERSITY)
TAKAGI, YOU KNOW YET?
I DON'T.
YOU'RE SUPPOSED TO ASK "KNOW WHAT?"
FINE. KNOW WHAT?
VRRR...
AH! A PHONE CALL. IT COULD BE THE FINAL REPORT...
YES, TAKAGI SPEAKING.
THE FINAL REPORT IS OUT.
PSST PSST
IT'S OUT...
YOU GOT NINTH PLACE.
WHAT...
Z! NINTH PLACE...
CLOP

OHBA'S STORYBOARD

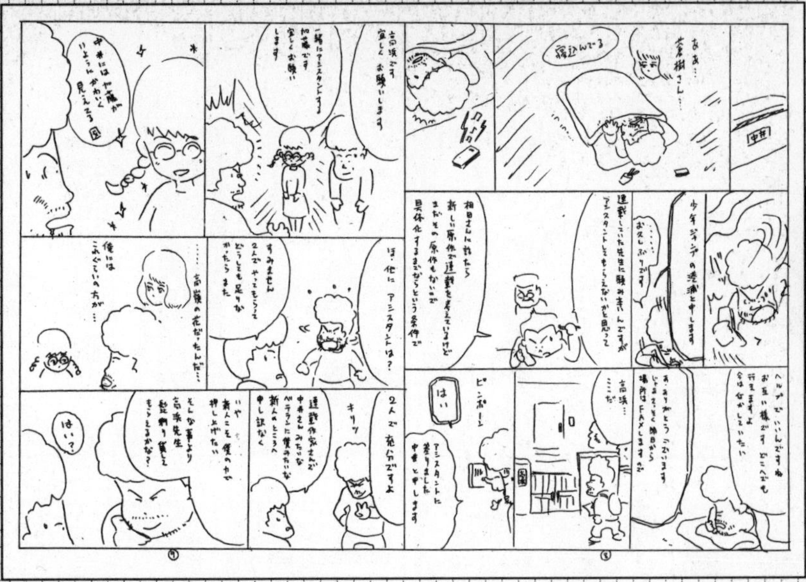
ああ…蒼樹さん…
寝込んでる
中井
お久しぶりです
高浜…ここだ
ピンポーン
はい
高浜です 宜しくお願いします
ほ・他にアシスタントは?
2人で充分ですよ
キリッ
はい?

OBATA'S STORYBOARD

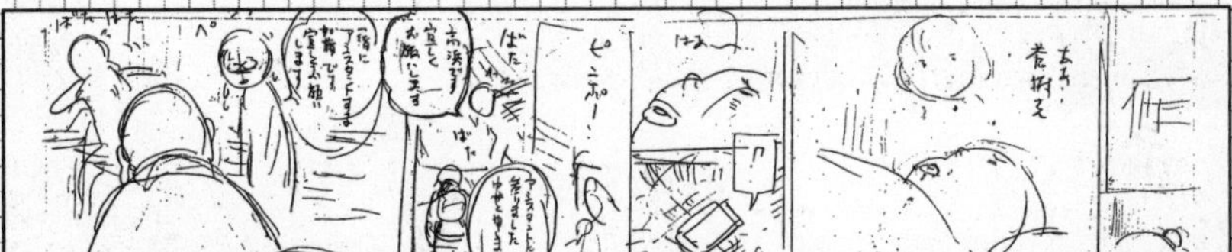

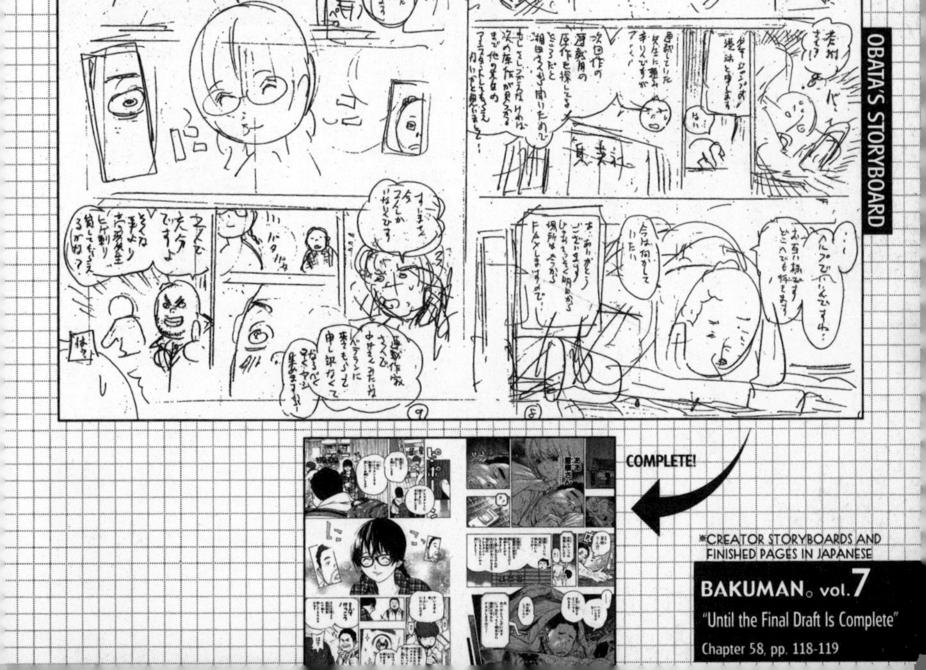

COMPLETE!

*CREATOR STORYBOARDS AND FINISHED PAGES IN JAPANESE

BAKUMAN。vol.7

"Until the Final Draft Is Complete"

Chapter 58, pp. 118-119

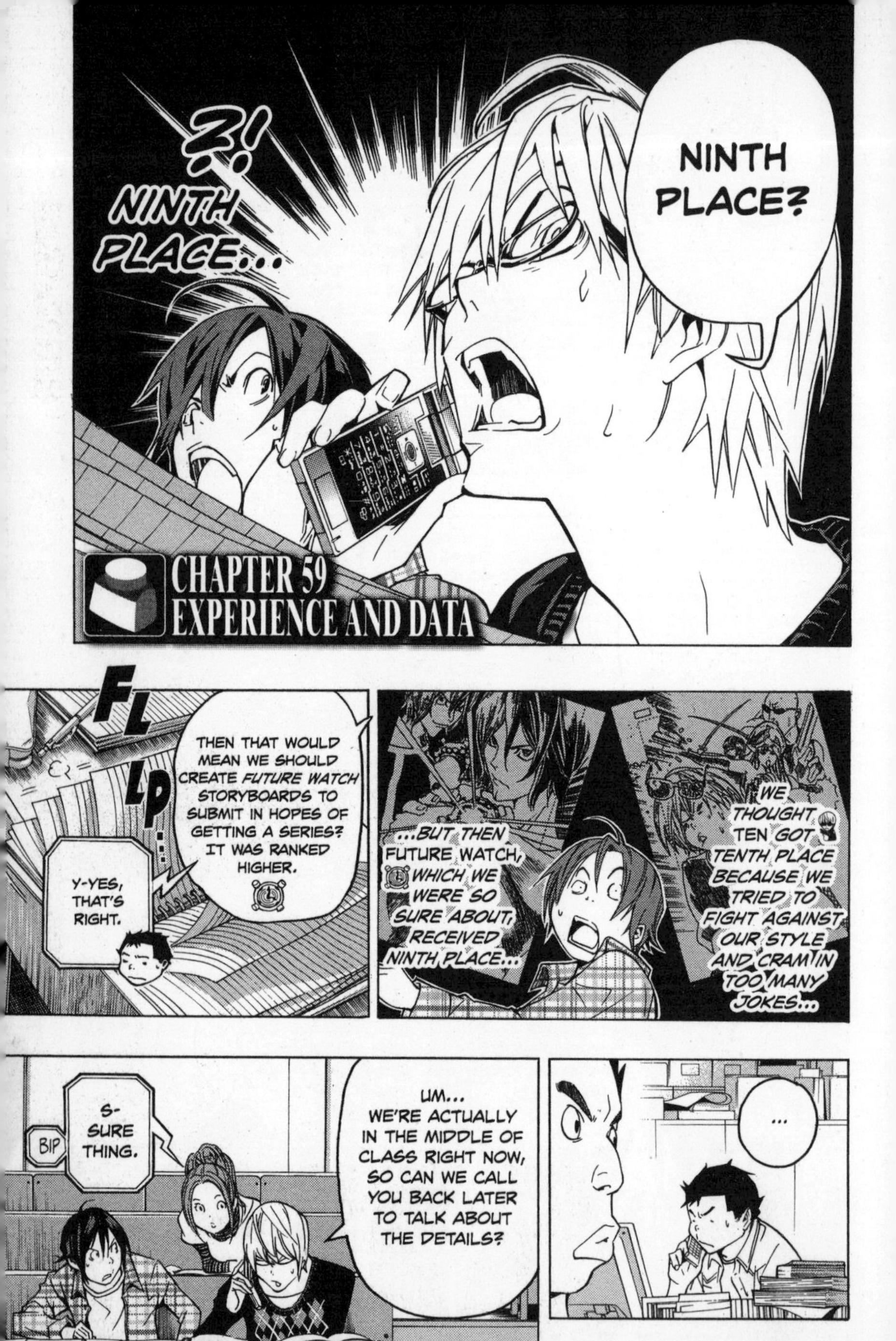
NINTH PLACE?
Z! NINTH PLACE...
CHAPTER 59 EXPERIENCE AND DATA
WE THOUGHT TEN GOT TENTH PLACE BECAUSE WE TRIED TO FIGHT AGAINST OUR STYLE AND CRAM IN TOO MANY JOKES...
...BUT THEN FUTURE WATCH, WHICH WE WERE SO SURE ABOUT, RECEIVED NINTH PLACE...
THEN THAT WOULD MEAN WE SHOULD CREATE FUTURE WATCH STORYBOARDS TO SUBMIT IN HOPES OF GETTING A SERIES? IT WAS RANKED HIGHER.
FLIP
Y-YES, THAT'S RIGHT.
...
UM... WE'RE ACTUALLY IN THE MIDDLE OF CLASS RIGHT NOW, SO CAN WE CALL YOU BACK LATER TO TALK ABOUT THE DETAILS?
S-SURE THING.
BIP

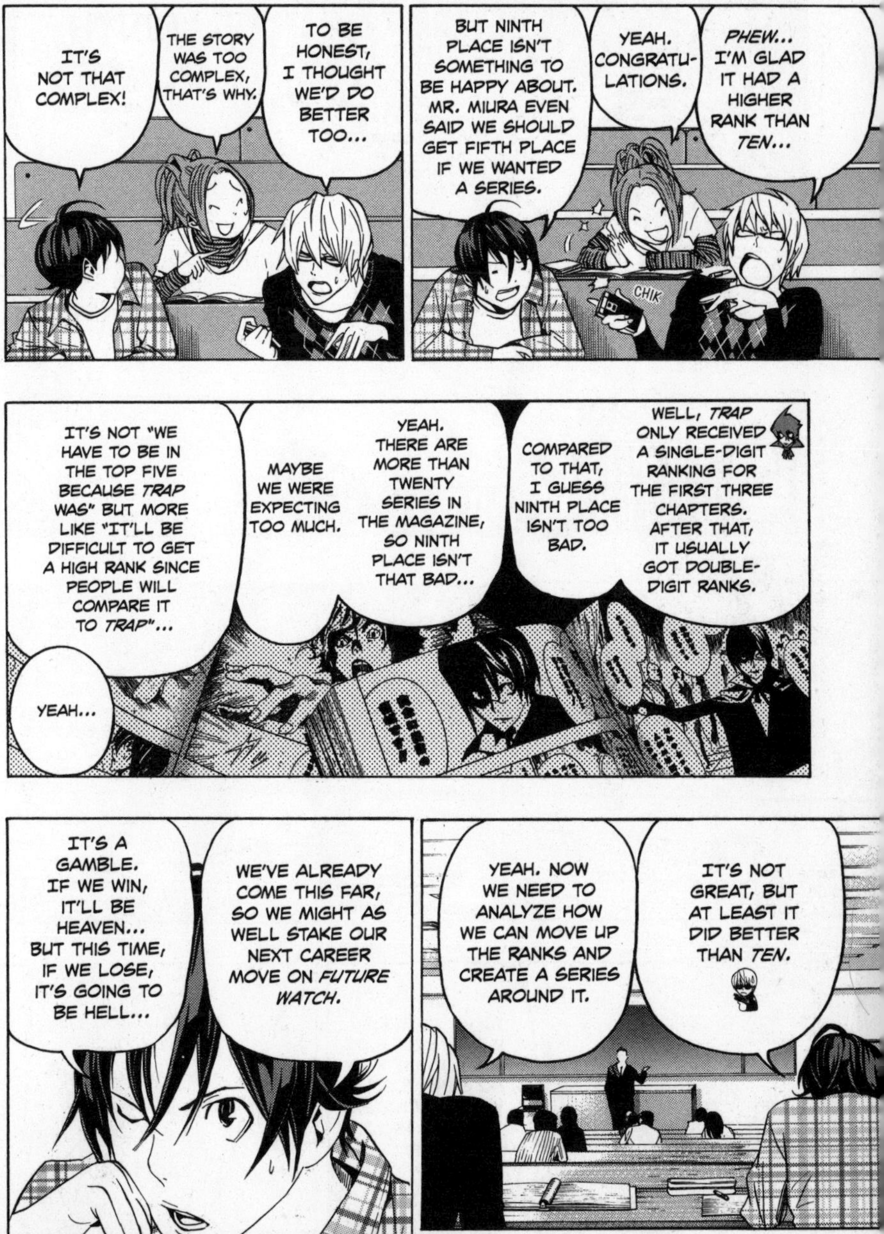
PHEW... I'M GLAD IT HAD A HIGHER RANK THAN TEN...
YEAH. CONGRATULATIONS.
BUT NINTH PLACE ISN'T SOMETHING TO BE HAPPY ABOUT. MR. MIURA EVEN SAID WE SHOULD GET FIFTH PLACE IF WE WANTED A SERIES.
CHIK
TO BE HONEST, I THOUGHT WE'D DO BETTER TOO...
THE STORY WAS TOO COMPLEX, THAT'S WHY.
IT'S NOT THAT COMPLEX!
WELL, TRAP ONLY RECEIVED A SINGLE-DIGIT RANKING FOR THE FIRST THREE CHAPTERS. AFTER THAT, IT USUALLY GOT DOUBLE-DIGIT RANKS.
COMPARED TO THAT, I GUESS NINTH PLACE ISN'T TOO BAD.
YEAH. THERE ARE MORE THAN TWENTY SERIES IN THE MAGAZINE, SO NINTH PLACE ISN'T THAT BAD...
MAYBE WE WERE EXPECTING TOO MUCH.
IT'S NOT "WE HAVE TO BE IN THE TOP FIVE BECAUSE TRAP WAS" BUT MORE LIKE "IT'LL BE DIFFICULT TO GET A HIGH RANK SINCE PEOPLE WILL COMPARE IT TO TRAP"...
YEAH...
IT'S NOT GREAT, BUT AT LEAST IT DID BETTER THAN TEN.
YEAH. NOW WE NEED TO ANALYZE HOW WE CAN MOVE UP THE RANKS AND CREATE A SERIES AROUND IT.
WE'VE ALREADY COME THIS FAR, SO WE MIGHT AS WELL STAKE OUR NEXT CAREER MOVE ON FUTURE WATCH.
IT'S A GAMBLE. IF WE WIN, IT'LL BE HEAVEN... BUT THIS TIME, IF WE LOSE, IT'S GOING TO BE HELL...

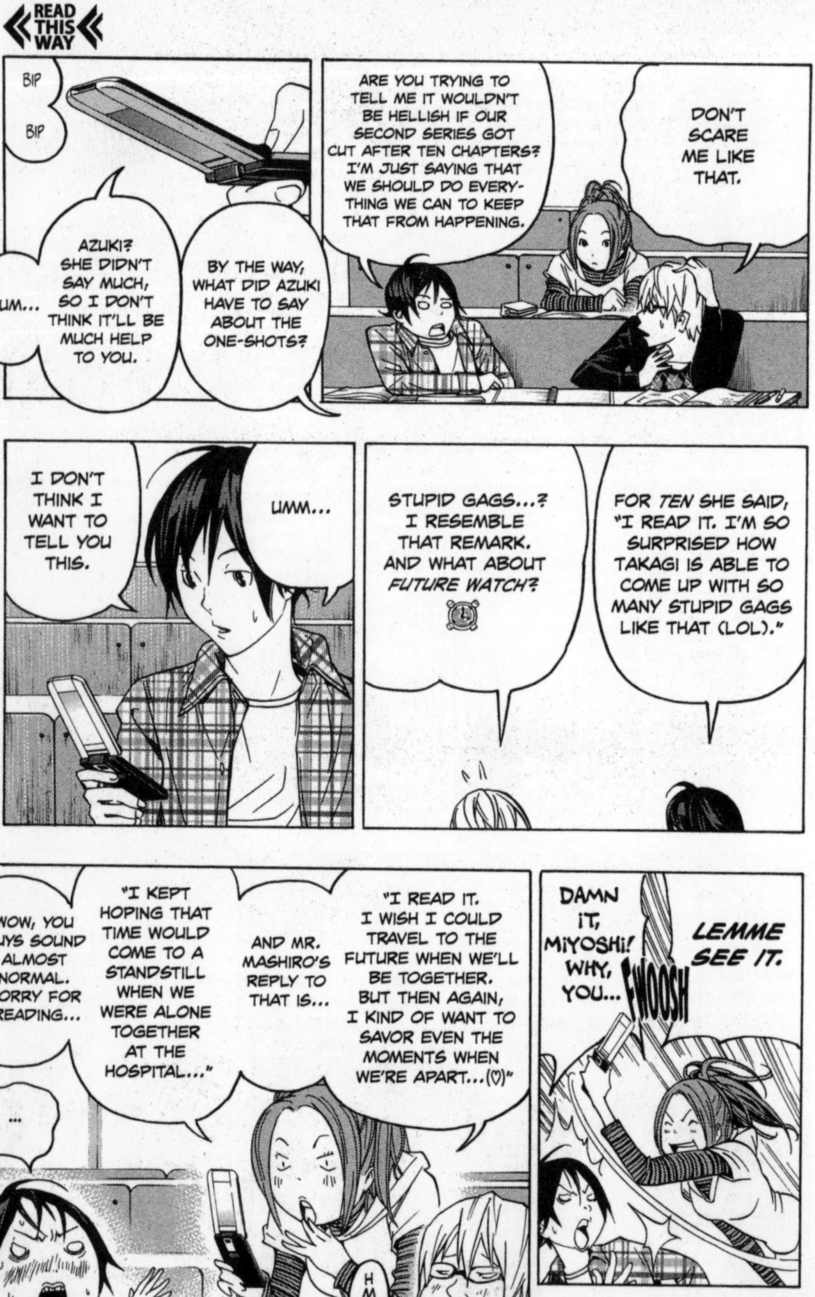
READ THIS WAY
DON'T SCARE ME LIKE THAT.
ARE YOU TRYING TO TELL ME IT WOULDN'T BE HELLISH IF OUR SECOND SERIES GOT CUT AFTER TEN CHAPTERS? I'M JUST SAYING THAT WE SHOULD DO EVERYTHING WE CAN TO KEEP THAT FROM HAPPENING.
BIP
BIP
BY THE WAY, WHAT DID AZUKI HAVE TO SAY ABOUT THE ONE-SHOTS?
AZUKI? SHE DIDN'T SAY MUCH, SO I DON'T THINK IT'LL BE MUCH HELP TO YOU.
UM...
FOR *TEN* SHE SAID, "I READ IT. I'M SO SURPRISED HOW TAKAGI IS ABLE TO COME UP WITH SO MANY STUPID GAGS LIKE THAT (LOL)."
STUPID GAGS...? I RESEMBLE THAT REMARK. AND WHAT ABOUT *FUTURE WATCH*?
UMM...
I DON'T THINK I WANT TO TELL YOU THIS.
LEMME SEE IT.
DAMN IT, MIYOSHI! WHY, YOU...
FWOOSH
"I READ IT. I WISH I COULD TRAVEL TO THE FUTURE WHEN WE'LL BE TOGETHER. BUT THEN AGAIN, I KIND OF WANT TO SAVOR EVEN THE MOMENTS WHEN WE'RE APART...(♡)"
AND MR. MASHIRO'S REPLY TO THAT IS...
"I KEPT HOPING THAT TIME WOULD COME TO A STANDSTILL WHEN WE WERE ALONE TOGETHER AT THE HOSPITAL..."
WOW, YOU GUYS SOUND ALMOST NORMAL. SORRY FOR READING...
...
HMM...

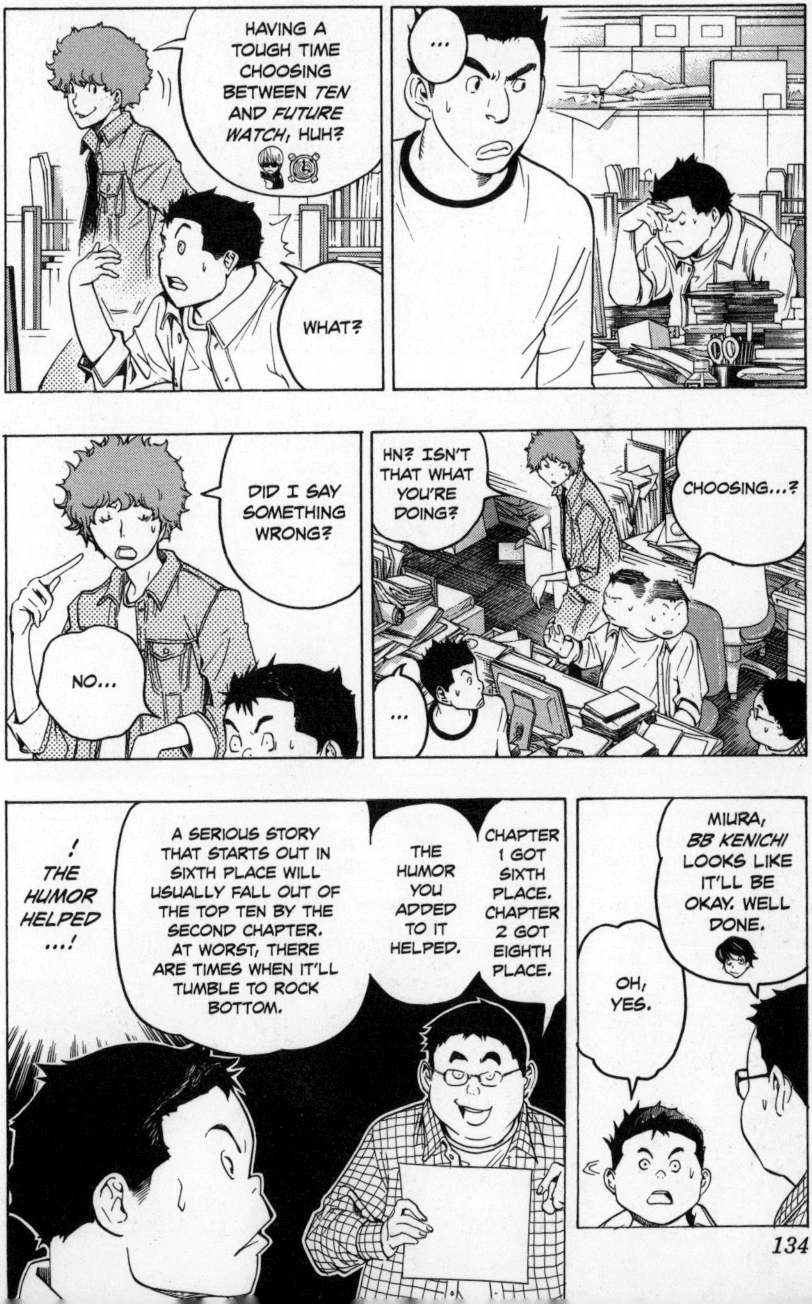
...
HAVING A TOUGH TIME CHOOSING BETWEEN *TEN* AND *FUTURE WATCH*, HUH?
WHAT?
CHOOSING...?
HN? ISN'T THAT WHAT YOU'RE DOING?
...
DID I SAY SOMETHING WRONG?
NO...
MIURA, *BB KENICHI* LOOKS LIKE IT'LL BE OKAY. WELL DONE.
OH, YES.
CHAPTER 1 GOT SIXTH PLACE. CHAPTER 2 GOT EIGHTH PLACE.
THE HUMOR YOU ADDED TO IT HELPED.
A SERIOUS STORY THAT STARTS OUT IN SIXTH PLACE WILL USUALLY FALL OUT OF THE TOP TEN BY THE SECOND CHAPTER. AT WORST, THERE ARE TIMES WHEN IT'LL TUMBLE TO ROCK BOTTOM.
! *THE HUMOR HELPED...!*

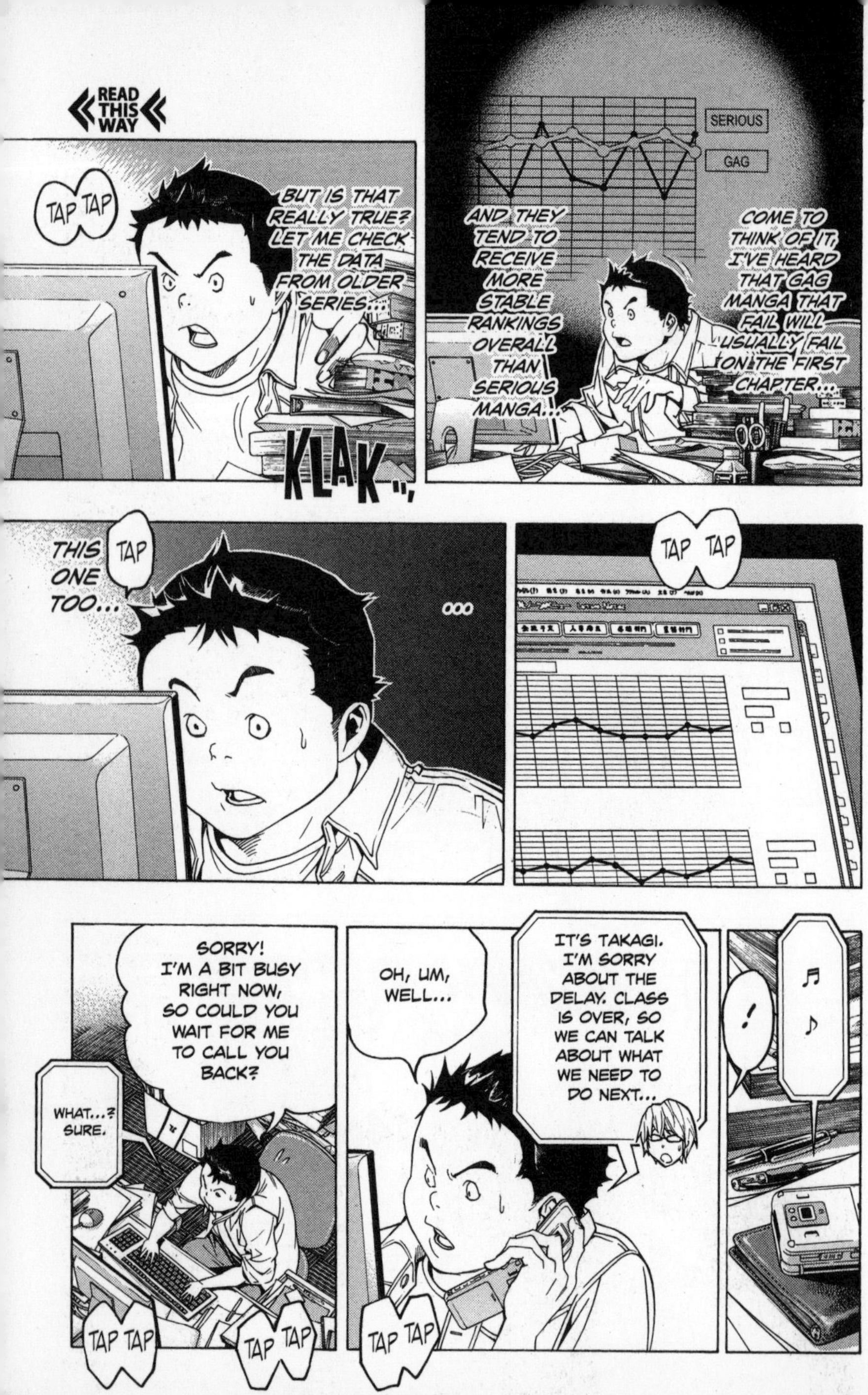
READ THIS WAY
SERIOUS
GAG
COME TO THINK OF IT, I'VE HEARD THAT GAG MANGA THAT FAIL WILL USUALLY FAIL ON THE FIRST CHAPTER...
AND THEY TEND TO RECEIVE MORE STABLE RANKINGS OVERALL THAN SERIOUS MANGA...
BUT IS THAT REALLY TRUE? LET ME CHECK THE DATA FROM OLDER SERIES...
TAP TAP
KLAK
TAP TAP
OOO
TAP
THIS ONE TOO...
♬ ♪
!
IT'S TAKAGI. I'M SORRY ABOUT THE DELAY. CLASS IS OVER, SO WE CAN TALK ABOUT WHAT WE NEED TO DO NEXT...
OH, UM, WELL...
TAP TAP
SORRY! I'M A BIT BUSY RIGHT NOW, SO COULD YOU WAIT FOR ME TO CALL YOU BACK?
WHAT...? SURE.
TAP TAP
TAP TAP

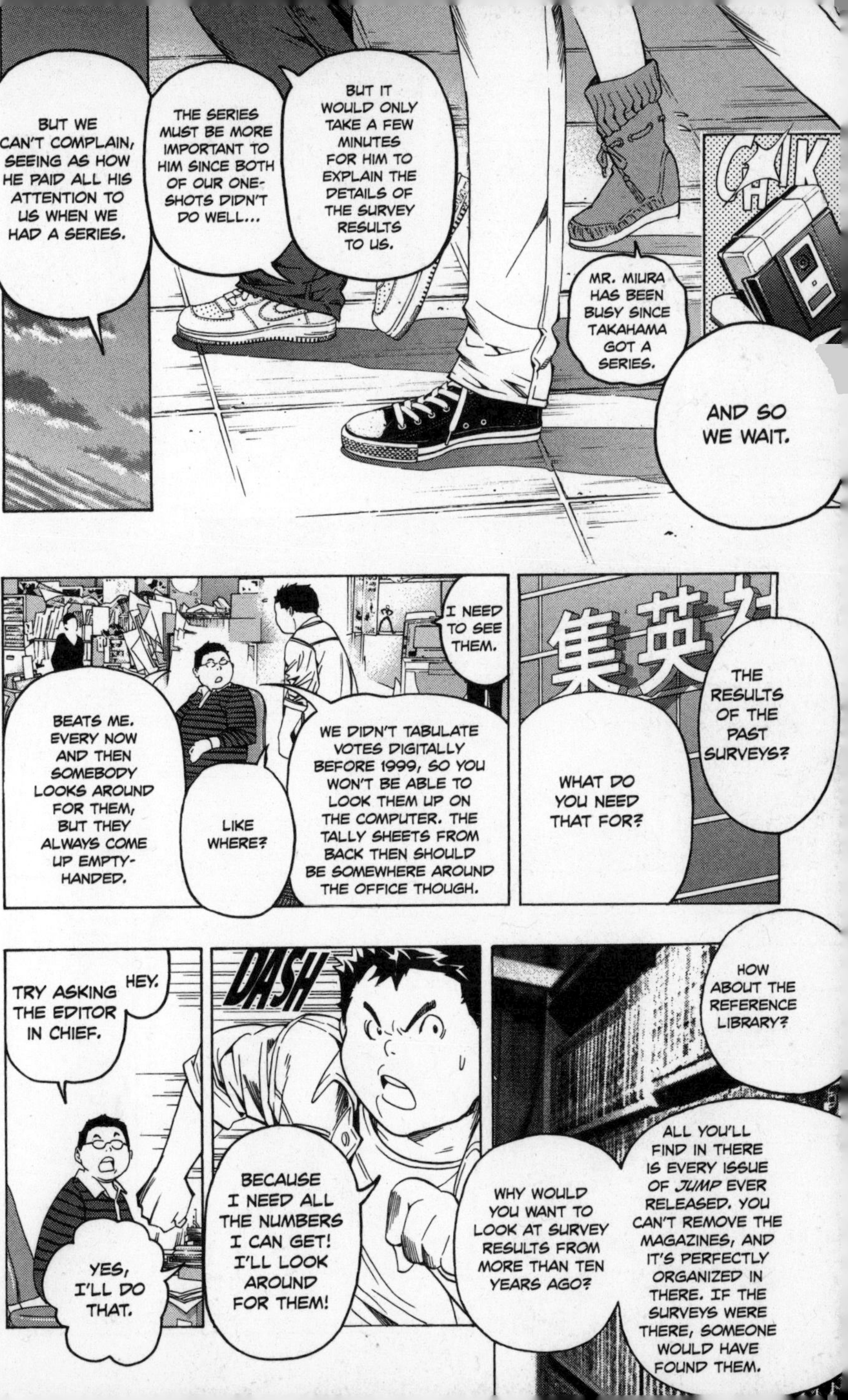
CHIK
MR. MIURA HAS BEEN BUSY SINCE TAKAHAMA GOT A SERIES.
BUT IT WOULD ONLY TAKE A FEW MINUTES FOR HIM TO EXPLAIN THE DETAILS OF THE SURVEY RESULTS TO US.
THE SERIES MUST BE MORE IMPORTANT TO HIM SINCE BOTH OF OUR ONE-SHOTS DIDN'T DO WELL...
BUT WE CAN'T COMPLAIN, SEEING AS HOW HE PAID ALL HIS ATTENTION TO US WHEN WE HAD A SERIES.
AND SO WE WAIT.
集英社
THE RESULTS OF THE PAST SURVEYS?
WHAT DO YOU NEED THAT FOR?
I NEED TO SEE THEM.
WE DIDN'T TABULATE VOTES DIGITALLY BEFORE 1999, SO YOU WON'T BE ABLE TO LOOK THEM UP ON THE COMPUTER. THE TALLY SHEETS FROM BACK THEN SHOULD BE SOMEWHERE AROUND THE OFFICE THOUGH.
LIKE WHERE?
BEATS ME. EVERY NOW AND THEN SOMEBODY LOOKS AROUND FOR THEM, BUT THEY ALWAYS COME UP EMPTY-HANDED.
HOW ABOUT THE REFERENCE LIBRARY?
ALL YOU'LL FIND IN THERE IS EVERY ISSUE OF *JUMP* EVER RELEASED. YOU CAN'T REMOVE THE MAGAZINES, AND IT'S PERFECTLY ORGANIZED IN THERE. IF THE SURVEYS WERE THERE, SOMEONE WOULD HAVE FOUND THEM.
WHY WOULD YOU WANT TO LOOK AT SURVEY RESULTS FROM MORE THAN TEN YEARS AGO?
DASH
BECAUSE I NEED ALL THE NUMBERS I CAN GET! I'LL LOOK AROUND FOR THEM!
HEY.
TRY ASKING THE EDITOR IN CHIEF.
YES, I'LL DO THAT.

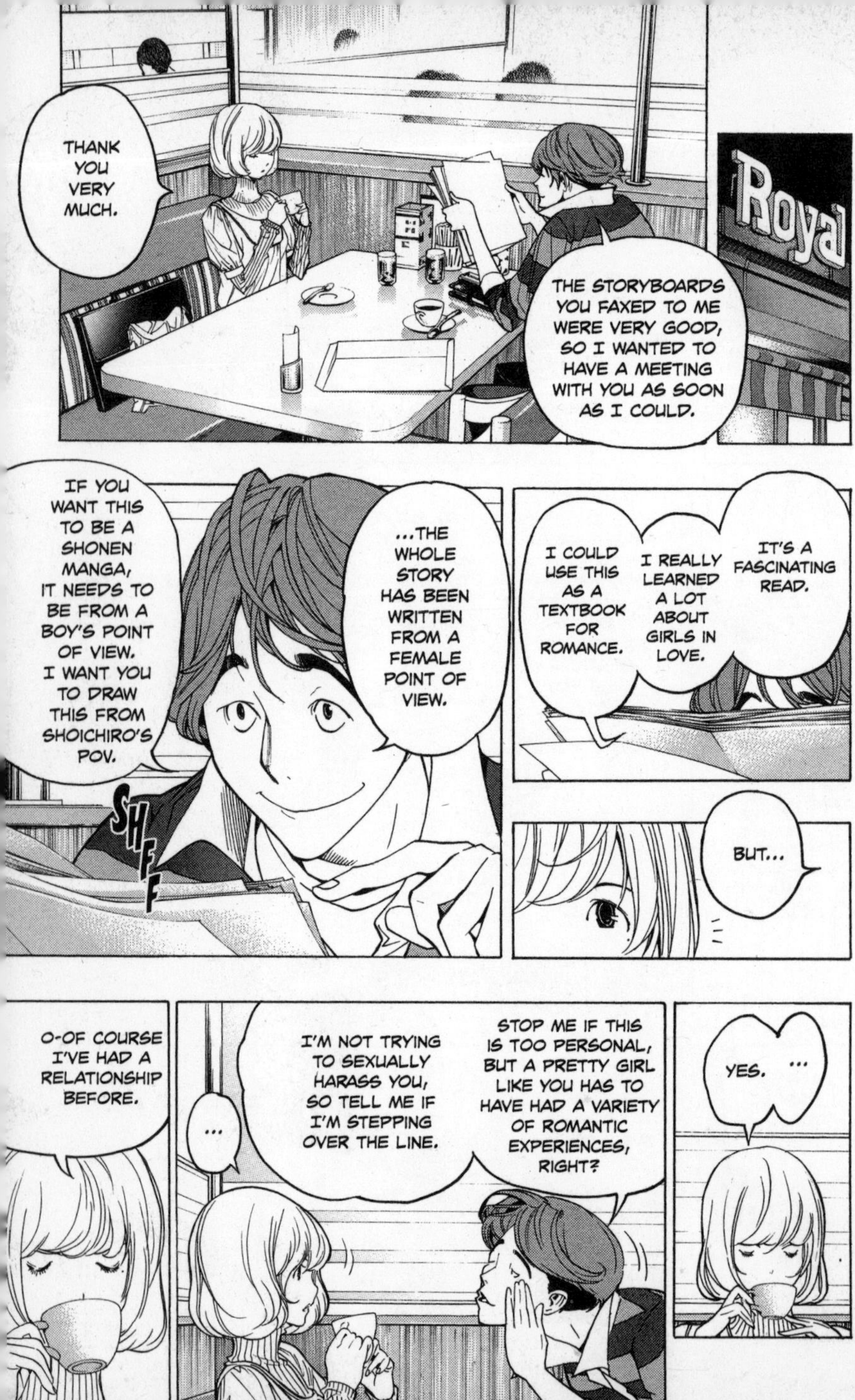
Royal
THE STORYBOARDS YOU FAXED TO ME WERE VERY GOOD, SO I WANTED TO HAVE A MEETING WITH YOU AS SOON AS I COULD.
THANK YOU VERY MUCH.
IT'S A FASCINATING READ.
I REALLY LEARNED A LOT ABOUT GIRLS IN LOVE.
I COULD USE THIS AS A TEXTBOOK FOR ROMANCE.
BUT...
...THE WHOLE STORY HAS BEEN WRITTEN FROM A FEMALE POINT OF VIEW.
IF YOU WANT THIS TO BE A SHONEN MANGA, IT NEEDS TO BE FROM A BOY'S POINT OF VIEW. I WANT YOU TO DRAW THIS FROM SHOICHIRO'S POV.
SHFF
YES. ...
STOP ME IF THIS IS TOO PERSONAL, BUT A PRETTY GIRL LIKE YOU HAS TO HAVE HAD A VARIETY OF ROMANTIC EXPERIENCES, RIGHT?
I'M NOT TRYING TO SEXUALLY HARASS YOU, SO TELL ME IF I'M STEPPING OVER THE LINE.
...
O-OF COURSE I'VE HAD A RELATIONSHIP BEFORE.

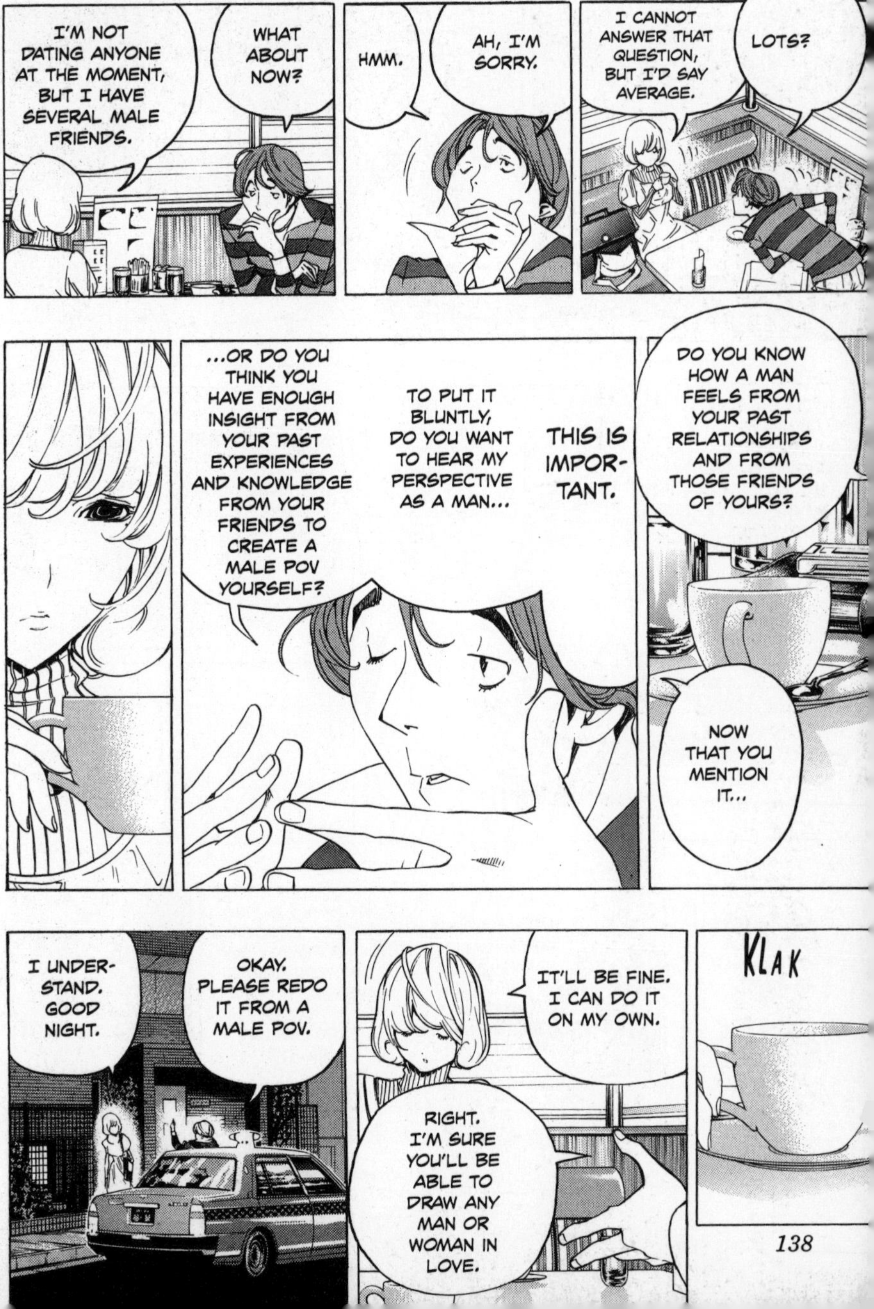
LOTS?
I CANNOT ANSWER THAT QUESTION, BUT I'D SAY AVERAGE.
AH, I'M SORRY.
HMM.
WHAT ABOUT NOW?
I'M NOT DATING ANYONE AT THE MOMENT, BUT I HAVE SEVERAL MALE FRIENDS.
DO YOU KNOW HOW A MAN FEELS FROM YOUR PAST RELATIONSHIPS AND FROM THOSE FRIENDS OF YOURS?
NOW THAT YOU MENTION IT...
THIS IS IMPOR-TANT.
TO PUT IT BLUNTLY, DO YOU WANT TO HEAR MY PERSPECTIVE AS A MAN...
...OR DO YOU THINK YOU HAVE ENOUGH INSIGHT FROM YOUR PAST EXPERIENCES AND KNOWLEDGE FROM YOUR FRIENDS TO CREATE A MALE POV YOURSELF?
KLAK
IT'LL BE FINE. I CAN DO IT ON MY OWN.
RIGHT. I'M SURE YOU'LL BE ABLE TO DRAW ANY MAN OR WOMAN IN LOVE.
OKAY. PLEASE REDO IT FROM A MALE POV.
I UNDER-STAND. GOOD NIGHT.

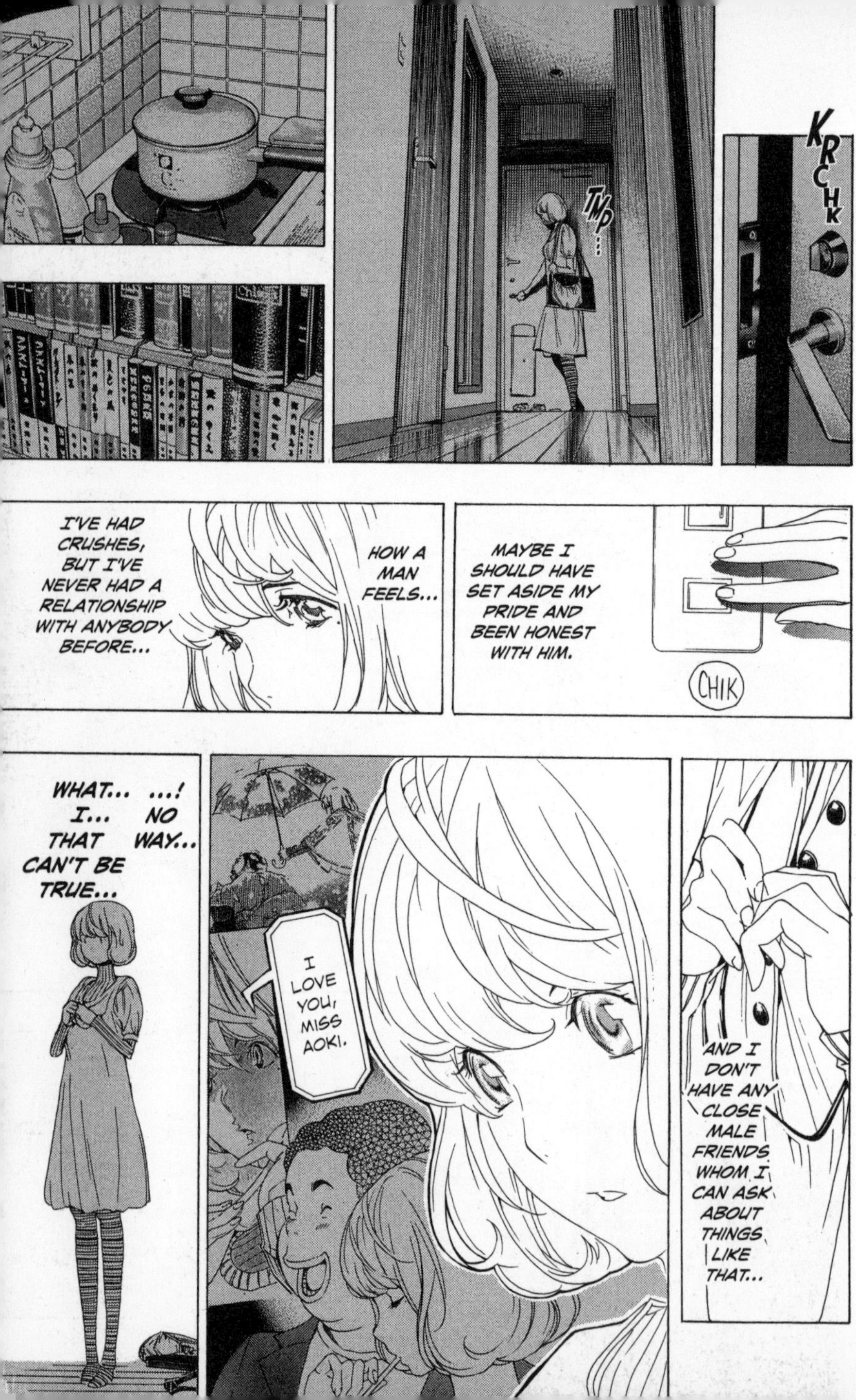
KRCHK
TMP...
MAYBE I SHOULD HAVE SET ASIDE MY PRIDE AND BEEN HONEST WITH HIM.
CHIK
HOW A MAN FEELS...
I'VE HAD CRUSHES, BUT I'VE NEVER HAD A RELATIONSHIP WITH ANYBODY BEFORE...
AND I DON'T HAVE ANY CLOSE MALE FRIENDS WHOM I CAN ASK ABOUT THINGS LIKE THAT...
I LOVE YOU, MISS AOKI.
...! NO WAY...
WHAT... I... THAT CAN'T BE TRUE...

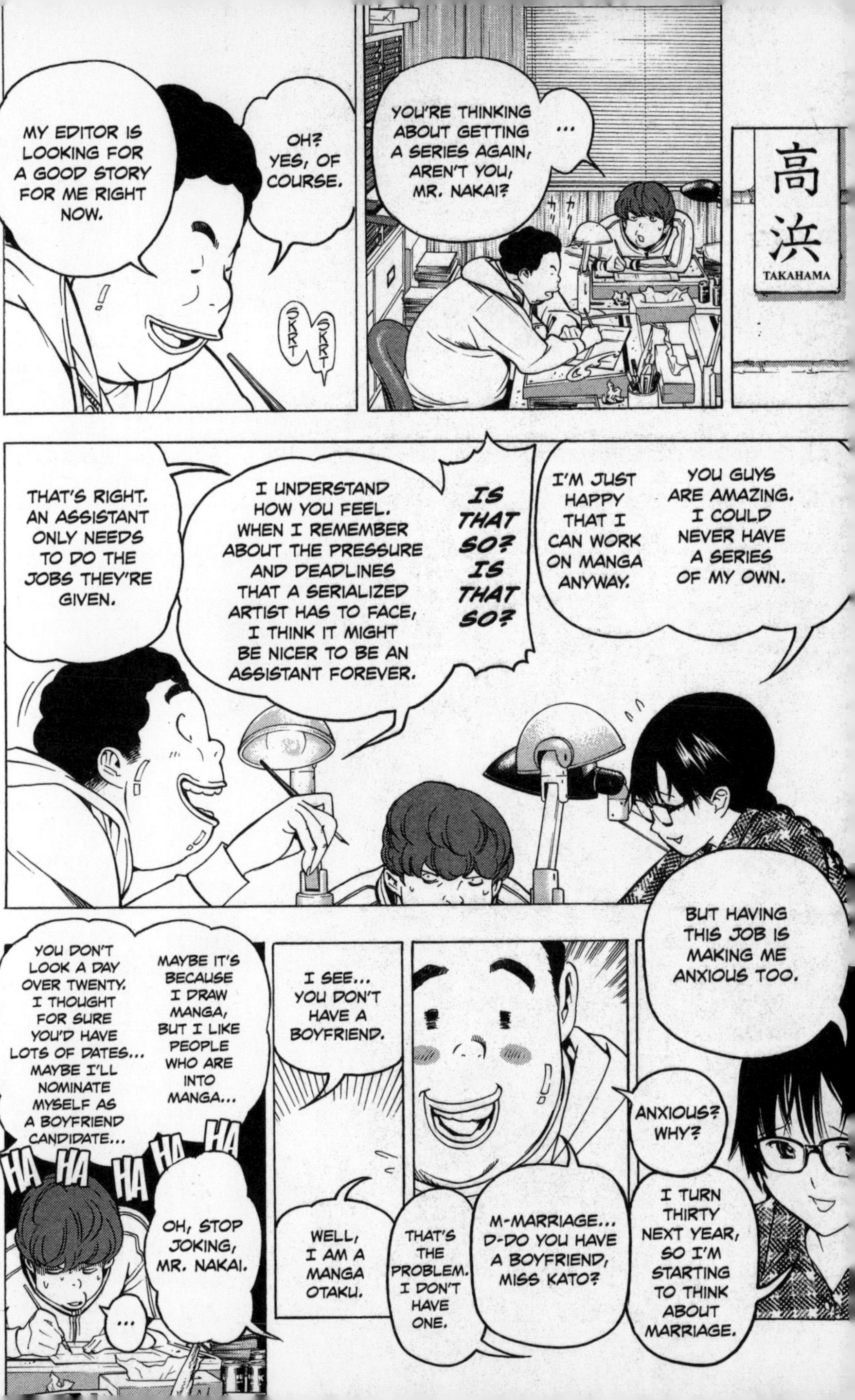
高浜
TAKAHAMA
...
YOU'RE THINKING ABOUT GETTING A SERIES AGAIN, AREN'T YOU, MR. NAKAI?
OH? YES, OF COURSE.
MY EDITOR IS LOOKING FOR A GOOD STORY FOR ME RIGHT NOW.
SKRT SKRT
YOU GUYS ARE AMAZING. I COULD NEVER HAVE A SERIES OF MY OWN.
I'M JUST HAPPY THAT I CAN WORK ON MANGA ANYWAY.
IS THAT SO? IS THAT SO?
I UNDERSTAND HOW YOU FEEL. WHEN I REMEMBER ABOUT THE PRESSURE AND DEADLINES THAT A SERIALIZED ARTIST HAS TO FACE, I THINK IT MIGHT BE NICER TO BE AN ASSISTANT FOREVER.
THAT'S RIGHT. AN ASSISTANT ONLY NEEDS TO DO THE JOBS THEY'RE GIVEN.
BUT HAVING THIS JOB IS MAKING ME ANXIOUS TOO.
ANXIOUS? WHY?
I TURN THIRTY NEXT YEAR, SO I'M STARTING TO THINK ABOUT MARRIAGE.
M-MARRIAGE... D-DO YOU HAVE A BOYFRIEND, MISS KATO?
THAT'S THE PROBLEM. I DON'T HAVE ONE.
I SEE... YOU DON'T HAVE A BOYFRIEND.
WELL, I AM A MANGA OTAKU.
MAYBE IT'S BECAUSE I DRAW MANGA, BUT I LIKE PEOPLE WHO ARE INTO MANGA...
YOU DON'T LOOK A DAY OVER TWENTY. I THOUGHT FOR SURE YOU'D HAVE LOTS OF DATES... MAYBE I'LL NOMINATE MYSELF AS A BOYFRIEND CANDIDATE...
HA HA HA HA HA
OH, STOP JOKING, MR. NAKAI.
...

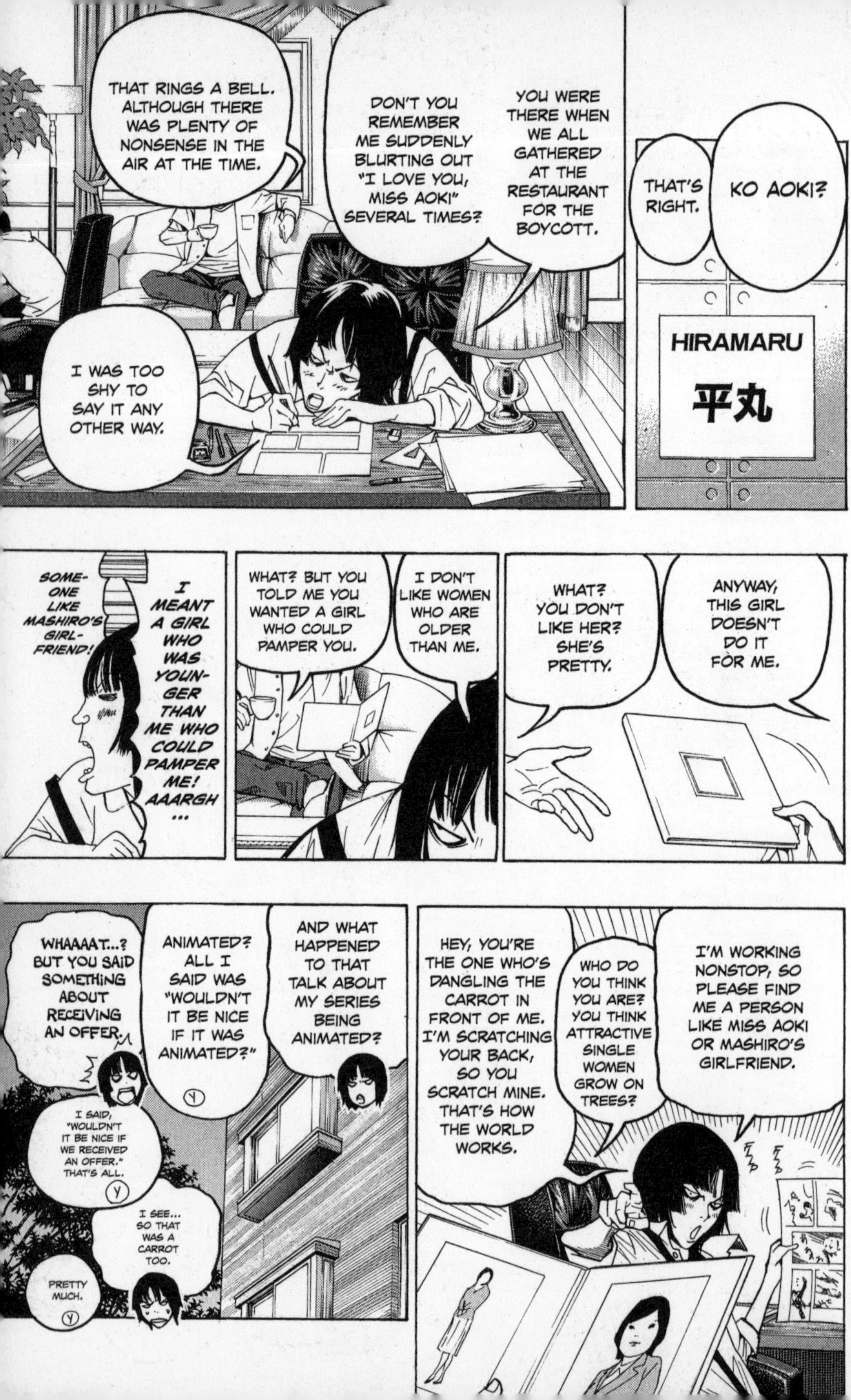
KO AOKI?
THAT'S RIGHT.
HIRAMARU
平丸
YOU WERE THERE WHEN WE ALL GATHERED AT THE RESTAURANT FOR THE BOYCOTT.
DON'T YOU REMEMBER ME SUDDENLY BLURTING OUT "I LOVE YOU, MISS AOKI" SEVERAL TIMES?
THAT RINGS A BELL. ALTHOUGH THERE WAS PLENTY OF NONSENSE IN THE AIR AT THE TIME.
I WAS TOO SHY TO SAY IT ANY OTHER WAY.
ANYWAY, THIS GIRL DOESN'T DO IT FOR ME.
WHAT? YOU DON'T LIKE HER? SHE'S PRETTY.
I DON'T LIKE WOMEN WHO ARE OLDER THAN ME.
WHAT? BUT YOU TOLD ME YOU WANTED A GIRL WHO COULD PAMPER YOU.
I MEANT A GIRL WHO WAS YOUNGER THAN ME WHO COULD PAMPER ME! AAARGH...
SOMEONE LIKE MASHIRO'S GIRLFRIEND!
I'M WORKING NONSTOP, SO PLEASE FIND ME A PERSON LIKE MISS AOKI OR MASHIRO'S GIRLFRIEND.
WHO DO YOU THINK YOU ARE? YOU THINK ATTRACTIVE SINGLE WOMEN GROW ON TREES?
HEY, YOU'RE THE ONE WHO'S DANGLING THE CARROT IN FRONT OF ME. I'M SCRATCHING YOUR BACK, SO YOU SCRATCH MINE. THAT'S HOW THE WORLD WORKS.
AND WHAT HAPPENED TO THAT TALK ABOUT MY SERIES BEING ANIMATED?
ANIMATED? ALL I SAID WAS "WOULDN'T IT BE NICE IF IT WAS ANIMATED?"
WHAAAAT...? BUT YOU SAID SOMETHING ABOUT RECEIVING AN OFFER.
I SAID, "WOULDN'T IT BE NICE IF WE RECEIVED AN OFFER." THAT'S ALL.
I SEE... SO THAT WAS A CARROT TOO.
PRETTY MUCH.

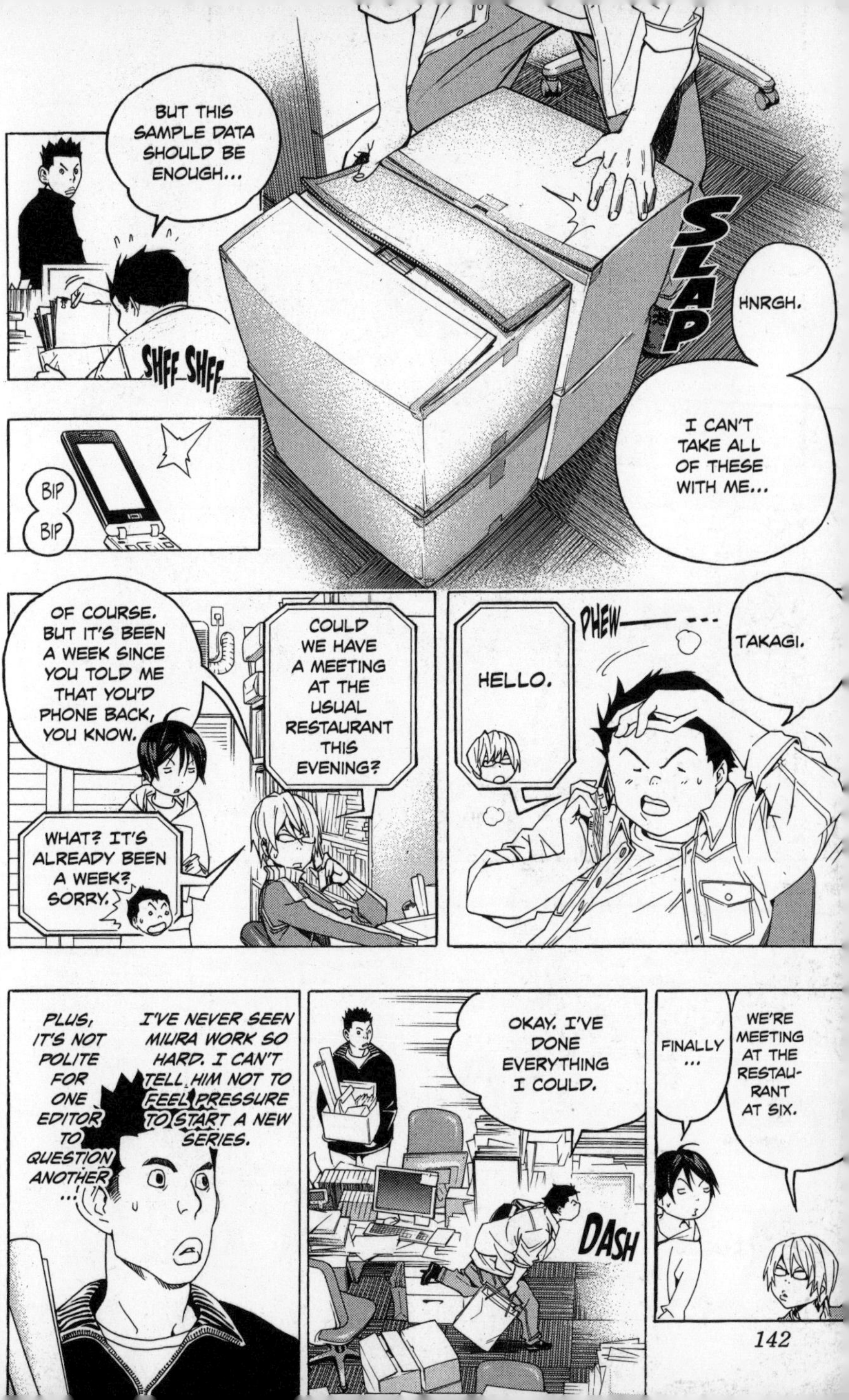
SLAP
HNRGH.
I CAN'T TAKE ALL OF THESE WITH ME...
BUT THIS SAMPLE DATA SHOULD BE ENOUGH...
SHFF SHFF
BIP
BIP
PHEW—— ...
TAKAGI.
HELLO.
COULD WE HAVE A MEETING AT THE USUAL RESTAURANT THIS EVENING?
OF COURSE. BUT IT'S BEEN A WEEK SINCE YOU TOLD ME THAT YOU'D PHONE BACK, YOU KNOW.
WHAT? IT'S ALREADY BEEN A WEEK? SORRY.
WE'RE MEETING AT THE RESTAU-RANT AT SIX.
FINALLY...
OKAY. I'VE DONE EVERYTHING I COULD.
DASH
I'VE NEVER SEEN MIURA WORK SO HARD. I CAN'T TELL HIM NOT TO FEEL PRESSURE TO START A NEW SERIES.
PLUS, IT'S NOT POLITE FOR ONE EDITOR TO QUESTION ANOTHER...!

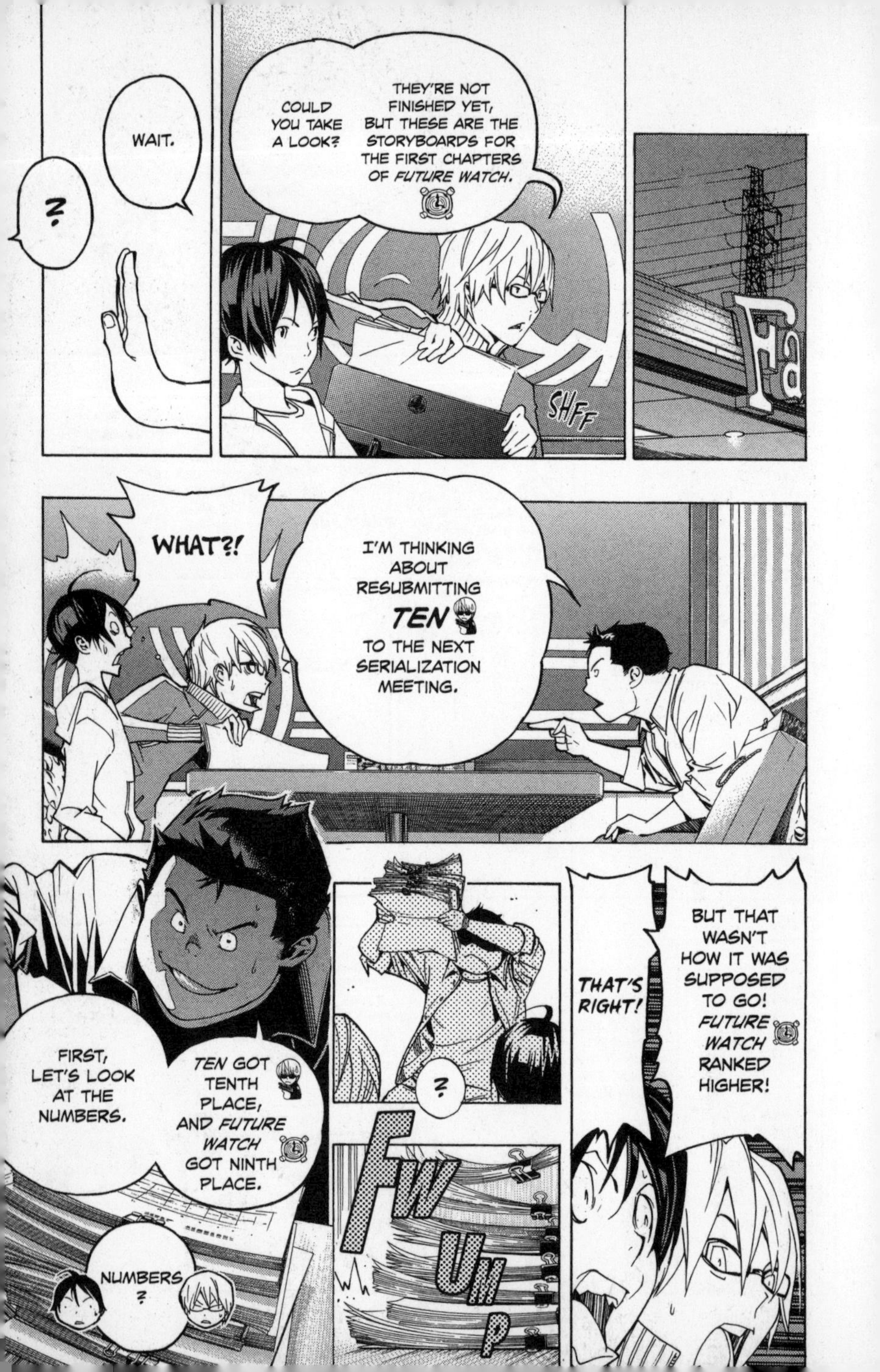
THEY'RE NOT FINISHED YET, BUT THESE ARE THE STORYBOARDS FOR THE FIRST CHAPTERS OF FUTURE WATCH.
COULD YOU TAKE A LOOK?
SHFF
WAIT.
?
I'M THINKING ABOUT RESUBMITTING TEN TO THE NEXT SERIALIZATION MEETING.
WHAT?!
BUT THAT WASN'T HOW IT WAS SUPPOSED TO GO! FUTURE WATCH RANKED HIGHER!
THAT'S RIGHT!
?
FWUUP
FIRST, LET'S LOOK AT THE NUMBERS.
TEN GOT TENTH PLACE, AND FUTURE WATCH GOT NINTH PLACE.
NUMBERS?

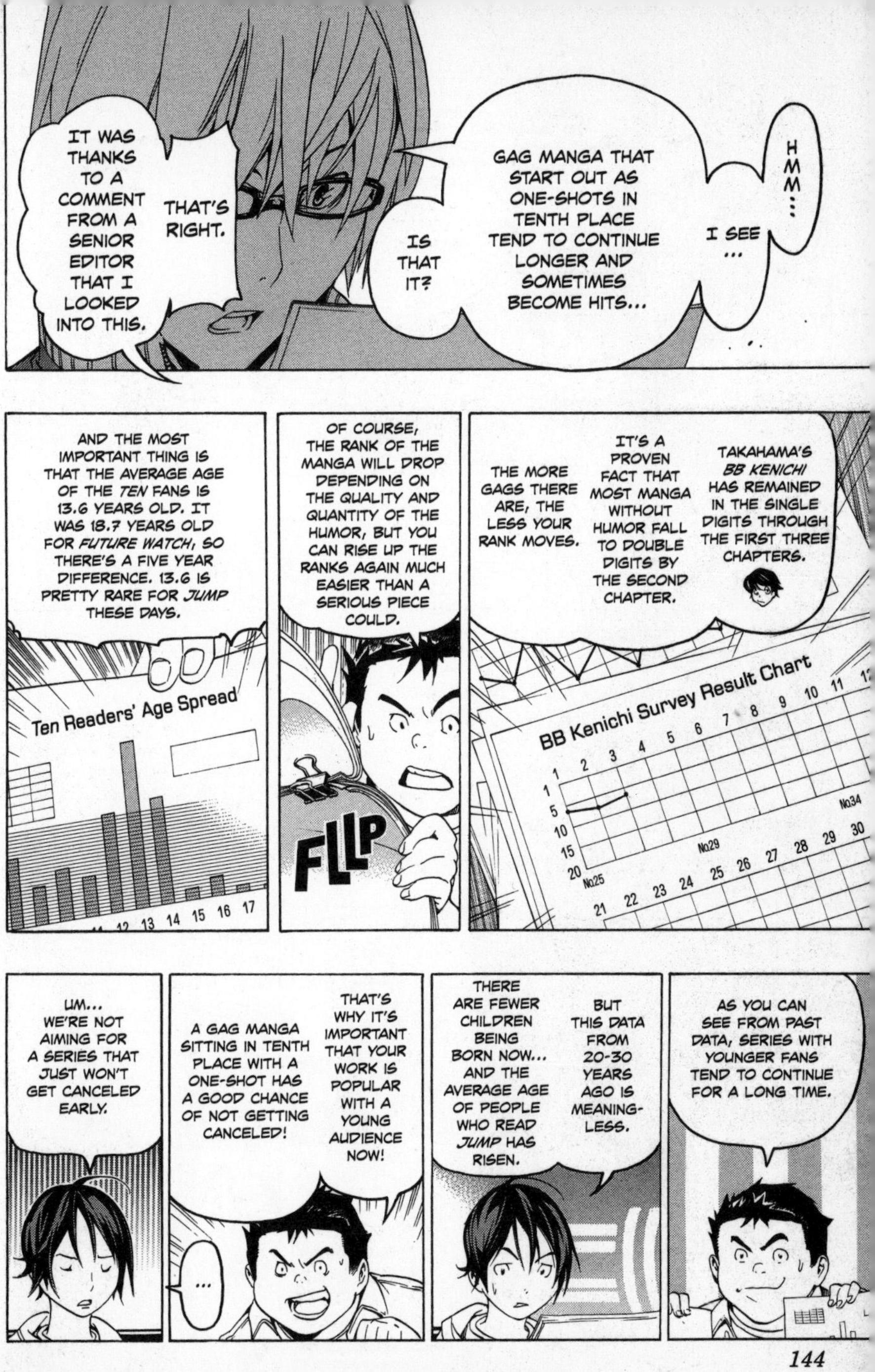
HMM...
I SEE...
GAG MANGA THAT START OUT AS ONE-SHOTS IN TENTH PLACE TEND TO CONTINUE LONGER AND SOMETIMES BECOME HITS...
IS THAT IT?
THAT'S RIGHT.
IT WAS THANKS TO A COMMENT FROM A SENIOR EDITOR THAT I LOOKED INTO THIS.
TAKAHAMA'S *BB KENICHI* HAS REMAINED IN THE SINGLE DIGITS THROUGH THE FIRST THREE CHAPTERS.
IT'S A PROVEN FACT THAT MOST MANGA WITHOUT HUMOR FALL TO DOUBLE DIGITS BY THE SECOND CHAPTER.
THE MORE GAGS THERE ARE, THE LESS YOUR RANK MOVES.
BB Kenichi Survey Result Chart
OF COURSE, THE RANK OF THE MANGA WILL DROP DEPENDING ON THE QUALITY AND QUANTITY OF THE HUMOR, BUT YOU CAN RISE UP THE RANKS AGAIN MUCH EASIER THAN A SERIOUS PIECE COULD.
FLLP
AND THE MOST IMPORTANT THING IS THAT THE AVERAGE AGE OF THE *TEN* FANS IS 13.6 YEARS OLD. IT WAS 18.7 YEARS OLD FOR *FUTURE WATCH*, SO THERE'S A FIVE YEAR DIFFERENCE. 13.6 IS PRETTY RARE FOR *JUMP* THESE DAYS.
Ten Readers' Age Spread
AS YOU CAN SEE FROM PAST DATA, SERIES WITH YOUNGER FANS TEND TO CONTINUE FOR A LONG TIME.
BUT THIS DATA FROM 20-30 YEARS AGO IS MEANINGLESS.
THERE ARE FEWER CHILDREN BEING BORN NOW... AND THE AVERAGE AGE OF PEOPLE WHO READ *JUMP* HAS RISEN.
THAT'S WHY IT'S IMPORTANT THAT YOUR WORK IS POPULAR WITH A YOUNG AUDIENCE NOW!
A GAG MANGA SITTING IN TENTH PLACE WITH A ONE-SHOT HAS A GOOD CHANCE OF NOT GETTING CANCELED!
...
UM... WE'RE NOT AIMING FOR A SERIES THAT JUST WON'T GET CANCELED EARLY.

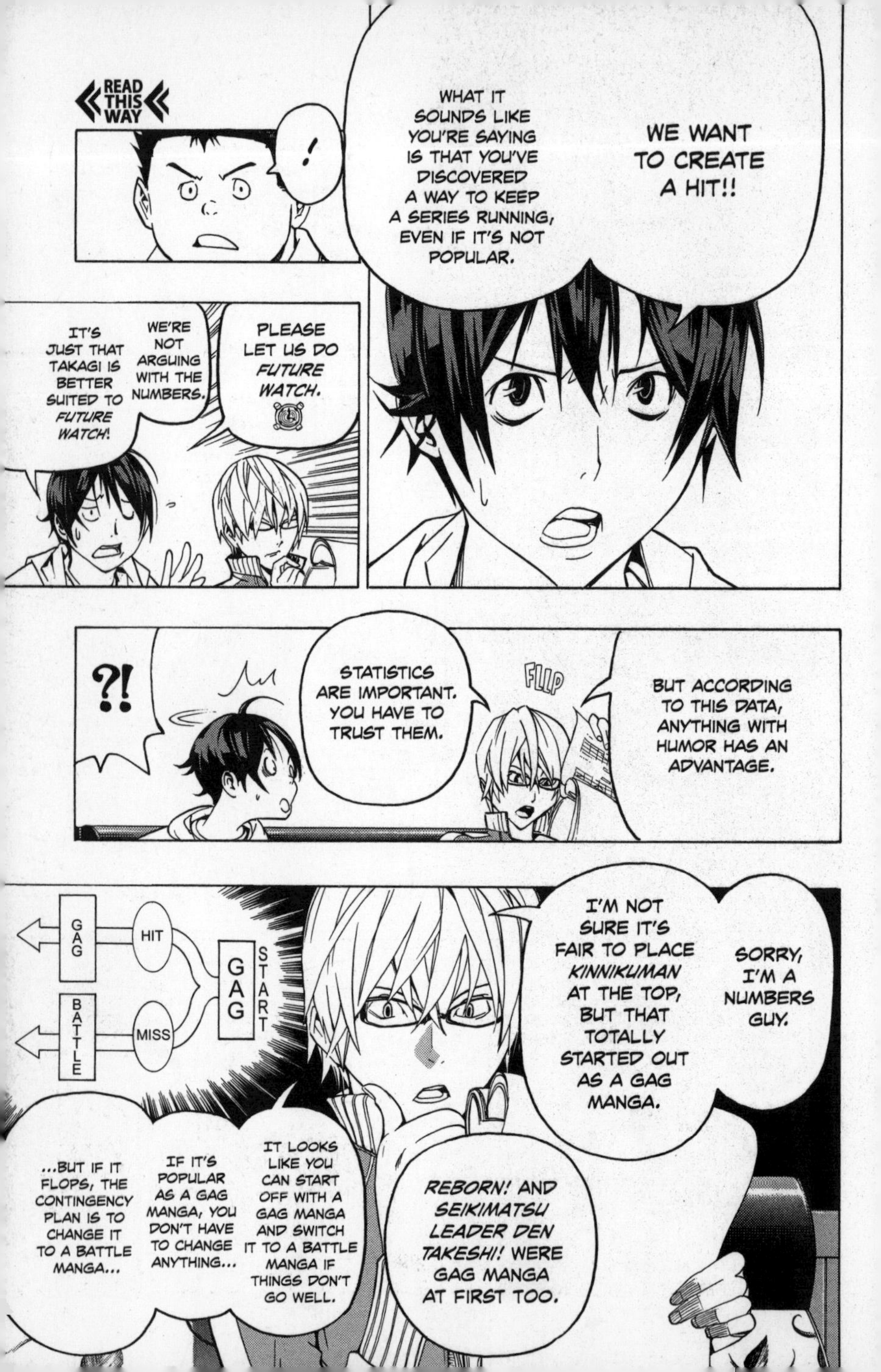
READ THIS WAY
WE WANT TO CREATE A HIT!!
WHAT IT SOUNDS LIKE YOU'RE SAYING IS THAT YOU'VE DISCOVERED A WAY TO KEEP A SERIES RUNNING, EVEN IF IT'S NOT POPULAR.
!
PLEASE LET US DO *FUTURE WATCH*.
WE'RE NOT ARGUING WITH THE NUMBERS.
IT'S JUST THAT TAKAGI IS BETTER SUITED TO *FUTURE WATCH*!
BUT ACCORDING TO THIS DATA, ANYTHING WITH HUMOR HAS AN ADVANTAGE.
FLIP
STATISTICS ARE IMPORTANT. YOU HAVE TO TRUST THEM.
?!
SORRY, I'M A NUMBERS GUY.
I'M NOT SURE IT'S FAIR TO PLACE *KINNIKUMAN* AT THE TOP, BUT THAT TOTALLY STARTED OUT AS A GAG MANGA.
REBORN! AND *SEIKIMATSU LEADER DEN TAKESHI!* WERE GAG MANGA AT FIRST TOO.
START
GAG
HIT
GAG
MISS
BATTLE
IT LOOKS LIKE YOU CAN START OFF WITH A GAG MANGA AND SWITCH IT TO A BATTLE MANGA IF THINGS DON'T GO WELL.
IF IT'S POPULAR AS A GAG MANGA, YOU DON'T HAVE TO CHANGE ANYTHING...
...BUT IF IT FLOPS, THE CONTINGENCY PLAN IS TO CHANGE IT TO A BATTLE MANGA...

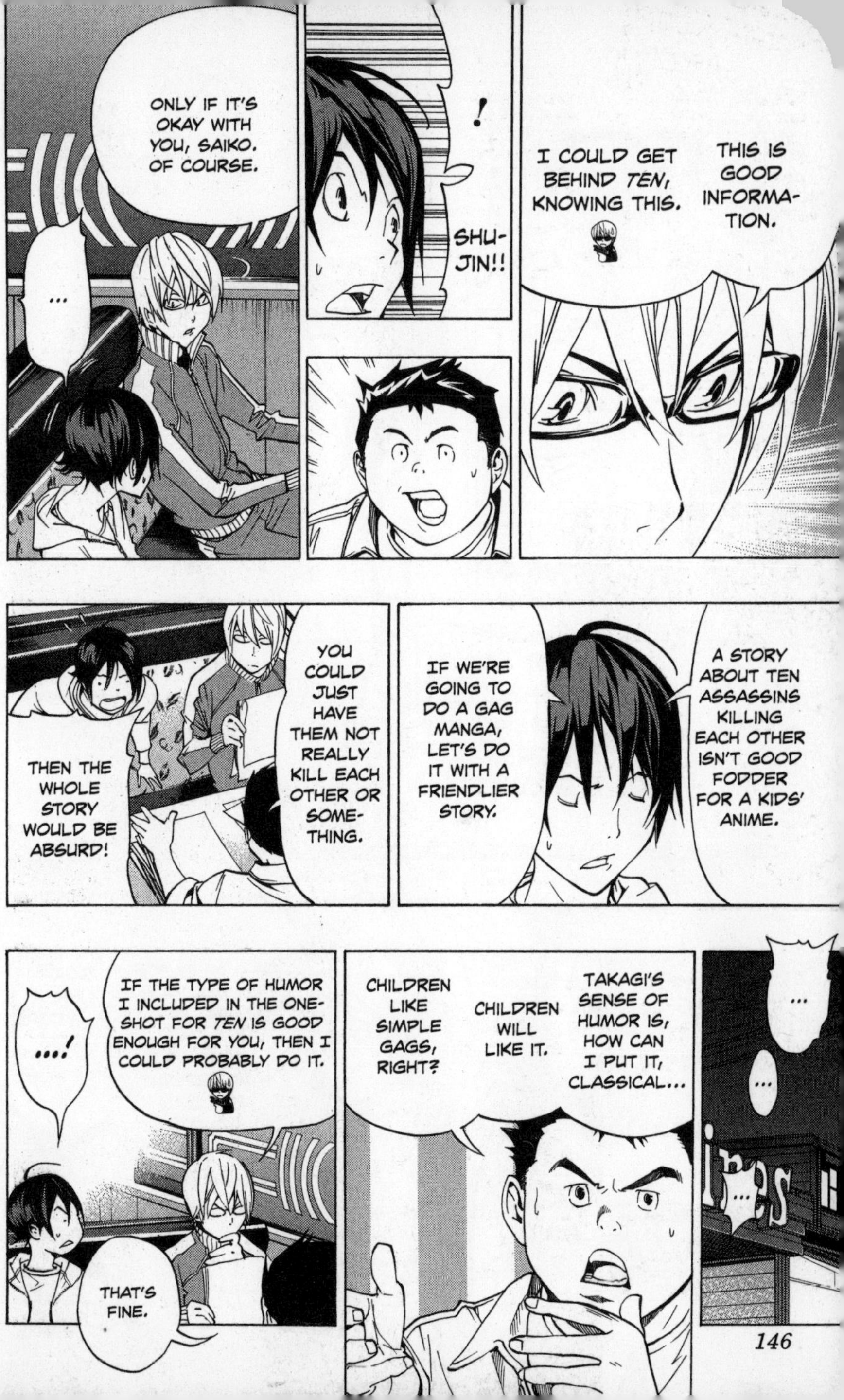
THIS IS GOOD INFORMATION.
I COULD GET BEHIND TEN, KNOWING THIS.
!
SHU-JIN!!
ONLY IF IT'S OKAY WITH YOU, SAIKO. OF COURSE.
...
A STORY ABOUT TEN ASSASSINS KILLING EACH OTHER ISN'T GOOD FODDER FOR A KIDS' ANIME.
IF WE'RE GOING TO DO A GAG MANGA, LET'S DO IT WITH A FRIENDLIER STORY.
YOU COULD JUST HAVE THEM NOT REALLY KILL EACH OTHER OR SOME-THING.
THEN THE WHOLE STORY WOULD BE ABSURD!
...
...
...
TAKAGI'S SENSE OF HUMOR IS, HOW CAN I PUT IT, CLASSICAL...
CHILDREN WILL LIKE IT.
CHILDREN LIKE SIMPLE GAGS, RIGHT?
IF THE TYPE OF HUMOR I INCLUDED IN THE ONE-SHOT FOR TEN IS GOOD ENOUGH FOR YOU, THEN I COULD PROBABLY DO IT.
....!
THAT'S FINE.

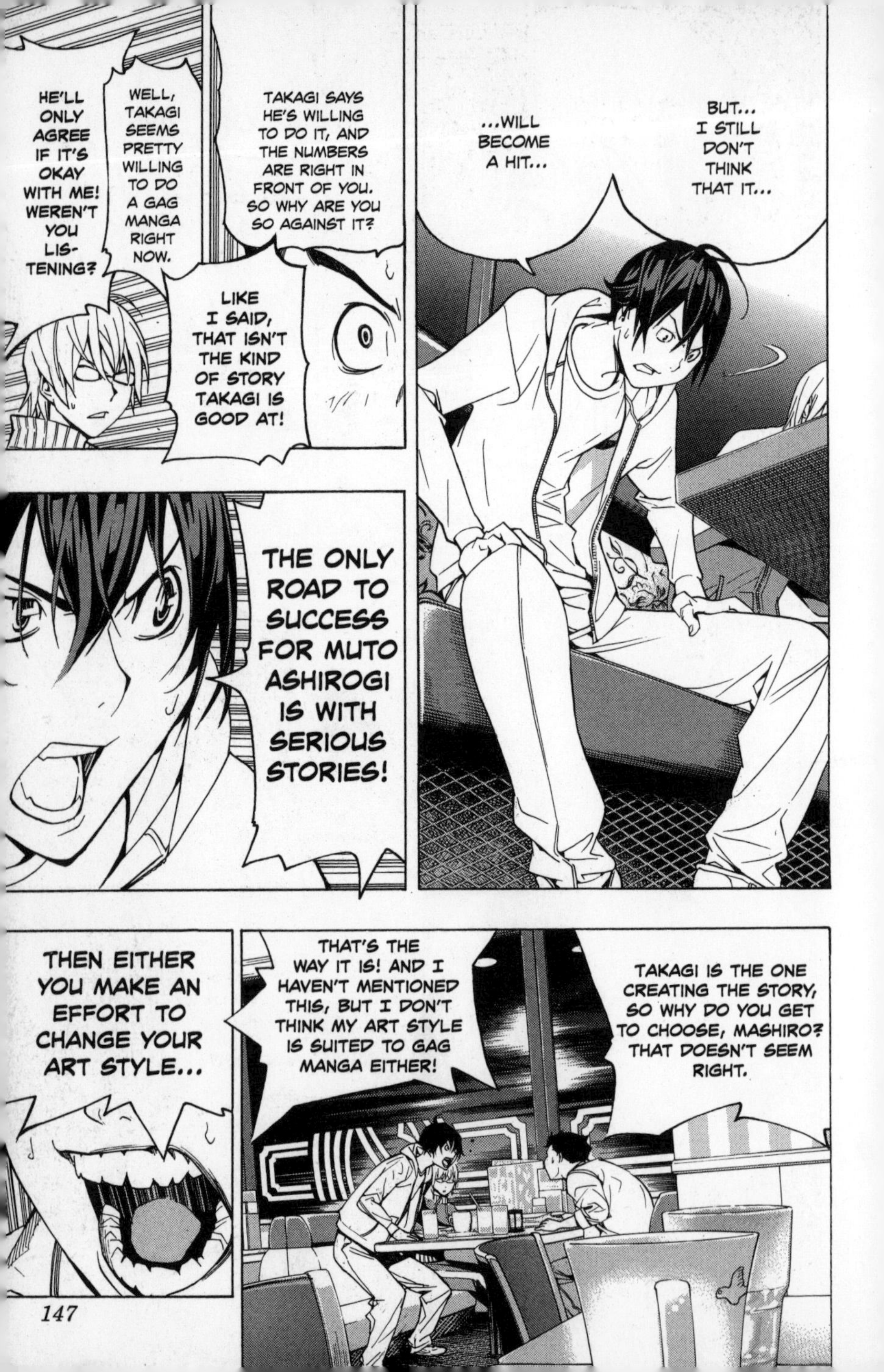
BUT... I STILL DON'T THINK THAT IT...
...WILL BECOME A HIT...
TAKAGI SAYS HE'S WILLING TO DO IT, AND THE NUMBERS ARE RIGHT IN FRONT OF YOU. SO WHY ARE YOU SO AGAINST IT?
WELL, TAKAGI SEEMS PRETTY WILLING TO DO A GAG MANGA RIGHT NOW.
HE'LL ONLY AGREE IF IT'S OKAY WITH ME! WEREN'T YOU LIS-TENING?
LIKE I SAID, THAT ISN'T THE KIND OF STORY TAKAGI IS GOOD AT!
THE ONLY ROAD TO SUCCESS FOR MUTO ASHIROGI IS WITH SERIOUS STORIES!
TAKAGI IS THE ONE CREATING THE STORY, SO WHY DO YOU GET TO CHOOSE, MASHIRO? THAT DOESN'T SEEM RIGHT.
THAT'S THE WAY IT IS! AND I HAVEN'T MENTIONED THIS, BUT I DON'T THINK MY ART STYLE IS SUITED TO GAG MANGA EITHER!
THEN EITHER YOU MAKE AN EFFORT TO CHANGE YOUR ART STYLE...

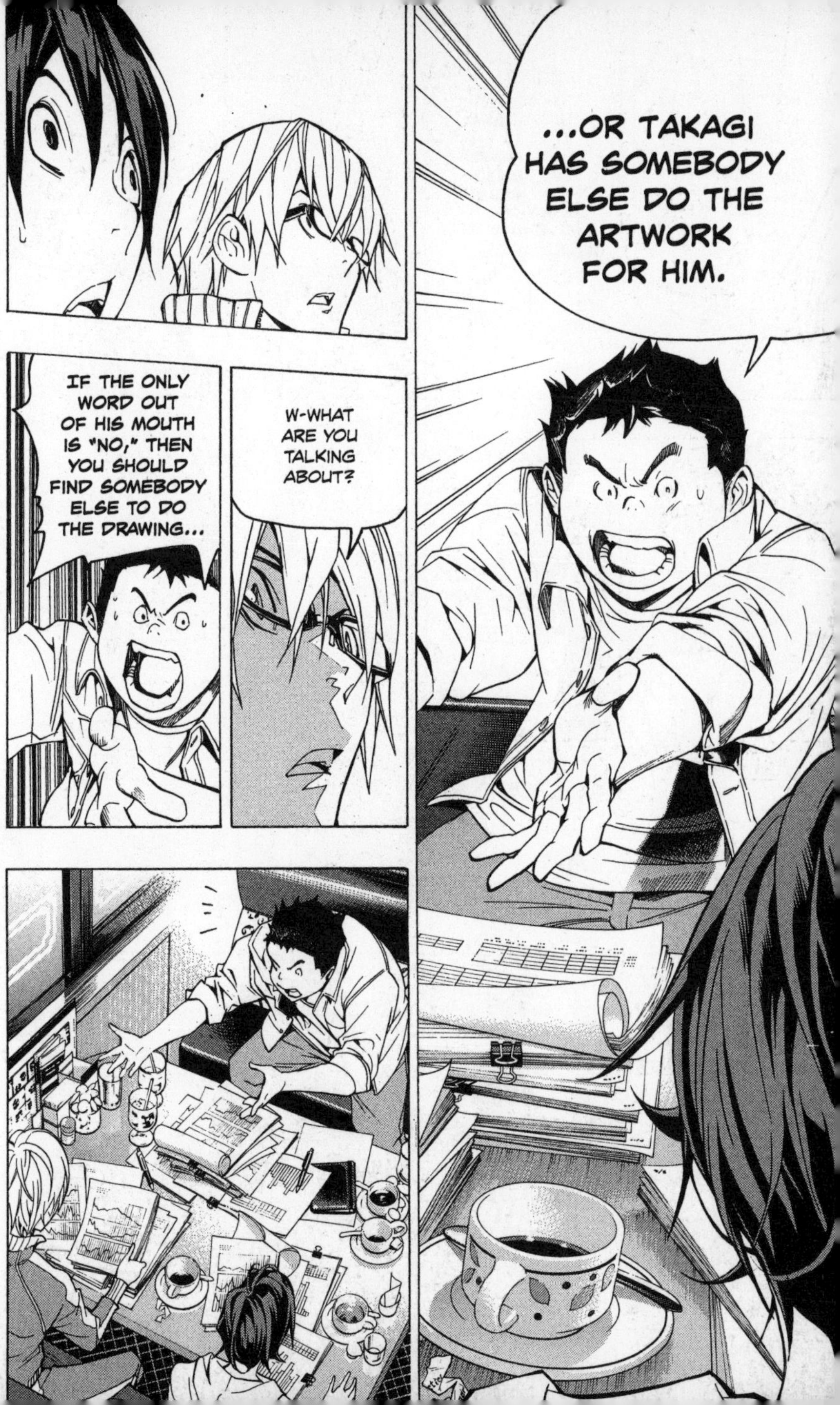
...OR TAKAGI HAS SOMEBODY ELSE DO THE ARTWORK FOR HIM.
W-WHAT ARE YOU TALKING ABOUT?
IF THE ONLY WORD OUT OF HIS MOUTH IS "NO," THEN YOU SHOULD FIND SOMEBODY ELSE TO DO THE DRAWING...

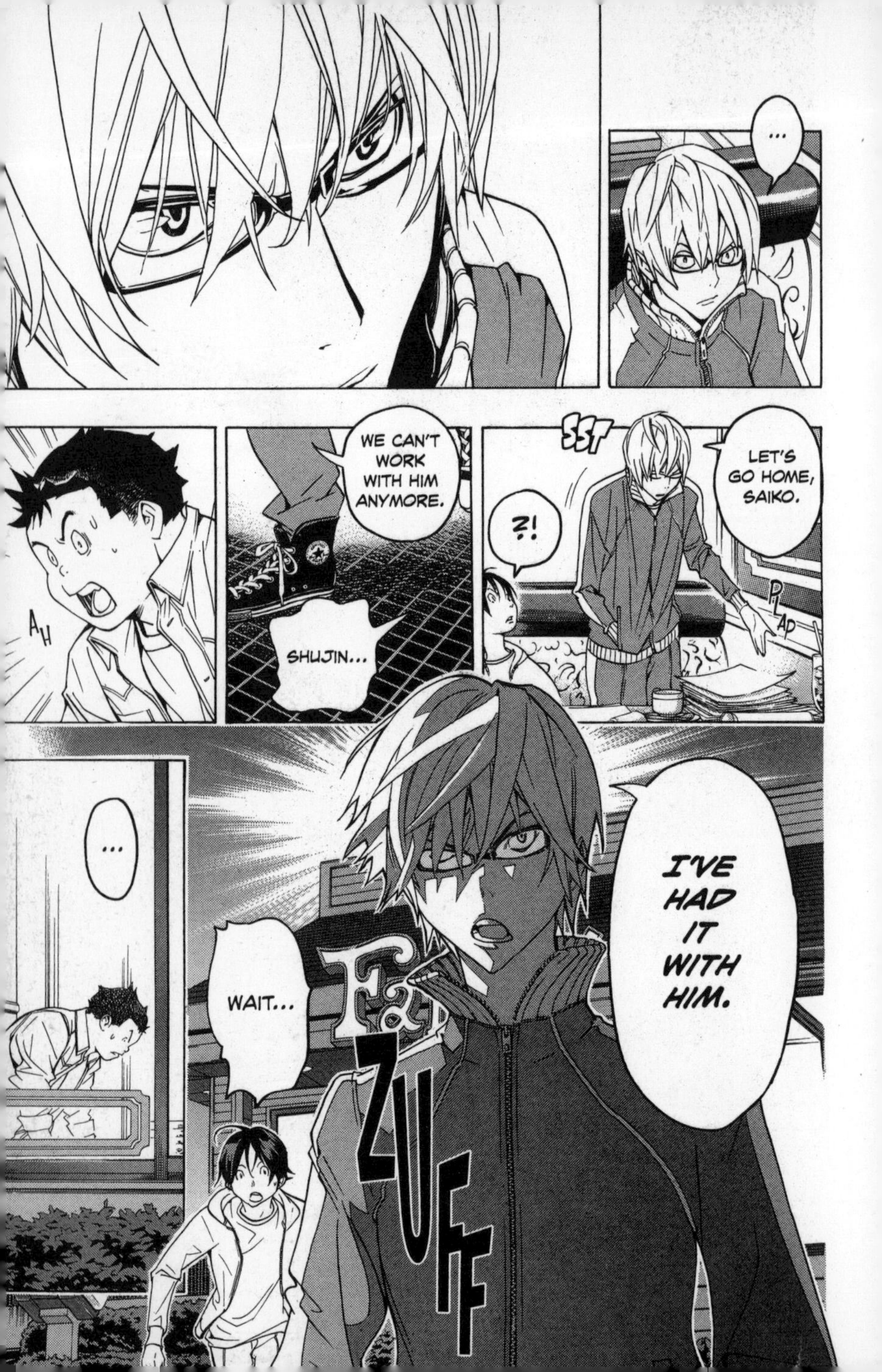
...
SST
LET'S GO HOME, SAIKO.
?!
PLAP
WE CAN'T WORK WITH HIM ANYMORE.
SHUJIN...
AH
I'VE HAD IT WITH HIM.
ZUFF
WAIT...
...

OHBA'S STORYBOARD

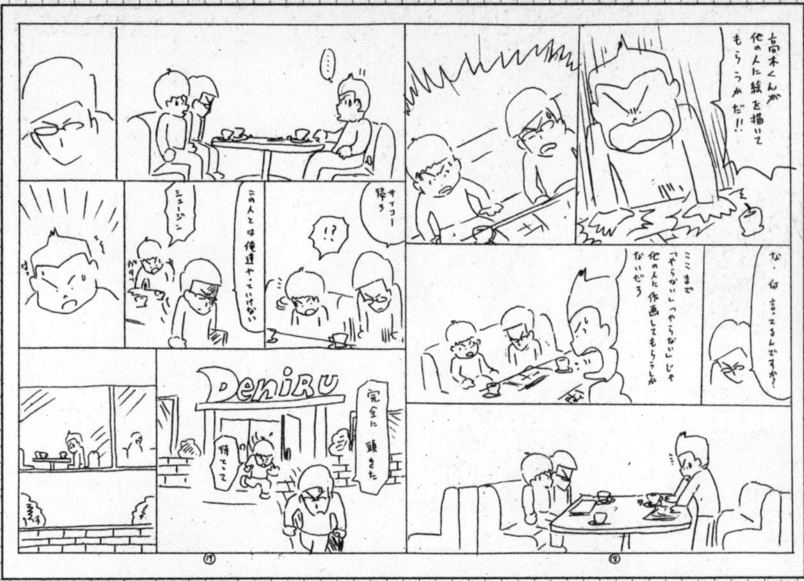

高木くんが他の人に絵を描いてもらうかだ!!
な・何言ってるんですか?
ここまで「やらない」「やらない」じゃ他の人に作画してもらうしかないだろ
サイコー帰ろ
!?
この人とは俺達やっていけない
シュージン
ガタッ
はっ
…
Deniru
完全に頭きた
待てって

OBATA'S STORYBOARD

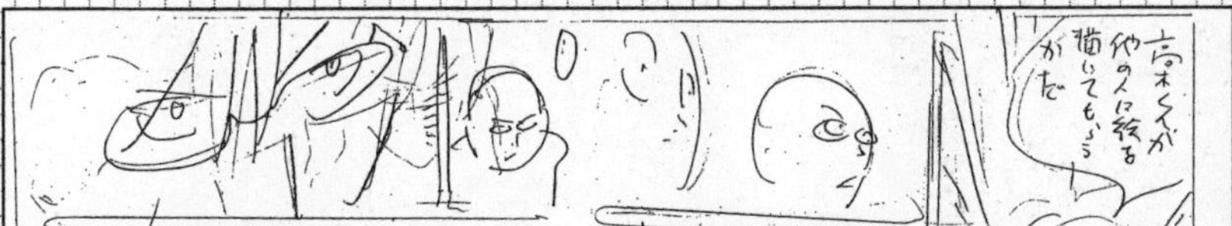

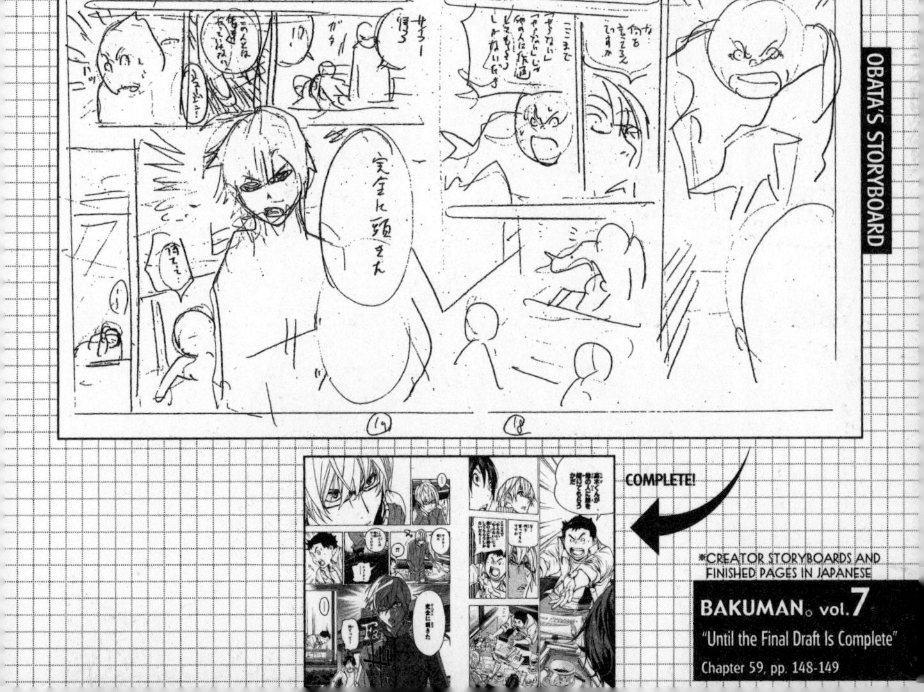

COMPLETE!

*CREATOR STORYBOARDS AND FINISHED PAGES IN JAPANESE

BAKUMAN。 vol. 7

"Until the Final Draft Is Complete"

Chapter 59, pp. 148-149

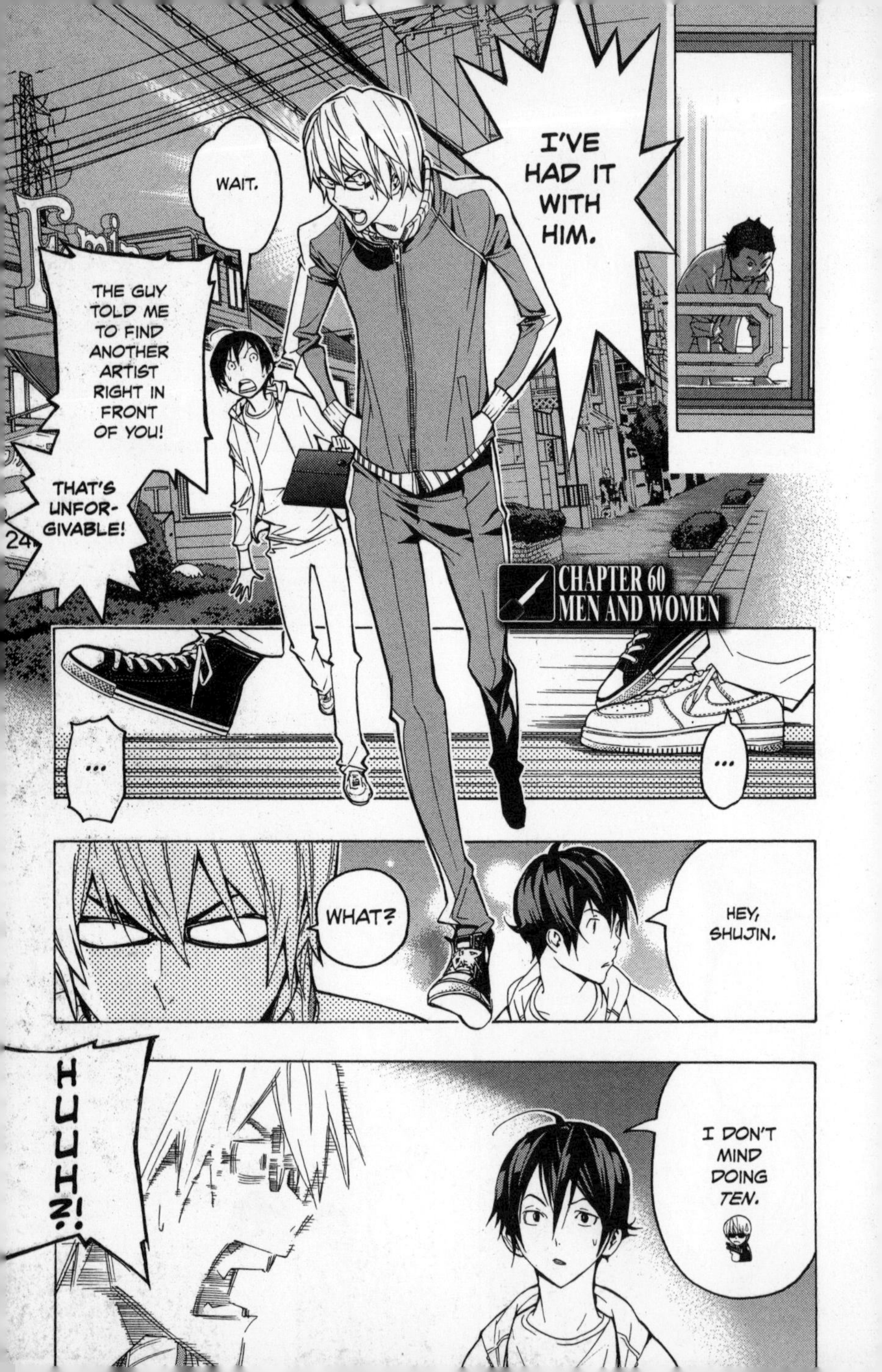
I'VE HAD IT WITH HIM.
WAIT.
THE GUY TOLD ME TO FIND ANOTHER ARTIST RIGHT IN FRONT OF YOU!
THAT'S UNFORGIVABLE!
CHAPTER 60
MEN AND WOMEN
...
...
HEY, SHUJIN.
WHAT?
I DON'T MIND DOING *TEN*.
HUUH?!

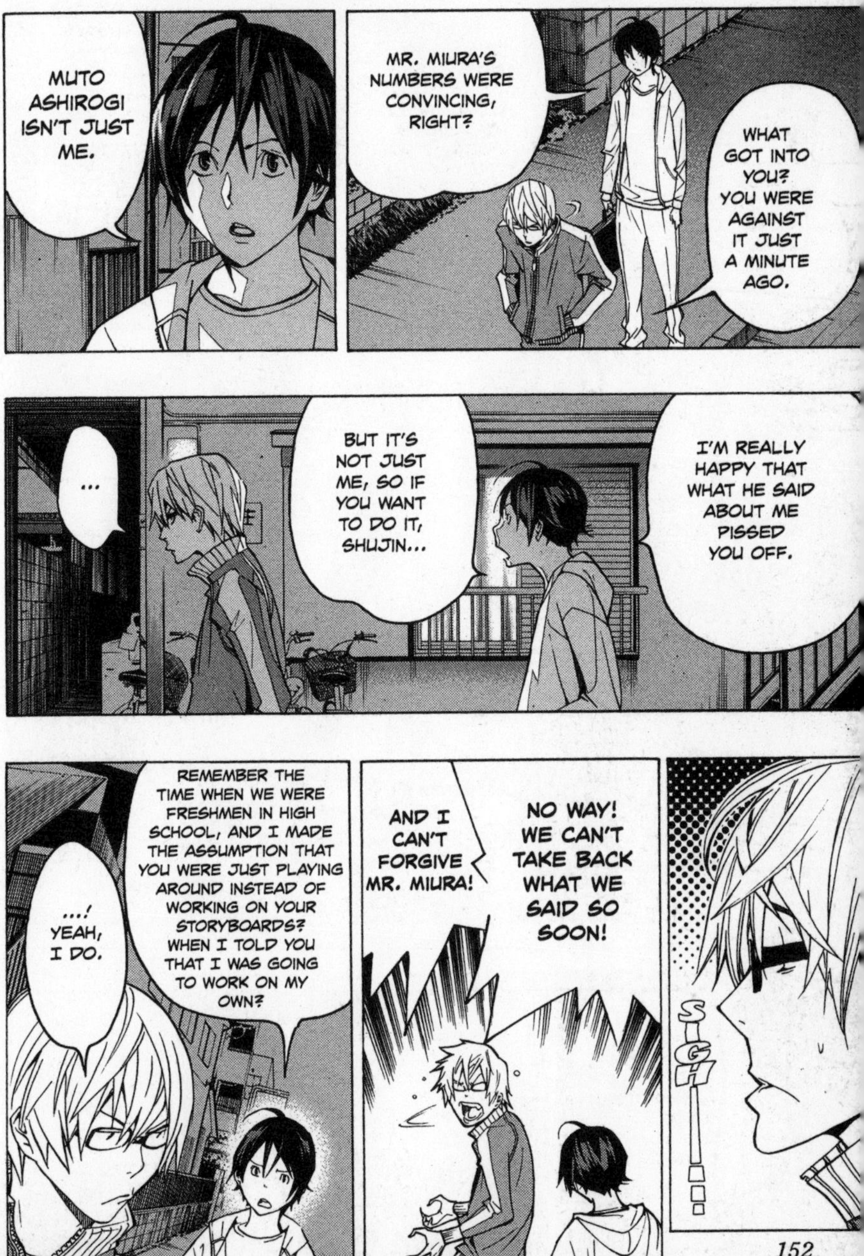
MR. MIURA'S NUMBERS WERE CONVINCING, RIGHT?
WHAT GOT INTO YOU? YOU WERE AGAINST IT JUST A MINUTE AGO.
MUTO ASHIROGI ISN'T JUST ME.
I'M REALLY HAPPY THAT WHAT HE SAID ABOUT ME PISSED YOU OFF.
BUT IT'S NOT JUST ME, SO IF YOU WANT TO DO IT, SHUJIN...
...
SIGH...
NO WAY! WE CAN'T TAKE BACK WHAT WE SAID SO SOON!
AND I CAN'T FORGIVE MR. MIURA!
REMEMBER THE TIME WHEN WE WERE FRESHMEN IN HIGH SCHOOL, AND I MADE THE ASSUMPTION THAT YOU WERE JUST PLAYING AROUND INSTEAD OF WORKING ON YOUR STORYBOARDS? WHEN I TOLD YOU THAT I WAS GOING TO WORK ON MY OWN?
...! YEAH, I DO.

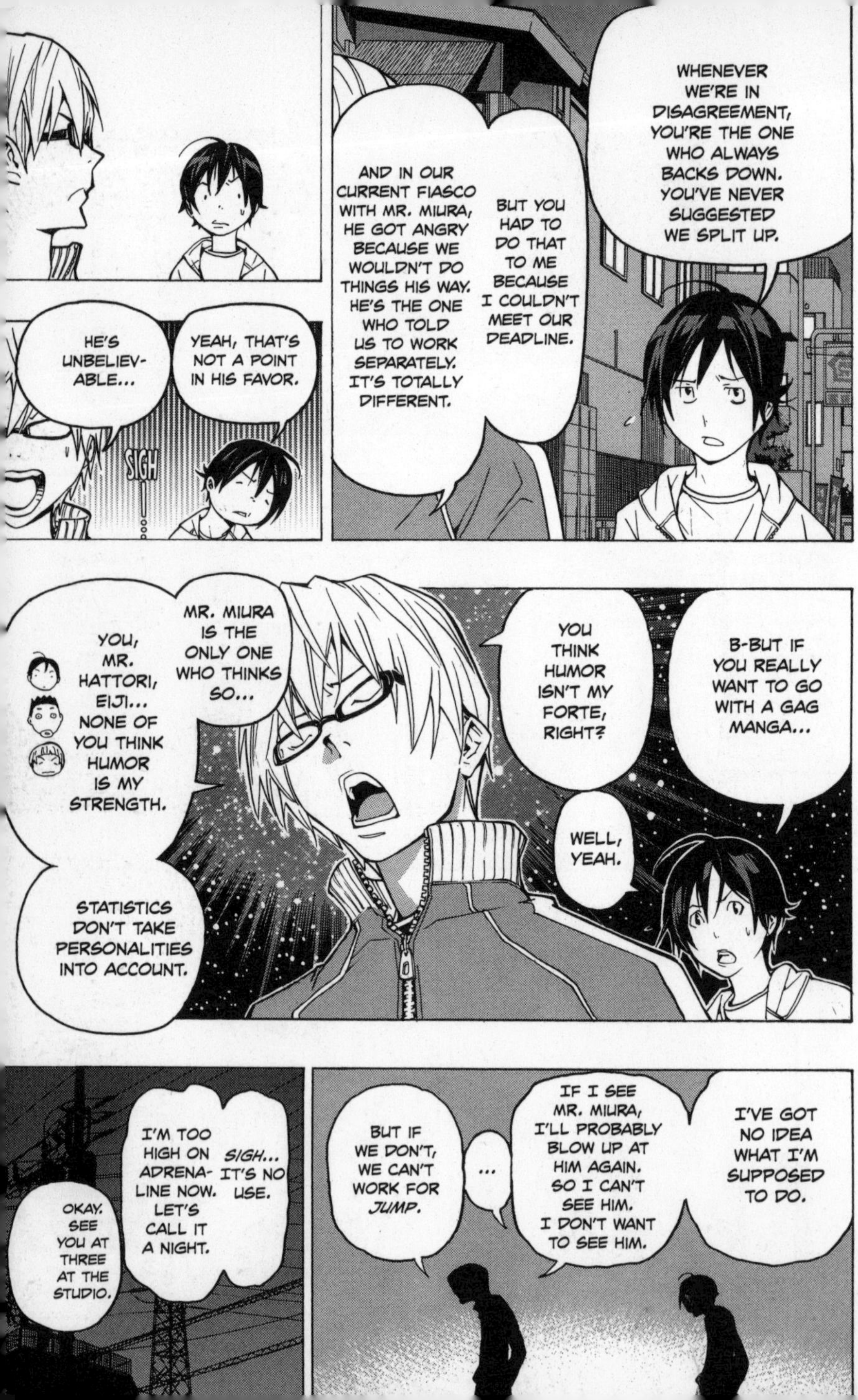
WHENEVER WE'RE IN DISAGREEMENT, YOU'RE THE ONE WHO ALWAYS BACKS DOWN. YOU'VE NEVER SUGGESTED WE SPLIT UP.
BUT YOU HAD TO DO THAT TO ME BECAUSE I COULDN'T MEET OUR DEADLINE.
AND IN OUR CURRENT FIASCO WITH MR. MIURA, HE GOT ANGRY BECAUSE WE WOULDN'T DO THINGS HIS WAY. HE'S THE ONE WHO TOLD US TO WORK SEPARATELY. IT'S TOTALLY DIFFERENT.
YEAH, THAT'S NOT A POINT IN HIS FAVOR.
HE'S UNBELIEV-ABLE...
SIGH
B-BUT IF YOU REALLY WANT TO GO WITH A GAG MANGA...
YOU THINK HUMOR ISN'T MY FORTE, RIGHT?
WELL, YEAH.
MR. MIURA IS THE ONLY ONE WHO THINKS SO...
YOU, MR. HATTORI, EIJI... NONE OF YOU THINK HUMOR IS MY STRENGTH.
STATISTICS DON'T TAKE PERSONALITIES INTO ACCOUNT.
I'VE GOT NO IDEA WHAT I'M SUPPOSED TO DO.
IF I SEE MR. MIURA, I'LL PROBABLY BLOW UP AT HIM AGAIN. SO I CAN'T SEE HIM. I DON'T WANT TO SEE HIM.
...
BUT IF WE DON'T, WE CAN'T WORK FOR *JUMP*.
SIGH... IT'S NO USE.
I'M TOO HIGH ON ADRENA-LINE NOW. LET'S CALL IT A NIGHT.
OKAY. SEE YOU AT THREE AT THE STUDIO.

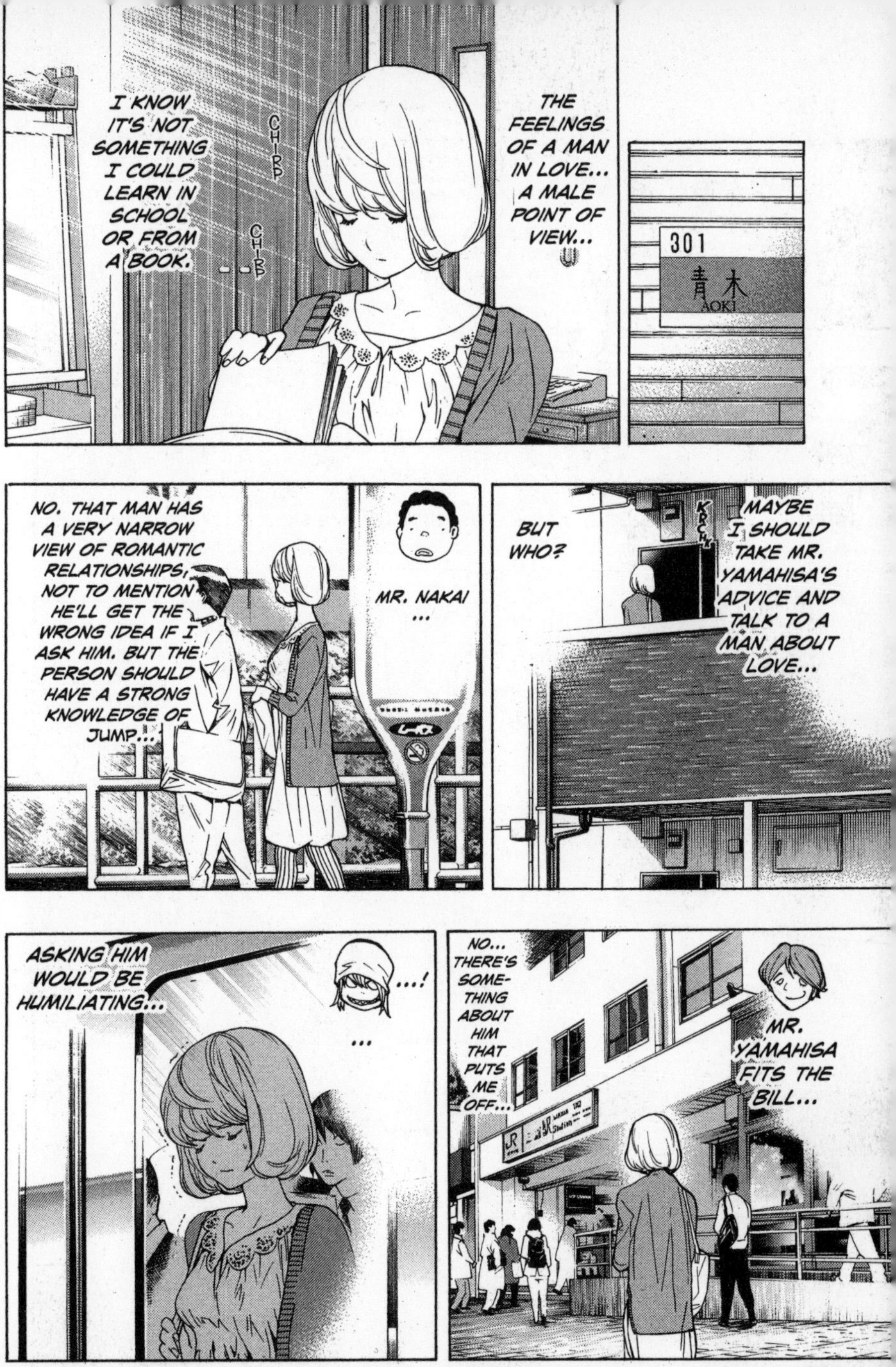
301
青木
AOKI
THE FEELINGS OF A MAN IN LOVE... A MALE POINT OF VIEW...
CHIRP
CHIRP
I KNOW IT'S NOT SOMETHING I COULD LEARN IN SCHOOL OR FROM A BOOK.
MAYBE I SHOULD TAKE MR. YAMAHISA'S ADVICE AND TALK TO A MAN ABOUT LOVE...
KRCHK
BUT WHO?
MR. NAKAI ...
NO. THAT MAN HAS A VERY NARROW VIEW OF ROMANTIC RELATIONSHIPS, NOT TO MENTION HE'LL GET THE WRONG IDEA IF I ASK HIM. BUT THE PERSON SHOULD HAVE A STRONG KNOWLEDGE OF JUMP...
MR. YAMAHISA FITS THE BILL...
NO... THERE'S SOME-THING ABOUT HIM THAT PUTS ME OFF...
...!
...
ASKING HIM WOULD BE HUMILIATING...

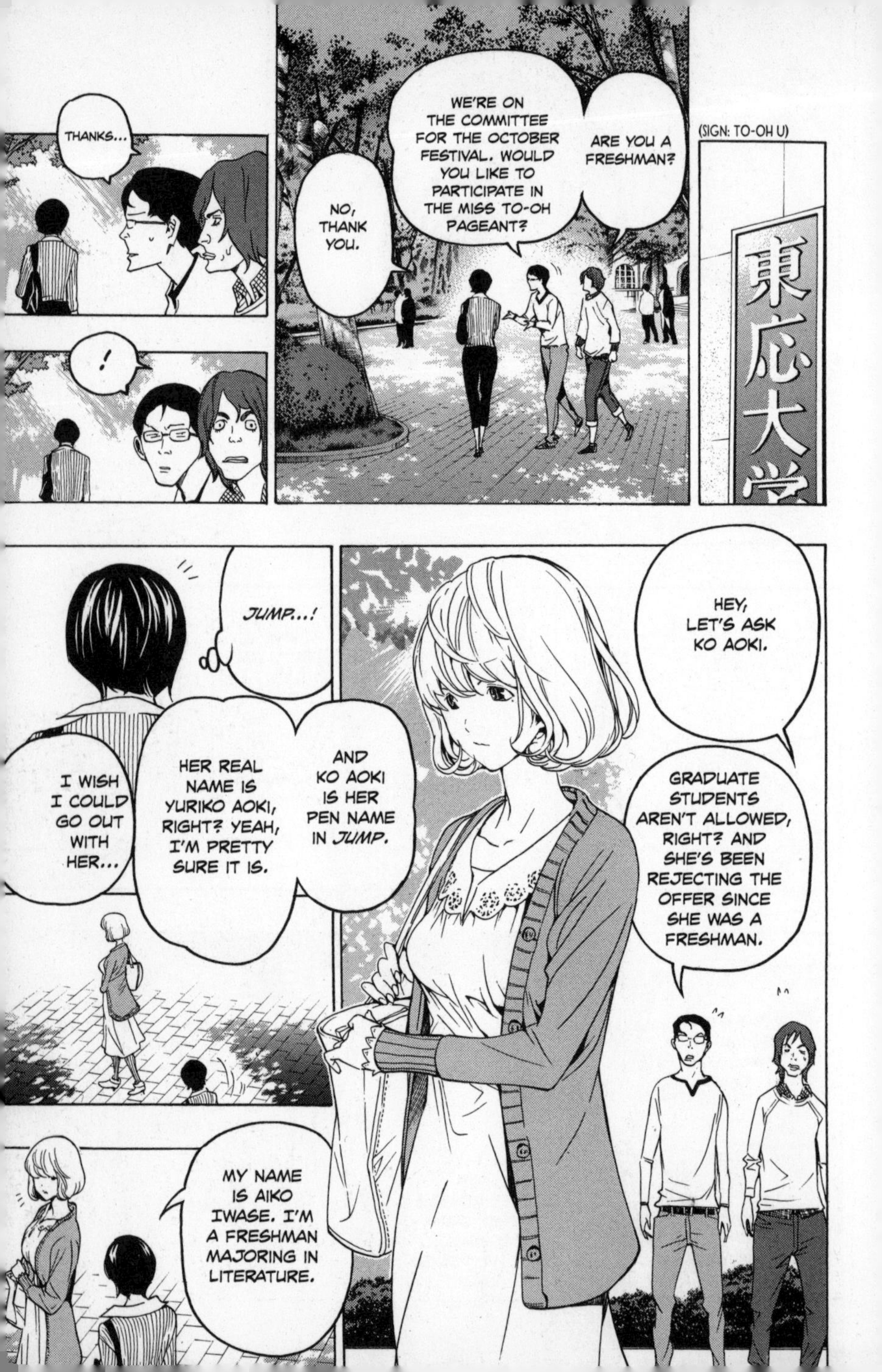
(SIGN: TO-OH U)
東応大
ARE YOU A FRESHMAN?
WE'RE ON THE COMMITTEE FOR THE OCTOBER FESTIVAL. WOULD YOU LIKE TO PARTICIPATE IN THE MISS TO-OH PAGEANT?
NO, THANK YOU.
THANKS...
!
HEY, LET'S ASK KO AOKI.
GRADUATE STUDENTS AREN'T ALLOWED, RIGHT? AND SHE'S BEEN REJECTING THE OFFER SINCE SHE WAS A FRESHMAN.
JUMP...!
AND KO AOKI IS HER PEN NAME IN *JUMP*.
HER REAL NAME IS YURIKO AOKI, RIGHT? YEAH, I'M PRETTY SURE IT IS.
I WISH I COULD GO OUT WITH HER...
MY NAME IS AIKO IWASE. I'M A FRESHMAN MAJORING IN LITERATURE.

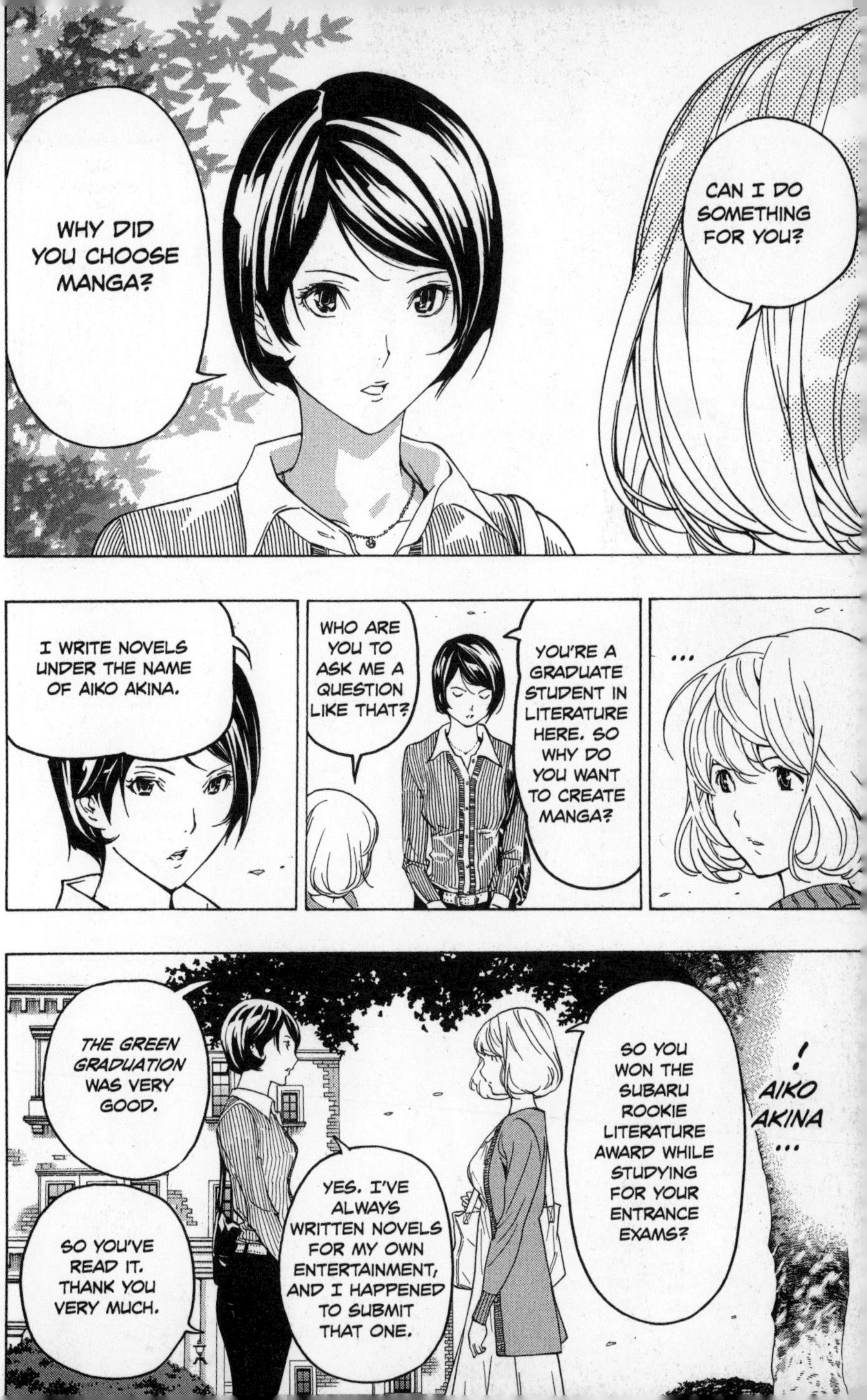
CAN I DO SOMETHING FOR YOU?
WHY DID YOU CHOOSE MANGA?
...
YOU'RE A GRADUATE STUDENT IN LITERATURE HERE. SO WHY DO YOU WANT TO CREATE MANGA?
WHO ARE YOU TO ASK ME A QUESTION LIKE THAT?
I WRITE NOVELS UNDER THE NAME OF AIKO AKINA.
! AIKO AKINA ...
SO YOU WON THE SUBARU ROOKIE LITERATURE AWARD WHILE STUDYING FOR YOUR ENTRANCE EXAMS?
THE GREEN GRADUATION WAS VERY GOOD.
YES. I'VE ALWAYS WRITTEN NOVELS FOR MY OWN ENTERTAINMENT, AND I HAPPENED TO SUBMIT THAT ONE.
SO YOU'VE READ IT. THANK YOU VERY MUCH.

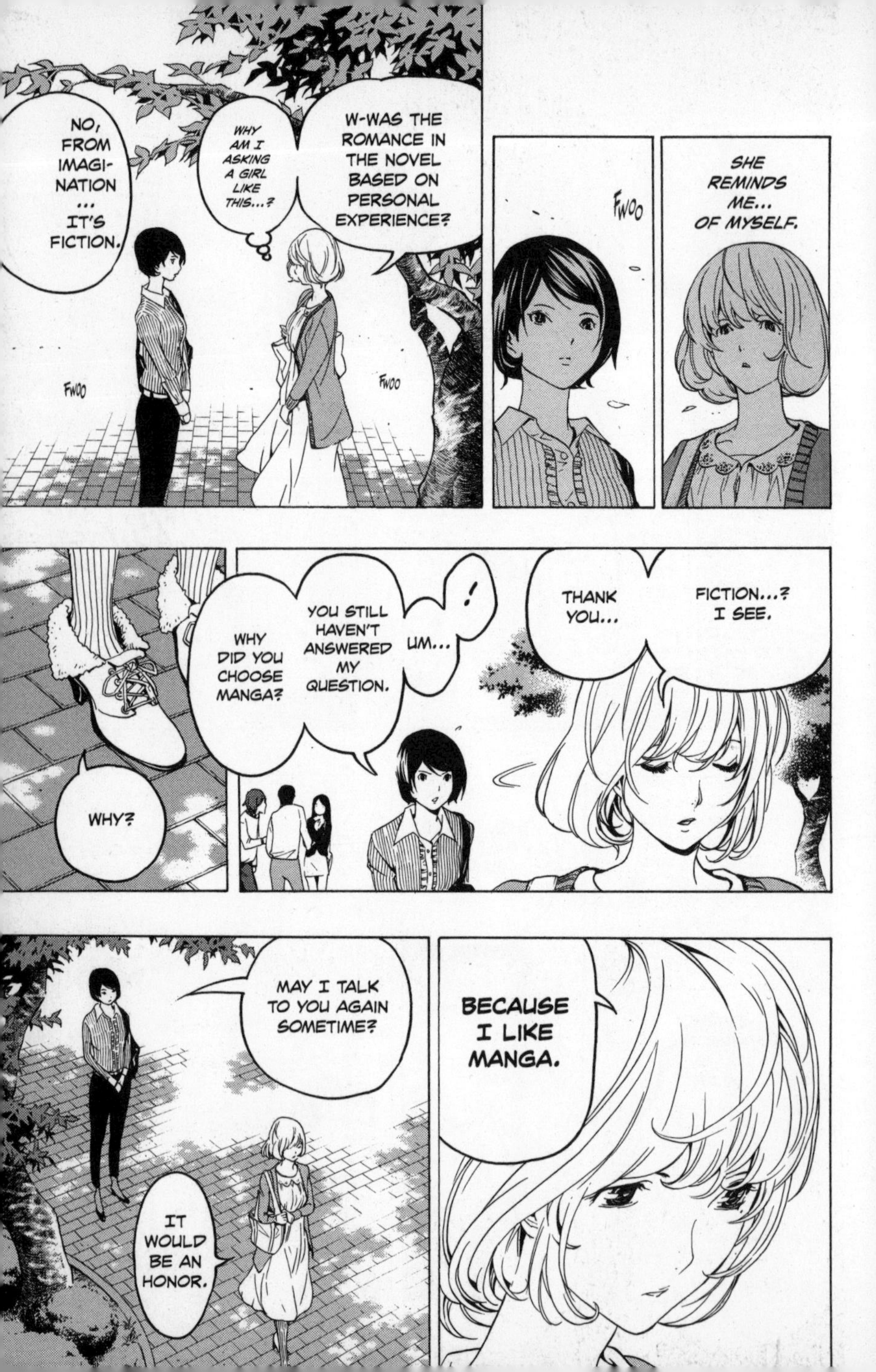
SHE REMINDS ME... OF MYSELF.
FWOO
W-WAS THE ROMANCE IN THE NOVEL BASED ON PERSONAL EXPERIENCE?
WHY AM I ASKING A GIRL LIKE THIS...?
NO, FROM IMAGI-NATION ... IT'S FICTION.
FWOO
FWOO
FICTION...? I SEE.
THANK YOU...
!
UM...
YOU STILL HAVEN'T ANSWERED MY QUESTION.
WHY DID YOU CHOOSE MANGA?
WHY?
BECAUSE I LIKE MANGA.
MAY I TALK TO YOU AGAIN SOMETIME?
IT WOULD BE AN HONOR.

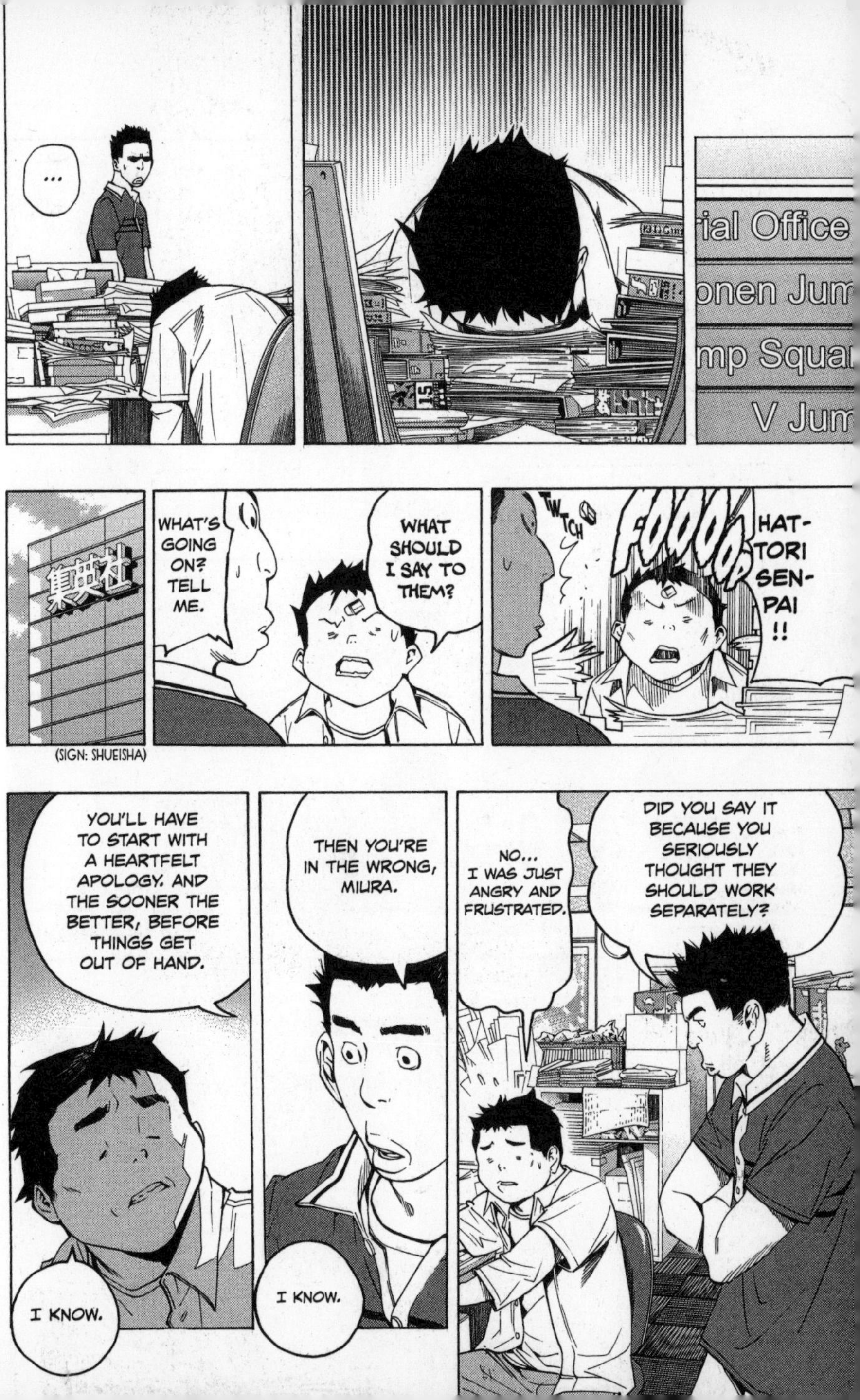
rial Office
onen Jum
mp Squa
V Jum
...
TWITCH
FOOOOP
HAT-TORI SEN-PAI!!
WHAT SHOULD I SAY TO THEM?
WHAT'S GOING ON? TELL ME.
集英社
DID YOU SAY IT BECAUSE YOU SERIOUSLY THOUGHT THEY SHOULD WORK SEPARATELY?
NO... I WAS JUST ANGRY AND FRUSTRATED.
THEN YOU'RE IN THE WRONG, MIURA.
I KNOW.
YOU'LL HAVE TO START WITH A HEARTFELT APOLOGY. AND THE SOONER THE BETTER, BEFORE THINGS GET OUT OF HAND.
I KNOW.
(SIGN: SHUEISHA)

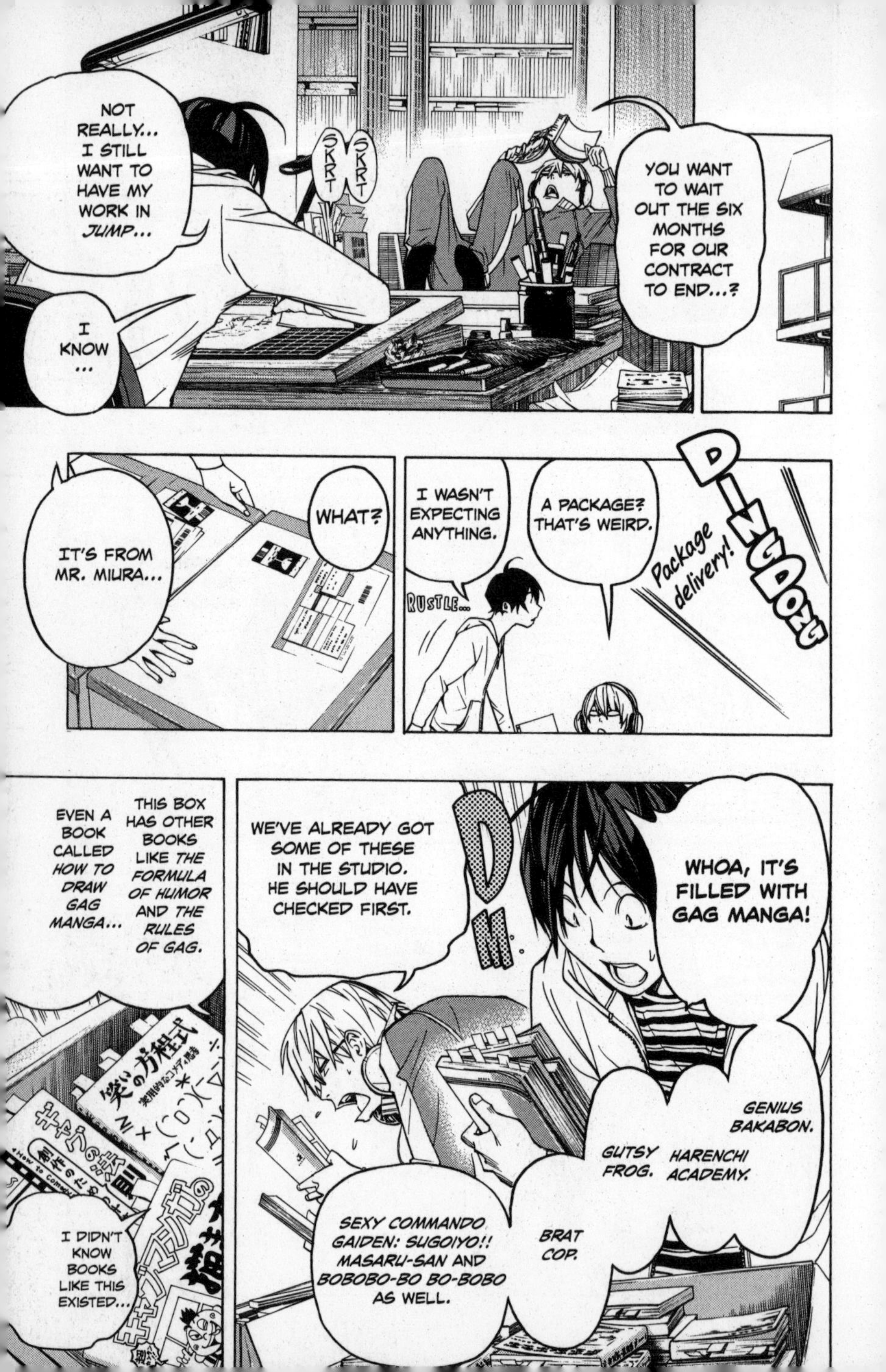
YOU WANT TO WAIT OUT THE SIX MONTHS FOR OUR CONTRACT TO END...?
SKRT SKRT
NOT REALLY... I STILL WANT TO HAVE MY WORK IN *JUMP*...
I KNOW...
DINGDONG
Package delivery!
A PACKAGE? THAT'S WEIRD.
I WASN'T EXPECTING ANYTHING.
RUSTLE...
WHAT?
IT'S FROM MR. MIURA...
WHOA, IT'S FILLED WITH GAG MANGA!
GENIUS BAKABON.
HARENCHI ACADEMY.
GUTSY FROG.
BRAT COP.
SEXY COMMANDO GAIDEN: SUGOIYO!! MASARU-SAN AND BOBOBO-BO BO-BOBO AS WELL.
WE'VE ALREADY GOT SOME OF THESE IN THE STUDIO. HE SHOULD HAVE CHECKED FIRST.
THIS BOX HAS OTHER BOOKS LIKE *THE FORMULA OF HUMOR* AND *THE RULES OF GAG*.
EVEN A BOOK CALLED *HOW TO DRAW GAG MANGA*...
笑いの方程式
I DIDN'T KNOW BOOKS LIKE THIS EXISTED...

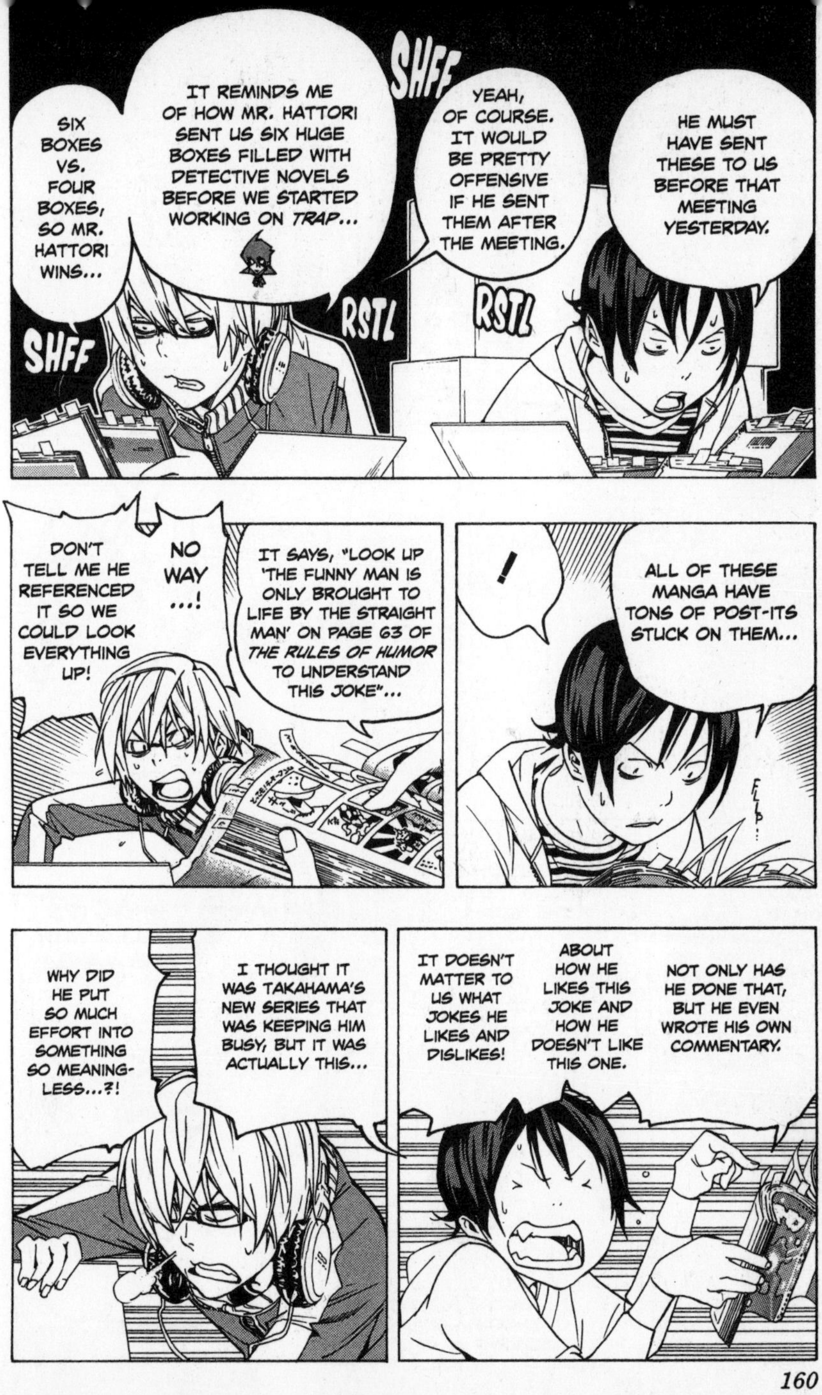
HE MUST HAVE SENT THESE TO US BEFORE THAT MEETING YESTERDAY.
SHFF
YEAH, OF COURSE. IT WOULD BE PRETTY OFFENSIVE IF HE SENT THEM AFTER THE MEETING.
RSTL
IT REMINDS ME OF HOW MR. HATTORI SENT US SIX HUGE BOXES FILLED WITH DETECTIVE NOVELS BEFORE WE STARTED WORKING ON *TRAP*...
RSTL
SIX BOXES VS. FOUR BOXES, SO MR. HATTORI WINS...
SHFF
ALL OF THESE MANGA HAVE TONS OF POST-ITS STUCK ON THEM...
!
FLIP...
IT SAYS, "LOOK UP 'THE FUNNY MAN IS ONLY BROUGHT TO LIFE BY THE STRAIGHT MAN' ON PAGE 63 OF *THE RULES OF HUMOR* TO UNDERSTAND THIS JOKE"...
NO WAY ...!
DON'T TELL ME HE REFERENCED IT SO WE COULD LOOK EVERYTHING UP!
NOT ONLY HAS HE DONE THAT, BUT HE EVEN WROTE HIS OWN COMMENTARY.
ABOUT HOW HE LIKES THIS JOKE AND HOW HE DOESN'T LIKE THIS ONE.
IT DOESN'T MATTER TO US WHAT JOKES HE LIKES AND DISLIKES!
I THOUGHT IT WAS TAKAHAMA'S NEW SERIES THAT WAS KEEPING HIM BUSY, BUT IT WAS ACTUALLY THIS...
WHY DID HE PUT SO MUCH EFFORT INTO SOMETHING SO MEANING-LESS...?!

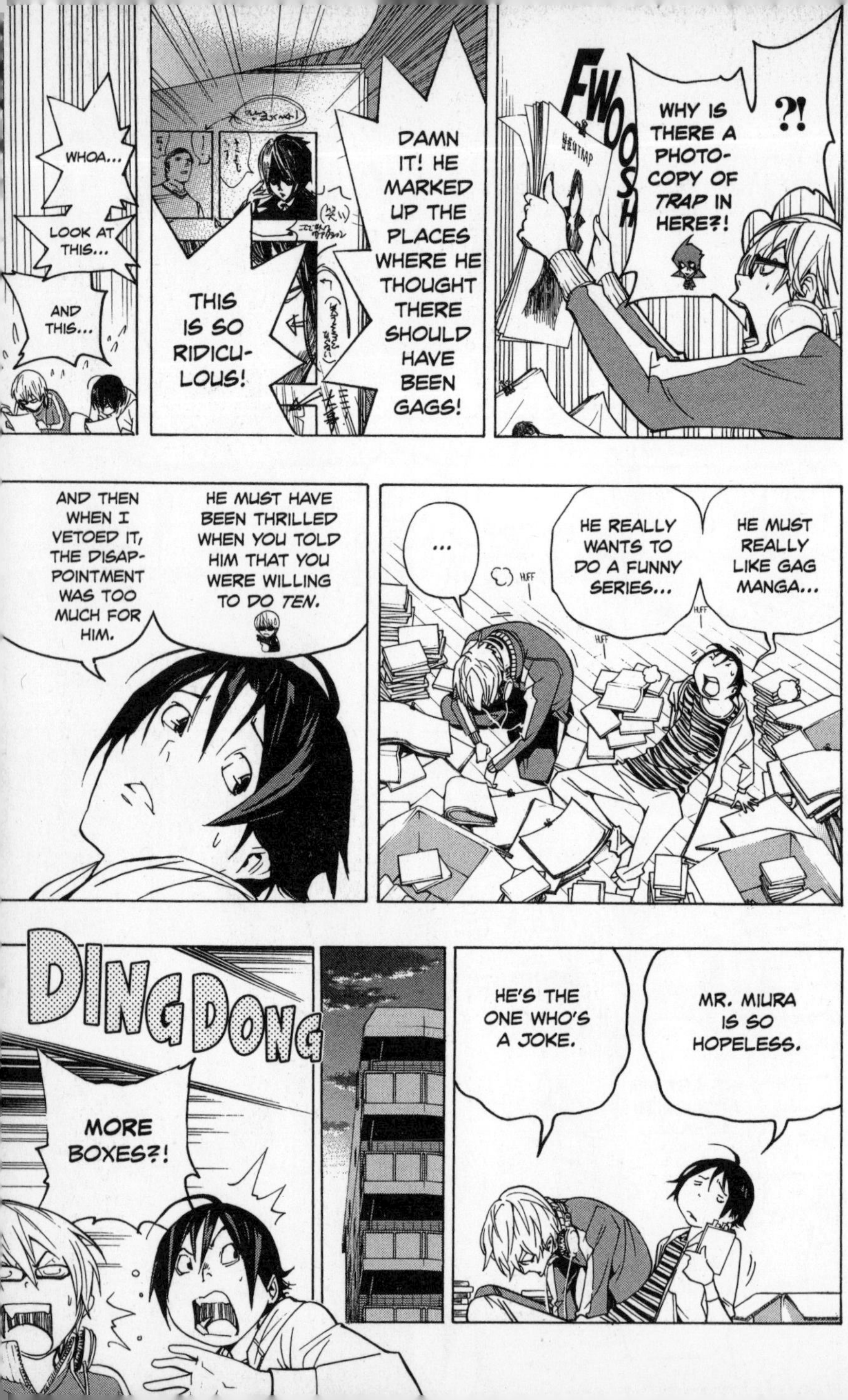
FWOOSH
WHY IS THERE A PHOTOCOPY OF TRAP IN HERE?!
?!
DAMN IT! HE MARKED UP THE PLACES WHERE HE THOUGHT THERE SHOULD HAVE BEEN GAGS!
THIS IS SO RIDICULOUS!
WHOA...
LOOK AT THIS...
AND THIS...
HE MUST REALLY LIKE GAG MANGA...
HE REALLY WANTS TO DO A FUNNY SERIES...
...
HUFF
HUFF
HUFF
HE MUST HAVE BEEN THRILLED WHEN YOU TOLD HIM THAT YOU WERE WILLING TO DO TEN.
AND THEN WHEN I VETOED IT, THE DISAPPOINTMENT WAS TOO MUCH FOR HIM.
MR. MIURA IS SO HOPELESS.
HE'S THE ONE WHO'S A JOKE.
DING DONG
MORE BOXES?!

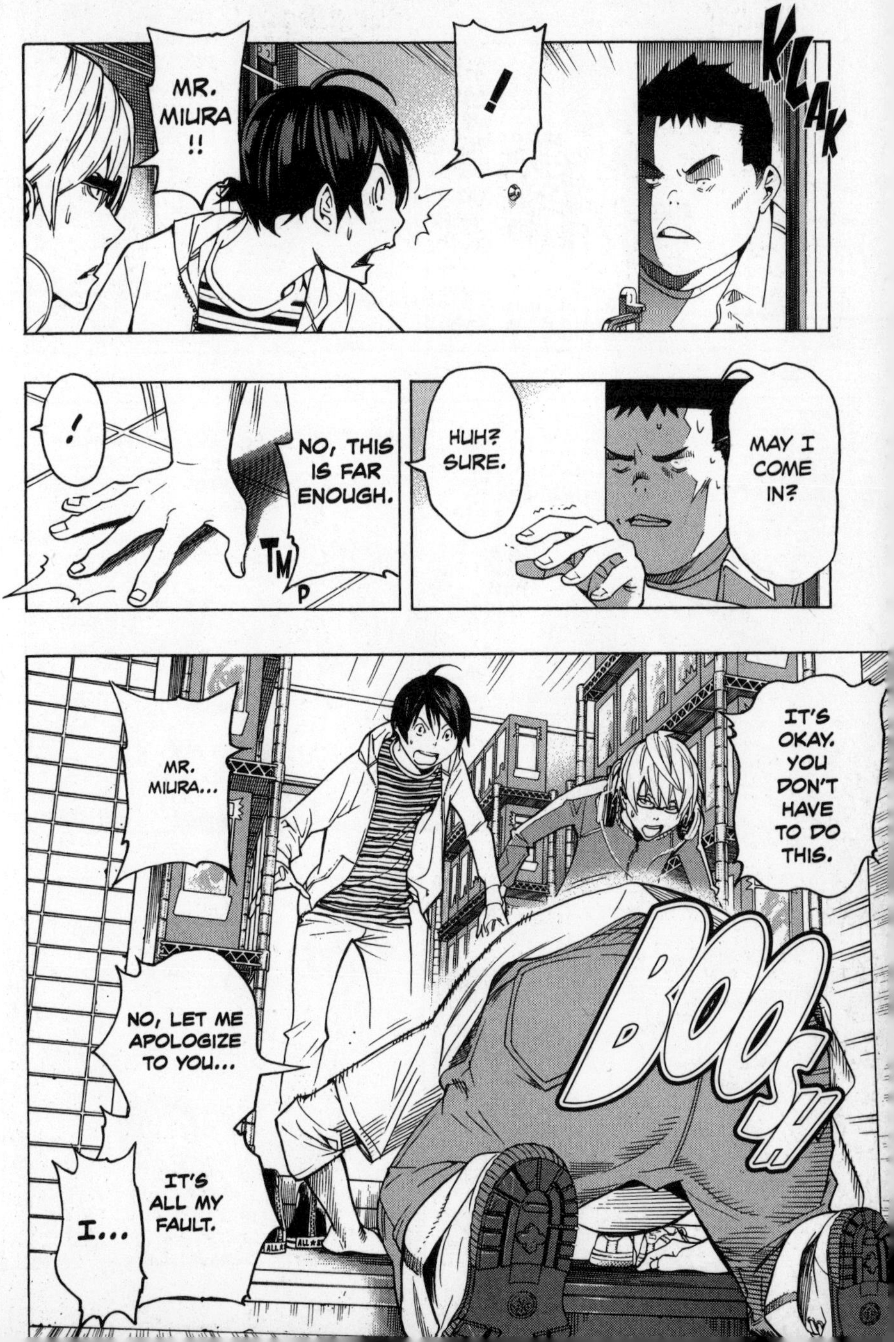
KLAK
!
MR. MIURA !!
MAY I COME IN?
HUH? SURE.
NO, THIS IS FAR ENOUGH.
TMP
!
IT'S OKAY. YOU DON'T HAVE TO DO THIS.
BOOSH
MR. MIURA...
NO, LET ME APOLOGIZE TO YOU...
IT'S ALL MY FAULT.
I...

READ THIS WAY

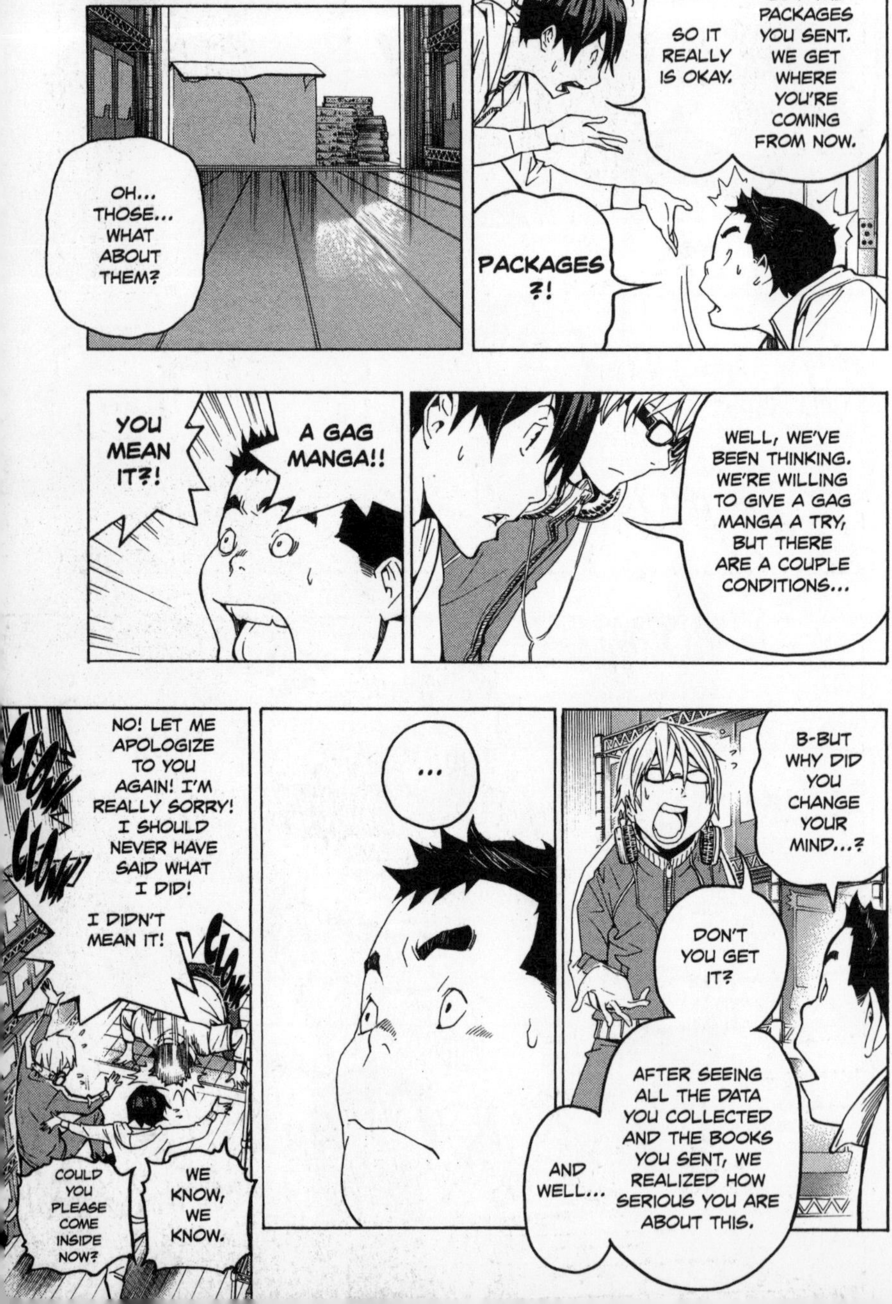
WE GOT THE PACKAGES YOU SENT. WE GET WHERE YOU'RE COMING FROM NOW.
SO IT REALLY IS OKAY.
PACKAGES?!
OH... THOSE... WHAT ABOUT THEM?
WELL, WE'VE BEEN THINKING. WE'RE WILLING TO GIVE A GAG MANGA A TRY, BUT THERE ARE A COUPLE CONDITIONS...
A GAG MANGA!!
YOU MEAN IT?!
B-BUT WHY DID YOU CHANGE YOUR MIND...?
DON'T YOU GET IT?
AFTER SEEING ALL THE DATA YOU COLLECTED AND THE BOOKS YOU SENT, WE REALIZED HOW SERIOUS YOU ARE ABOUT THIS.
AND WELL...
...
NO! LET ME APOLOGIZE TO YOU AGAIN! I'M REALLY SORRY! I SHOULD NEVER HAVE SAID WHAT I DID!
I DIDN'T MEAN IT!
CLONK
CLONK
CLONK
WE KNOW, WE KNOW.
COULD YOU PLEASE COME INSIDE NOW?

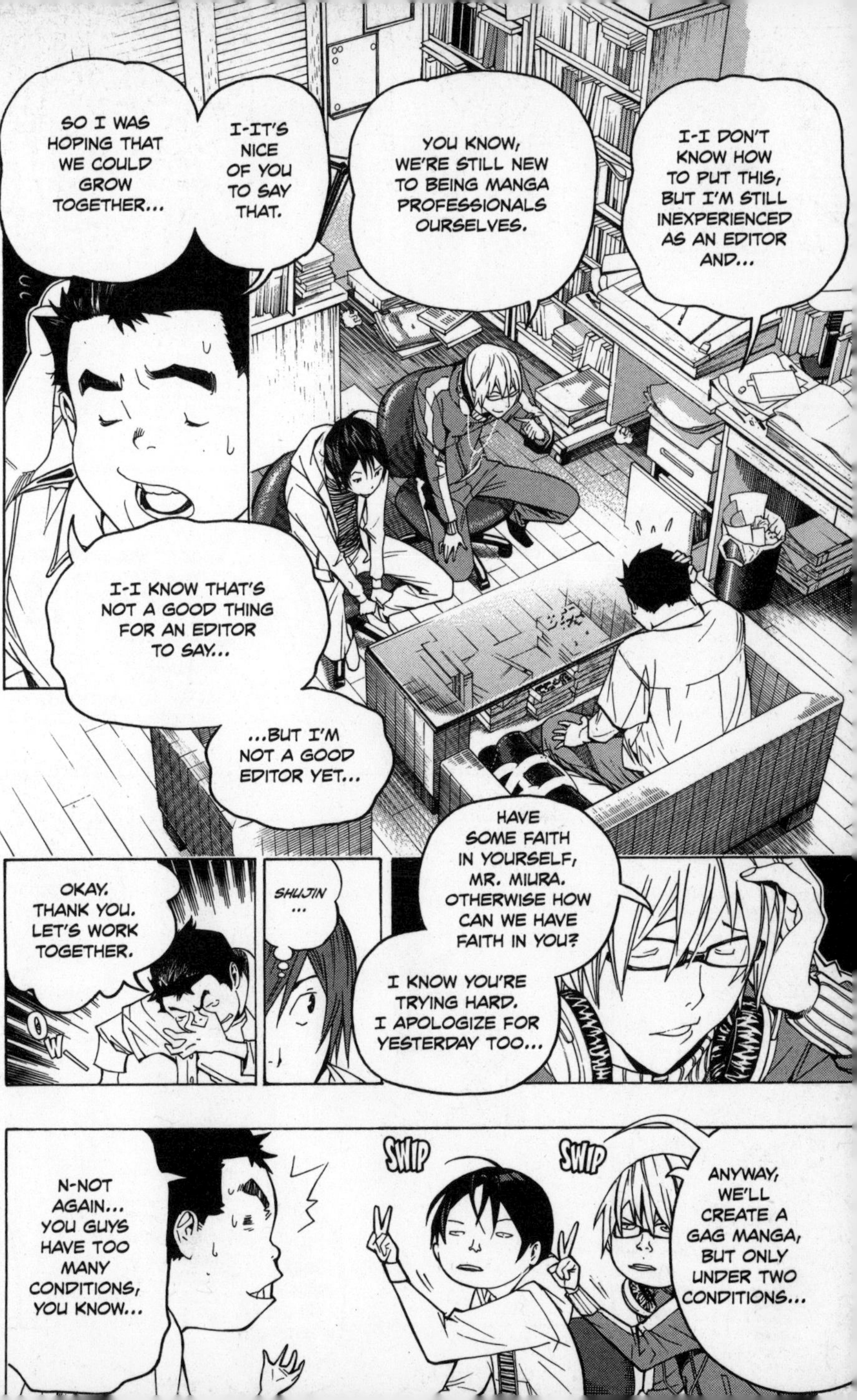
I-I DON'T KNOW HOW TO PUT THIS, BUT I'M STILL INEXPERIENCED AS AN EDITOR AND...
YOU KNOW, WE'RE STILL NEW TO BEING MANGA PROFESSIONALS OURSELVES.
I-IT'S NICE OF YOU TO SAY THAT.
SO I WAS HOPING THAT WE COULD GROW TOGETHER...
I-I KNOW THAT'S NOT A GOOD THING FOR AN EDITOR TO SAY...
...BUT I'M NOT A GOOD EDITOR YET...
HAVE SOME FAITH IN YOURSELF, MR. MIURA. OTHERWISE HOW CAN WE HAVE FAITH IN YOU?
I KNOW YOU'RE TRYING HARD. I APOLOGIZE FOR YESTERDAY TOO...
SHUJIN ...
OKAY. THANK YOU. LET'S WORK TOGETHER.
OW
SWIP
SWIP
ANYWAY, WE'LL CREATE A GAG MANGA, BUT ONLY UNDER TWO CONDITIONS...
N-NOT AGAIN... YOU GUYS HAVE TOO MANY CONDITIONS, YOU KNOW...

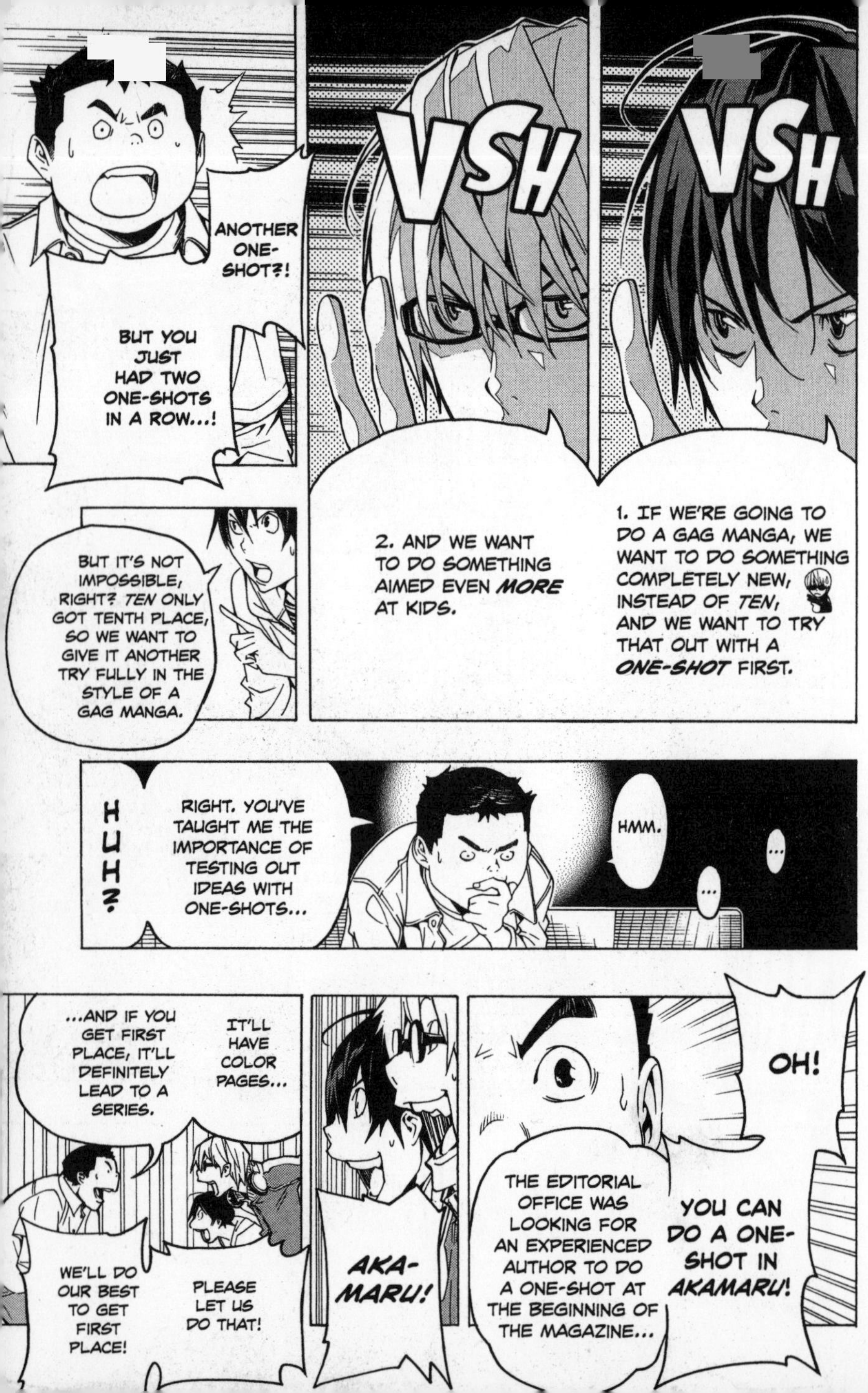
VSH
VSH
1. IF WE'RE GOING TO DO A GAG MANGA, WE WANT TO DO SOMETHING COMPLETELY NEW, INSTEAD OF *TEN*, AND WE WANT TO TRY THAT OUT WITH A *ONE-SHOT* FIRST.
2. AND WE WANT TO DO SOMETHING AIMED EVEN *MORE* AT KIDS.
ANOTHER ONE-SHOT?!
BUT YOU JUST HAD TWO ONE-SHOTS IN A ROW...!
BUT IT'S NOT IMPOSSIBLE, RIGHT? *TEN* ONLY GOT TENTH PLACE, SO WE WANT TO GIVE IT ANOTHER TRY FULLY IN THE STYLE OF A GAG MANGA.
HMM.
...
...
RIGHT. YOU'VE TAUGHT ME THE IMPORTANCE OF TESTING OUT IDEAS WITH ONE-SHOTS...
HUH?
OH!
YOU CAN DO A ONE-SHOT IN *AKAMARU*!
THE EDITORIAL OFFICE WAS LOOKING FOR AN EXPERIENCED AUTHOR TO DO A ONE-SHOT AT THE BEGINNING OF THE MAGAZINE...
AKA-MARU!
IT'LL HAVE COLOR PAGES...
...AND IF YOU GET FIRST PLACE, IT'LL DEFINITELY LEAD TO A SERIES.
PLEASE LET US DO THAT!
WE'LL DO OUR BEST TO GET FIRST PLACE!

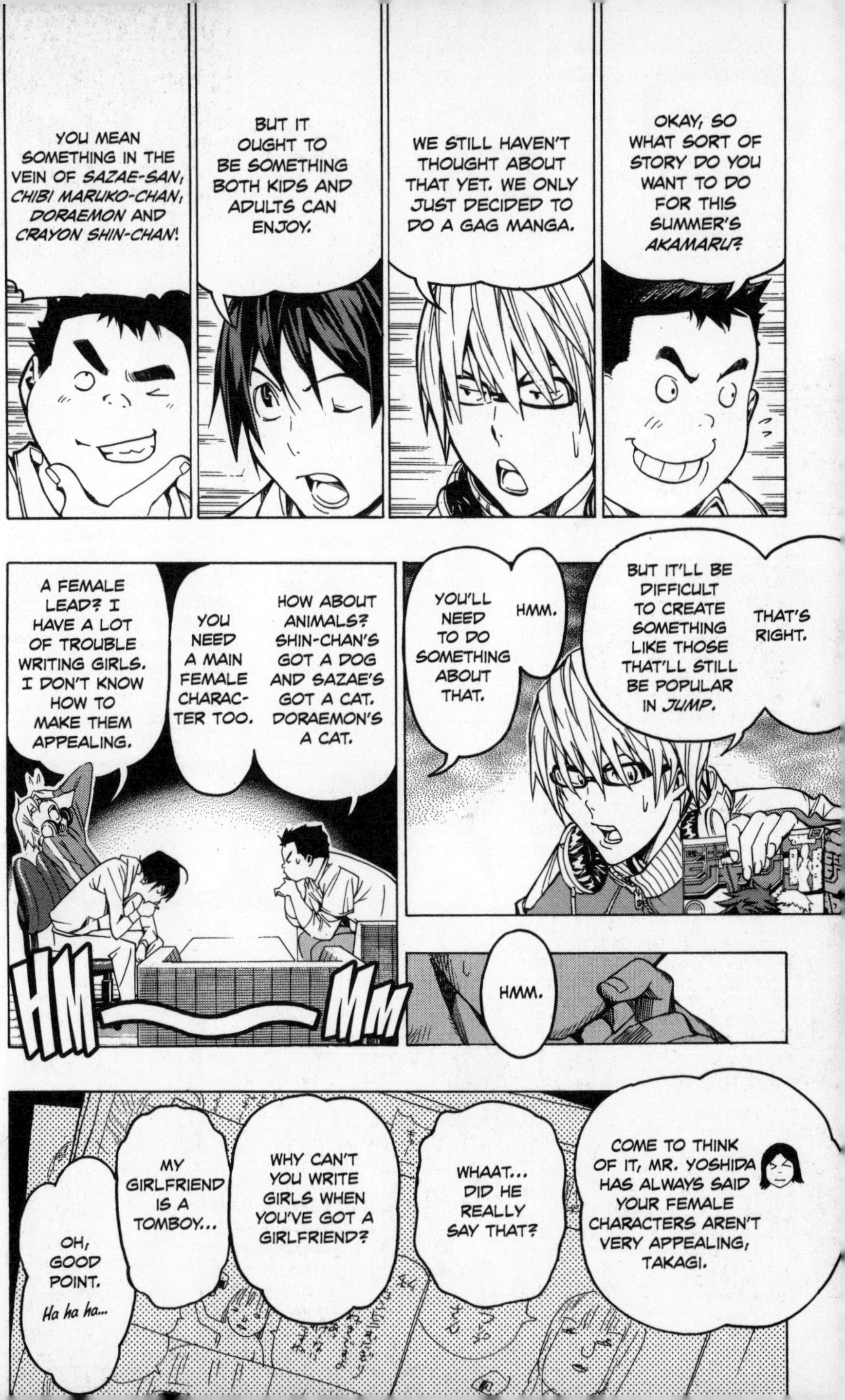
OKAY, SO WHAT SORT OF STORY DO YOU WANT TO DO FOR THIS SUMMER'S *AKAMARU*?
WE STILL HAVEN'T THOUGHT ABOUT THAT YET. WE ONLY JUST DECIDED TO DO A GAG MANGA.
BUT IT OUGHT TO BE SOMETHING BOTH KIDS AND ADULTS CAN ENJOY.
YOU MEAN SOMETHING IN THE VEIN OF *SAZAE-SAN*, *CHIBI MARUKO-CHAN*, *DORAEMON* AND *CRAYON SHIN-CHAN*!
THAT'S RIGHT.
BUT IT'LL BE DIFFICULT TO CREATE SOMETHING LIKE THOSE THAT'LL STILL BE POPULAR IN *JUMP*.
HMM.
YOU'LL NEED TO DO SOMETHING ABOUT THAT.
HMM.
HOW ABOUT ANIMALS? SHIN-CHAN'S GOT A DOG AND SAZAE'S GOT A CAT. DORAEMON'S A CAT.
YOU NEED A MAIN FEMALE CHARACTER TOO.
A FEMALE LEAD? I HAVE A LOT OF TROUBLE WRITING GIRLS. I DON'T KNOW HOW TO MAKE THEM APPEALING.
HM—MM
COME TO THINK OF IT, MR. YOSHIDA HAS ALWAYS SAID YOUR FEMALE CHARACTERS AREN'T VERY APPEALING, TAKAGI.
WHAAT... DID HE REALLY SAY THAT?
WHY CAN'T YOU WRITE GIRLS WHEN YOU'VE GOT A GIRLFRIEND?
MY GIRLFRIEND IS A TOMBOY...
OH, GOOD POINT.
Ha ha ha...

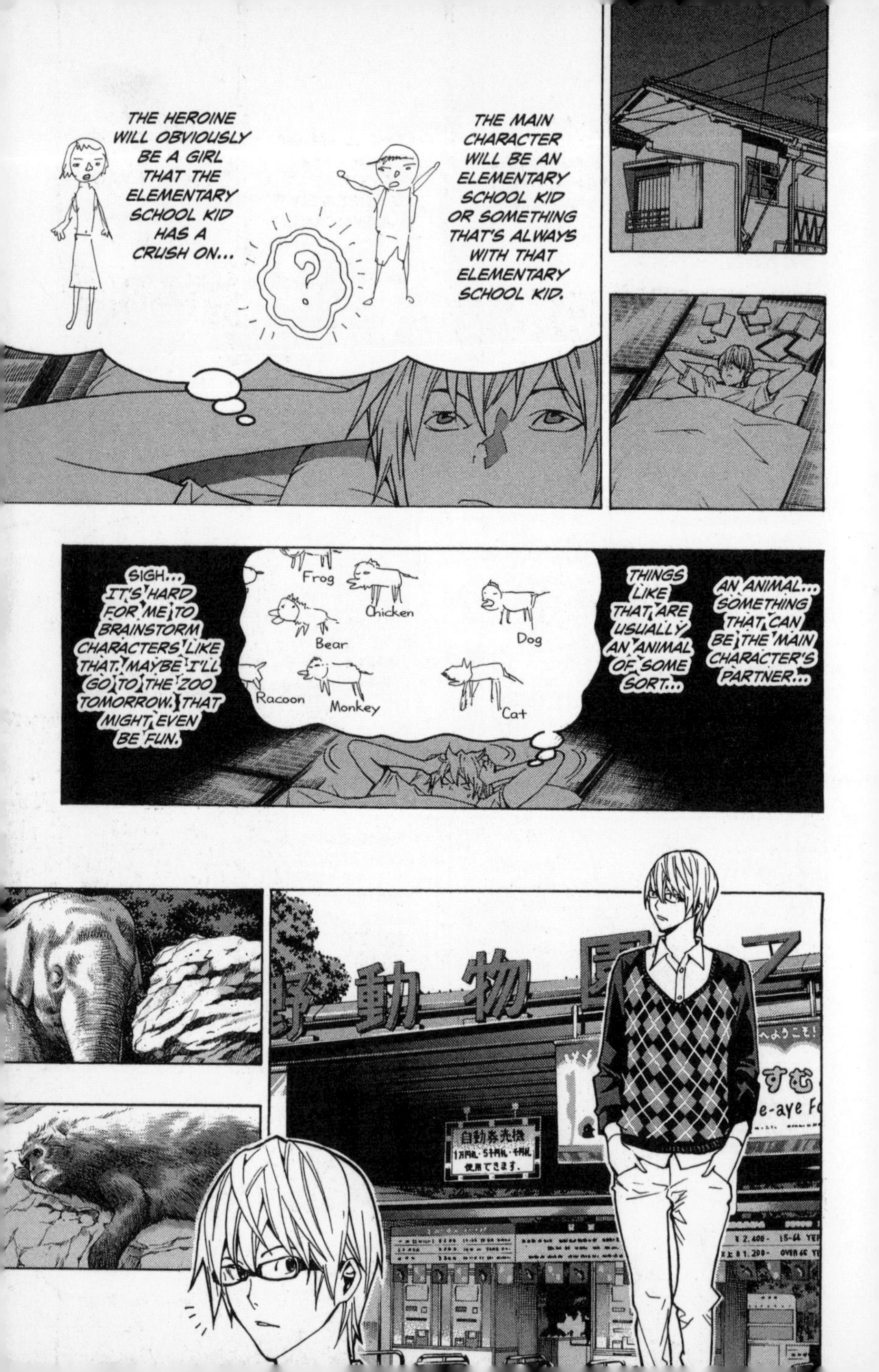
THE MAIN CHARACTER WILL BE AN ELEMENTARY SCHOOL KID OR SOMETHING THAT'S ALWAYS WITH THAT ELEMENTARY SCHOOL KID.
THE HEROINE WILL OBVIOUSLY BE A GIRL THAT THE ELEMENTARY SCHOOL KID HAS A CRUSH ON...
?
AN ANIMAL... SOMETHING THAT CAN BE THE MAIN CHARACTER'S PARTNER...
THINGS LIKE THAT ARE USUALLY AN ANIMAL OF SOME SORT...
Dog
Frog
Chicken
Bear
Cat
Monkey
Racoon
SIGH... IT'S HARD FOR ME TO BRAINSTORM CHARACTERS LIKE THAT. MAYBE I'LL GO TO THE ZOO TOMORROW. THAT MIGHT EVEN BE FUN.
動物園
自動券売機
使用できます。

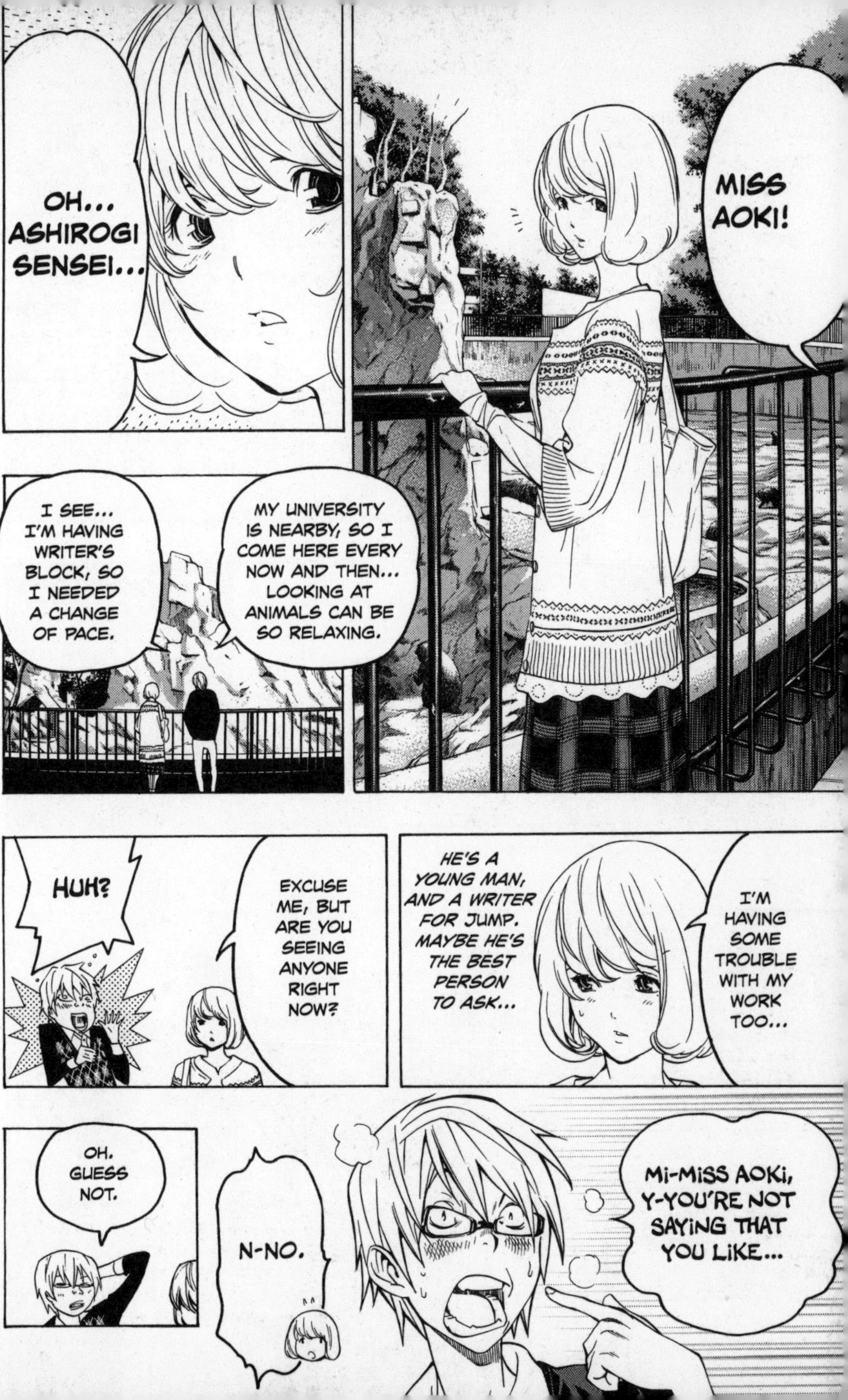
MISS AOKI!
OH... ASHIROGI SENSEI...
MY UNIVERSITY IS NEARBY, SO I COME HERE EVERY NOW AND THEN... LOOKING AT ANIMALS CAN BE SO RELAXING.
I SEE... I'M HAVING WRITER'S BLOCK, SO I NEEDED A CHANGE OF PACE.
I'M HAVING SOME TROUBLE WITH MY WORK TOO...
HE'S A YOUNG MAN, AND A WRITER FOR JUMP. MAYBE HE'S THE BEST PERSON TO ASK...
EXCUSE ME, BUT ARE YOU SEEING ANYONE RIGHT NOW?
HUH?
MI-MISS AOKI, Y-YOU'RE NOT SAYING THAT YOU LIKE...
N-NO.
OH. GUESS NOT.

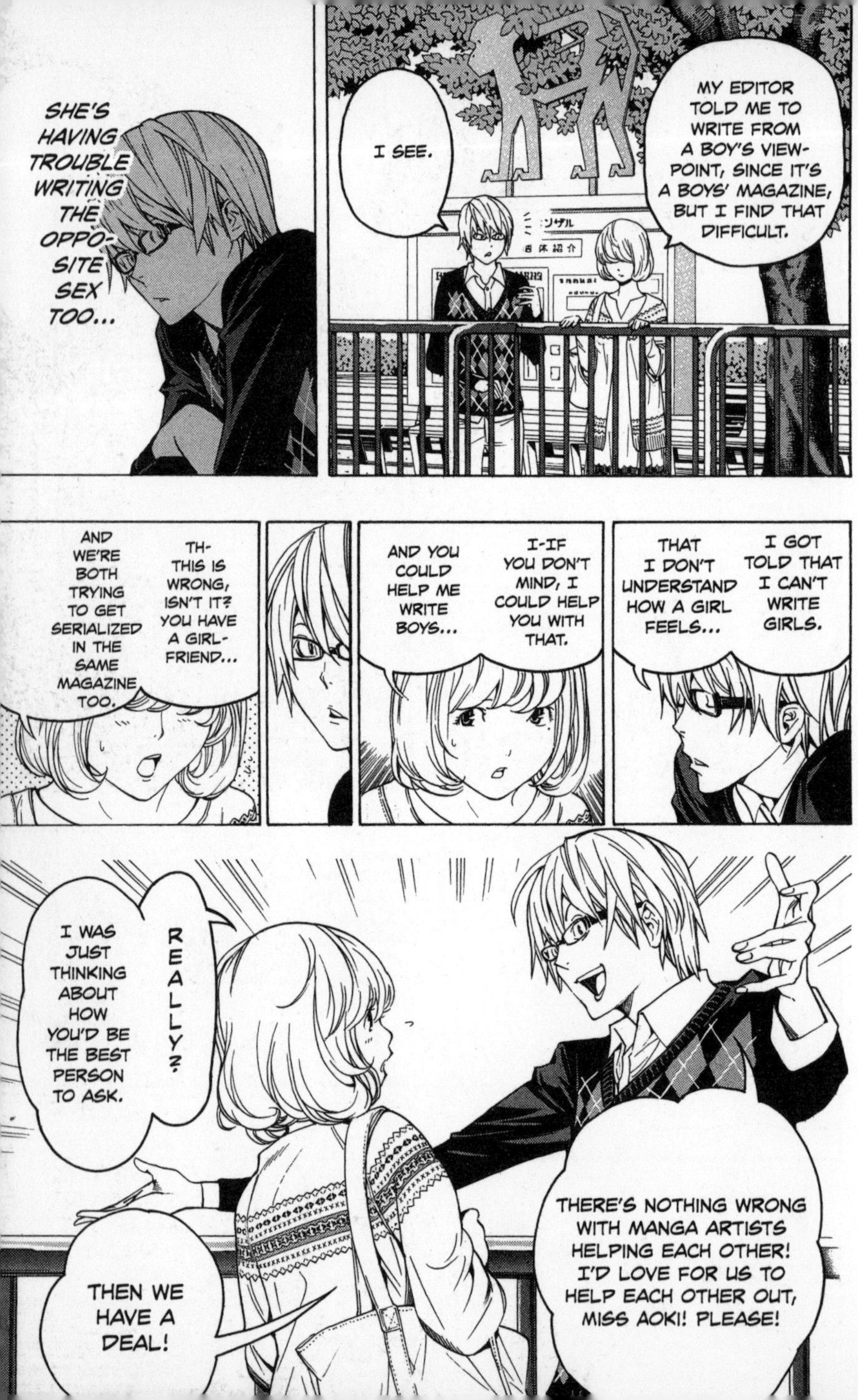
MY EDITOR TOLD ME TO WRITE FROM A BOY'S VIEWPOINT, SINCE IT'S A BOYS' MAGAZINE, BUT I FIND THAT DIFFICULT.
I SEE.
SHE'S HAVING TROUBLE WRITING THE OPPOSITE SEX TOO...
I GOT TOLD THAT I CAN'T WRITE GIRLS.
THAT I DON'T UNDERSTAND HOW A GIRL FEELS...
I-IF YOU DON'T MIND, I COULD HELP YOU WITH THAT.
AND YOU COULD HELP ME WRITE BOYS...
TH- THIS IS WRONG, ISN'T IT? YOU HAVE A GIRLFRIEND...
AND WE'RE BOTH TRYING TO GET SERIALIZED IN THE SAME MAGAZINE TOO.
REALLY?
I WAS JUST THINKING ABOUT HOW YOU'D BE THE BEST PERSON TO ASK.
THERE'S NOTHING WRONG WITH MANGA ARTISTS HELPING EACH OTHER! I'D LOVE FOR US TO HELP EACH OTHER OUT, MISS AOKI! PLEASE!
THEN WE HAVE A DEAL!

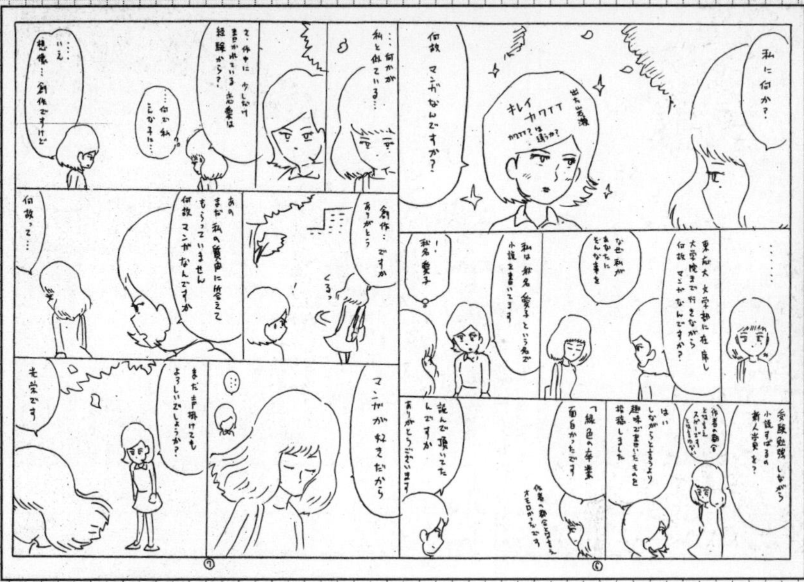

私に何か？
キレイ カワイイ
何故 マンガなんですか？
……
東応大文学部に在席し大学院まで行きながら何故 マンガなんですか？
なぜ私があなたにそんな事を
私は秋名愛子という名で小説を書いてます
秋名 愛子！
受験勉強しながら小説すばるの新人賞を？
はい しながらと言うより趣味で書いたものを投稿しました
「緑色の卒業」面白かったです
読んで頂いてたんですか ありがとうございます
…何かが私と似ている…
さ・作中に少しだけ書かれている恋愛は経験から？
……何か私こんな子に…
…いえ 想像…創作ですけど
創作…ですか ありがとう
くるっ
あの まだ私の質問に答えてもらっていません 何故マンガなんですか
何故って…
マンガが好きだから
まだ声掛けてもよろしいでしょうか？
光栄です

OHBA'S STORYBOARD

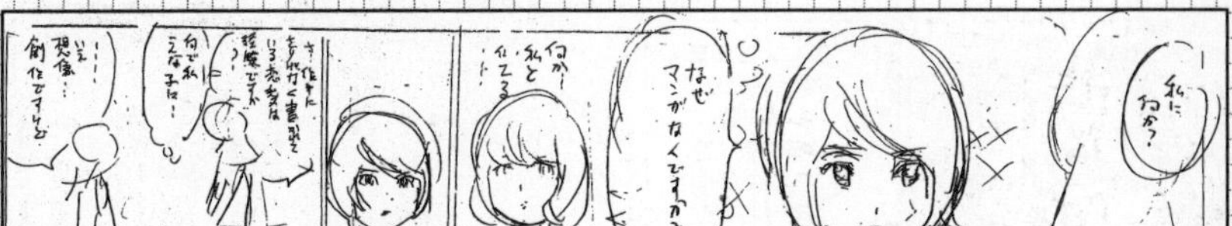

OBATA'S STORYBOARD

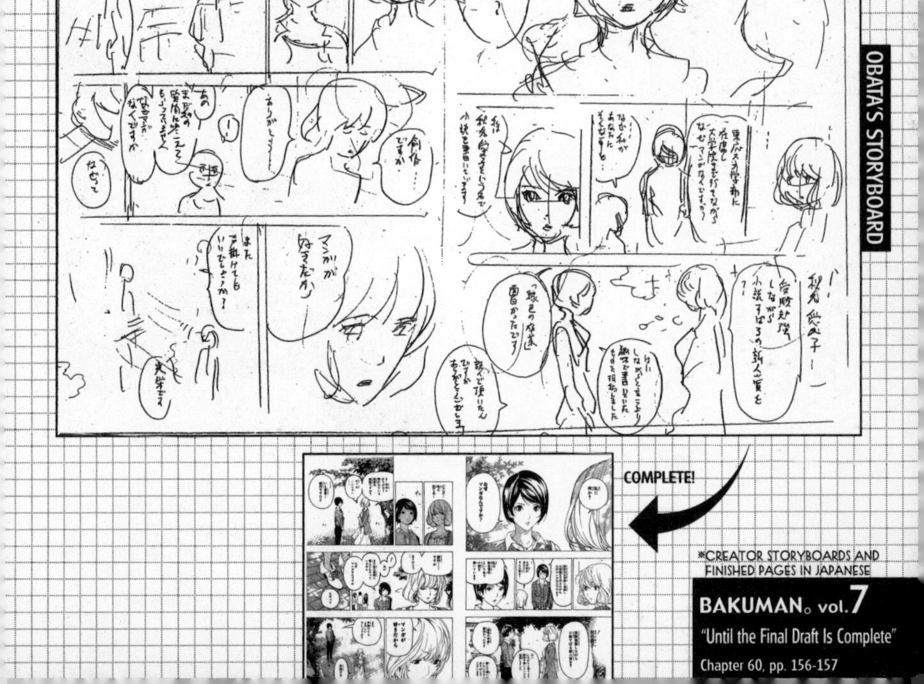

COMPLETE!

※CREATOR STORYBOARDS AND FINISHED PAGES IN JAPANESE

BAKUMAN。 vol.7

"Until the Final Draft Is Complete"

Chapter 60, pp. 156-157

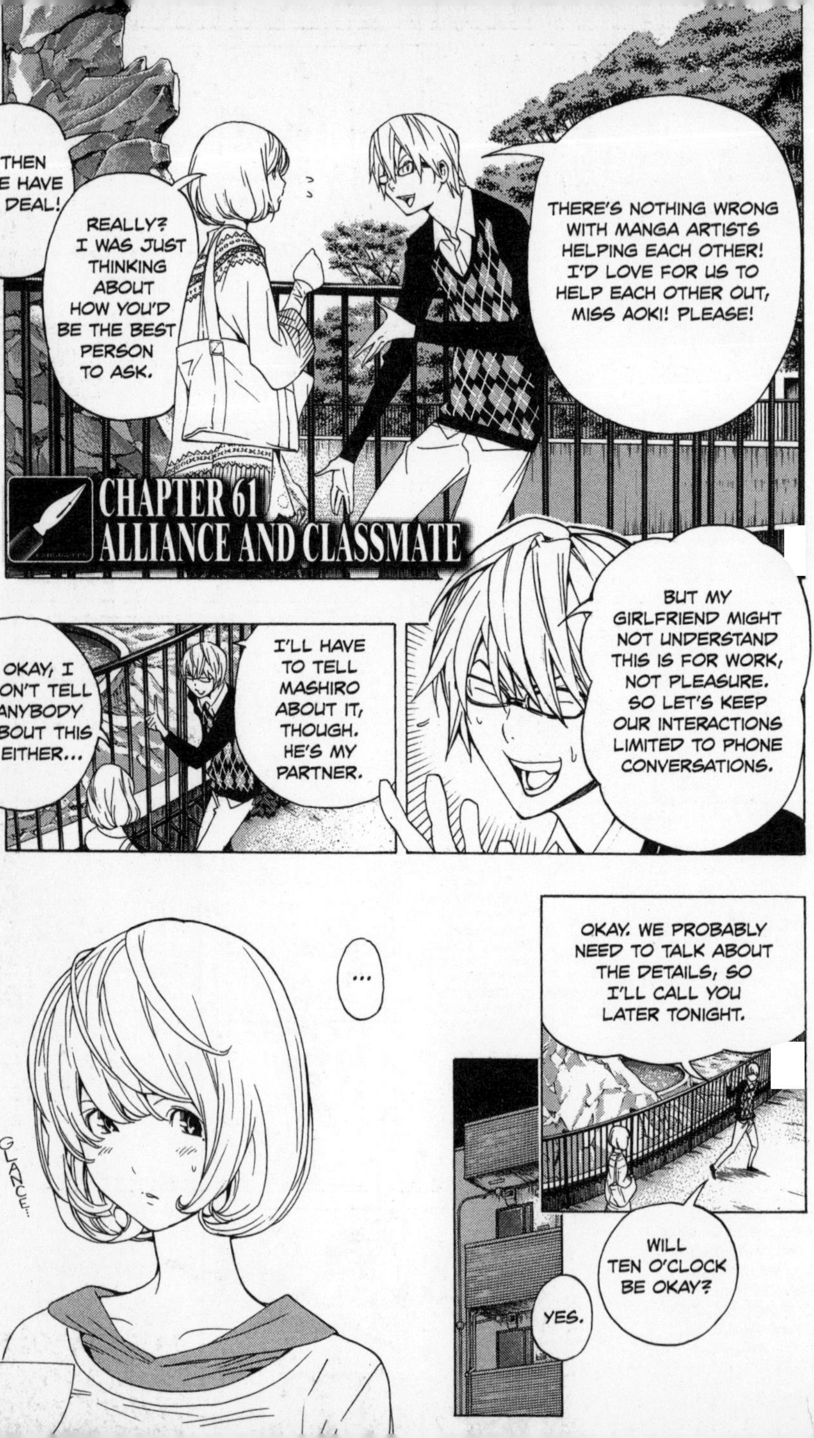
THERE'S NOTHING WRONG WITH MANGA ARTISTS HELPING EACH OTHER! I'D LOVE FOR US TO HELP EACH OTHER OUT, MISS AOKI! PLEASE!
REALLY? I WAS JUST THINKING ABOUT HOW YOU'D BE THE BEST PERSON TO ASK.
THEN WE HAVE A DEAL!
CHAPTER 61
ALLIANCE AND CLASSMATE
BUT MY GIRLFRIEND MIGHT NOT UNDERSTAND THIS IS FOR WORK, NOT PLEASURE. SO LET'S KEEP OUR INTERACTIONS LIMITED TO PHONE CONVERSATIONS.
I'LL HAVE TO TELL MASHIRO ABOUT IT, THOUGH. HE'S MY PARTNER.
OKAY, I WON'T TELL ANYBODY ABOUT THIS EITHER...
OKAY. WE PROBABLY NEED TO TALK ABOUT THE DETAILS, SO I'LL CALL YOU LATER TONIGHT.
WILL TEN O'CLOCK BE OKAY?
YES.
...
GLANCE...

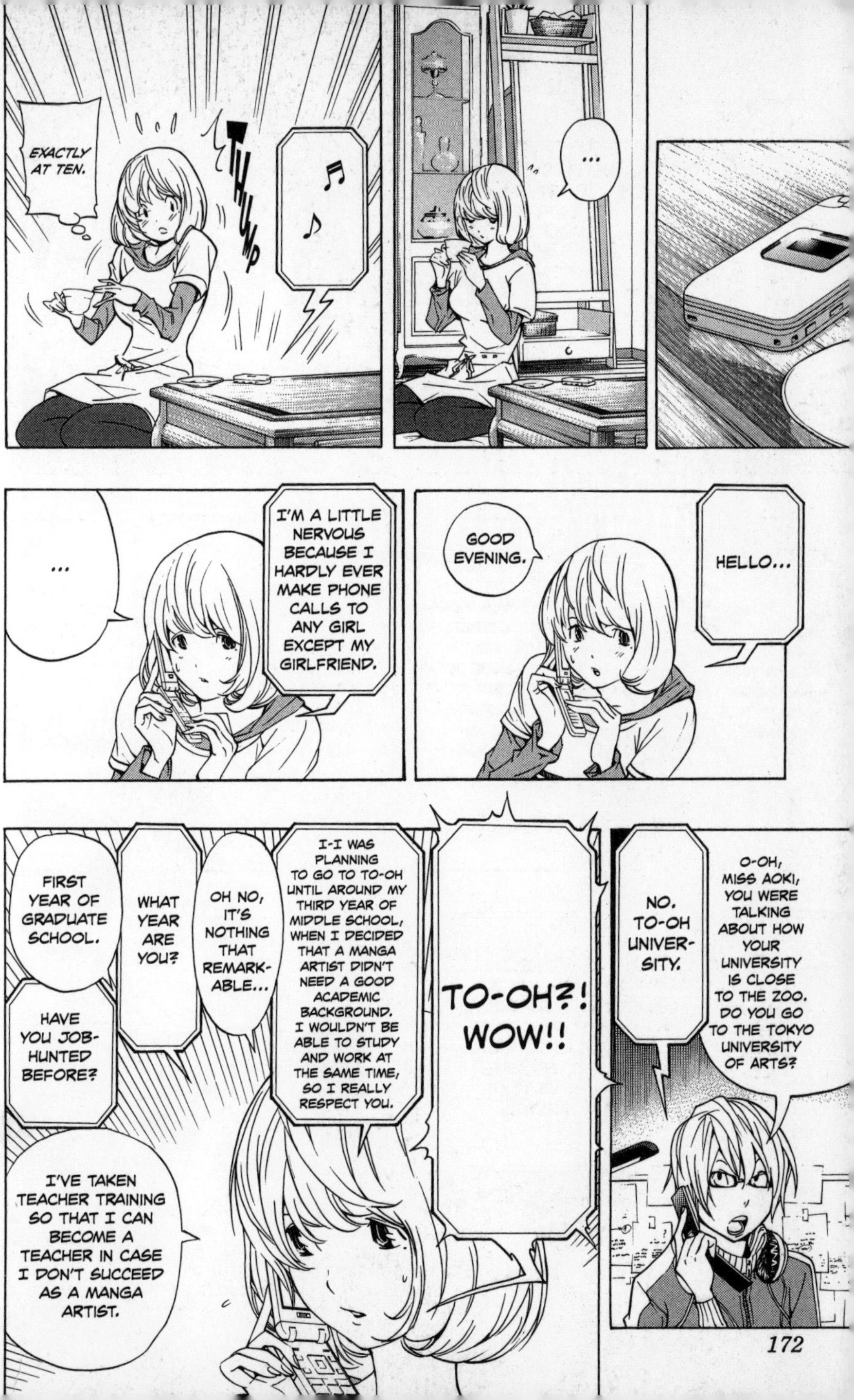
...
♫ ♪
THUMP
EXACTLY AT TEN.
HELLO...
GOOD EVENING.
I'M A LITTLE NERVOUS BECAUSE I HARDLY EVER MAKE PHONE CALLS TO ANY GIRL EXCEPT MY GIRLFRIEND.
...
O-OH, MISS AOKI, YOU WERE TALKING ABOUT HOW YOUR UNIVERSITY IS CLOSE TO THE ZOO. DO YOU GO TO THE TOKYO UNIVERSITY OF ARTS?
NO. TO-OH UNIVER-SITY.
TO-OH?! WOW!!
I-I WAS PLANNING TO GO TO TO-OH UNTIL AROUND MY THIRD YEAR OF MIDDLE SCHOOL, WHEN I DECIDED THAT A MANGA ARTIST DIDN'T NEED A GOOD ACADEMIC BACKGROUND. I WOULDN'T BE ABLE TO STUDY AND WORK AT THE SAME TIME, SO I REALLY RESPECT YOU.
OH NO, IT'S NOTHING THAT REMARK-ABLE...
WHAT YEAR ARE YOU?
FIRST YEAR OF GRADUATE SCHOOL.
HAVE YOU JOB-HUNTED BEFORE?
I'VE TAKEN TEACHER TRAINING SO THAT I CAN BECOME A TEACHER IN CASE I DON'T SUCCEED AS A MANGA ARTIST.

READ THIS WAY

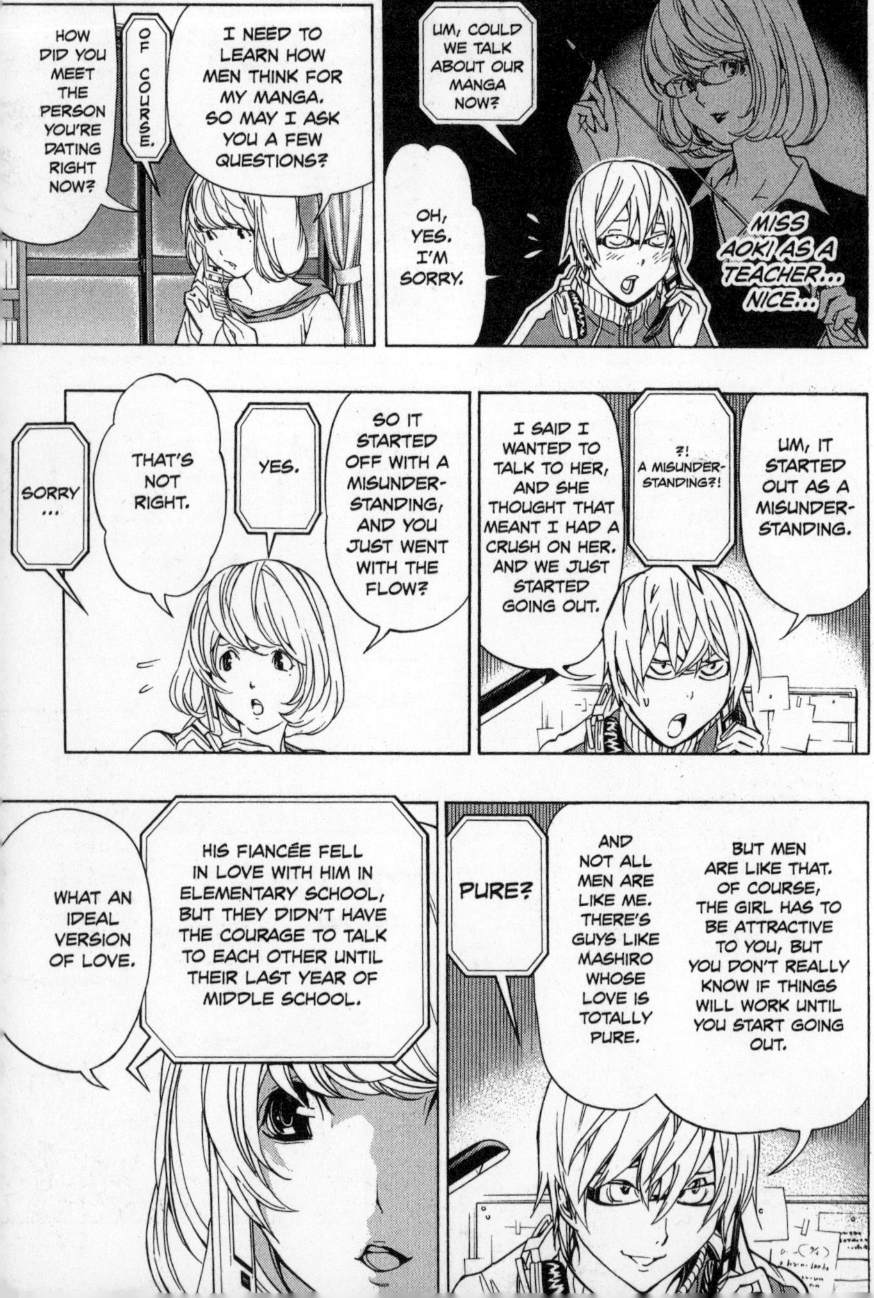
MISS AOKI AS A TEACHER... NICE...
UM, COULD WE TALK ABOUT OUR MANGA NOW?
OH, YES. I'M SORRY.
I NEED TO LEARN HOW MEN THINK FOR MY MANGA. SO MAY I ASK YOU A FEW QUESTIONS?
OF COURSE.
HOW DID YOU MEET THE PERSON YOU'RE DATING RIGHT NOW?
UM, IT STARTED OUT AS A MISUNDERSTANDING.
?! A MISUNDERSTANDING?!
I SAID I WANTED TO TALK TO HER, AND SHE THOUGHT THAT MEANT I HAD A CRUSH ON HER. AND WE JUST STARTED GOING OUT.
SO IT STARTED OFF WITH A MISUNDERSTANDING, AND YOU JUST WENT WITH THE FLOW?
YES.
THAT'S NOT RIGHT.
SORRY...
BUT MEN ARE LIKE THAT. OF COURSE, THE GIRL HAS TO BE ATTRACTIVE TO YOU, BUT YOU DON'T REALLY KNOW IF THINGS WILL WORK UNTIL YOU START GOING OUT.
AND NOT ALL MEN ARE LIKE ME. THERE'S GUYS LIKE MASHIRO WHOSE LOVE IS TOTALLY PURE.
PURE?
HIS FIANCÉE FELL IN LOVE WITH HIM IN ELEMENTARY SCHOOL, BUT THEY DIDN'T HAVE THE COURAGE TO TALK TO EACH OTHER UNTIL THEIR LAST YEAR OF MIDDLE SCHOOL.
WHAT AN IDEAL VERSION OF LOVE.

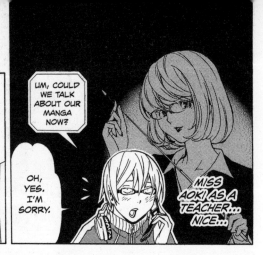

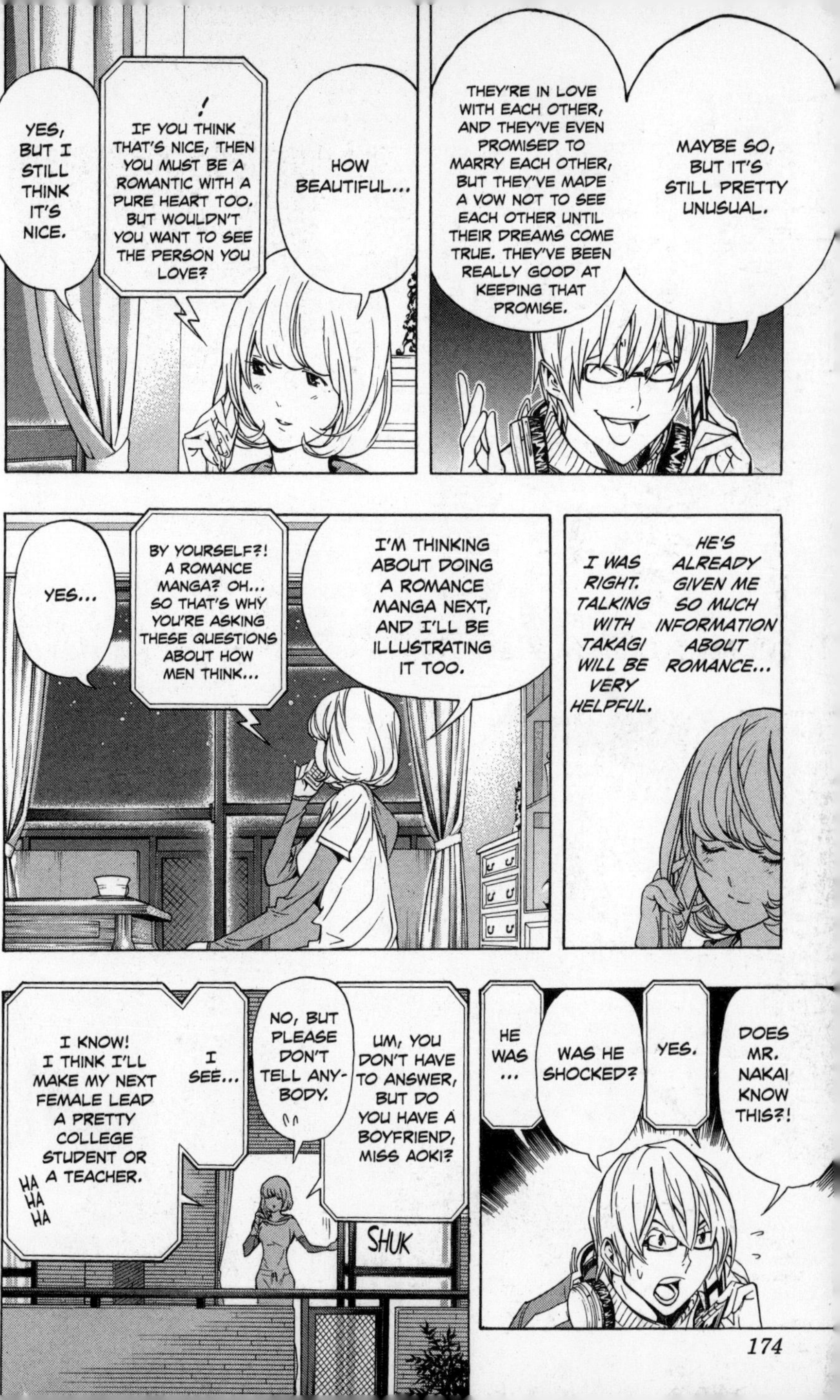
MAYBE SO, BUT IT'S STILL PRETTY UNUSUAL.
THEY'RE IN LOVE WITH EACH OTHER, AND THEY'VE EVEN PROMISED TO MARRY EACH OTHER, BUT THEY'VE MADE A VOW NOT TO SEE EACH OTHER UNTIL THEIR DREAMS COME TRUE. THEY'VE BEEN REALLY GOOD AT KEEPING THAT PROMISE.
HOW BEAUTIFUL...
!
IF YOU THINK THAT'S NICE, THEN YOU MUST BE A ROMANTIC WITH A PURE HEART TOO. BUT WOULDN'T YOU WANT TO SEE THE PERSON YOU LOVE?
YES, BUT I STILL THINK IT'S NICE.
HE'S ALREADY GIVEN ME SO MUCH INFORMATION ABOUT ROMANCE...
I WAS RIGHT. TALKING WITH TAKAGI WILL BE VERY HELPFUL.
I'M THINKING ABOUT DOING A ROMANCE MANGA NEXT, AND I'LL BE ILLUSTRATING IT TOO.
BY YOURSELF?! A ROMANCE MANGA? OH... SO THAT'S WHY YOU'RE ASKING THESE QUESTIONS ABOUT HOW MEN THINK...
YES...
DOES MR. NAKAI KNOW THIS?!
YES.
WAS HE SHOCKED?
HE WAS...
UM, YOU DON'T HAVE TO ANSWER, BUT DO YOU HAVE A BOYFRIEND, MISS AOKI?
NO, BUT PLEASE DON'T TELL ANYBODY.
SHUK
I SEE...
I KNOW! I THINK I'LL MAKE MY NEXT FEMALE LEAD A PRETTY COLLEGE STUDENT OR A TEACHER.
HA HA HA

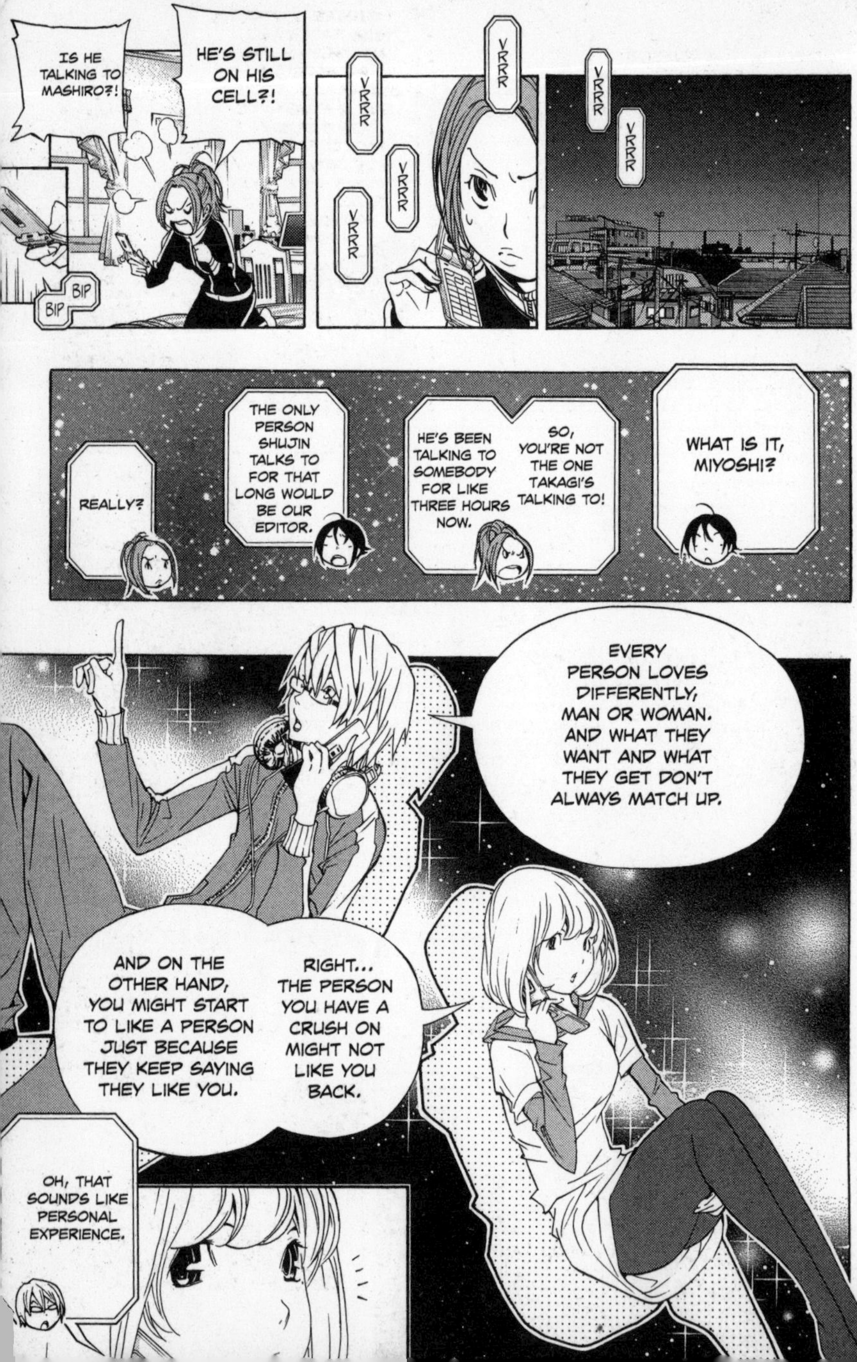
VRRR
VRRR
VRRR
VRRR
VRRR
VRRR
HE'S STILL ON HIS CELL?!
IS HE TALKING TO MASHIRO?!
BIP
BIP
WHAT IS IT, MIYOSHI?
SO, YOU'RE NOT THE ONE TAKAGI'S TALKING TO!
HE'S BEEN TALKING TO SOMEBODY FOR LIKE THREE HOURS NOW.
THE ONLY PERSON SHUJIN TALKS TO FOR THAT LONG WOULD BE OUR EDITOR.
REALLY?
EVERY PERSON LOVES DIFFERENTLY, MAN OR WOMAN. AND WHAT THEY WANT AND WHAT THEY GET DON'T ALWAYS MATCH UP.
RIGHT... THE PERSON YOU HAVE A CRUSH ON MIGHT NOT LIKE YOU BACK.
AND ON THE OTHER HAND, YOU MIGHT START TO LIKE A PERSON JUST BECAUSE THEY KEEP SAYING THEY LIKE YOU.
OH, THAT SOUNDS LIKE PERSONAL EXPERIENCE.

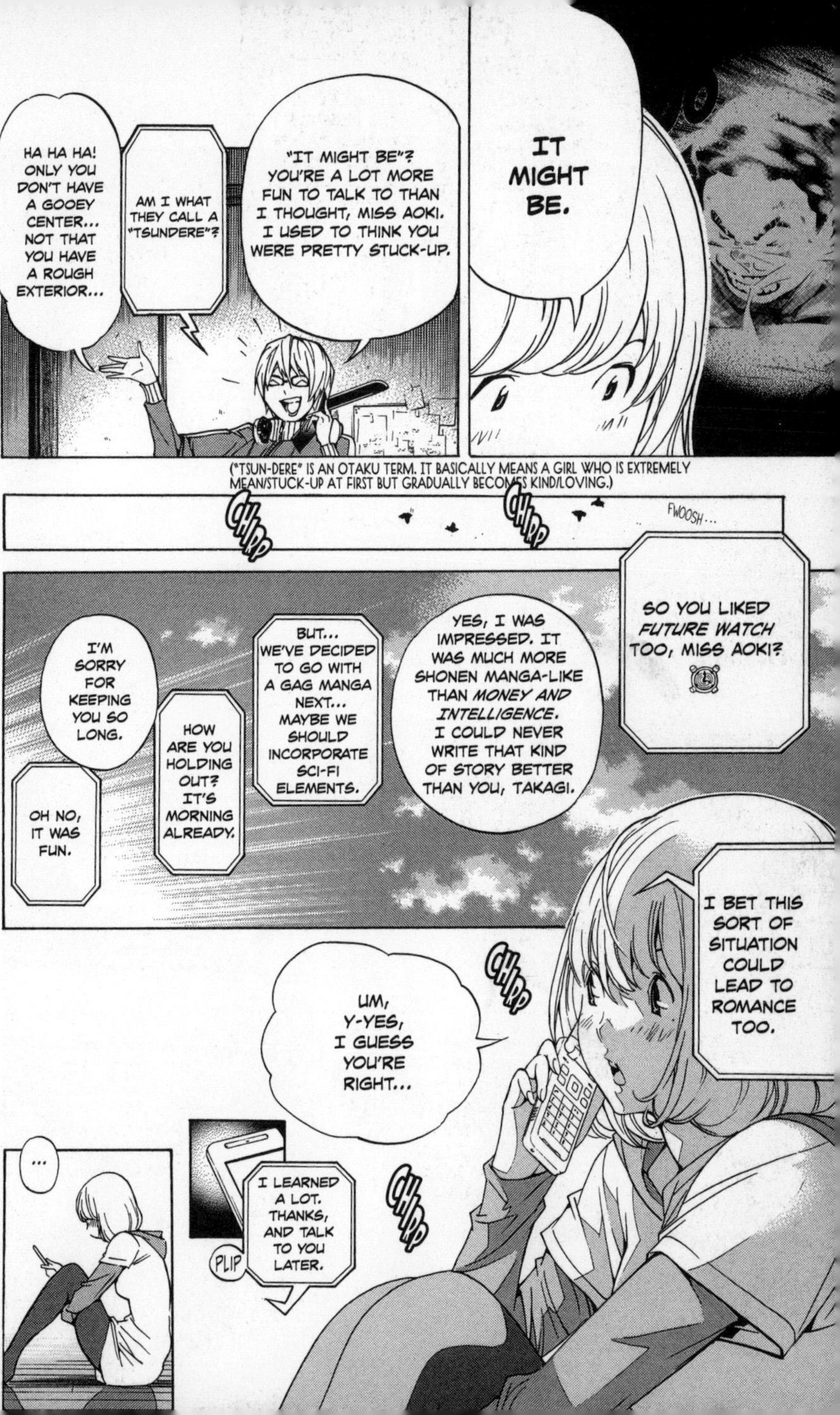
IT MIGHT BE.
"IT MIGHT BE"? YOU'RE A LOT MORE FUN TO TALK TO THAN I THOUGHT, MISS AOKI. I USED TO THINK YOU WERE PRETTY STUCK-UP.
AM I WHAT THEY CALL A "TSUNDERE"?
HA HA HA! ONLY YOU DON'T HAVE A GOOEY CENTER... NOT THAT YOU HAVE A ROUGH EXTERIOR...
("TSUN-DERE" IS AN OTAKU TERM. IT BASICALLY MEANS A GIRL WHO IS EXTREMELY MEAN/STUCK-UP AT FIRST BUT GRADUALLY BECOMES KIND/LOVING.)
FWOOSH...
CHIRP
CHIRP
SO YOU LIKED *FUTURE WATCH* TOO, MISS AOKI?
YES, I WAS IMPRESSED. IT WAS MUCH MORE SHONEN MANGA-LIKE THAN *MONEY AND INTELLIGENCE*. I COULD NEVER WRITE THAT KIND OF STORY BETTER THAN YOU, TAKAGI.
BUT... WE'VE DECIDED TO GO WITH A GAG MANGA NEXT... MAYBE WE SHOULD INCORPORATE SCI-FI ELEMENTS.
HOW ARE YOU HOLDING OUT? IT'S MORNING ALREADY.
I'M SORRY FOR KEEPING YOU SO LONG.
OH NO, IT WAS FUN.
I BET THIS SORT OF SITUATION COULD LEAD TO ROMANCE TOO.
CHIRP
UM, Y-YES, I GUESS YOU'RE RIGHT...
CHIRP
I LEARNED A LOT. THANKS, AND TALK TO YOU LATER.
PLIP
...

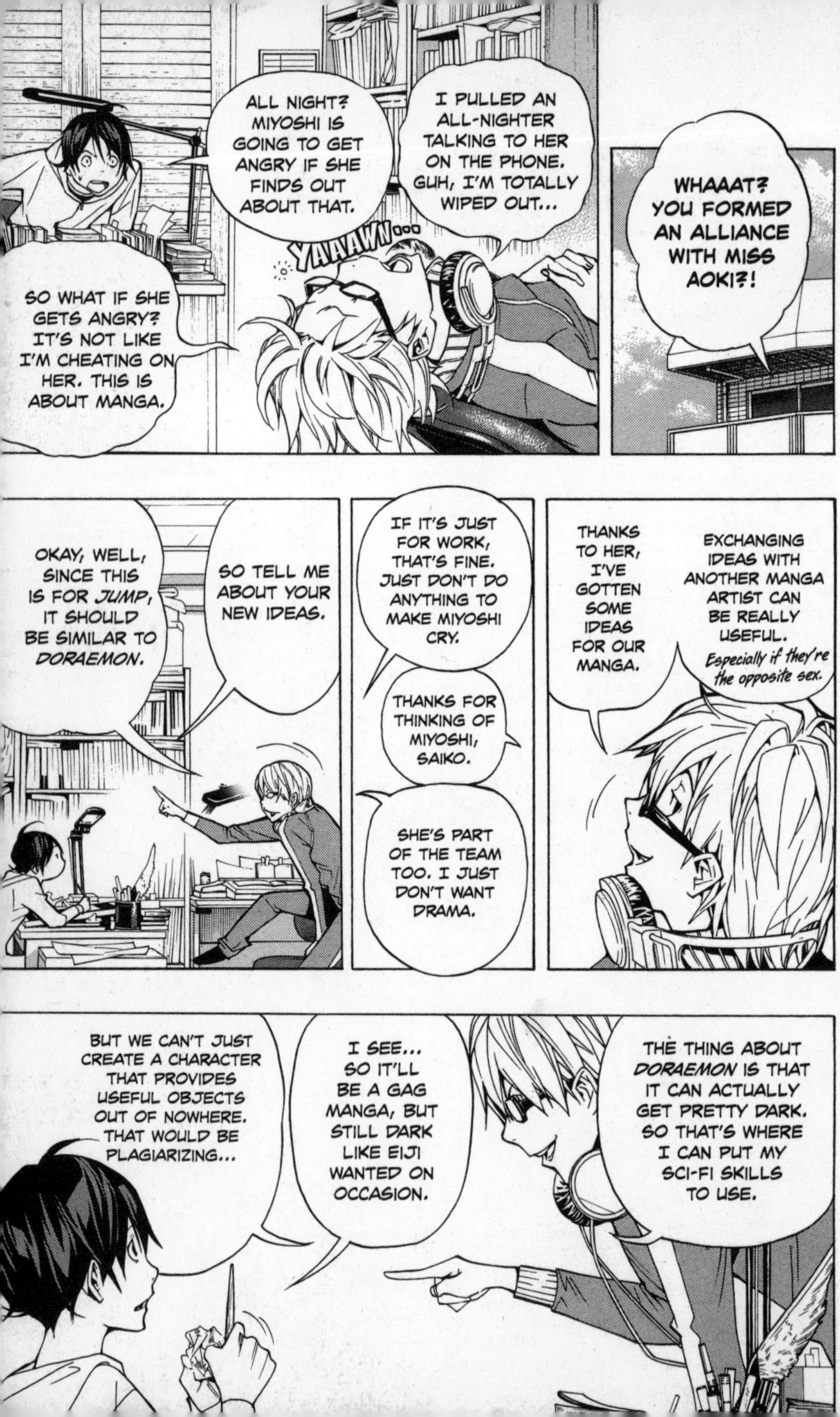
WHAAAT? YOU FORMED AN ALLIANCE WITH MISS AOKI?!
I PULLED AN ALL-NIGHTER TALKING TO HER ON THE PHONE. GUH, I'M TOTALLY WIPED OUT...
ALL NIGHT? MIYOSHI IS GOING TO GET ANGRY IF SHE FINDS OUT ABOUT THAT.
YAAAWN...
SO WHAT IF SHE GETS ANGRY? IT'S NOT LIKE I'M CHEATING ON HER. THIS IS ABOUT MANGA.
EXCHANGING IDEAS WITH ANOTHER MANGA ARTIST CAN BE REALLY USEFUL. *Especially if they're the opposite sex.*
THANKS TO HER, I'VE GOTTEN SOME IDEAS FOR OUR MANGA.
IF IT'S JUST FOR WORK, THAT'S FINE. JUST DON'T DO ANYTHING TO MAKE MIYOSHI CRY.
THANKS FOR THINKING OF MIYOSHI, SAIKO.
SHE'S PART OF THE TEAM TOO. I JUST DON'T WANT DRAMA.
SO TELL ME ABOUT YOUR NEW IDEAS.
OKAY, WELL, SINCE THIS IS FOR *JUMP*, IT SHOULD BE SIMILAR TO *DORAEMON*.
THE THING ABOUT *DORAEMON* IS THAT IT CAN ACTUALLY GET PRETTY DARK. SO THAT'S WHERE I CAN PUT MY SCI-FI SKILLS TO USE.
I SEE... SO IT'LL BE A GAG MANGA, BUT STILL DARK LIKE EIJI WANTED ON OCCASION.
BUT WE CAN'T JUST CREATE A CHARACTER THAT PROVIDES USEFUL OBJECTS OUT OF NOWHERE. THAT WOULD BE PLAGIARIZING...

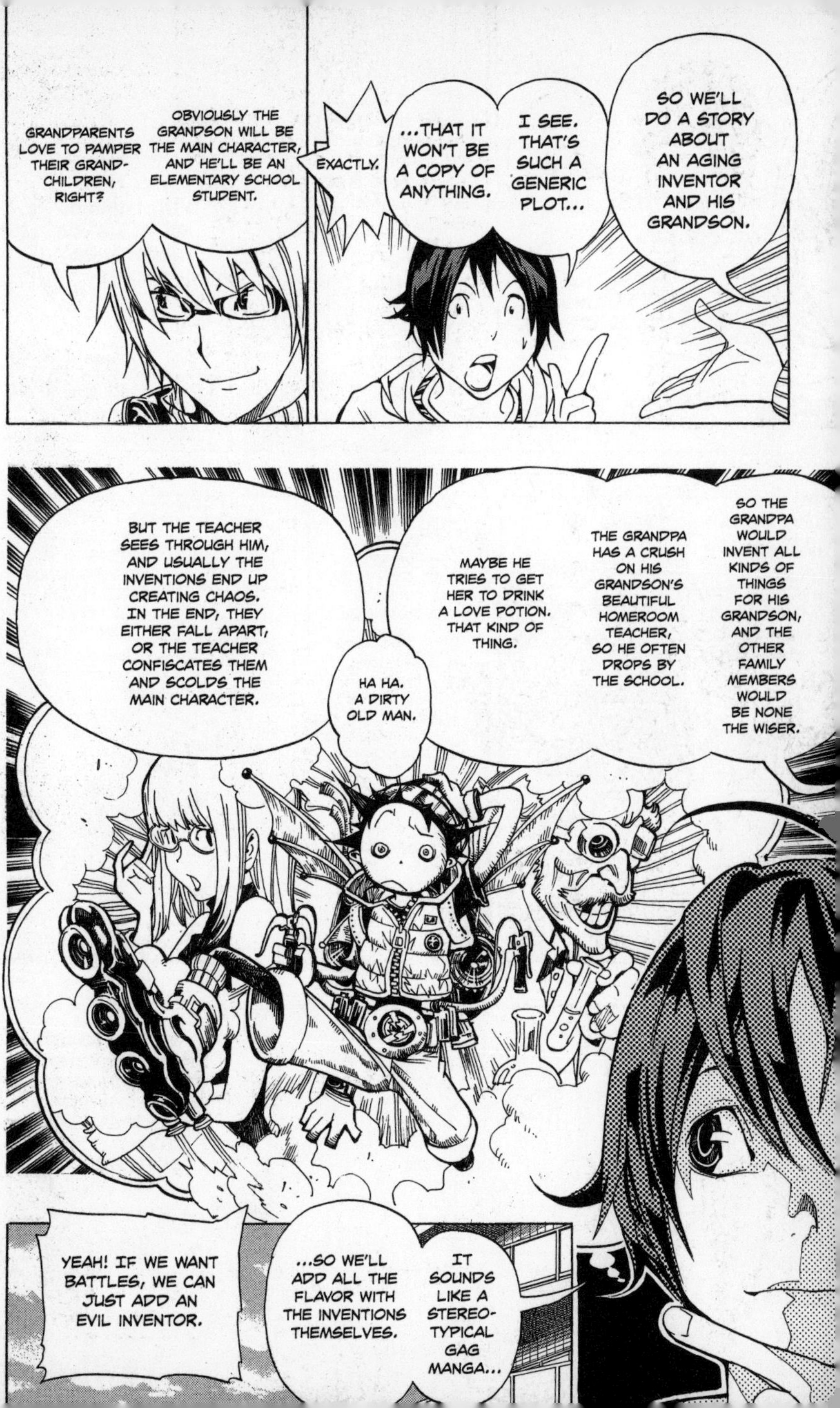
SO WE'LL DO A STORY ABOUT AN AGING INVENTOR AND HIS GRANDSON.
I SEE. THAT'S SUCH A GENERIC PLOT...
...THAT IT WON'T BE A COPY OF ANYTHING.
EXACTLY.
OBVIOUSLY THE GRANDSON WILL BE THE MAIN CHARACTER, AND HE'LL BE AN ELEMENTARY SCHOOL STUDENT.
GRANDPARENTS LOVE TO PAMPER THEIR GRAND-CHILDREN, RIGHT?
SO THE GRANDPA WOULD INVENT ALL KINDS OF THINGS FOR HIS GRANDSON, AND THE OTHER FAMILY MEMBERS WOULD BE NONE THE WISER.
THE GRANDPA HAS A CRUSH ON HIS GRANDSON'S BEAUTIFUL HOMEROOM TEACHER, SO HE OFTEN DROPS BY THE SCHOOL.
MAYBE HE TRIES TO GET HER TO DRINK A LOVE POTION. THAT KIND OF THING.
HA HA. A DIRTY OLD MAN.
BUT THE TEACHER SEES THROUGH HIM, AND USUALLY THE INVENTIONS END UP CREATING CHAOS. IN THE END, THEY EITHER FALL APART, OR THE TEACHER CONFISCATES THEM AND SCOLDS THE MAIN CHARACTER.
IT SOUNDS LIKE A STEREO-TYPICAL GAG MANGA...
...SO WE'LL ADD ALL THE FLAVOR WITH THE INVENTIONS THEMSELVES.
YEAH! IF WE WANT BATTLES, WE CAN JUST ADD AN EVIL INVENTOR.

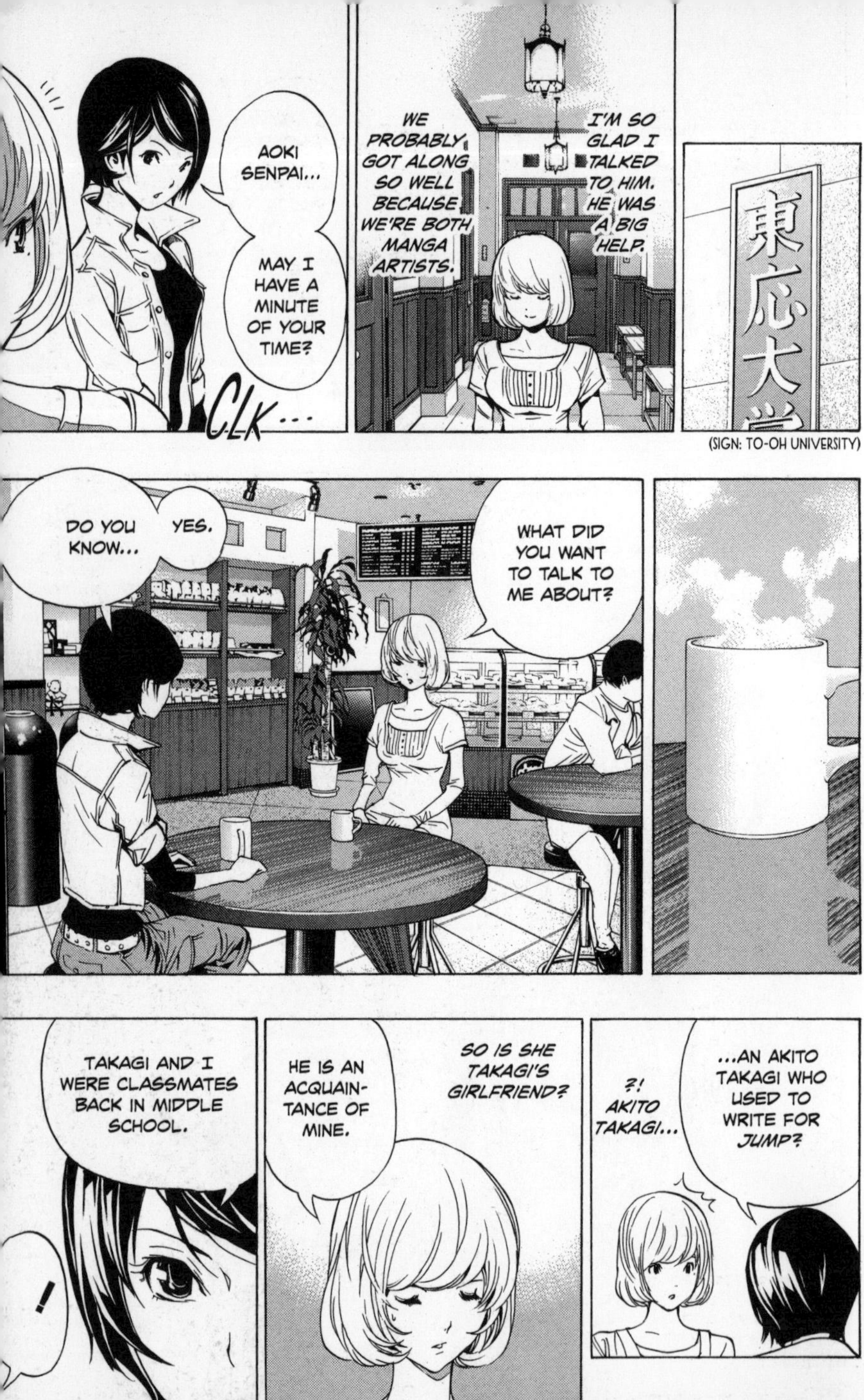
東応大学
(SIGN: TO-OH UNIVERSITY)
I'M SO GLAD I TALKED TO HIM. HE WAS A BIG HELP.
WE PROBABLY GOT ALONG SO WELL BECAUSE WE'RE BOTH MANGA ARTISTS.
AOKI SENPAI...
MAY I HAVE A MINUTE OF YOUR TIME?
CLK...
WHAT DID YOU WANT TO TALK TO ME ABOUT?
YES.
DO YOU KNOW...
...AN AKITO TAKAGI WHO USED TO WRITE FOR *JUMP*?
?! AKITO TAKAGI...
SO IS SHE TAKAGI'S GIRLFRIEND?
HE IS AN ACQUAINTANCE OF MINE.
TAKAGI AND I WERE CLASSMATES BACK IN MIDDLE SCHOOL.
!

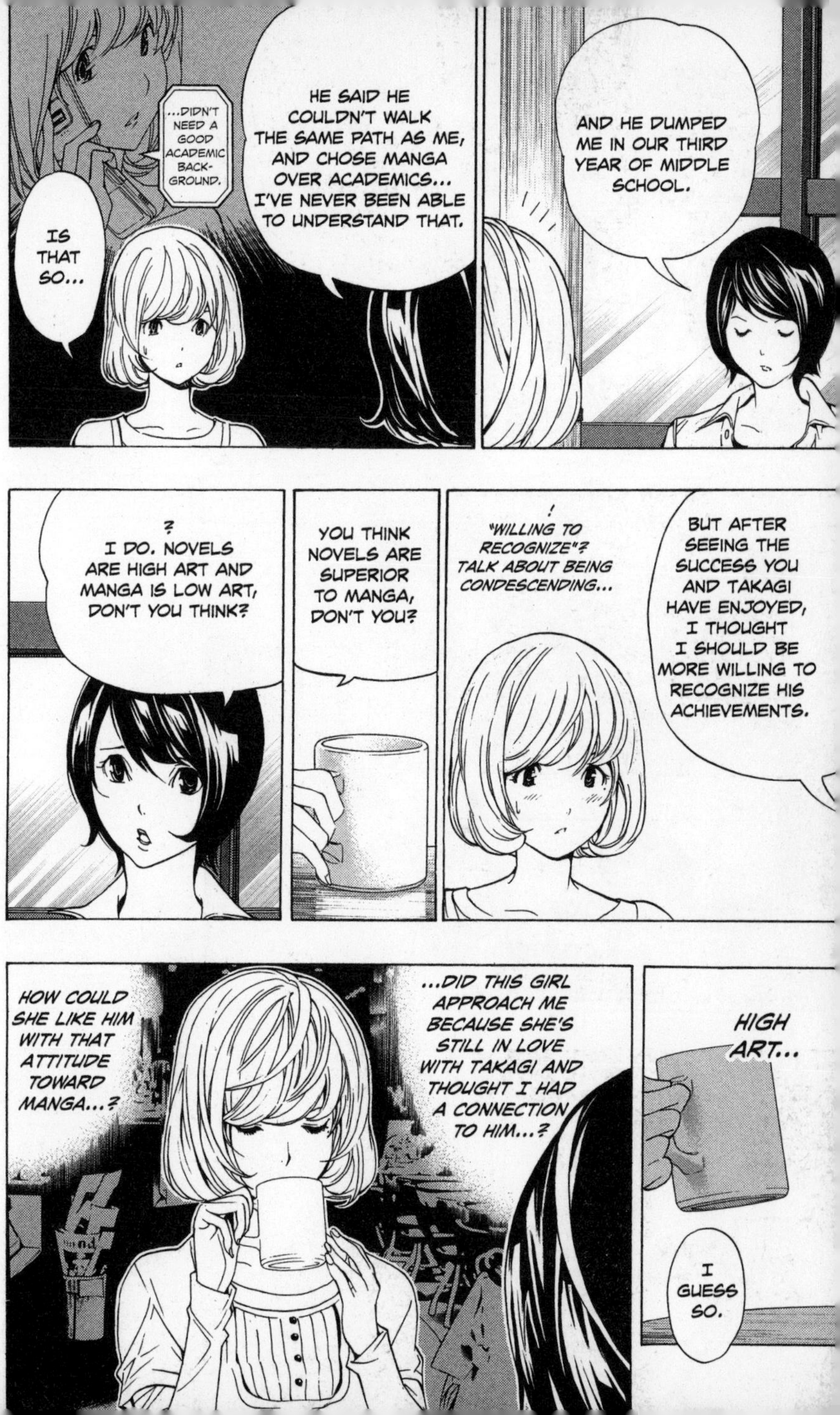
AND HE DUMPED ME IN OUR THIRD YEAR OF MIDDLE SCHOOL.
HE SAID HE COULDN'T WALK THE SAME PATH AS ME, AND CHOSE MANGA OVER ACADEMICS... I'VE NEVER BEEN ABLE TO UNDERSTAND THAT.
...DIDN'T NEED A GOOD ACADEMIC BACK-GROUND.
IS THAT SO...
BUT AFTER SEEING THE SUCCESS YOU AND TAKAGI HAVE ENJOYED, I THOUGHT I SHOULD BE MORE WILLING TO RECOGNIZE HIS ACHIEVEMENTS.
!
"WILLING TO RECOGNIZE"? TALK ABOUT BEING CONDESCENDING...
YOU THINK NOVELS ARE SUPERIOR TO MANGA, DON'T YOU?
?
I DO. NOVELS ARE HIGH ART AND MANGA IS LOW ART, DON'T YOU THINK?
HIGH ART...
I GUESS SO.
...DID THIS GIRL APPROACH ME BECAUSE SHE'S STILL IN LOVE WITH TAKAGI AND THOUGHT I HAD A CONNECTION TO HIM...?
HOW COULD SHE LIKE HIM WITH THAT ATTITUDE TOWARD MANGA...?

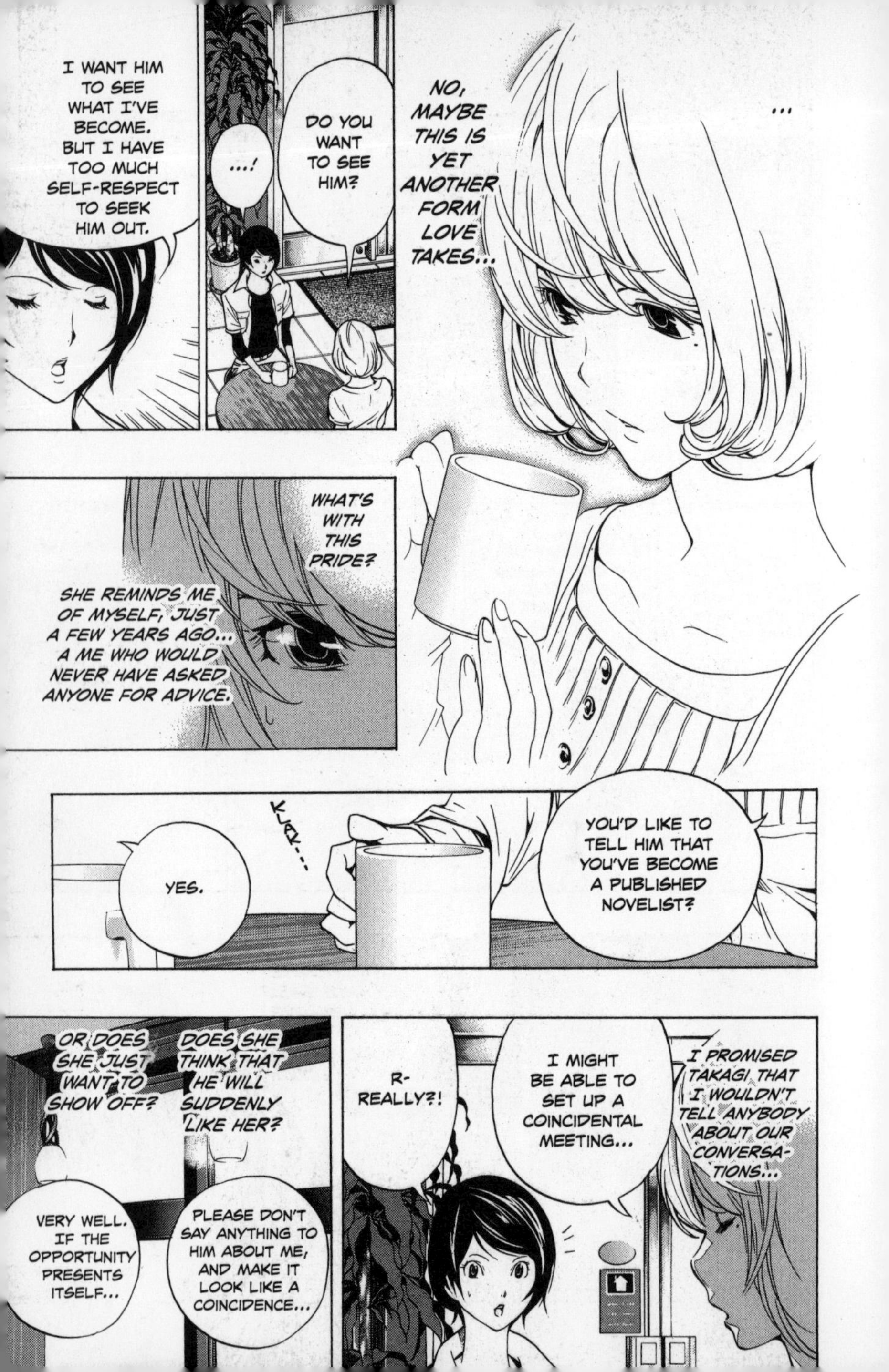
...
NO, MAYBE THIS IS YET ANOTHER FORM LOVE TAKES...
DO YOU WANT TO SEE HIM?
...!
I WANT HIM TO SEE WHAT I'VE BECOME. BUT I HAVE TOO MUCH SELF-RESPECT TO SEEK HIM OUT.
WHAT'S WITH THIS PRIDE?
SHE REMINDS ME OF MYSELF, JUST A FEW YEARS AGO... A ME WHO WOULD NEVER HAVE ASKED ANYONE FOR ADVICE.
YOU'D LIKE TO TELL HIM THAT YOU'VE BECOME A PUBLISHED NOVELIST?
KLAK...
YES.
I PROMISED TAKAGI THAT I WOULDN'T TELL ANYBODY ABOUT OUR CONVERSA-TIONS...
I MIGHT BE ABLE TO SET UP A COINCIDENTAL MEETING...
R-REALLY?!
DOES SHE THINK THAT HE WILL SUDDENLY LIKE HER?
OR DOES SHE JUST WANT TO SHOW OFF?
PLEASE DON'T SAY ANYTHING TO HIM ABOUT ME, AND MAKE IT LOOK LIKE A COINCIDENCE...
VERY WELL. IF THE OPPORTUNITY PRESENTS ITSELF...

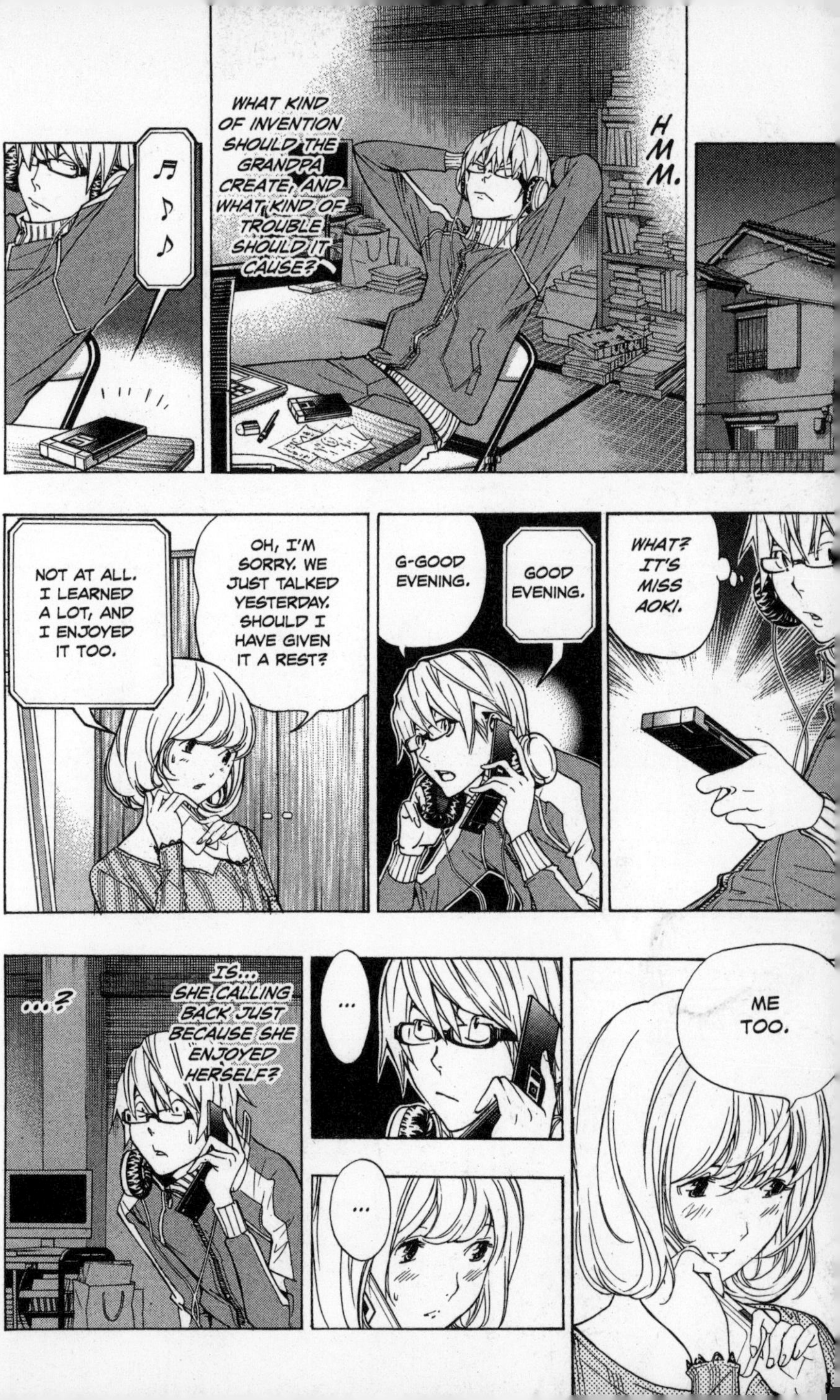
HMM.
WHAT KIND OF INVENTION SHOULD THE GRANDPA CREATE, AND WHAT KIND OF TROUBLE SHOULD IT CAUSE?
♬ ♪ ♪
WHAT? IT'S MISS AOKI.
GOOD EVENING.
G-GOOD EVENING.
OH, I'M SORRY. WE JUST TALKED YESTERDAY. SHOULD I HAVE GIVEN IT A REST?
NOT AT ALL. I LEARNED A LOT, AND I ENJOYED IT TOO.
ME TOO.
...
...
IS... SHE CALLING BACK JUST BECAUSE SHE ENJOYED HERSELF?
...?

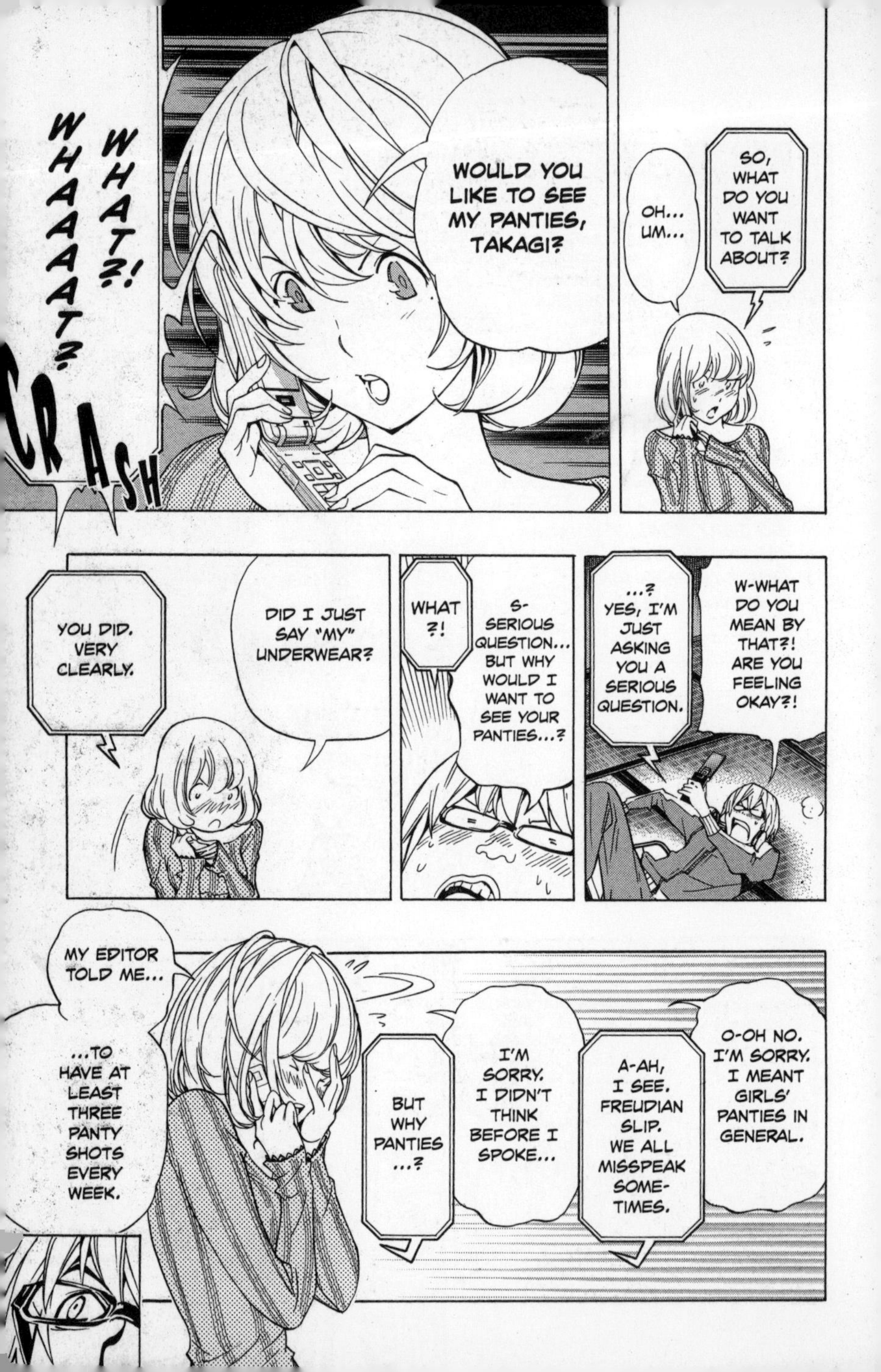
SO, WHAT DO YOU WANT TO TALK ABOUT?
OH... UM...
WOULD YOU LIKE TO SEE MY PANTIES, TAKAGI?
WHAT?!
WHAAAAAT?
CRASH
W-WHAT DO YOU MEAN BY THAT?! ARE YOU FEELING OKAY?!
...? YES, I'M JUST ASKING YOU A SERIOUS QUESTION.
S-SERIOUS QUESTION... BUT WHY WOULD I WANT TO SEE YOUR PANTIES...?
WHAT?!
DID I JUST SAY "MY" UNDERWEAR?
YOU DID. VERY CLEARLY.
O-OH NO. I'M SORRY. I MEANT GIRLS' PANTIES IN GENERAL.
A-AH, I SEE. FREUDIAN SLIP. WE ALL MISSPEAK SOME-TIMES.
I'M SORRY. I DIDN'T THINK BEFORE I SPOKE...
BUT WHY PANTIES...?
MY EDITOR TOLD ME...
...TO HAVE AT LEAST THREE PANTY SHOTS EVERY WEEK.

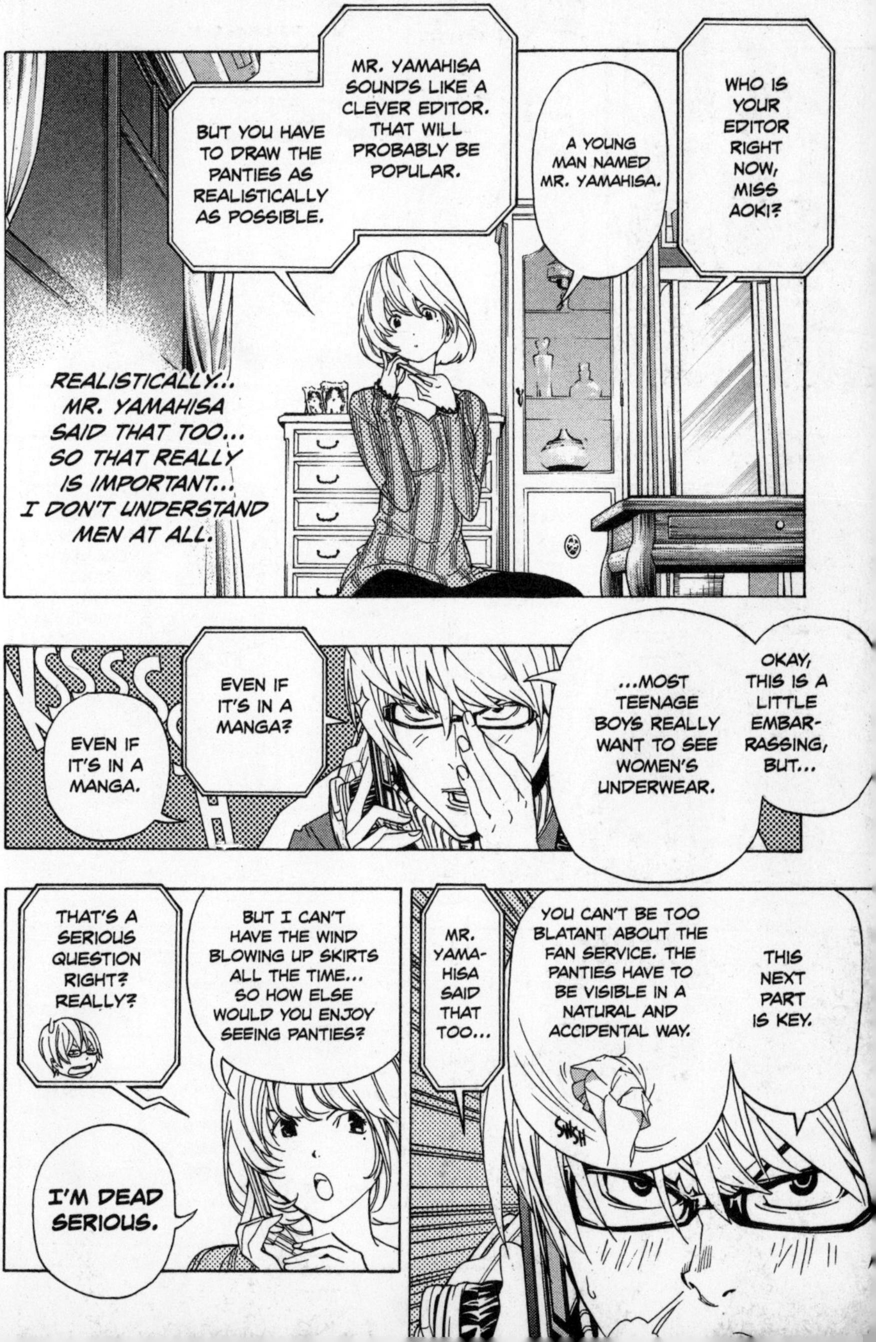
WHO IS YOUR EDITOR RIGHT NOW, MISS AOKI?
A YOUNG MAN NAMED MR. YAMAHISA.
MR. YAMAHISA SOUNDS LIKE A CLEVER EDITOR. THAT WILL PROBABLY BE POPULAR.
BUT YOU HAVE TO DRAW THE PANTIES AS REALISTICALLY AS POSSIBLE.
REALISTICALLY... MR. YAMAHISA SAID THAT TOO... SO THAT REALLY IS IMPORTANT... I DON'T UNDERSTAND MEN AT ALL.
OKAY, THIS IS A LITTLE EMBARRASSING, BUT...
...MOST TEENAGE BOYS REALLY WANT TO SEE WOMEN'S UNDERWEAR.
EVEN IF IT'S IN A MANGA?
EVEN IF IT'S IN A MANGA.
THIS NEXT PART IS KEY.
YOU CAN'T BE TOO BLATANT ABOUT THE FAN SERVICE. THE PANTIES HAVE TO BE VISIBLE IN A NATURAL AND ACCIDENTAL WAY.
MR. YAMAHISA SAID THAT TOO...
BUT I CAN'T HAVE THE WIND BLOWING UP SKIRTS ALL THE TIME... SO HOW ELSE WOULD YOU ENJOY SEEING PANTIES?
THAT'S A SERIOUS QUESTION RIGHT? REALLY?
I'M DEAD SERIOUS.

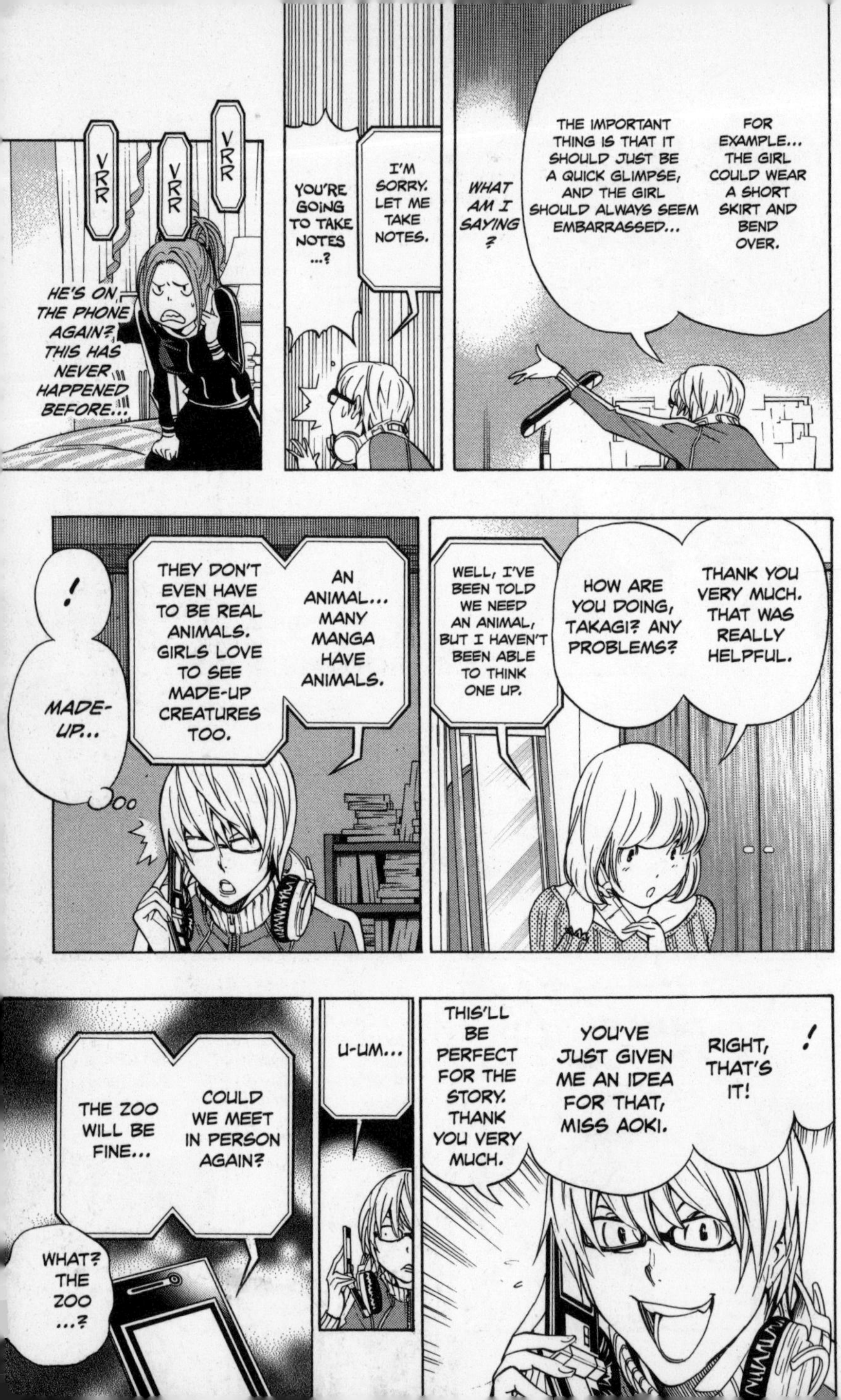
THE IMPORTANT THING IS THAT IT SHOULD JUST BE A QUICK GLIMPSE, AND THE GIRL SHOULD ALWAYS SEEM EMBARRASSED...
FOR EXAMPLE... THE GIRL COULD WEAR A SHORT SKIRT AND BEND OVER.
WHAT AM I SAYING?
I'M SORRY. LET ME TAKE NOTES.
YOU'RE GOING TO TAKE NOTES...?
VRR
VRR
VRR
HE'S ON THE PHONE AGAIN? THIS HAS NEVER HAPPENED BEFORE...
THANK YOU VERY MUCH. THAT WAS REALLY HELPFUL.
HOW ARE YOU DOING, TAKAGI? ANY PROBLEMS?
WELL, I'VE BEEN TOLD WE NEED AN ANIMAL, BUT I HAVEN'T BEEN ABLE TO THINK ONE UP.
AN ANIMAL... MANY MANGA HAVE ANIMALS.
THEY DON'T EVEN HAVE TO BE REAL ANIMALS. GIRLS LOVE TO SEE MADE-UP CREATURES TOO.
!
MADE-UP...
!
RIGHT, THAT'S IT!
YOU'VE JUST GIVEN ME AN IDEA FOR THAT, MISS AOKI.
THIS'LL BE PERFECT FOR THE STORY. THANK YOU VERY MUCH.
U-UM...
COULD WE MEET IN PERSON AGAIN?
THE ZOO WILL BE FINE...
WHAT? THE ZOO...?

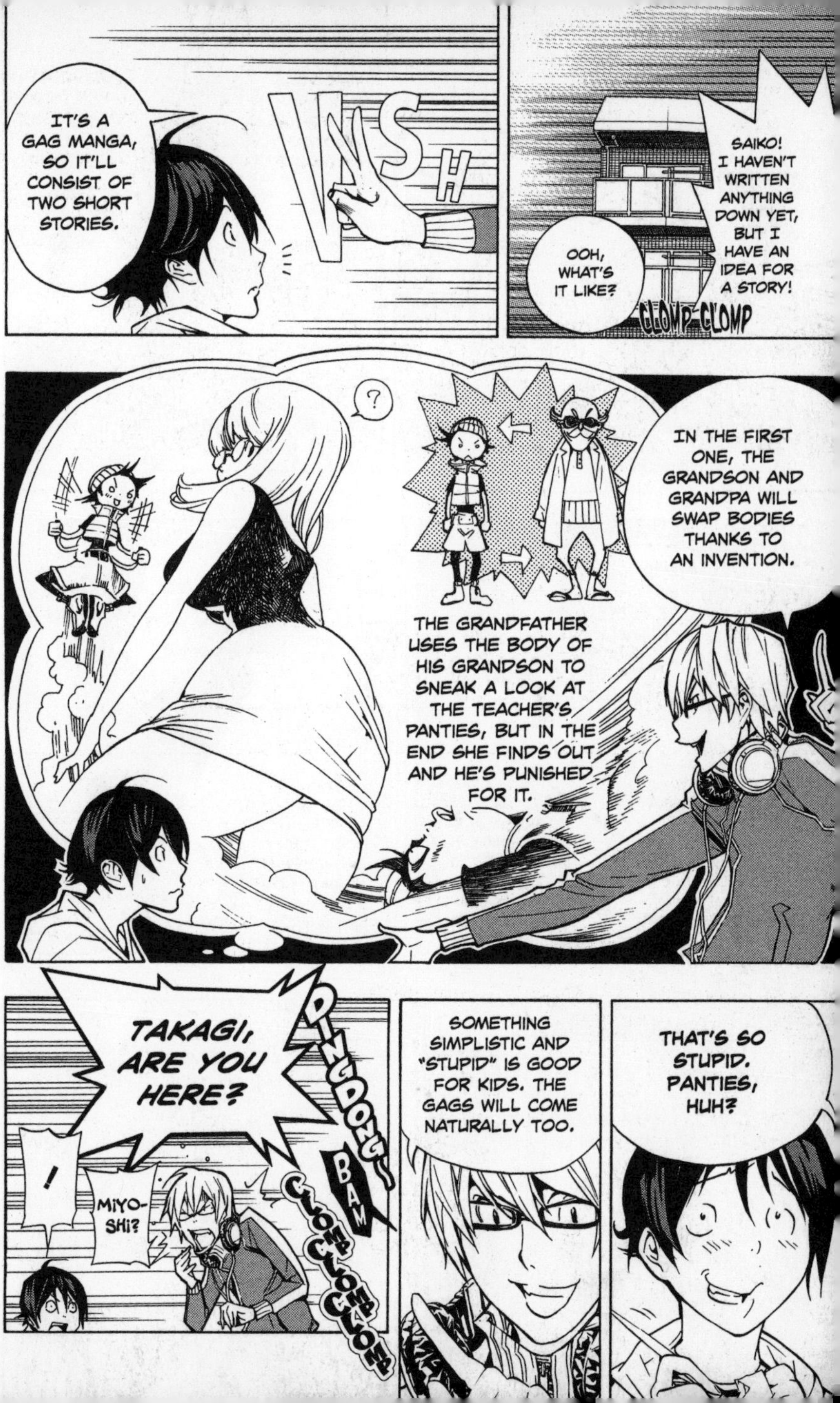
SAIKO! I HAVEN'T WRITTEN ANYTHING DOWN YET, BUT I HAVE AN IDEA FOR A STORY!
OOH, WHAT'S IT LIKE?
CLOMP CLOMP
VSH
IT'S A GAG MANGA, SO IT'LL CONSIST OF TWO SHORT STORIES.
IN THE FIRST ONE, THE GRANDSON AND GRANDPA WILL SWAP BODIES THANKS TO AN INVENTION.
?
THE GRANDFATHER USES THE BODY OF HIS GRANDSON TO SNEAK A LOOK AT THE TEACHER'S PANTIES, BUT IN THE END SHE FINDS OUT AND HE'S PUNISHED FOR IT.
THAT'S SO STUPID. PANTIES, HUH?
SOMETHING SIMPLISTIC AND "STUPID" IS GOOD FOR KIDS. THE GAGS WILL COME NATURALLY TOO.
DINGDONG
TAKAGI, ARE YOU HERE?
BAM
CLOMP CLOMP CLOMP
!
MIYO-SHI?

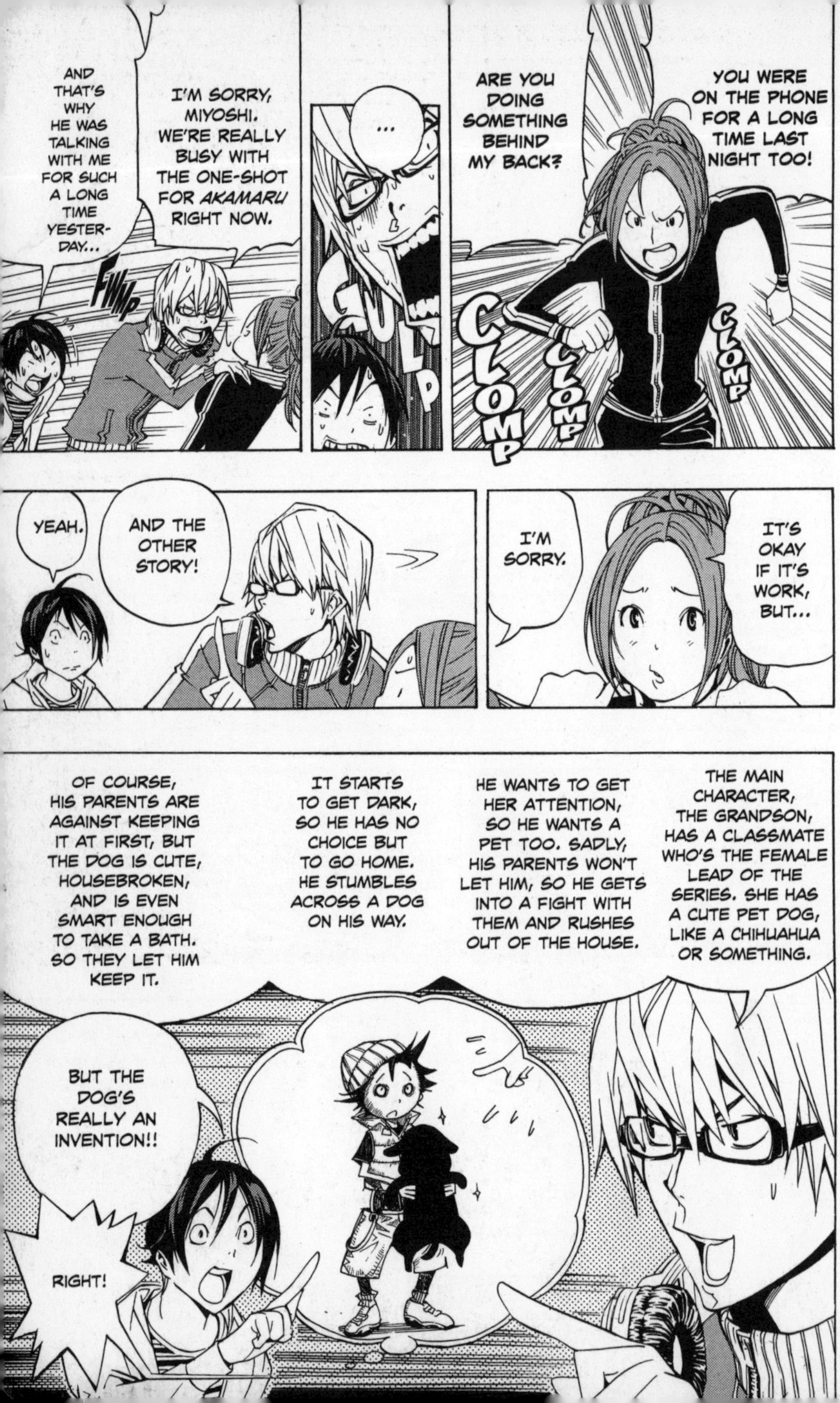
YOU WERE ON THE PHONE FOR A LONG TIME LAST NIGHT TOO!
ARE YOU DOING SOMETHING BEHIND MY BACK?
CLOMP
CLOMP
CLOMP
...
GULP
I'M SORRY, MIYOSHI. WE'RE REALLY BUSY WITH THE ONE-SHOT FOR *AKAMARU* RIGHT NOW.
FWMP
AND THAT'S WHY HE WAS TALKING WITH ME FOR SUCH A LONG TIME YESTER-DAY...
IT'S OKAY IF IT'S WORK, BUT...
I'M SORRY.
AND THE OTHER STORY!
YEAH.
THE MAIN CHARACTER, THE GRANDSON, HAS A CLASSMATE WHO'S THE FEMALE LEAD OF THE SERIES. SHE HAS A CUTE PET DOG, LIKE A CHIHUAHUA OR SOMETHING.
HE WANTS TO GET HER ATTENTION, SO HE WANTS A PET TOO. SADLY, HIS PARENTS WON'T LET HIM, SO HE GETS INTO A FIGHT WITH THEM AND RUSHES OUT OF THE HOUSE.
IT STARTS TO GET DARK, SO HE HAS NO CHOICE BUT TO GO HOME. HE STUMBLES ACROSS A DOG ON HIS WAY.
OF COURSE, HIS PARENTS ARE AGAINST KEEPING IT AT FIRST, BUT THE DOG IS CUTE, HOUSEBROKEN, AND IS EVEN SMART ENOUGH TO TAKE A BATH. SO THEY LET HIM KEEP IT.
BUT THE DOG'S REALLY AN INVENTION!!
RIGHT!

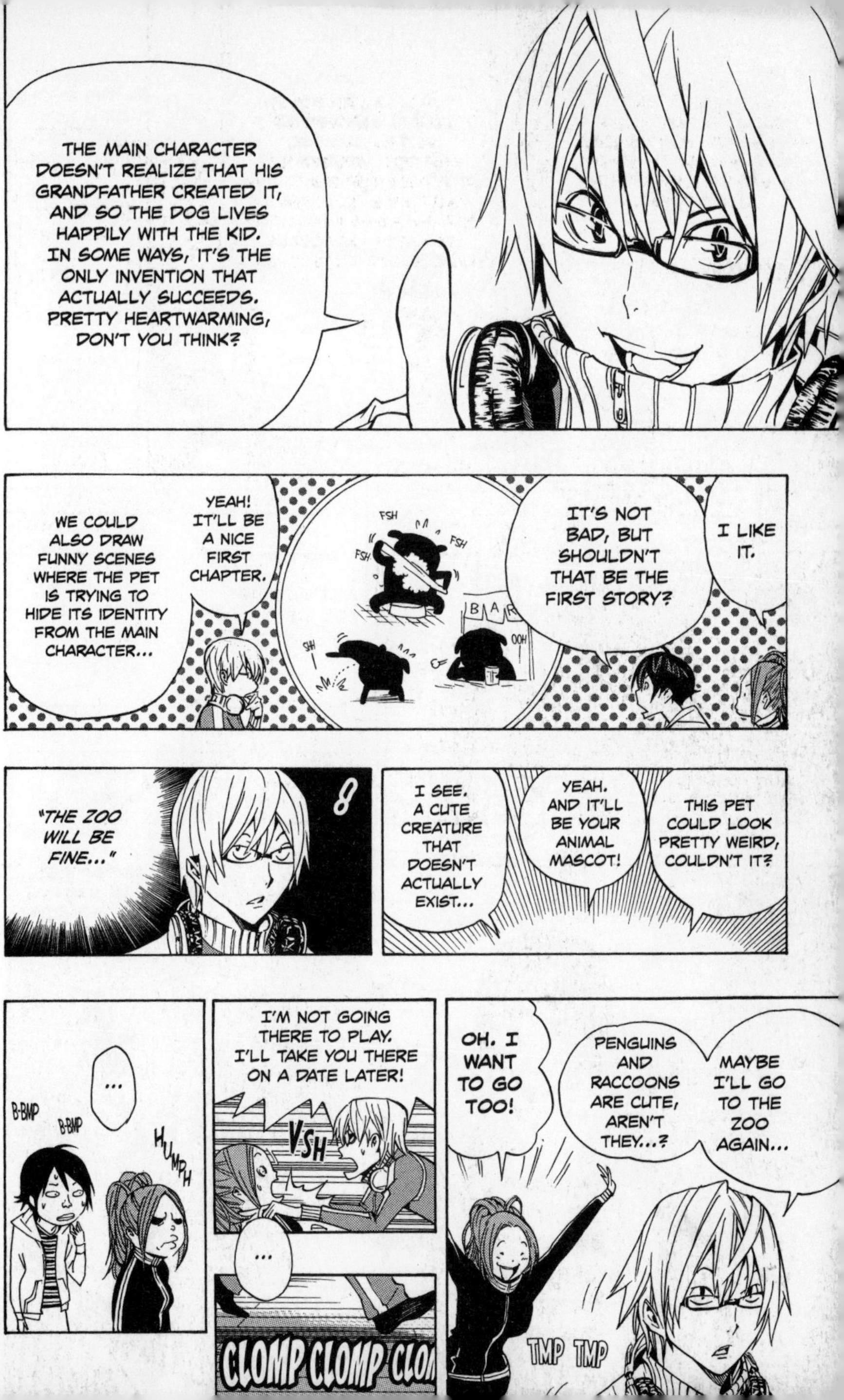
THE MAIN CHARACTER DOESN'T REALIZE THAT HIS GRANDFATHER CREATED IT, AND SO THE DOG LIVES HAPPILY WITH THE KID. IN SOME WAYS, IT'S THE ONLY INVENTION THAT ACTUALLY SUCCEEDS. PRETTY HEARTWARMING, DON'T YOU THINK?
I LIKE IT.
IT'S NOT BAD, BUT SHOULDN'T THAT BE THE FIRST STORY?
FSH
FSH
FSH
BAR
OOH
SHH
YEAH! IT'LL BE A NICE FIRST CHAPTER.
WE COULD ALSO DRAW FUNNY SCENES WHERE THE PET IS TRYING TO HIDE ITS IDENTITY FROM THE MAIN CHARACTER...
THIS PET COULD LOOK PRETTY WEIRD, COULDN'T IT?
YEAH. AND IT'LL BE YOUR ANIMAL MASCOT!
I SEE. A CUTE CREATURE THAT DOESN'T ACTUALLY EXIST...
"THE ZOO WILL BE FINE..."
MAYBE I'LL GO TO THE ZOO AGAIN...
PENGUINS AND RACCOONS ARE CUTE, AREN'T THEY...?
OH. I WANT TO GO TOO!
TMP TMP
I'M NOT GOING THERE TO PLAY. I'LL TAKE YOU THERE ON A DATE LATER!
VSH
...
CLOMP CLOMP CLOM
...
B-BMP
B-BMP
HUMPH

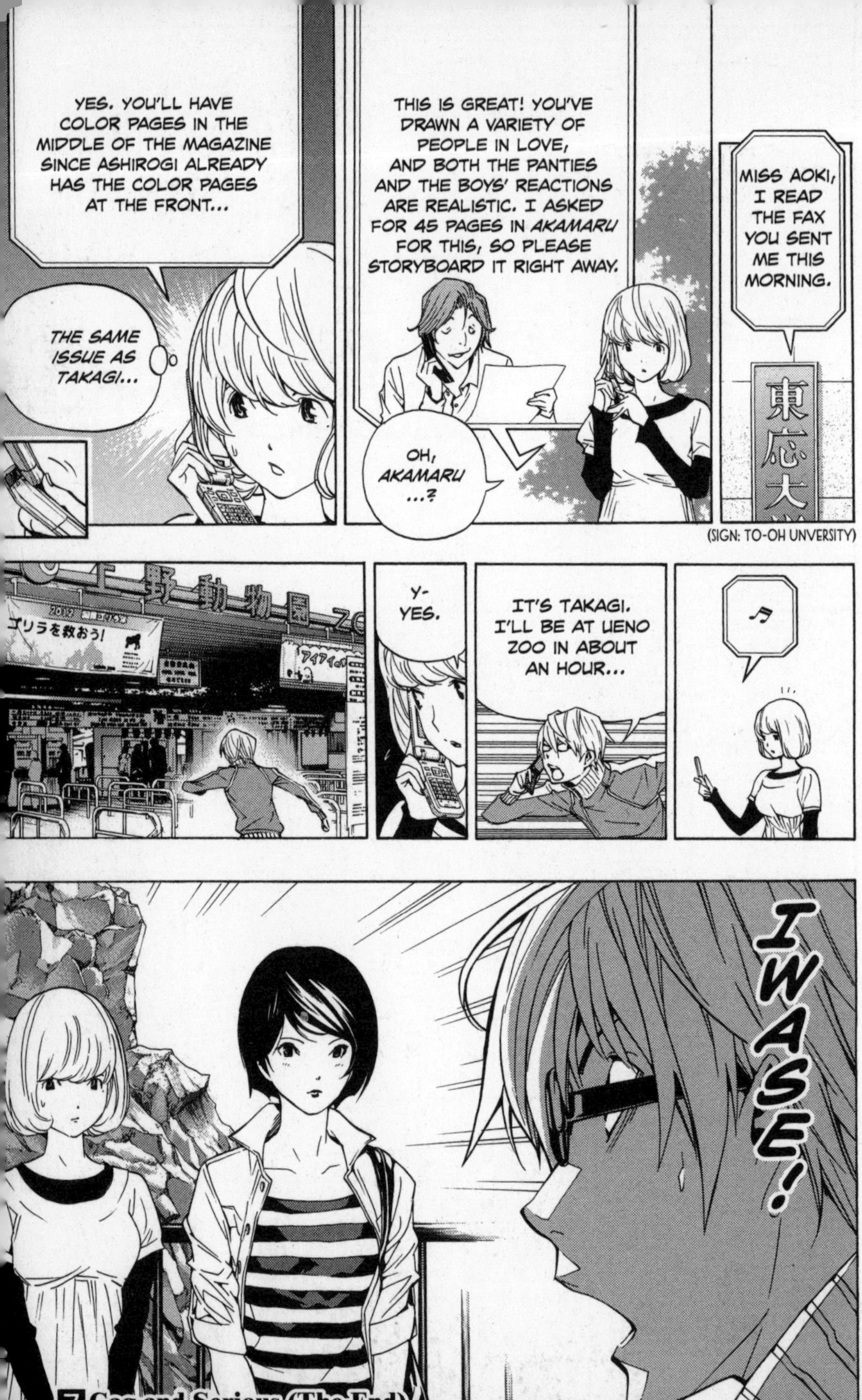
MISS AOKI, I READ THE FAX YOU SENT ME THIS MORNING.
東応大
(SIGN: TO-OH UNVERSITY)
THIS IS GREAT! YOU'VE DRAWN A VARIETY OF PEOPLE IN LOVE, AND BOTH THE PANTIES AND THE BOYS' REACTIONS ARE REALISTIC. I ASKED FOR 45 PAGES IN *AKAMARU* FOR THIS, SO PLEASE STORYBOARD IT RIGHT AWAY.
OH, *AKAMARU* ...?
YES. YOU'LL HAVE COLOR PAGES IN THE MIDDLE OF THE MAGAZINE SINCE ASHIROGI ALREADY HAS THE COLOR PAGES AT THE FRONT...
THE SAME ISSUE AS TAKAGI...
♪
IT'S TAKAGI. I'LL BE AT UENO ZOO IN ABOUT AN HOUR...
Y- YES.
ゴリラを救おう!
IWASE!
7 Gag and Serious (The End)

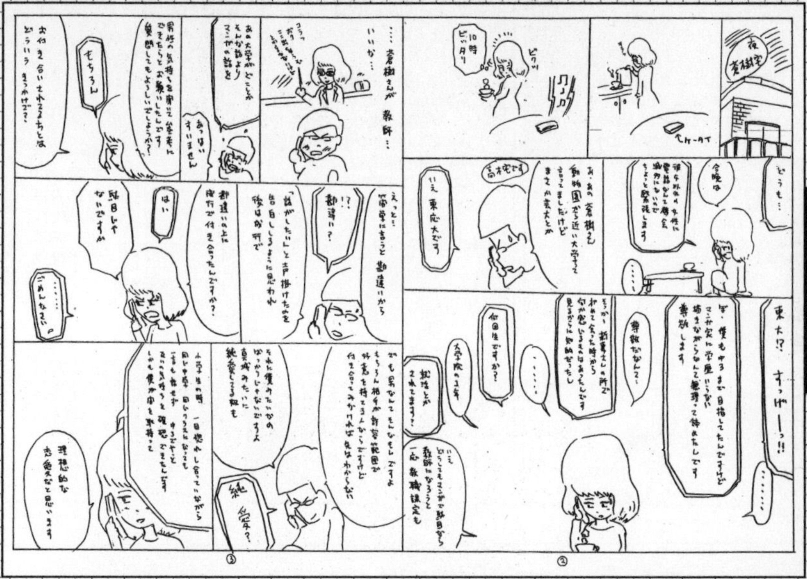

OHBA'S STORYBOARD

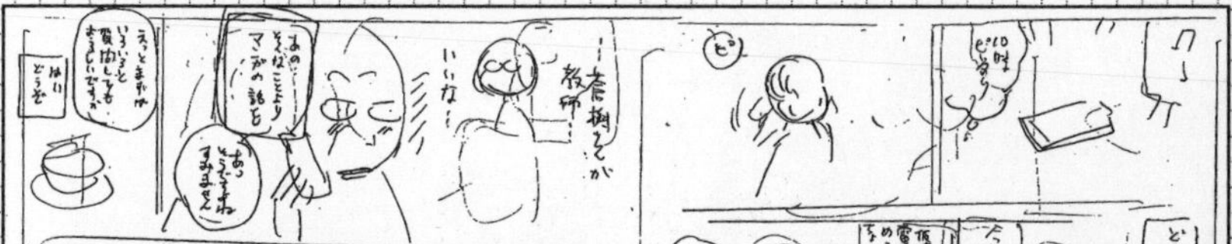

OBATA'S STORYBOARD

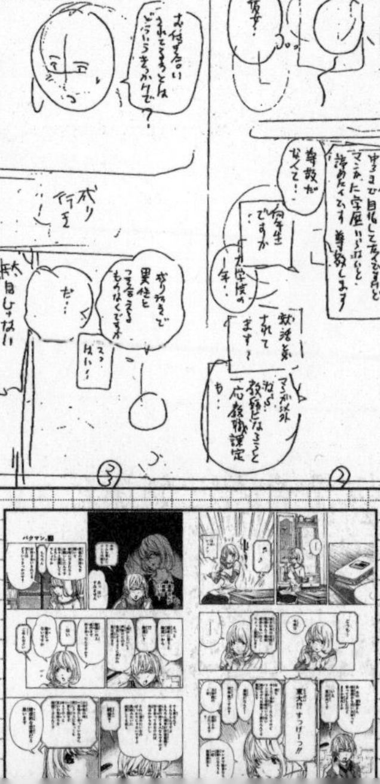

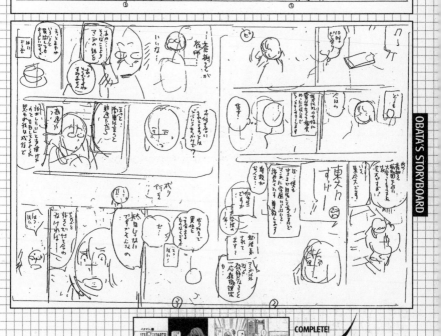

COMPLETE!

※CREATOR STORYBOARDS AND FINISHED PAGES IN JAPANESE

BAKUMAN。vol.7

"Until the Final Draft Is Complete"

Chapter 61, pp. 172-173

BAKUMAN。

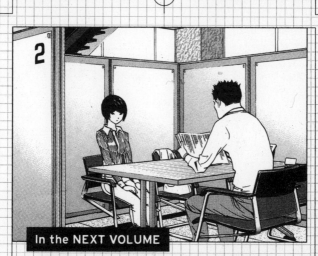

In the NEXT VOLUME

As the boys work hard on creating a new series, Miyoshi finds out that Akito's been meeting with other girls. Will the misunderstanding end their relationship? And when Iwase decides to become a manga storywriter, she'll team up with an artist nobody could have predicted!

Available December 2011

next_volume.dd

09.1.5 7:25:52 PM